Value Chain Development and the Poor

Praise for this book

'Value chains need not and often do not include or benefit poor people, but there are a number of collections of case studies about those that do. This book by three acknowledged experts who have many years of field experience in appraising and developing value chains goes further. It includes some important cases, from Latin America, Africa and SE Asia, but most of the book is about what has been learned, how value chains can be developed so that they do include poor people, and do not exclude them. Let us hope that the book is read, and acted upon, not only by the 'development community' but by the management of the businesses who actually design and manage the value chains, so that they include and benefit the poor.'

Malcolm Harper, Emeritus Professor, Cranfield School of Management

'This collection offers unique perspectives on value chain development, exploring how VCD is implemented in the field, options for innovation in design, and the potential for VCD to achieve impact at scale.'

Shaun Ferris, Technical Director Agriculture and Livelihoods,
Catholic Relief Services

'In my many years as a researcher I have learned that analysts with different backgrounds will generate unique insights into tackling common problems and it is the collection of those insights that lead to progress. The editors of this book have pulled together not only interesting case studies on agricultural value chain development, but have drawn together an impressive calibre and diversity of authors, both researchers and practitioners. The book focuses on how to make value chains work better for the poor, especially the millions of smallholder farmers in developing countries. Readers will come away with a firm understanding of the challenges, what has been achieved so far, and what still requires attention to make value chains work for the poor.'

Frank Place, Director of the CGIAR Research Program on Policies,
Institutions, and Markets

Value Chain Development and the Poor

Promise, delivery, and opportunities
for impact at scale

Edited by
Jason Donovan, Dietmar Stoian, and Jon Hellin

Practical
ACTION
PUBLISHING

Practical Action Publishing Ltd
27a, Albert Street, Rugby, Warwickshire, CV21 2SG, UK
www.practicalactionpublishing.com

A catalogue record for this book is available from the British Library.

A catalogue record for this book has been requested from the Library of Congress.

ISBN 978-1-78853-055-2 Hardback
ISBN 978-1-78853-056-9 Paperback
ISBN 978-1-78853-058-3 Epub
ISBN 978-1-78853-057-6 PDF

Citation: Donovan, J., Stoian, D., Hellin, J., (ed) (2020) *Value Chain Development and the Poor: Promise, delivery, and opportunities for impact at scale,* Rugby, UK: Practical Action Publishing <http://dx.doi. org/10.3362/9781788530576>.

Since 1974, Practical Action Publishing has published and disseminated books and information in support of international development work throughout the world. Practical Action Publishing is a trading name of Practical Action Publishing Ltd (Company Reg. No. 1159018), the wholly owned publishing company of Practical Action. Practical Action Publishing trades only in support of its parent charity objectives and any profits are covenanted back to Practical Action (Charity Reg. No. 247257, Group VAT Registration No. 880 9924 76).

This work was undertaken as part of the CGIAR Research Programmes on Maize Agri-Food Systems (MAIZE), led by CIMMYT, and Policies, Institutions and Markets (PIM), led by IFPRI. The opinions expressed here belong to the authors, and do not necessarily reflect those of CIMMYT, IFPRI, MAIZE, PIM, CGIAR, Practical Action Publishing Ltd or its parent charity Practical Action.

Reasonable efforts have been made to publish reliable data and information, but the authors and publisher cannot assume responsibility for the validity of all materials or for the consequences of their use.

Cover photos shows from top: Banana nursery, Philippines, by Dietmar Stoian; Coffee bean production, Peru, by Francis Salas, Practical Action; Sawmill in Carmelita, Guatemala, by Jason Houston for USAID.
Cover design by Practical Action Publishing

Contents

http://dx.doi.org/10.3362/9781788530576.000

Acknowledgements

This book was supported by the CGIAR Research Program on Policies, Institutions and Markets (PIM) and the CGIAR Research Program on Maize Agrifood Systems (MAIZE). We thank the donors who support PIM and MAIZE through their contributions to the CGIAR Fund.

Introducing value chain development and the poor: Promise, delivery, and opportunities for impact at scale

Jason Donovan, Dietmar Stoian, and Jon Hellin

Abstract

Since the early 2000s, value chain development (VCD) has figured prominently on the agendas of donors, governments, and NGOs in pursuit of market-based options to poverty reduction, food security, gender equity, and other goals. Researchers have shown interest in value chains as a theoretical construct for studying interactions between farmers and markets, while practitioners have focused their attention on approaches and tools for applying VCD in the field. Despite considerable investments in VCD, limited evidence exists on the extent to which different approaches to VCD have advanced diverse development goals. This knowledge gap sounds alarms, not least because of the complexities involved and the multitude of options for getting it right (or wrong). The 16 chapters in this book offer unique perspectives on VCD from both practitioners and researchers. They explore how VCD is implemented in the field, options for innovation in design, and the potential for VCD to achieve impact at scale. Altogether, the book provides a timely critique of current approaches, pointing at options for more reflexive learning, new collaborative frameworks, and faster innovation of VCD. Here we introduce the chapters and extract some of their principal lessons in terms of the promise, delivery, and opportunities for impact at scale.

Keywords: value chains, rural development, smallholders, private sector, development practice

Why this book on value chains

Since the late 1990s, the topic of value chains has captured the attention of researchers and practitioners alike. While the former have tended to study globalizing markets and their effects on farmers, businesses, and consumers, the latter have sought to leverage value chains in their efforts to reduce poverty and, more recently, advance broader development goals and the environmental and social performance of enterprises (Taglioni and Winkler, 2014). At its core, the concept of value chains refers to the processes, actors, and institutional arrangements needed to move products from primary production to final consumption (Rayport and Sviokla, 1995). The operationalization of the concept has differed across academic disciplines and according to the specific goals of practitioners.

Early value chain research, for example, examined how 'lead firms' (often large-scale retailers and processors headquartered in Europe or North America) established the conditions for the production and marketing of agricultural commodities in the global South (e.g. Gereffi, 1994; Gereffi and Kaplinsky 2001). Numerous case studies looked at smallholder engagement in higher value crops, such as horticulture and coffee (e.g. Fitter and Kaplinsky, 2001; Barrientos et al., 2003). A number of these painted a bleak scenario for long-term smallholder engagement and the prospects for increasing the benefits smallholders derived from it, given their limited capacities, demanding quality and volume requirements of other value chain actors, and the reduced role of governments and international agreements. Researchers then turned to structural and regulatory changes in agri-food value chains, including retail and logistics as well as food safety and other standards (e.g. Reardon et al., 2003; Swinnen and Maertens, 2007; Henson and Humphrey, 2010). Over the years, the focus has thus shifted away from lead firms and their suppliers to a broader view on the role processors, distributors, and retailers play in agri-food value chains. More recently, researchers have looked beyond value chains to food systems as a broader framework for identifying opportunities for both the urban poor (as consumers) and the rural poor (as producers) (e.g. Mount, 2012; Kennedy et al., 2017). At the same time, value chain frameworks have branched off to address specific topics such as nutrition, climate change, and gender equity (see Dekens and Dazé, 2016; Allen and de Brauw, 2018; Stoian et al., 2018).

Practitioners, in turn, have advanced their own approaches to VCD, at times in line with contemporary academic debate, but frequently quite independent of it. In the early 2000s, the market-based development strategies of bi- and multilateral donors, government agencies, NGOs, and, in some cases, large-scale processors and retailers, began to converge under the label of 'value chain development'. This reflected, in part, the advance of influential development paradigms and frameworks, such as poverty reduction and the Millennium Development Goals (MDGs). Shortly thereafter institutional branding emerged, reflected in the titles of methodological guides and training courses like Making Markets Work for the Poor by the Springfield Centre, ValueLinks by GTZ (now GIZ), Inclusive Business by SNV, and Market Systems by USAID. Despite potential differences suggested by these titles, the frameworks shared a focus on resource-poor smallholders, employed similar sets of indicators for measuring change, and held similar assumptions about how such change occurred. A review of well-known guides for designing VCD showed that, in spite of their general support for design, many of them fell short in providing guidance for differentiated implementation in response to the diversity and variation of smallholder livelihood strategies and capacities, agroecological conditions, and market, political-legal, and institutional environments (Donovan et al., 2015). The potential pitfalls of overlooking the diversity within populations, their livelihoods and the larger forces which shape values, capacities, and decision-making have been well established (Chambers, 1994; Bebbington, 1999).

Whether practitioners have the right tools and guidance for effective design, targeting, and implementation of VCD therefore remains an open question (Donovan et al., 2016). The few studies that have examined VCD design and implementation suggest that more work is needed in this area. A recent review of guides for gender-equitable VCD, for example, highlighted gaps in adequate coverage of gender-based constraints in collective enterprises, the influence of norms on gender relations, and processes to transform inequitable relations through VCD (Stoian et al., 2018). Similar gaps have existed with regard to monitoring and evaluation (M&E) of VCD. In many cases, M&E has tended to focus largely on activities and outputs, leaving significant gaps in terms of credible evidence on the outcomes and impacts of VCD.[1] Another impediment to incremental improvement in VCD design lies in project frameworks, which are the typical modus operandi of VCD initiatives, and whose short-term implementation cycles discourage a more strategic view on the long-term support needed for small- and medium-sized enterprise (SME) and value chain development (Donovan et al., 2008) as well as the flexibility and creativity needed to address the complexity of VCD processes (Orr et al., 2018). Further constraints lie in the lack of structured processes for critical reflection and learning around VCD. It is acknowledged, though, that such processes are a challenge given the nature of value chains as open, multi-layered systems in which development outcomes and impacts are multi-dimensional and contingent on contextual particularities (Ton et al., 2011).

It is in this context that this book has been conceptualized. Our primary motivation is to draw attention to recent and noteworthy contributions in the field of VCD, and the role of smallholders and their business partners therein, with the aim to synthesize options for achieving impact at scale. While previous books on value chains have provided valuable overviews of contemporary issues linked with VCD, they have paid little attention to the debates and interactions between researchers and practitioners, and how these have helped overcome the shortcomings of VCD approaches or left blind spots yet to be addressed. This unique collection of contributions from researchers and practitioners explores the promise of VCD, the extent to which it has lived up to its expectations, and opportunities for more impactful design, implementation, and assessment of VCD. The focus of this book is practical; less about macro-level policy design and more about shaping and targeting field-level strategies by funders, NGOs, and businesses looking to expand or deepen their engagement with smallholders and SMEs. Considerable content is drawn from the practitioner-oriented journal *Enterprise Development and Microfinance (EDM)*, which for nearly 30 years has provided a platform for debate on market-based development approaches for researchers and practitioners. *EDM* articles are complemented by those published in other development journals and invited contributions published for the first time here.

Chapters in this book

The book is divided into three parts, each containing five to six chapters (see Table 1 for an overview).

Part I contains five chapters which explore the context in which value chains operate in the *global South* and in which interventions for VCD are carried out. The first chapter, by Stoian and Donovan, explores the evolution of market-based development approaches, from non-traditional agricultural export strategies to VCD, through the lens of 'issue-attention cycles'. The authors highlight the shifts in terms of goals, stakeholder groups, and the extent to which genuine improvements and impact have been achieved. Chapter 2, by Hellin and colleagues, discusses the challenges to advance VCD goals in the context of western Guatemala, a place with high levels of poverty where food security remains a primary objective of farming households. Chapter 3, by Krauss, provides a critical view on sustainability initiatives in the cocoa sector, arguing that the strong bargaining position of international buyers results in reduced benefits for farmers and their organizations. Chapter 4, by Belt and colleagues, highlights the potential of development impact bonds to inject funding and increased accountability into VCD interventions. The authors caution that more reflection among stakeholders is needed to address the ambiguities in the terms of engagement. The final chapter in this part, by Blare and Donovan, calls attention to the high expectations for cooperatives engaged in VCD processes, given their position in the chain between farmers and exporters/importers, along with persistent challenges that coops face in growing and developing over time.

Part II comprises six chapters which explore *VCD design and field implementation*. In Chapter 6 Stoian and fellow CGIAR researchers scrutinize well-known guides for incorporating gender into VCD, drawing attention to conceptual advances in their design, but also important gaps in coverage. Chapter 7, by Norell at World Vision, reflects on the challenges of building capacity among 'frontline' project staff for engagement on VCD, leading to practical recommendations for achieving better results. In their exploration of how VCD is actually implemented by local project teams, Donovan and colleagues, in Chapter 8, advocate a broader approach to VCD, based on a combination of tools to account for multiple, context-specific needs of diverse stakeholders, deeper collaboration between key actors within and outside the value chain, and evidence-based reflection and learning. Similar research on VCD in Vietnam in support of smallholder participation in high-value, fast-growing markets (Chapter 9), led by Even, finds that, despite the conceptualizations of VCD in terms of multi-dimensional strategies including the private sector, VCD interventions tend to focus on a narrow set of activities, mainly around upgrading smallholder production capacities and establishing producer associations. In Chapter 10, Faveri and Wilson from MEDA and Shaikh from the Entrepreneurship and Community Development Institute, argue that VCD that embraces a more nuanced approach to women's engagement, including 'push' and 'pull' tactics, holds greater promise for achieving such engagement over time. Finally, Florey and colleagues from the International Rice Research Institute (IRRI) focus on the contribution of digital agriculture to VCD and rural development. Using the example of a digital agriculture decision support tool (Rice Crop Manager), the authors emphasize the importance of careful targeting of smallholders and other resource-poor value chain actors to avoid a digital divide that risks exacerbating social and economic inequalities.

Part III presents five chapters that examine *learning processes and mechanisms in VCD around the outcomes of VCD interventions*. In Chapter 12, Stoian and colleagues argue the case for greater attention to multi-stakeholder learning within and across VCD initiatives, with special attention paid to the variation in livelihood strategies and the endowment of smallholders with livelihood assets. Where smallholder capacities were especially limited, they advocate for non-market-based approaches in support of resource-poor farmers to facilitate their 'value chain readiness'. With a focus on Nicaragua, Chapter 13, by Bastiaensen and colleagues, shows the limitations of integrated microfinance interventions (the combination of financial, advisory, and other services) for incentivizing the delivery of ecosystem services by farmers when interventions fail to address the broader social and market context in which they take place and where farm-level engagement does not occur in a persistent way. Chapter 14, by Rutherford and colleagues, presents the findings from a longitudinal quasi-experimental assessment of VCD in Liberia. The authors report positive outcomes for farming households in terms of production (improved yields and income) and access to food, though without significant changes for children, suggesting the limits of VCD to improve overall household wellbeing. Lomboll, of the Natural Resources Institute (NRI), and colleagues (Chapter 15) review experiences in a large-scale project in sub-Saharan Africa to strengthen value chains for high-quality cassava flour. They highlight various challenges to advance VCD goals within project frameworks and advocate more reflective and adaptive implementation processes. Finally, in Chapter 16, Mayoux examines the need and potential for advancing both gender equity goals and value chain performance by explicitly targeting gender inequalities in terms of gender-based violence, division of labour, and land ownership.

Promise, delivery, and opportunities for impact at scale

This collection of 16 chapters provides much needed fresh perspective on VCD, which was put forth with considerable fanfare roughly two decades ago. Practitioners had declared a 'value chain revolution' for advancing rural development goals (Hulm, 2004), and researchers largely echoed their enthusiasm, with only a few cautionary notes (Timmer et al., 2013; Barrett et al., 2019). Several chapters presented here, along with the publications referenced therein, provide evidence of progress towards the multiple goals associated with VCD, such as poverty reduction, food and nutrition security, and gender equity. At the same time, the dearth of evidence of broad-based impact becomes manifest and various suggestions are made on how to improve this apparent shortcoming. This echoes the findings of recent value chain studies which question the evidence for VCD initiatives adequately addressing the context in which value chains operate, or for the alleged 'inclusiveness' of farmers' engagement in value chains. Ros-Tonen et al., (2019), for example, pointed at the lack of literature which would shed light on the operationalization of the concept of inclusiveness in VCD. Similarly, Hainzer et al., (2019) argued that the interaction between context, socio-economic constraints, and intervention strategies is still a poorly understood feature in VCD, and that a greater understanding of these interactions is crucial to the success of value chain interventions.

Notwithstanding the important contributions VCD has made to rural development over the past two decades, the chapters assembled here identify several limitations and shortcomings that should be addressed for VCD initiatives to be more impactful:

- existence of issue-attention cycles, paired with lack of self-critical reflection, which go against processes of continuous improvement;
- deployment of multiple guides and tools, without adequate guidance for their selection, combination, and adaptation according to the VCD goals and context;
- reductionist approaches to VCD, reflected in single tools, focus on single value chains, and limited sets of interventions that do not do justice to the complexity of VCD processes and the diversity of smallholder livelihoods;
- branding of organizations, guides, and tools which leads to siloed implementation approaches;
- limited leverage of private sector experience and investments in VCD with a view on multiple actors and nodes along the chain; and
- absence of broader collaborative frameworks that allow for pooling of capacities and resources among public and private sector and civil society organizations in support of the Sustainable Development Goals (particularly SDGs 1, 2, 5, 8, 9, 12, 13, 15, and 17).

Looking forward, there is an urgent need for diverse stakeholders in VCD to recognize their respective roles and responsibilities by building shared visions and systemic theories of change (Douthwaite et al., 2017; Blundo-Canto et al., 2019). The challenge of ensuring that VCD contributes to a broad set of development goals requires transdisciplinary, multisector collaboration within broader frameworks, such as integrated rural–urban development, food system transformation, and green recovery of the economy in the post Covid-19 era. Systemic approaches to VCD will require bundling of resources of multiple stakeholders beyond the budgets and timelines of 'projects', along with their genuine interest in joint learning based on critical reflection on what works, what doesn't, and why. Closer collaboration between practitioners and researchers could be at the heart of systemic, reflective approaches to VCD. Such progress, however, will only be achieved to the extent that key players in VCD, from the NGOs and private businesses that implement in the field to the programme officers at major funding agencies who define the parameters within which VCD interventions are designed, recognize the challenges at hand, and make the changes needed.

While important contributions to this book are provided by practitioners working in NGOs or consulting firms, there remains an urgent need for more critical reflection by a broader group of stakeholders engaged in VCD including INGOs, funding agencies, and private companies operating around the globe. Much of their experiences and insights rest outside of the public domain or are scattered and available only in grey literature which is often difficult to access. This leaves a space to be filled by researchers with their reflections on the state of affairs, and what could and should be done differently. Many researchers, however, have shied away from critical debate on VCD and close engagement with those operating in the field. Scholars working at the interface between research and development, like those in the CGIAR, would be well positioned to fill this space. But even they have limited access to M&E data collected routinely by practitioners as part of their project activities. A self-selected portion of this information finds its way into reports to funding agencies which, in turn, often show limited interest in requiring grantees to implement more reflective evaluation processes. With few incentives for critical reflection, such reports rarely provide a complete picture of progress and setbacks and their underlying factors – a missed opportunity for evidence-based redesigning of VCD interventions to increase their efficiency and impact.

As a way forward, there is both the potential and need for strategic partnerships between practitioners and development-oriented researchers for joint analyses, evidence-based design, and data-supported scaling. This will imply a change in culture within implementing organizations, businesses, and funding agencies; from one epitomized by 'We are generally doing well despite a few challenges', to one that embraces mistakes as a source of learning and eventual improvement. Development-oriented researchers, in turn, would need to come forward with broader approaches like systematic reviews, stronger focus on real-world issues in VCD, and constructive engagement with practitioners as part of shared impact pathways. We hope you enjoy reading this book and look forward to compiling experiences and insights on the impact of VCD initiatives based on such researcher–practitioner alliances and novel approaches in a few years' time.

Table 0.1 Summary of book chapters

Chapter title	Reference	VCD focus point(s)	Methodological approach	Main contribution
Part 1: Context for value chain development				
1. Putting value chain development into perspective: Evolution, blind spots, and promising avenues	Stoian and Donovan, 2020	Learning and innovation in VCD by donors, NGOs, private sector, and researchers	Literature review on VCD and earlier market-based development approaches	Case for deeper and more sustained engagement among donors, practitioners, and researchers on VCD
2. Maize diversity, market access, and poverty reduction in the Western Highlands of Guatemala	Hellin et al., 2017	VCD options for speciality maize grain	Case study; mixed methods, including survey of 989 farmers in four departments	Limitations of VCD to achieve goals with smallholders for speciality crops in areas of high poverty
3. What is cocoa sustainability? Mapping stakeholders' socio-economic, environmental, and commercial constellations of priorities	Krauss, 2018	Sustainability standards in shaping value chain engagement, cocoa	Qualitative research with cocoa buyers and sellers	Outsized influence of buyers in shaping the terms of market engagement for smallholders, which undermines the goals of sustainability standards
4. Development impact bonds: Learning from the Ashaninka cocoa and coffee case in Peru	Belt et al., 2017	Innovative financing options for VCD, cocoa and coffee, Peru		Role of development impact bonds in reshaping the interactions of donors, NGOs, and private sector agents
5. Stuck in a rut: Emerging cocoa cooperatives in Peru and factors that influence their performance	Donovan et al., 2017a	Role of agricultural cooperatives in VCD, Peru	Comparative case studies based on interviews with cooperative leaders and members	Challenges for coops to engage in higher value markets and implications for VCD design

Part 2: Design and implementation of VCD

6. Fit for purpose? Review of tools for gender-equitable value chain development	Stoian et al., 2018	Incorporation of gender in VCD design	Comparative review of guides for incorporating gender into VCD	Options for conceptual and methodological innovation to address the roles, needs, and aspirations of women and men in VCD
7. Building frontline market facilitators' capacity: The case of the *Integrating Very Poor Producers into Value Chains Field Guide*	Norell, 2014	Capacity building of VCD project staff, Ghana and Malawi	Qualitative assessment from training participants from six projects	Recommendations for increasing the effectiveness of capacity building efforts with staff of VCD projects
8. Value chain development in Nicaragua: Prevailing approaches and tools and persistent gaps	Donovan et al., 2017b	Implementation of VCD projects by NGOs, Nicaragua	Comparative case studies of four projects by large NGOs that aimed to link smallholders to higher value markets	VCD implementation based on reductionist approaches, suggesting the need for deeper collaboration among stakeholders and evidence-based reflection and learning
9. Value chain development in Vietnam: A look at approaches used and options for improved impact	Even and Donovan, 2017	Implementation of VCD projects by NGOs and government agencies, Vietnam	Comparative case studies of five projects that worked with smallholders to facilitate market access	VCD interventions focused on supply-side areas of engagement (boosting production and producer associations)
10. Making markets work for women: How push and pull strategies can support women's economic empowerment	Faveri et al., 2015	Implementation of VCD projects with an explicit gender orientation, Afghanistan, Ghana, and Pakistan	Case studies of three MEDA implemented projects	Engagement of women in VCD enhanced by nuanced implementation strategies including 'push' and 'pull' tactics
11. Digital agriculture and pathways out of poverty: The need for appropriate design, targeting, and scaling	Florey et al., 2020	Potential contribution of digital agriculture to VCD and rural development	Case study of a digital agriculture decision support tool	Importance of judicious design and targeting of digital agriculture to support VCD and minimize a 'digital divide'

(Continues)

Table 0.1 (*Continued*)

Chapter title	Reference	VCD focus point(s)	Methodological approach	Main contribution
Part 3: Assessment and outcomes of VCD				
12. Value chain development for poverty reduction: A reality check and a warning	Stoian et al., 2012	Monitoring and assessment of interventions in support of VCD	Review of grey and academic literatures	Understanding variations in asset endowments and livelihood strategies of farming households improves VCD design and expands opportunities for learning
13. Microfinance plus for ecosystem services: A territorial perspective on Proyecto CAMBio in Nicaragua	Bastiaensen et al., 2015	Design of interventions that use financial and other means to promote environmentally responsible businesses	Case study, with survey data from farmers	Integrated microfinance interventions will benefit from greater awareness of differences in capacities among producers, critical reflection on intervention design, and broader engagement with local stakeholders
14. Impact of an agricultural value chain project on smallholder farmers, households, and children in Liberia	Rutherford et al., 2016	Reach of outcomes and impacts from VCD within households	Longitudinal quasi-experimental survey, combined with qualitative methods	Potential for VCD to deliver positive impacts in production and food security, but limitations of VCD to deliver changes in child welfare
15. Practical lessons on scaling up smallholder-inclusive and sustainable cassava value chains in Africa	Lamboll et al., 2015	Scaling and impact from VCD in sub-Saharan Africa	Case study, with review of project documentation and interviews with project stakeholders	Need for more reflective design and implementation of VCD initiatives, with attention to variation in the capacities of smallholders, service providers, and government agencies
16. Gender mainstreaming in value chain development: Experience with Gender Action Learning System in Uganda	Mayoux, 2012	Gender equity in value chains, Uganda	Case studies on implementation of the Gender Action Learning Systems (GALS)	Interventions specially targeting gender inequities potentially generate benefits for households and value chains as a whole

Note

1. This situation persists despite the availability of field-tested tools for assessing the outcomes and impacts of VCD. For examples, see Donovan and Stoian (2012), Sheck et al., (2013), and Torero (2016).

Acknowledgements

This work was undertaken as part of the CGIAR Research Programs (CRPs) on Policies, Institutions and Markets (PIM) and Maize. We thank PIM and MAIZE CRPs for funding the study and all donors who support PIM and Maize CRPs through their contributions to the CGIAR Fund.

References

Allen, S. and de Brauw, A. (2018) 'Nutrition sensitive value chains: theory, progress, and open questions', *Global Food Security* 16: 22–8. <https://doi.org/10.1016/j.gfs.2017.07.002>

Barrett, C., Reardon, T., Swinnen, J., and Zilberman, D. (2019) *Structural Transformation and Economic Development: Insights from the Agri-food Value Chain Revolution*, Working Paper, Dyson School of Applied Economics and Management, Cornell University, Ithaca, New York.

Barrientos, S., Dolan, C., and Tallontire, A. (2003) 'A gendered value chain approach to codes of conduct in African horticulture', *World Development* 31(9): 1511–26. <https://doi.org/10.1016/S0305-750X(03)00110-4>

Bastiaensen, J., Huybrechs, F., Forcella, D., and Van Hecken, G. (2015) 'Microfinance plus for ecosystem services: a territorial perspective on Proyecto CAMBio in Nicaragua', *Enterprise Development and Microfinance* 26(3): 292–306. <https://doi.org/10.3362/1755-1986.2015.025>

Bebbington, A. (1999) 'Capitals and capabilities: a framework for analyzing peasant viability, rural livelihoods and poverty', *World Development* 27(12): 2021–44. <https://doi.org/10.1016/S0305-750X(99)00104-7>

Belt, J., Kuleshov, A., and Minneboo, E. (2017) 'Development impact bonds: learning from the Ashaninka cocoa and coffee case in Peru', *Enterprise Development and Microfinance* 28(1–2): 130–44. <https://doi.org/10.3362/1755-1986.16-00029>

Blundo-Canto, G., Triomphe, B., Faure, G., Barret, D., De Romemont, A., and Hainzelin, E. (2019) 'Building a culture of impact in an international agricultural research organization: process and reflective learning', *Research Evaluation* 28(2): 136–44. <https://doi.org/10.1093/reseval/rvy033>

Chambers, R. (1994) 'The origins and practice of participatory rural appraisal', *World Development* 22(7): 953–69. <https://doi.org/10.1016/0305-750X(94)90141-4>

Dekens, J. and Dazé, A. (2016) *How Small Businesses Can Support Climate-Resilient Value Chains: Lessons from Uganda*, International Institute for Sustainable Development (IISD), Winnipeg, Canada.

Donovan, J., Stoian, D., and Poole, N. (2008) *Global Review of Rural Community Enterprises: The Long and Winding Road to Creating Viable Businesses, and*

Potential Shortcuts, Technical Bulletin 29, Rural Enterprise Development Collection 2, CATIE, Turrialba, Costa Rica.

Donovan, J., Franzel, S., Cunha, M., Gyau A., and Mithofer, D. (2015) 'Guides for value chain development: a comparative review', *Journal of Agribusiness in Developing and Emerging Economies* 5(1): 1–22. <https://doi.org/10.1108/JADEE-07-2013-0025>

Donovan, J., Stoian, D., and Lundy, M. (2016) 'Inclusive value-chain development: challenges and approaches (introduction)', in A. Devaux, M. Torero, J. Donovan, and D. Horton (eds), *Innovation for Inclusive Value-Chain Development: Successes and Challenges*, pp. 37–46, IFPRI, Washington, DC.

Donovan, J., Blare, T., and Poole, N. (2017a) 'Stuck in a rut: emerging cocoa cooperatives in Peru and factors that influence their performance', *International Journal of Agricultural Sustainability* 15(2): 169–84. <https://doi.org/10.1080/14735903.2017.1286831>

Donovan, J., Stoian, D., and Poe, K. (2017b) 'Value chain development in Nicaragua: prevailing approaches and tools and persistent gaps', *Enterprise Development and Microfinance* 28(1–2): 10–27. <https://doi.org/10.3362/1755-1986.00036>

Douthwaite, B., Mur, R., Audouin, S., Wopereis, M., Hellin, J., Moussa, A., Karbo, N., Kasten, W., and Bouyer, J. (2017) *Agricultural Research for Development to Intervene Effectively in Complex Systems and the Implications for Research Organizations*, KIT Working Paper 2017-12, Royal Tropical Institute, Amsterdam.

Even, B. and Donovan, J. (2017) 'Value chain development in Vietnam: a look at approaches used and options for improved impact', *Enterprise Development and Microfinance* 28(1–2): 28–43. <https://doi.org/10.3362/1755-1986.16-00034>

Faveri, C., Wilson, M.J., and Shaikh, P. (2015) 'Making markets work for women: how push and pull strategies can support women's economic empowerment', *Enterprise Development and Microfinance* 26(1): 11–22. <https://doi.org/10.3362/1755-1986.2015.003>

Fitter, R. and Kaplinksy, R. (2001) 'Who gains from product rents as the coffee market becomes more differentiated? A value-chain analysis', *IDS Bulletin* 32(3): 69–82. <https://doi.org/10.1111/j.1759-5436.2001.mp32003008.x>

Florey, C., Hellin, J., and Balié, J. (2020) 'Digital agriculture and pathways out of poverty: the need for appropriate design, targeting, and scaling', *Enterprise Development and Microfinance* 31(2): 126-140. <http://dx.doi.org/10.3362/1755-1986.20-00007>

Gereffi, G. (1994) 'The organisation of buyer-driven global commodity chains: how US retailers shape overseas production networks', in G. Gereffi and M. Korzeniewicz (eds), *Commodity Chains and Global Capitalism*, pp. 95–122, Praeger, Westport, CT.

Gereffi, G. and Kaplinsky, R. (2001) 'Introduction: globalisation, value chains and development', *IDS Bulletin* 32(3): 1–8. <https://doi.org/10.1111/j.1759-5436.2001.mp32003001.x>

Hainzer, K., Best, T., and Brown, P.H. (2019) 'Local value chain interventions: a systematic review', *Journal of Agribusiness in Developing and Emerging Economies* 9(4): 369–90. <https://doi.org/10.1108/JADEE-11-2018-0153>

Hellin, J., Cox, R., and Lopez-Ridaura, S. (2017) 'Maize diversity, market access and poverty reduction in the Western Highlands of Guatemala', *Mountain Development and Research* 37(2): 188–97.

Henson, S. and Humphrey, J. (2010) 'Understanding the complexities of private standards in global agri-food chains as they impact developing countries', *The Journal of Development Studies* 46(9): 1628–46. <https://doi.org/10.1659/MRD-JOURNAL-D-16-00065.1>

Hulm, P. (2004) 'The value chain revolution', *International Trade Forum* 1: 22.

Kennedy, G., Stoian, D., Hunter, D., Kikulwe, E., and Termote, C., with contributions from Alders, R., Burlingame, B., Jamnadass, R., McMullin, S., and Thilsted, S. (2017) 'Food biodiversity for healthy, diverse diets', in Bioversity International, *Mainstreaming Agrobiodiversity in Sustainable Food Systems: Scientific Foundations for an Agrobiodiversity Index*, pp. 23–52, Bioversity International, Rome.

Krauss, J. (2018) 'What is cocoa sustainability? Mapping stakeholders' socio-economic, environmental, and commercial constellations of priorities', *Enterprise Development and Microfinance* 28(3): 228–50. <https://doi.org/10.3362/1755-1986.17-000JK>

Lamboll, R., Nelson, V., Posthumus, H., Martin, A., Adebayo, K., Alacho, F., Dziedzoave, N., Mahende, G., Sandifolo, V., Sanni, L., Abayomi, L., Graffham, A., Hillocks, R., and Westby, A. (2015) 'Practical lessons on scaling up smallholder-inclusive and sustainable cassava value chains in Africa', *Food Chain* 5(1-2): 28–52. <https://doi.org/10.3362/2046-1887.2015.004>

Mayoux, L. (2012) 'Gender mainstreaming in value chain development: experience with gender action learning system in Uganda', *Enterprise Development and Microfinance* 23(4): 319–37. <https://doi.org/10.3362/1755-1986.2012.031>

Mount, P. (2012) 'Growing local food: scale and local food systems governance', *Agriculture and Human Values* 29(1): 107–21. <https://doi.org/10.1007/s10460-011-9331-0>

Norell, D. (2014) 'Building frontline market facilitators' capacity: the case of the "Integrating Very Poor Producers into Value Chains Field Guide"', *Enterprise Development and Microfinance* 25(2): 163–78. <https://doi.org/10.3362/1755-1986.2014.015>

Orr, A., Donovan, J. and Stoian, D. (2018) 'Small value chains as complex adaptive systems: a conceptual framework', *Journal of Agribusiness in Developing and Emerging Economies* 8(1): 14-33. <https:// DOI 10.1108/JADEE-03-2017-0031>

Rayport, J.F. and Sviokla, J.J. (1995) 'Exploiting the virtual value chain', *Harvard Business Review* 73(6): 75–85.

Reardon, T., Timmer, C.P., Barrett, C.B., and Berdegue, J. (2003) 'The rise of supermarkets in Africa, Asia, and Latin America', *American Journal of Agricultural Economics* 85(5): 1140–6. <https://www.jstor.org/stable/1244885>

Ros-Tonen, M.A., Bitzer, V., Laven, A., de Leth, D.O., Van Leynseele, Y., and Vos, A. (2019) 'Conceptualizing inclusiveness of smallholder value chain integration', *Current Opinion in Environmental Sustainability* 41: 10–17. <https://doi.org/10.1016/j.cosust.2019.08.006>

Rutherford, D.D., Burke, H., Cheung, K., and Field, S. (2016) 'Impact of an agricultural value chain project on smallholder farmers, households, and children in Liberia', *World Development* 83: 70–83. <https://doi.org/10.1016/j.worlddev.2016.03.004>

Stoian, D., Donovan, J., Fisk, J., and Muldoon, M. (2012) 'Value chain development for rural poverty reduction: a reality check and a warning', *Enterprise Development and Microfinance* 23(1): 54–69. <https://doi.org/10.3362/1755-1986.2012.006>

Stoian, D., Donovan, J., Elias, M., and Blare, T. (2018) 'Fit for purpose? Review of tools for gender–equitable value chain development', *Development in Practice* 24(4): 494–509. <https://doi.org/10.1080/09614524.2018.1447550>

Stoian, D. and Donovan, J.(2020) 'Putting value chain development into perspective: evolution, blind spots and promising avenues', in (eds) Donovan, J., Stoian, D. and Hellin, J. *Value chain development and the poor: promise, delivery, and opportunities for impact at scale*, Practical Action Publishing, Rugby, UK.

Maertens, M. (2007) 'Globalization, privatization, and vertical coordination in food value chains in developing and transition countries', *Agricultural Economics* 37: 89–102. <https://doi.org/10.1111/j.1574-0862.2007.00237.x>

Taglioni, D. and Winkler, D. (2014) *Making Global Value Chains Work for Development*, Economic Premise 143, World Bank, Washington, DC.

Timmer, M., Los, B., Stehrer, R., and De Vries, G. (2013) 'Rethinking competitiveness: the global value chain revolution' [online], CEPR's Policy Portal <https://voxeu.org/article/rethinking-competitiveness-global-value-chain-revolution> [accessed 23 June 2020].

Ton, G., Vellema, S. & De Ruyter De Wildt, M. (2011) 'Development impacts of value chain interventions: how to collect credible evidence and draw valid conclusions in impact evaluations?', *Journal on Chain and Network Science* 11(1): 69-84. <http://dx.doi.org/10.2139/ssrn.1609680>

Torero, M. (2016) 'Evaluating inclusive value-chain development', in A. Devaux, M. Torero, J. Donovan, and D. Horton (eds), *Innovation for Inclusive Value-Chain Development: Successes and Challenges*, pp. 329–42, IFPRI, Washington, DC.

About the authors

Jason Donovan, PhD (j.donovan@cgiar.org), Senior Economist, Research Theme Leader for Markets and Value Chains, International Maize and Wheat Improvement Center (CIMMYT), Texcoco, Mexico

Dietmar Stoian, PhD (d.stoian@cgiar.org), Lead Scientist, Value Chains, Private Sector Engagement and Investments, World Agroforestry (ICRAF), Bonn, Germany

Jon Hellin, PhD (j.hellin@irri.org), Platform Leader, Sustainable Impact, International Rice Research Institute (IRRI), Los Baños, Philippines

PART I
Context for value chain development

CHAPTER 1

Putting value chain development into perspective: Evolution, blind spots, and promising avenues

Dietmar Stoian and Jason Donovan

Abstract

Donors, NGOs, and government agencies have long embraced market-based development approaches for achieving economic growth and poverty reduction. Over the past two decades, value chain development (VCD) has taken the lead among such approaches. This chapter reviews the evolution of these approaches since the 1980s, with emphasis on the contributions and interactions of researchers and practitioners. Adopting the lens of 'issue-attention cycles', we show how 1) excitement is built up over a given approach, funding becomes available, and proliferation kicks in; 2) disenchantment follows as awareness builds on the complexity, trade-offs, and resources required to address these; and 3) interest declines, funding sources dry up, and attention moves to new (or rebranded) approaches. Researchers have spurred these cycles by coining new terms, designing tools, and assessing impact, with limited accountability for VCD outcomes. Practitioners, in turn, have promoted own VCD frameworks and tools and trumpeted their success in implementation, while showing limited appetite for scrutiny. More impactful VCD will require productive interactions between researchers, practitioners, and funding agencies, lasting presence on the ground for supporting smallholders and SMEs, and safe spaces for (self-)critical reflection. Review of what has worked in previous cycles, and what has not, is needed to build on proven elements of VCD approaches while addressing evident shortcomings. Shared commitment to continuous improvement with a long-term view and evidence-based achievements will extend the length of issue-attention cycles, if not eliminate them altogether.

Keywords: agri-food value chains, market-based development approaches, issue-attention cycles, smallholders, private sector, CGIAR

Introduction

Value chain development (VCD) emerged as a major concept for economic development in the late 1990s and gained momentum in the mid-2000s. Researchers had laid the foundation by developing the theoretical constructs of value chains, emphasizing the actual and potential role of smallholders

http://dx.doi.org/10.3362/9781788530576.001

in tropical countries in dynamic and increasingly globalized agri-food markets. With support from bi- and multilateral donor agencies and based on concepts, methodologies, and tools advocated by development-oriented research institutions, think tanks, and the CGIAR, development practitioners implemented VCD projects across the global South, often with a focus on smallholder engagement in the evolving agri-food sector. The spread of VCD in rural development programming, in turn, inspired researchers to examine different ways of designing, implementing, and assessing VCD initiatives. Compared with earlier market-based development approaches (MBDA), the emergence of VCD implied major changes in terms of goals and associated impact pathways, the role of government agencies and NGOs, and the forms of engagement with the private sector. Starting off with a strong focus on rural poverty reduction, with emphasis on economic development, job creation, and inclusive growth, VCD has evolved over time to address a wider range of social and environmental development issues (Stamm and Von Drachenfels, 2011).

This chapter reviews the discussions on MBDA over recent decades, with special attention to VCD in the agri-food sector. It sheds light on interactions between funding agencies, practitioners, and researchers in how MBDA are designed, implemented, and assessed, and the extent to which genuine learning and improvement has happened. We view these discussions through the lens of 'issue-attention cycles', first employed by Downs (1972) to describe the cyclical nature of issues that dominate public and academic debate. While researchers have called out the fickleness of funding priorities for development (Riddell, 1999), little has been said about how researchers, practitioners, and donors have engaged to advance development approaches, and their respective roles in fostering issue-attention cycles. The existence of these cycles in development programming can reflect positive outcomes from engagements, for example, cycles based on innovation in design that recognize lessons learned in previous approaches. However, cycles may also reflect a lack of learning from implementation given the overall complexity in which development projects are carried out, and the strong competition among implementers who operate under tight budgets and short time horizons. Funding agencies, under pressure to show impact from their use of taxpayers' money, may also play a role by favouring grantees capable of generating something 'new', without demanding sound analysis of what has worked or not in previous approaches. The extent to which issue-attention cycles in discussions on VCD and other forms of MBDA result from scattered and uncoordinated efforts, potentially leading to inefficient use of resources and, ultimately, reduced impact, rather than genuine learning based on engagement between practitioners, donors, and researchers, merits inquiry.

Against this backdrop, this chapter seeks to answer three questions: 1) What have been the principal issue-attention cycles in MBDA over recent decades? 2) To what extent have interactions between researchers and practitioners extended or shortened such cycles? and 3) How have these contributed to, or distracted from, achieving overall development goals? In addressing these questions, we look back at the debates around MBDA in the global South since the 1960s and the way these have been driven by overarching development paradigms (Box 1.1). Section 2 introduces the concept of issue-attention cycles that have shaped the evolutionary process from earlier MBDA to the more recent VCD approaches. Section 3 explores these cycles from both a research-er's and a practitioner's perspective, looking into their interactions and iden-tifying blind spots in VCD design and implementation. Section 4 concludes with promising avenues for further conceptual and operational development in pursuit of impact at scale.

Box 1.1 The imprint of development paradigms on market-based development approaches

Market-based development approaches have played a central role in development agendas since the 1960s, shaped largely by overarching development paradigms (Stoian et al., 2019). Based on Rostow's (1959) theory of a dual economy, 'tradi-tional' societies were assumed to follow an evolutionary path to 'modern' societies. This 'modernization theory' equated industrial transformation with 'economic growth' which, in turn, was expected to generate broader societal wealth through trickle-down effects (Thornton et al., 1978). Consequently, governments invested in processing facilities and other infrastructure, export promotion, and improvements of overall trade capacity. By the 1970s, disillusionment over the theory and its implications had grown in view of the non-linearity of development processes (Tipps, 1973), as well as the private sector's disinterest in resource conservation and the rural poor. This gave way to development strategies focusing on 'basic needs' (Samater, 1984), which emphasized the preconditions required before people in the global South would be receptive to conventional economic stimuli by focusing on human development, along with the recognition that economic development does not take place in a social vacuum (Keeton, 1984).

In the 1990s, after prioritizing economic goals of development (1950s/1960s) and a stronger focus on its social dimension (1970s/1980s), the time was ripe for approaches to 'sustainable development' which integrated the environment as a third pillar. Such approaches were particularly promoted by NGOs whose numbers had been mushrooming since the mid-1980s in response to structural adjustment programmes promoted by the World Bank and International Monetary Fund which had resulted in downscaling of the governmental sector and dismantling of agricultural extension services. The emerging NGO sector brought a shift away from government-backed investment programmes to more participatory initiatives focused on rural communities and households (Farrington, 1994). While such approaches were laudable, they also proved challenging as assumed win-win-win scenarios mostly turned out to be elusive. In the late 1990s, development programming increasingly reflected a reorientation to the economic foundations of development. What had started as an academic topic under the label 'value chain' would subsequently become a key area of 'integrated' and 'inclusive' development approaches. Over the next two decades, value chain development would take different forms and shapes driven by a series of issue-attention cycles.

Issue-attention cycles

The concept of 'issue-attention cycles' owes to Downs (1972) who observed the systematic cycle characterized by heightened public interest in major issues followed by increasing boredom, despite any changes in the underlying conditions that had sparked the interest in the issues in first place. Traditionally, research looking at issue-attention cycles has focused on interactions between major communications media and the general public as well as the practical implications for advancing policy and societal change (Peters and Hogwood, 1985; Shih et al., 2008; Petersen, 2009). We adapt the concept of issue-attention cycles to examine the evolution of discussions on MBDA by distinguishing the following stages:

1. *Pre-proliferation*, where a few researchers or practitioners seek to address a given problem by developing an approach (and associated methodologies and tools).
2. *Proliferation*, where, propelled by euphoric enthusiasm, a broader group of researchers and practitioners becomes aware of a particular problem and a yet larger group adopts the new approach as a proposed solution, facilitated by funding from donor agencies in search of promising avenues for achieving much needed impact.
3. *Levelling off* as scepticism kicks in, given the lack of evidenced impact, realization of the real cost, and growing awareness of trade-offs.
4. *Gradual decline* of donor interest and enthusiasm among practitioners and researchers alike.
5. *Post-proliferation*, where the funding agencies, practitioners, and researchers move into 'a prolonged limbo – a twilight realm of lesser attention or spasmodic recurrences of interest', as Downs (1972: 40) puts it, and eventually move on to the next issue-attention cycle.

Figure 1.1 shows the evolution issues cycles in MBDA since the 1980s, each depicted by an 'expectation curve' which shows the proliferation, levelling off, and gradual decline of each cycle. In some cases, issues were driven by researchers with limited engagement by practitioners (e.g. commodity chain), while in other cases researcher-led issue cycles were picked up by practitioners for the design of interventions (e.g. rural livelihoods and value chains). Various cycles were largely driven by practitioners, to include those related to microfinance and small and medium enterprise (SME) development, non-traditional agricultural exports, and VCD. Within each cycle, and between some of them, multiple streams of debate and interactions existed. For example, discussions on 'Making Markets Work for the Poor' (M4P) developed by the Springfield Centre in the 2000s evolved into 'Market Systems' as promoted by USAID and others in the 2010s. In other cases, discussions proved to be short lived in the context of rural development, such as Base of the Pyramid. Cross-fertilization between the researchers' and practitioners' realms occurred for overarching topics, such as gender, livelihoods, and poverty reduction. In these cases,

Prominence / Expectations

Practice driven
Trade capacity
Non-traditional ag. exports

Microfinance
SME development
Business development services

M4P (Springfield)
Value links (GTZ/GIZ)
VC finance
Base of Pyramid
Risk management

Market Systems (USAID)
Inclusive VC
Gender-equitable VC
Branching out —Nutrition-sensitive VC
Climate-resilient VC
Responsible finance / Impact investments

Concern: smallholder competitiveness

Concern: Poorest left behind in VCD

Research driven

Rural livelihoods & poverty reduction

Agriculture/nutrition/market linkages

Commodity chain debate
Market & trade distortions
French filière approach
Wallerstein's world system

Global value chain debate
Upgrading value chains
Value chain governance
Porter's value chain

Climate risks and impact
Inclusive business models
VC as complex systems

1980   1990   2000   2010   2020

Earlier market-based development approaches

Value chain development

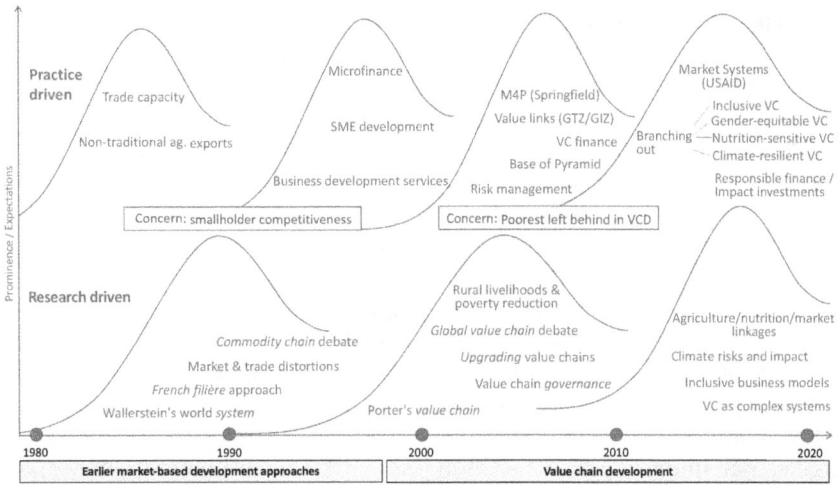

Figure 1.1 Issue-attention cycles in earlier market-based development approaches and value chain development, 1980–2020.

researchers highlighted the relevance of the topics which stimulated practitioners to design more nuanced VCD initiatives and associated monitoring systems. With a view on smallholders, a general shift can be observed from a focus on their competitiveness in earlier MBDA to prioritizing specific measures so that the poorest among them are not left behind in VCD. The next section sheds light on the main proponents of these approaches, interactions between researchers and practitioners, and the extent to which genuine progress was made.

Issue-attention cycles in value chain research and development

Approaches preceding value chain development, early 1980s–late 1990s

During the 1980s and 1990s, encouraging private sector engagement in development efforts in the global South became a central element of development cooperation strategies, with investments mostly focused at the micro level (Schulpen and Gibbon, 2002). Two early strategies were non-traditional agricultural exports (NTAE) and SME development. The former sought to encourage smallholder engagement in newly expanding export markets for high-value agricultural products, often horticultural products. The public sector provided subsidies, infrastructure development, and others means of support for export promotion, often directed at large-scale companies equipped to ship agricultural commodities to international markets. SME development, in turn, and related discussions on microfinance and business development services (BDS), shifted the focus to small and medium enterprises with the expectation that the urban and rural poor would benefit from income-generating activities, either as business owners or as employees. As the discussions below highlight, both approaches started with a strong push from funding agencies and governmental agencies and NGOs supported by them, but ultimately fell out of favour after a few years.

Non-traditional agricultural exports. In the 1980s, following large-scale investments in road construction, expanded power grids, and processing facilities for agricultural, forest, and other products in the 1960s and 1970s, attention shifted towards interventions in support of NTAE. Associated strategies sought to capitalize on preferential access of tropical countries to export markets for agricultural products, such as the United States for Latin America or the European Economic Community for the countries of Africa, the Caribbean, and the Pacific. NTAE promotion also dovetailed with the implementation of structural adjustment and market liberalization programmes which dominated political and development agendas around the mid-1980s. Proponents argued that, under appropriate conditions (e.g. favourable policy frameworks), smallholders could successfully participate in NTAE, increase their incomes and, eventually, move out of poverty. Interventions were typically large scale, involving thousands of farmers, relied heavily on agricultural inputs to meet volume and quality requirements, and were coupled with costly infrastructure improvements (Barham et al., 1995). Some funding agencies (e.g. USAID) were so convinced about NTAE as a solution to the economic ills of tropical countries that they requested their agriculture offices to modify projects such that they directly contributed to NTAE (Rosset, 1991).

Despite positive impacts in some cases (e.g. Von Braun et al., 1989; Hamilton and Fischer, 2003), the appropriateness of NTAE for smallholders attracted scrutiny in light of its high demand for economies of scale which often led to social differentiation and, over time, expelling of large numbers of smallholders from their lands (Rosset, 1991). Concern was also raised that income generation focusing on a single crop was too risky for poor farming households (Mannon, 2005). Others argued that smallholder engagement in export-oriented horticultural production provoked pesticide resistance and encouraged increased application of chemical inputs over time, resulting in high costs for growers and health problems (Murray, 1991; Murray and Hoppin, 1992). Where governments strongly invested in support of NTAE, political tensions arose over scarce public resources being directed at large-scale exporters, while at the same time government support for smallholder production and marketing had been declining (Barham et al., 1992). Overall, NTAE proved a viable strategy for farmers with sufficient asset endowments and prepared to take risks, for example in relation to horticultural production. For many smallholders, however, benefits were limited in view of poor rural services and highly demanding regulatory and market requirements (see Carletto et al., 2007; Okello et al., 2011).

SME development. Unlike NTAE strategies, which supported limited numbers of large-scale exporters in hopes that they would engage smallholders over time, SME development targeted hundreds, sometimes thousands, of SMEs as agents of local economic development. As early as the 1970s, some economists had considered SME development a viable pathway out of poverty (Gibb, 1993). In the mid-1980s and early 1990s, discussions intensified on the income-generating potential of SME development. This reflected the growing concern over unequal distribution of income, linked partially with large-scale businesses and NTAE promotion, and the recognition of the public sector's limitations in effectively addressing persistent underemployment and poverty (Liedholm and Mead, 1987; Mahajan and Dichter, 1990). Bilateral donors and UN agencies were especially active in supporting SMEs through a combination of credit, training, and technical assistance. In the mid-1980s, USAID alone financed close to 100 SME development projects (Meyer, 1991) and, between 1980 and 1990, the World Bank lent roughly US$200 m a year for the same purpose (Webster, 1990). The underlying rationale considered: 1) the sheer number of SMEs and their relevance to the rural economy; 2) their nature as a critical source of income for the rural poor, especially those with limited access to land; and 3) the lack of government support, due partially to the informality prevalent in the SME sector. Advocates of SME development argued that this type of enterprise used capital more efficiently, generated more employment, and was more evenly distributed geographically than larger businesses (Liedholm and Mead, 1987; Webster, 1990).

With growing support for SME development there was a felt need for sharing lessons learned and a critical reflection on what could be done differently for increased impact. In response to this need, the practitioner-oriented journal *Small Enterprise Development*[1] was launched in 1990, with financing from the World Bank, USAID, and others. The journal would become a platform for fruitful, at times passionate, debate between researchers and practitioners on SME development and associated topics. Representatives of funding agencies engaged periodically in the journal, often to lay out and clarify their strategies for SME development (Frenz, 1990; Webster, 1990; Tomecko and Kolshorn, 1996; Wolfensohn, 2000). Donors' support for and active participation in discussions on SME development pathways marked an important change from the previous NTAE era. Practitioners, for their part, shared their experiences in addressing crucial issues in relation to SME development, for example the design of capacity building programmes (Agar, 1999; Grierson, 2000) or the assessment of occupational health and safety conditions (Scott, 1999). Unlike many donors and practitioners, researchers would adopt a more critical stance by addressing policy issues hampering SME development (Abuodha and Bowles, 2000; Bateman, 2000), or by conducting thorough impact assessments of SME support programmes (Dunn and Arbuckle, 2001; Daniels, 2001). They also pointed at blind spots in contemporary debate and practice, for example the role gender plays in accessing credit for microenterprise development (Johnson and Kidder, 1999).

After more than a decade of strong support for SME development, attention started to decline among donors, practitioners, and researchers alike. Meyer's

(1991) comprehensive review of SME programmes provided insight into the factors leading to donor decline in interest:

- growing concern over project sustainability, with a shift in focus to sustainability in microfinance services that would become decoupled from the development of formal SMEs (discussed below);
- broad consensus on the importance of the macroeconomic environment, notwithstanding minimal evidence on the extent to which it effectively contributed to a given programme's success or failure;
- increasing doubts about the capacity of NGOs as principal implementers of SME programmes to respond to the multiple services needed by SMEs; and
- minimal support provided by funding agencies for critical analysis of the role SMEs play in development processes.

Microfinance. While many associate microfinance with the Grameen Bank in Bangladesh in the early 1980s, its origins date back to the early 18th century and it has evolved in various ways since (Seibel, 2003). Contemporary microfinance spans both urban and rural businesses across diverse sectors. Early efforts to promote microfinance aimed to facilitate access by the poor to finance, thus overcoming their lack of collateral and jump-starting their engagement in markets as small-scale traders, producers, or processors. The underlying rationale was that even the poorest people could escape poverty by becoming entrepreneurs, albeit in the informal sector, with microfinance being the 'missing link'. In this context, early discussions on microfinance ran in parallel to SME development. Depending on the programme or initiative, links between SME development and microfinance were strong in some cases or nearly absent in others. The attention cycle for SME development ended earlier though and, by the early 2000s, microfinance had fully eclipsed SME development as a key focus area of rural development.

During the 1990s and 2000s, expectations with regard to the poverty-reducing potential of microfinance ran high. An important role in the process accrued to microfinance institutions (MFIs) which began to mushroom as donors made available significant amounts of money to be channelled to low-income households through them. After a few years, however, MFIs faced strong pressure to become less dependent on donor funding in line with the latter's policy shifts. As a result, MFIs increased their commercial orientation, charging higher interest rates to an increasingly urban clientele. Concerns were also raised over the potential for MFIs to encourage poor people to take on excessive debt burdens and reduce their support for microenterprise development and the harder-to-service rural sector (Dichter and Harper, 2007; Mersland and Strøm, 2010). Overall, however, the microfinance movement has shown that high transactions costs and the lack of collateral do not necessarily impede profitable lending to low-income households, and even relatively poor households have demonstrated their ability to save in quantity when given attractive saving vehicles (Morduch, 1999). In addition, donor investments in building the microfinance industry can be considered successful in the sense that MFIs demonstrated their ability to wean themselves from donor assistance and establish themselves as viable commercial operations. At the same time, strong voices have been raised regarding the 'mission-drift' of MFIs and their weakened commitment to the poor (e.g. Arrassen, 2017). The microfinance attention cycle was one of the MBDA-related cycles which took longest until *levelling off* and entering the *phase of decline*. In fact, there is still a number of programmes with explicit or implicit focus on microfinance but, by and large, attention has shifted to alternative forms of rural finance beyond the scale and scope of microenterprises, such as social lending for SMEs and impact investments that target both SMEs and larger companies.

Business development services. In the late 1990s, donors and NGOs embraced the idea of business development services (BDS) to enhance the effectiveness of microfinance in spurring SME growth and development. Promoted heavily by bi- and multilateral funding agencies (e.g. SDC, GTZ, USAID, World Bank, and UN agencies), BDS strategies emphasized the need to spur market development for specialized services which were non-financial in nature (e.g. management consulting, logistics support, and marketing services). Such services were expected to support the building of business skills to run SMEs, including the capacity to access and manage rural finance. The BDS attention cycle responded to two major concerns: 1) financial services alone were insufficient to support SME growth at scale; and 2) government and NGO-led service provision within project frameworks was considered unaccountable and unsustainable. Over nearly a decade, funding agencies supported mainly NGOs to facilitate BDS market development, working both on the supply (e.g. building service capacity) and the demand side (e.g. subsidy and voucher programmes). With the aim to create a critical mass of service demanders, the owners of micro, small, and other enterprises were sensitized, and at times subsidized, to increase their willingness and capacity to pay for such services. It was expected that, over time, they would become aware of the potential and actual benefits of such services and, based on that, demand them proactively and pay the providers for their delivery. In practice, however, BDS providers often found it difficult to offer cost-effective services that micro and small businesses would demand (and pay for), while at the same time reducing their dependence on donor support (Tanburn, 1999; Bear et al., 2003). Despite the challenges to establish a self-sustaining BDS market (Gibson, 1997), the underlying 'BDS paradigm' brought needed attention to the sustainability problem inherent in project-facilitated service provision and the need for quality services to be affordable and available when required. However, donor interest and *proliferation quickly levelled off* and soon gave way to other priorities. As a result, BDS investments and productive exchange on how to improve such services and associated delivery mechanisms diminished rapidly as the shortcomings of

BDS programmes became more pronounced – after all, they were perceived as too ambitious, and proponents were criticized for lacking a fundamental understanding of how markets actually develop (Caniels et al., 2006).

Academics debate 'commodity chains'. Just before practitioners embraced SME development, microfinance, and BDS, the sociologists Hopkins and Wallerstein had begun to draw attention to the power imbalances between rich and poor countries and the structures that fostered these imbalances. They coined the term 'commodity chain' in a 1977 article outlining a research framework to study patterns of development of the modern 'world-system'. World-systems theory was an offshoot of dependency theory which, in turn, had emerged as a critique of modernization theory as laid out earlier. Unlike Rostow (1959) who assumed a linear, deterministic path to modernization of all national economies, world-systems theory emphasized the division of labour as a key organizing principle in a world-system comprising core (developed), semi-peripheral (middle income), and peripheral (underdeveloped) nations – a principle that would become key for commodity chain analysis as well (Dougherty, 2008).

By the mid-1990s, inspired by advancing free trade agreements and economic globalization, commodity chain researchers explored relationships among businesses in the downstream segments of the chain in the global North (the 'core') and opportunities for value chain actors in the upstream segments in the global South (the 'periphery') to move into higher skill and higher value activities. In light of successful export-orientation of the East and South-east Asian 'tiger states' and outsourcing of critical manufacturing operations by Northern firms, researchers focused on a 'new global manufacturing system' entailing coordinated activities along the nodes of given chains (Raikes et al., 2000). One of the primary concerns of commodity chain analysis was to understand how powerful 'lead firms', usually headquartered in the global North, set up and maintain their production and trade networks including the sourcing of raw materials and semi-finished products from the global South (Staritz, 2012). Rather than trying to understand how commodity chains are structured and reproduced in a 'stratified and hierarchical world-system' (i.e. the original focus of Hopkins and Wallerstein), attention focused on the influence of lead firms and their presumed importance as potential agents of upgrading and development in the global South (Gereffi, 1999). The commodity chain concept rightfully highlighted the roles of materiality and governance structures in shaping globalization, but ultimately failed to adequately address price mechanisms, issues of terms of trade, the key role of state policy in influencing commodity trajectories, and non-physical commodities such as services and knowledge (Dougherty, 2008). By the early 2000s, the attention cycle around commodity chains and the potential power imbalances between northern and southern-based firms had largely vanished, giving way to the conceptualization of value chains and associated research and practice.

Emergence of value chain development, early 2000s

The previous section described how earlier MBDA underwent a *phase of gradual decline* and eventually entered into the *post-proliferation stage*. This does not imply, however, that the interests and concerns in relation to earlier MBDA disappeared altogether. Some of these have been modified and continue to form, one way or another, elements of what would become VCD in the early 2000s. At the heart of VCD was the concept of 'value chain' which was first picked up by researchers before it was incorporated in development approaches and *proliferation* would kick in. The shift towards VCD implied effective changes in terms of the goals of market interventions, the roles of government agencies, NGOs, and value chain actors (including smallholders) and, particularly, the way engagement was sought with the private sector.

Academics shift debate to 'value chains'. Starting in the late 1990s, the term 'value chain' began to gradually replace 'commodity chain' in the literature. It is often claimed that the term value chain was derived from Porter's work (1985), though it had been in use since at least the early 1980s (see, for example, Prigogine et al., 1982). Porter's value chain concept did not consider specific issues among firms, nor those in relation to production, processing, and marketing in the global South. Rather, the emerging value chain literature adopted a modified view of commodity chains in the early 2000s. The extent to which the new terminology reflected genuine conceptual progress is debatable. According to Gereffi et al., (2001: 3), the term '(global) value chain' was chosen 'because it was perceived as being the most inclusive of the full range of possible chain activities and end products'. In a way, the shift in terminology also reflected a desire to avoid misleading associations with primary agricultural products that the term 'commodity chain' implied. Another layer of confusion was added through the term 'supply chain' which was commonly used in the marketing literature and by practitioners in the early 2000s. Rather than clarifying the difference in terminology and underlying concepts, researchers did their part to add to the confusion (see, for example, Al-Mudimigh et al., 2004). By the mid-2000s, both researchers and practitioners tended to employ the term 'value chain', without resolving the key differences in the nomenclature and conceptualization.

For the *pre-proliferation* and *proliferation* stages of VCD, two major strands of discussion can be distinguished in the scientific literature. The first was dominated by sociologists and development economists and the other by agricultural economists, both with different entry points and interests. The first strand examined the ability of 'lead' firms (usually Northern-based large-scale retailers and brand-name companies operating in higher value segments of the chain) to determine the terms of trade for smallholders and SMEs involved in the production, processing, and marketing of a given product. Lead firms acquired their status due to their proximity to final consumers and access to capital and technology. Key areas of this type of value chain research were governance and upgrading. Governance referred to the coordination by lead firms of activities carried out by farmers and firms in the global South (Gereffi, 1999; Humphrey and Schmitz, 2001). Analysis of governance dealt with the influence of lead firms on the organization of production, logistics, and marketing systems in the South (Humphrey and Schmitz, 2004). In theory, participation in value chains allowed businesses and farmers in the global South to acquire the skills and resources needed to 'upgrade', i.e. to reduce costs, increase the level of processing, or produce new types of goods or services (Gereffi, 1999). In this light, upgrading was primarily about technological change that would render new value-adding opportunities for farmers and businesses. Case studies examined governance structures and upgrading potential for smallholders and SMEs, particularly in sub-Saharan Africa, though their findings left little reason for optimism (Dolan and Humphrey, 2000; Raikes and Gibbon, 2000; Ponte, 2002; Gibbon and Ponte, 2005; Challies and Murray, 2011).

A second strand of early value chain research, put forward by agricultural economists, focused on the changing dynamics of global agribusinesses in response to rapid urbanization and income growth trends in the global South. In this context, the concept of value chain was freed from assumptions about unequal power dynamics between lead firms and their suppliers, and served to stress the role of processors, distributors, and retailers in getting high-value food to consumers. With the adoption of the value chain concept agricultural economists highlighted their interest to look beyond their traditional domain (e.g. farm-level production technologies and competitiveness of commodity markets) and explore the contributions of diverse value chain actors to formal food systems. In particular, they focused on four major trends in value chains, each with important implications for how agricultural products are produced, sourced, processed, and sold: 1) rapid growth of high value agri-food for export; 2) consolidation in the global agri-food industry; 3) diversification of food retail (supermarkets) and service outlets (e.g. expansion of fast food chains); and 4) the transformation of intermediation (e.g. logistical services, cold storage facilities) (Maertens and Swinnen, 2015; Barrett et al., 2020). The extent to which these changes have included, or excluded, smallholders remains an open question; case studies have suggested that formalization of commercial relations has enticed buyers to seek out medium- to large-scale suppliers over smallholders, while others have shown that smallholders hold their position despite the changing business environment.

The two predominant strands of early value chain research ran largely in parallel to each other. The recent review of value chain research by Barrett and colleagues (2020), for example, made few references to concerns expressed in previous value chain work by sociologists and development economists. However, the basic ideas behind both strands of value chain research, namely, that the rules of the game were changing and that Northern-based firms were willing to engage smallholders and SMEs in the global South to respond to demanding consumers in the global North, piqued the interest of funding agencies and NGOs with respect to the design of projects to advance VCD.

With a view on emerging opportunities in global agri-food markets, imple-menters focused on building the capacities of smallholders and SMEs in the global South to better respond to demand-side requirements in the global North.

Proliferation of value chain development, mid- to late 2000s

Donors, NGOs, and governments embrace value chains. Proliferation of VCD started around the mid-2000s, fuelled by donor interest in poverty reduction and increased funding for national poverty reduction strategies. The rise of VCD programming also reflected broader trends in development, including a reaccentuation of economic considerations in addition to environmental and social aspects which had dominated development agendas during most of the 1990s. This move 'back to the roots' prepared the ground for VCD and implied stronger engagement with the private sector. VCD programming rapidly gained momentum among donor agencies, NGOs, and national governments eager to leverage the private sector's resources, networks, and experiences in local economic development. A basic assumption of VCD interventions in the agri-food industry was that large-scale private companies would provide mar-ket opportunities or employment for smallholders. The role of development was to identify these opportunities and to support smallholders and SMEs that engaged with them to respond to the demands of large-scale buyers. Examples include USAID's support to NGOs for building value chains for horticultural products involving retailer outlets which would later become Walmart (Koica USAID, 2014); funding provided by GTZ (now GIZ) to German chocolate manufacturer Ritter for building a cacao value chain involving smallholders in Nicaragua (Rabe, 2004); USAID's and USDA's support to US coffee buyers for establishing supply links with Central American smallholders (Simmons, 2002); and Italian cooperation supporting the establishment of a milk supply network for Italian dairy processor Parmalat (Dobson, 2003). In these exam-ples, NGOs were called upon to develop a supplier base, strengthen the links between producers and processors, create infrastructure, and provide other support to develop the value chains. Overall, this new approach to VCD aimed at local economic development through leveraging private sector engagement and investments.

The growing importance of VCD was also reflected in donor strategy doc-uments (Camagni and Kherallah, 2014; DFID, 2017), commissioned papers, project development, and significant amounts of money made available for VCD implementation. Influential think tanks, such as the Institute of Development Studies, The Springfield Centre, and the donor-funded Donor Committee for Enterprise Development, oriented their work to support NGOs and governments in the design, implementation, and assessment of VCD. Further boost was received through national and international responses to important events and trends in global agricultural markets, such as: substantial price fluctuations in major agricultural commodities (e.g. coffee price crisis, recovery of cocoa prices); increasing opportunities for value adding to primary production; the growth of markets for certified and other speciality products in the global North; and the expanding engagement of multinational companies into food processing and retail in the global South. The latter was largely facilitated by the expansion of supermarkets in Africa, Latin America, and Asia (Weatherspoon and Reardon, 2003; Reardon et al., 2005).

Advancement of guides and tools. With increased funding for and implementation of VCD programmes, development-oriented research organizations saw an opportunity for developing methodologies and tools for value chain analysis as an input for the design, implementation, and assessment of interventions. Most guides concentrated at the micro-level, facilitating the design of relatively small-scale interventions, although some take a broader approach by considering policy change and human rights issues (e.g. Offenheiser and Holcombe, 2003; Shriver and Abdalah, 2012). Among the micro-level guides that attracted widespread attention were those by CGIAR centres (e.g. Bernet et al., 2006; Lundy et al., 2007), development think tanks (e.g. Vermeulen et al., 2008), bilateral donor agencies (e.g. Purcell, 2008; Springer-Heinze, 2008), and UN agencies (e.g. Herr and Muzira, 2009). The guides differed in terms of the focus of VCD interventions (e.g. strengthening market links for smallholders vs. improving the overall business environment), goals (poverty reduction, creation of employment and income, decent work), and targeted users (government agencies, NGOs, smallholder organizations, private sector). They also varied in terms of their information requirements, degree of complexity, conceptualization of VCD, and engagement with multi-sector stakeholders. Two reviews have documented the respective strengths and weaknesses of well-known generic guides for VCD (Donovan et al., 2015) and those with a specific focus on gender-equitable VCD (Stoian et al., 2018), including the identification of opportunities for conceptual and methodological innovation. Others have pointed out challenges to secure active engagement from the private sector in VCD design processes, and to refine guides and their underlying theories of change over time, due to lapses and adaptation (infidelities) in their application (Horton et al., 2013).

Academics scrutinize the tenets of VCD. Not long after the early studies of value chains by sociologists and development economists emerged, a cadre of academics began to critically reflect on the potential of value chains and related VCD efforts to advance development goals, and in doing so contributed to a *levelling off* of expectations. One area of contention centred on the concept of governance and the role actually played by Northern-based firms in establishing the conditions under which smallholders and SMEs engaged in markets. For example, Gellert (2003) argued that the notion of governance failed to consider the underlying conditions that gave rise to a particular form of inter-firm relation or that allowed it to change over time. Looking at Mozambique's cashew sector, Cramer (1999) found that national-level political constraints on the development of agro-processing industries (e.g. bureaucratic interference with production relations, restricted access to credit, lack of skills, and labour supply unreliability) explained more about development prospects than externally determined governance structures. Others cast doubt on the idea that power was unilaterally exerted by Northern firms through the establishment and enforcement of standards. Sverrisson (2003: 27) argued, 'Rather than assuming the [Northern] actors control chains and invariably get what they want, we can also surmise that rather often they learn to want what they get and to select from among the available suppliers'. In addition, drawing on experiences in the Bangladesh garment industry, it was observed that suppliers upgraded their capacities and activities in the chain without any explicit coordination with buyers and their suppliers (Gereffi, 1999).

Researchers also began to highlight the challenges for smallholders to benefit from closer engagement with large-scale buyers and processors. Tallontire et al., (2005) described how social criteria put in place by European buyers on African suppliers reduced the benefits for women and informal workers, thus highlighting the role of the local context in limiting the reach of value chain governance. A meta-analysis of third-party certification for agri-food products – a requirement by Northern-based processors and retailers for access to the value chain – showed mixed outcomes for smallholders across key indicators, including household income growth (Oya et al., 2018). Others have looked at the willingness and capacity of smallholders to expand their production and build assets in response to value chain engagement, bringing to light potential trade-offs between livelihood needs and strategies and the demands of the value chain (Sheck et al., 2013; Donovan and Poole, 2014).

Maturation of value chain development, 2010s

VCD branches out. The sharp focus on poverty reduction, which had characterized VCD for about a decade, began to soften in the early 2010s in response to an increasingly diverse development agenda, which included interests related to climate change, health and nutrition, and gender equity. The branching out of interests and expectations around VCD was reflected in the publication of various articles and methodological guides and tools that merged VCD with nutrition-sensitive agriculture, climate-resilience, and gender equity (Table 1.1). In addition, new frameworks emerged that guided thinking about smallholder engagement in markets, such as 'inclusive business models' and 'market systems development'. These have been driven mainly by practitioners and, to some extent, funding agencies. While they suggest an advancement in terms of conceptual thinking, much of what appears under a new label draws on existing features of VCD. On one hand, these variations of VCD direct attention to aspects of smallholder market engagement considered to be particularly relevant by funding and implementing agencies. On the other hand, they carry an even greater risk of being overly reductionist in thinking on how to support smallholder market engagement, especially in light of recent discussions on the complexity of value chains and the need for systemic approaches and adaptive management (Orr et al., 2018).

Academics expand the discussion on VCD. Over the past decade, economists at CGIAR and elsewhere have zoomed in on various features of value chains relevant for improved design and implementation of VCD programming. One stream of discussion has focused on the role of cooperatives in providing services to smallholders to facilitate engagement in value chains (Bernard et al., 2008; Hellin et al., 2009; Poole and Donovan, 2014). Researchers also made the case for incorporating the dimension of sustainable rural livelihoods into VCD programming, recognizing that smallholder households pursue diversified strategies to make a living and have varied resource endowments which influence their capacity to engage in and benefit from value chains (Dorward et al., 2003; Stoian et al., 2012; Neilson and Shonk, 2014). They also tackled issues around how chain actors access and share knowledge and the implications for innovation along the chain (Pietrobelli and Rabellotti, 2011; Thiele et al., 2011; Devaux et al., 2018). Others highlighted the unique challenges faced by stakeholders in value chains for lesser-known foods characterized, for example, by weak demand, limited investment, infrastructure deficiencies, and dispersed production (Blare and Donovan, 2016). Discussions also highlighted the uncertainty in which value chains operate, the capacities of smallholders and SMEs to respond to shocks, and the implications for how interventions are designed and implemented (Lamboll et al., 2018; Orr et al., 2018). Overall, these studies have addressed important issues related to value chains and

Table 1.1 Branching out of VCD in the 2010s

Extension of VCD	Organizational proponents	Selected citations
Value chains and nutrition	CGIAR, IFAD	Hawkes and Ruel (2011) Maestre et al., (2017) Gelli et al., (2019)
Value chains and gender equity	AgriProFocus, BMGF, DCED, FAO, ILO, SNV, USAID, CGIAR	Stoian et al., (2018)
Value chains and climate change	IFAD, IISD, CGIAR	Vermeulen (2015) Daze and Dekens (2016)
Market systems development	USAID, SDC, ACIAR	Downing et al., (2018) Campbell (2014)
Inclusive business models	SNV, CGIAR, FAO, Wageningen University	Kelly et al., (2015) Sopov et al., (2014)

ACIAR = Australian Centre for International Agricultural Research, BMGF = Bill and Melinda Gates Foundation, DCED = Donor Committee for Enterprise Development, FAO = Food and Agricultural Organization of the United Nations, IFAD = International Fund for Agricultural Development, ILO = International Labour Organization, IISD = International Institute for Sustainable Development, SDC = Swiss Agency for Development and Cooperation, SNV = Netherlands Development Organization, USAID = United States Agency for International Development smallholder engagement in them. However, the extent to which these lessons have reached practitioners remains largely unknown. In some cases, the articles employed theoretical considerations and abstract language without direct links to development practices, which may lead to the work being dismissed outright by those in the field. In most cases, studies were carried out outside of project frameworks or without direct collaboration with government agencies, NGOs or businesses, thus reducing options for joint learning around research findings and suggested improvements for implementation.

Evolution, blind spots, and promising avenues

Applying the concept of 'issue-attention cycles' to the discussions on VCD and earlier MBDA provides valuable insights on how a perceived gap in approaches to rural development has been addressed by diverse research and development organizations, how both groups have inspired (or ignored) each other, and how 'real-life issues' have effectively been solved or debate has deviated due to relabelling and rebranding without addressing these issues. We present these insights in response to the three key questions posed earlier.

Issue-attention cycles in relation to value chain development

We identified seven issue-attention cycles in relation to VCD and earlier MBDA over the past 40 years, with dozens of frameworks and topics brought forward by practitioners and researchers. A few methodologies and tools for VCD stood out which have mainly been promoted by development organizations, though researchers often contributed to their conceptual foundation and development of methodologies and tools for their application. Prominent frameworks for VCD reflect commonalities with regard to some key focus areas, while important differences exist in terms of others (Table 1.2). Thinking around VCD places emphasis on poverty reduction through inclusion of smallholders and other marginalized groups in value chains and the development of SMEs that provides support and services to smallholders. Despite the supposed focus on the demand side in VCD, however, surprisingly few frameworks or guides place a strong focus on consumers. Institutional arrangements among value chain actors and in the enabling environment of value chains are addressed, but little attention is paid to legal or voluntary sustainability standards, such as food safety and environmental regulations, certifications and ecolabels, and industry-wide or company standards. Similarly, a thorough assessment of the political-legal framework for business development has rarely been a key focus area of VCD approaches, nor has the provision of VCD services. Particularly notable is the lack of attention paid to the diversity of VCD services in terms of service type (technical, business, financial), providers (government agencies, NGOs, firms), and delivery mechanisms (for profit, cost-recovering, subsidized). This comes as a surprise in view of the diverse needs of smallholders for such services over longer periods of time (see Donovan et al., 2008, 2018).

Table 1.2 Overview of key areas of interest among principal frameworks for VCD

VCD approach	Smallholders/ small-scale entrepreneurs	SME development	Consumers	Poverty reduction	Inclusion	Institutional arrangements	Sustainability standards	Political-legal framework	Technical and business services	Financial services
Base of the Pyramid	+	++	+++	+++	+++	++	+	+	++	+
M4P	+++	++	+	+++	+++	++	+	++	+	++
Value chain development (e.g. ValueLinks by GIZ, PMCA and 5Capitals by CGIAR)	++	++	+	++	++	++	+	+	++	++
Market systems	+++	+++	++	+++	++	++	+	++	++	++
Inclusive business models (e.g. LINK by CGIAR)	+++	++	+	++	+++	++	++	+	++	++
Nutrition-sensitive value chains	++	+	+++	++	++	++	+	++	++	+
Climate-resilient value chains	++	+	++	+	+	+++	++	+++	+	++
Gender-equitable value chains	++	+	+	+++	+++	++	+	++	+	+

+++ = principal focus, ++ = some focus, + = limited/no focus

GIZ = German Corporation for International Cooperation, M4P = Making Markets Work for the Poor, PMCA = Participatory Market Chain Approach

This shortcoming can be linked to the way many research and development organizations support VCD – typically in the form of projects that rarely last for more than three years. While some projects may include training of service providers, both the breadth and depth of such efforts hardly allow for building service delivery capacity that meets the needs of smallholders and SMEs once a project has terminated. Equally challenging is the integration of services related to production, processing and environmental management, business and marketing, and finance, ranging from microfinance in the order of a few hundred dollars to multi-million dollar impact investments. These services are often required in combination, although the right mix will vary according to the local context. In addition, the potential for high transaction costs in the provision of services to micro and small enterprises needs to be recognized. To date, thinking around VCD design has yet to consider how to design delivery modes that ensure reliable access by smallholders and SMEs to integrated and dynamic services. After roughly two decades of discussions around how to design VCD, this blind spot has yet to attract attention on a larger scale.

The issue-attention cycles linked with MBDA have had fairly short lifespans, mostly in the range of 5 to 7 and rarely up to 10 years. This can also be attributed to funding agencies expecting constant 'innovation' and the way practitioners and researchers seek to meet this expectation. By its very nature, innovation implies approaches, methodologies, and tools that have yet to demonstrate 'proof of concept' and 'scalability'. Ironically, despite much needed impact at scale, donor funding is rarely made available over longer periods of time for approaches which have proven their impact and uptake at scale. To the contrary, by following issue-attention cycles and calling for frequent 'innovation', donors effectively discourage continued work with successful approaches and tools or, indirectly, provide incentives for relabelling what already exists ('old wine in new bottles'). Drying up of donor funding is a key factor driving the at times abrupt *decline of VCD approaches* and the moving on to the next issue-attention cycle, usually without effectively addressing emerging issues and shortcomings. This phenomenon was described by Downs (1972: 40) as follows:

> As more and more people realize how difficult, and how costly to themselves, a solution to the problem would be, three reactions set in. Some people just get discouraged. Others feel positively threatened by thinking about the problem; so they suppress such thoughts. Still others become bored by the issue. Most people experience some combination of these feelings. Consequently, public desire to keep attention focused on the issue wanes. And by this time, some other issue is usually entering Stage Two; so it exerts a more novel and thus more powerful claim upon public attention.

Replacing 'people' with 'funding agencies, practitioners, and researchers' in the above quotation encapsulates the essence of the issue-attention cycles associated with MBDA, including VCD. As highlighted throughout this chapter, we are dealing with a patchwork of seemingly rushed attempts of trial and error, rather than a process of continuous improvement in the Hegelian sense of thesis, antithesis, and synthesis.

Interactions between researchers and practitioners

NGOs, government agencies, and CGIAR, among others, are under mounting pressure from funders to demonstrate impact at scale. While experience suggests that achieving large-scale impact on overarching issues such as poverty reduction requires systems approaches involving diverse stakeholders from public and private sector and civil society, there is an expectation that a given implementing organization alone can convene diverse stakeholder groups and 'go to scale'. This expectation is often linked to a 'track record' an organization needs to build to be successful in mobilizing resources for its work. This, in turn, provides an incentive for branding own approaches, methodologies, and tools, rather than incorporating or adapting existing ones in new VCD initiatives. A good part of the diversity found in approaches, methodologies, and tools for VCD has its roots in the competition generated among researchers and practitioners and the need to stand out among peers. This is reflected in the confusing mix of branded methodological guidelines available for the design of VCD (M4P, ValueLinks, Market Systems, Participatory Market Chain Approach), which share a basic notion of what smallholders and SMEs need and how to achieve it. Such silos are reinforced through branded building capacity events and training-of-trainers (ToT) approaches, which provide reference to complementary methodologies or tools and potential perils that have been discussed in the wider value chain literature.

On the upside, innovative ideas have captured the attention of researchers, donors, and practitioners, which have been intergraded into VCD thinking and practice to varying degrees. Perhaps most notable is the influence of the sustainable livelihoods framework developed by DFID and others in the late 1990s which was picked up by social scientists who, in turn, provided practitioners with valuable insights from a multitude of livelihood studies around the globe. This helped raise awareness about the importance of gender-differentiated approaches to VCD, outcomes to be sought beyond employment and income (for example, in the form of nutrition) and, in general, asset-based approaches to VCD (see Stoian et al., 2012, 2018; Devaux et al., 2018). Such approaches also found their way into methodological guides for assessing the poverty impacts of VCD (Donovan and Stoian, 2012). Relatedly, standard bodies have reached out to researchers to study the impact of voluntary sustainability standards (including certifications) on smallholders and the environment which has produced a growing body of literature over the past few years (see EVIDENSIA (n.d.) which was launched by ISEAL, Rainforest Alliance and WWF in 2019). Practitioners, in turn, pointed at the difficulty to include the poorest of the poor in VCD initiatives, particularly landless people, migrant labourers, and ethnic minorities, among others (Mitchell et al., 2009). This spurred researchers to suggest non-market based approaches to asset building among such groups before these would become 'value chain ready' (Stoian and Donovan, 2013).

In recent years, some scepticism has been expressed by both researchers and practitioners as regards the linearity underlying the value chain concept. While it is evident that there is a linear flow of raw materials, semi-finished, and finished products from producers via processors to consumers, there are various horizontal linkages among value chain actors and between them and service providers operating from outside the chain. In addition, there are linkage points between value chains in a given geography, for example in the form of technical or financial services provided to smallholders operating in different value chains. This has led to concepts such as 'value webs' or 'value networks' which seek to overcome the limitations of the value chain concept (see Li and Whalley, 2002; Kelly and Marchese, 2015; Scheiterle et al., 2018). These ideas have been picked up by recent frameworks proposed for VCD, such as Market Systems as promoted by USAID and others. While the concept of looking into both vertical and horizontal linkages within and across value chains is a step forward, it still falls short of addressing persistent blind spots of VCD. Among these are:

- The focus of most interventions on a single value chain, thereby failing to recognize the diversified livelihood strategies of smallholders who balance portfolios of market and non-market oriented activities.
- Understanding and addressing trade-offs and risks facing smallholders when required to bundle their resources for participation in value chains.
- The complex and dynamic nature of value chains which requires a systems approach and adaptive management including contingency plans when something goes wrong.
- Insufficient mechanisms for sharing information, benefits, and risks between smallholders and their business partners in the mid- and downstream segments of value chains.
- Incomplete integration of technical, business, and financial services whose orientation and combination need to be adapted as smallholders and the enterprises they are linked with develop.
- Inconsistency between public and private sustainability standards governing value chains (e.g. voluntary standards for 'deforestation free' value chains vs. what is considered illegal deforestation by law).
- Lack of collaborative frameworks for joint learning among value chain actors, service providers, political decision makers, and researchers for continuous improvement.

VCD contributions to achieving development goals

Undoubtedly, the emergence and evolution of VCD have been important catalysts of development processes that address multiple development goals. While in the past support to smallholders was largely confined to on-farm interventions, it is now common practice to consider market and value chain linkages in rural development interventions. In particular, the capacity of the private sector to leverage networks, investments, and other resources is better taken advantage of. Combining this capacity with that of public sector entities, for example through public-private partnerships fostered as integral elements of VCD, has strong potential to make significant contributions to the SDGs.

At the same time, surprisingly little is known about how VCD initiatives have effectively been carried out by different types of practitioners, the main challenges in their application, and the resulting outcomes and impacts for smallholders, SMEs, and others (Devaux et al., 2020). One reason is that VCD interventions are often time, place and commodity specific and unlikely to be repeated in a similar way, while VCD outcomes are multi-dimensional and contingent on contextual particularities given the nature of value chains as open, multi-layered systems (Ton et al., 2011). Moreover, there are few, if any, incentives for implementing organizations to be (self-)critical, and most of their experiences and results are confined to unpublished reports for funding agencies. Independent third-party assessments are rare and there is an urgent need for systematic reviews for broad-based learning across value chains and diverse contexts in which they are operating. Similarly, ex-post impact evaluation needs to be applied more broadly and systematically to determine value-for-money from VCD interventions (Torero, 2016).

To date, few studies have examined the implementation processes by NGOs and government agencies. In Nicaragua, for example, typical approaches to VCD were found to be very basic, reflected in: 1) reliance on a single tool for design and implementation; 2) expected outcomes based on technical assistance and training, without linkages to business and financial services; and 3) limited engagement with other value chain actors, service providers, and researchers (Donovan et al., 2017). In Vietnam, after identification of opportunities for linking smallholders with markets for high-value agricultural products (e.g. dairy, horticulture), NGOs focused on traditional areas of engagement, namely technical assistance to farmers for boosting production and organizational support for establishing producer associations (Even and Donovan, 2017). Similar restrictions apply for recent approaches to more focused VCD, emphasizing climate resilience, nutrition outcomes, or gender equity. In a review of principal guides for gender-equitable VCD, for example, it was found that while making important contributions to sensitizing practitioners regarding the importance of gender in VCD, most guides failed to provide indications of how they could be combined with other methodologies or tools for VCD (Stoian et al., 2018). This is striking as none of the existing guides claims to be the only tool for VCD. One the hand, there is a multitude of VCD frameworks and tools which have been proposed by researchers and practitioners alike. Given different foci, they provide for a multitude of contexts within which VCD can be promoted. On the other hand, the sheer number of such guides is overwhelming and for only a handful of them is there evidence of their outcomes and impact.

After about two decades of VCD, it should go without saying that VCD requires more than a technological focus on agricultural production, or zooming in on one topic (e.g. climate, nutrition, gender). Researchers have admonished donors and NGOs over the lack of attention to learning within VCD programmes, especially given the strong assumptions that underpin intervention designs. Where recommendations for assessment had been provided in methodological guides, the focus has tended to be on describing activities, thus leaving limited scope for learning around the underlying impact pathways of VCD. These combined factors work strongly against what is needed for successful VCD: 1) cross-sector collaboration, rather than competition; 2) pooling of experiences and resources; and 3) critical reflection and genuine learning for continuous improvement over time.

Looking forward, it is highly likely that the factors underlying the issue-attention cycles described here will persist. At the beginning of a new decade, a number of topics are looming on the horizon which have entered, or will soon enter, the *pre-proliferation stage*. The role of value chains as an integral element of local and global food systems has already gained momentum. Additional topics of interest in the near future may include: 1) value chains in the circular economy; 2) 'green' (and 'white') value chains with strong environmental (and social) credentials; and, in view of the Covid-19 pandemic, 3) green recovery of value chains; and 4) reshoring value chains (focus on domestic agri-food value chains to decrease reliance on global value chains). This list could be extended ad infinitum; the bottom line is that genuine progress in terms of VCD and its impact will only happen if the blind spots identified above are adequately addressed. More systematic reviews of what has worked, what has not, and why, will also go a long way to minimize the risk that errors are repeated, silos perpetuated, and shortcomings not addressed. Funding agencies, impact investors, and other agents of responsible finance have a strong role to play to support such reviews, collaborative frameworks for joint learning, and a long-term vision of what is needed for VCD to achieve impact at scale. With these ingredients combined, the duration of issue-attention cycles can be significantly extended and resources be bundled for impactful interventions. Without these, however, important impediments, such as cacophonic discourse, navel-gazing reflection, and self-serving branding, are likely to persist.

Note

1. In 2004, the journal changed its name from *Small Enterprise Development* to *Enterprise Development and Microfinance*.

Acknowledgement

This study was supported by the CGIAR Research Program on Policies, Institutions and Markets (PIM). We thank the donors who support PIM through their contributions to the CGIAR Fund. We are also grateful to the anonymous reviewers whose suggestions improved this chapter.

References

Abuodha, C. and Bowles, R. (2000) 'Business license reform in Kenya and its impact on small enterprises', *Small Enterprise Development* 11(3): 16–24. <https://doi.org/10.3362/0957-1329.2000.028>

Adhikari, R. (2019) 'Agricultural marketing and high-value chains: enhanced role for private sector towards value chain integration', in G. Thapa, P.K. Joshe, and A. Kumar (eds), *Agricultural Transformation in Nepal: Trends, Prospects and Policy Options*, Springer, Singapore.

Agar, J. (1999) 'Marketing for the local market: what does it mean in practice?' *Small Enterprise Development* 10(4): 4–15. <https://doi.org/10.3362/0957-1329.1999.038>

Al-Mudimigh, A.S., Zairi, M., and Ahmed, A.M.M. (2004) 'Extending the concept of supply chain: the effective management of value chains', *International Journal of Production Economics* 87(3): 309–20. <https://doi.org/10.1016/j.ijpe.2003.08.004>

Arrassen, W. (2017) 'The determinates of MFIs' social and financial performances in sub-Saharan Africa: has mission driven occurred?' *Annals of Finance* 13: 205–35. <https://doi.org/10.1007/s10436-017-0296-x>

Barham, B., Clark, M., Katz, E., and Schurman, R. (1992) 'Nontraditional agricultural exports in Latin America', *Latin American Research Review* 27(2): 43–82. <http://www.jstor.com/stable/2503749>

Barham, B., Carter, M., and Sigelko, W. (1995) 'Agro-export production and peasant land access: examining the dynamic between adoption and accumulation', *Journal of Development Economics* 46(1): 85–107. <https://doi.org/10.1016/0304-3878(94)00049-I>

Barrett, C.B., Reardon, T., Swinnen, J., and Zilberman, D. (2020) *Agri-food Value Chain Revolutions in Low-and Middle-Income Countries*, June 2020 revised version [pdf] <http://barrett.dyson.cornell.edu/files/papers/BRSZ%20revision%2018%20June%20resubmitted.pdf> <http://barrett.dyson.cornell.edu/files/papers/BRSZ%2013%20Aug%202019.pdf> [accessed 18 August 2020].

Bateman, M. (2000) 'Business support centers in the transition economies: progress with the wrong model', *Small Enterprise Development* 11(2): 50–9. <https://doi.org/10.3362/0957-1329.2000.020>

Bear, M., Gibson, A., and Hitchins, R. (2003) 'From principles to practice: ten critical challenges for BDS market development', *Small Enterprise Development* 14(4): 10–23. <https://doi.org/10.3362/0957-1329.2003.042>

Bernard, T., Taffesse, A.S., and Gabre-Madhin, E. (2008) 'Impact of cooperatives on smallholders' commercialization behavior: evidence from Ethiopia', *Agricultural Economics* 39(2998): 147–61. <https://doi.org/10.1111/j.1574-0862.2008.00324.x>

Bernet, T., Thiele, G., and Zschocke, T. (2006) *Participatory Market Chain Approach*, CIP, Lima, Peru.

Blare, T. and Donovan, J. (2016) 'Building value chains for indigenous fruits: lessons from camu-camu in Peru', *Renewable Agriculture and Food Systems* 33(1): 6–18. <https://doi.org/10.1017/S1742170516000181>

Camagni, M. and Kherallah, M. (2014) *Commodity Value Chain Development Projects: Sustainable Inclusion of Smallholders in Agricultural Value Chains*, IFAD, Rome, Italy.

Campbell, R. (2014) 'A framework for inclusive market systems development' [online], USAID <https://www.marketlinks.org/sites/marketlinks.org/files/resource/files/Market_Systems_Framework.pdf> [accessed 18 August 2020].

Caniels, M., Romijn, H., and Ruijter-De Wildt, M. (2006) 'Can business development service practitioners learn from theories of innovation and services marketing?' *Development in Practice* 16(5): 425–40. <https://www.jstor.org/stable/4030038>

Carletto, C., Kirk, A., Winters, P., and Davis, B. (2007) *Non-Traditional Exports, Traditional Constraints: The Adoption and Diffusion of Cash Crops among Smallholders in Guatemala*, ESA Working Paper 07-03, FAO, Rome.

Challies, E. and Murray, W. (2011) 'The interaction of global value chains and rural livelihoods: the case of smallholder raspberry growers in Chile', *Journal of Agrarian Change* 11(1): 29–59. <https://doi.org/10.1111/j.1471-0366.2010.00282.x>

Cramer, C. (1999) 'Can Africa industrialize by processing primary commodities? The case of Mozambican cashew nuts', *World Development* 27(7): 1247–64. <https://doi.org/10.1016/S0305-750X(99)00053-4>

Daniels, L. (2001) 'A guide to measuring microenterprise profits and net worth', *Small Enterprise Development* 12(4): 54–66.

Daze, A. and Dekens, J. (2016) *Enabling Climate Risk Management along Agricultural Value Chains: Insights from the Rice Value Chain in Uganda*, IISD, Winnipeg.

Devaux, A., Torero, M., Donovan, J., and Horton, D. (2018) 'Agricultural innovation and inclusive value chain development: a review', *Journal of Agribusiness in Developing and Emerging Economies* 8(1): 99–123. <https://doi.org/10.1108/JADEE-06-2017-0065>

Devaux, A., Velasco, C., Ordinola, M., and Naziri, D. (2020) 'Enhancing value chain innovation through collective action: lessons from the Andes, Africa, and Asia', in H. Campos and O. Ortiz (eds), *The Potato Crop*, pp. 75–106, Springer, Cham.

DFID (2017) *Economic Development Strategy: Prosperity, Poverty and Meeting Global Challenges* [pdf], DIFD, London <http://pubdocs.worldbank.org/en/822011487174249256/DFID-Economic-Development-Strategy-2017.pdf> [accessed 5 August 2020].

Dichter, T.W. and Harper, M. (2007) 'What's wrong with microfinance?' In T.W. Dichter and M. Harper (eds.), *What's Wrong with Microfinance?* Practical Action Publishing, Rugby, UK.

Dobson, W.D. (2003) *Strategies for Developing Domestic and International Markets for Nicaragua's Dairy Products*, Babcock Institute Discussion Paper 2003-1, University of Wisconsin, Madison, WI.

Dolan, C. and Humphrey, J. (2000) 'Governance and trade in fresh vegetables: the impact of UK supermarkets in the African horticulture industry', *Journal of Development Studies* 37(2): 147–76. <https://doi.org/10.1080/713600072>

Donovan, J., Stoian, D., and Poole, N. (2008) *Global Review of Rural Community Enterprises: The Long and Winding Road to Creating Viable Businesses, and Potential Shortcuts*, Technical Series, Technical Bulletin 29, Rural Enterprise Development Collection 2, CATIE, Turrialba, Costa Rica.

Donovan, J. and Poole, N. (2014) 'Changing asset endowments and smallholder participation in markets: evidence from certified coffee producers in Nicaragua', *Food Policy* 44: 1–13. <https://doi.org/10.1016/j. foodpol.2013.09.010>

Donovan, J. and Stoian, D. (2012) *5Capitals: A Tool for Assessing the Poverty Impacts of Value Chain Development*, Technical Bulletin 55, Rural Enterprise Development Collection 7, CATIE, Turrialba, Costa Rica.

Donovan, J., Franzel, S., Cunha, M., Gyau, A., and Mithöfer, D. (2015) 'Guides for value chain development: a comparative review', *Journal of Agribusiness in Developing and Emerging Economies* 5(1): 1–22. <https://doi. org/10.1108/JADEE-07-2013-0025>

Donovan, J., Stoian, D., and Poe, K. (2017) Value chain development in Nicaragua: prevailing approaches and tools used for design and implementation', *Enterprise Development and Microfinance* 28(1–2): 10–27. <http://dx. doi.org/10.3362/1755-1986.16-00035>

Donovan, J., Stoian, D., Foundjem, D., and Blare, T. (2018) 'Service provision by agri-cooperatives engaged in high value markets', in K. Davis, A. Bohn, S. Franzel, M. Blum, U. Rieckmann, S. Raj, K. Hussein, and N. Ernst (eds), *What Works in Rural Advisory Services?*, pp. 73–6, Global Forum for Rural Advisory Services, Lausanne, Switzerland.

Dorward, A., Poole, N., Morrison, J. Kydd, J., and Urey, I. (2003) 'Markets, institutions and technology: missing links in livelihoods analysis', *Development Policy Review* 21(3): 319–32. <https://doi.org/10.1111/1467-7679.00213>

Dougherty, M.L. (2008) 'Theorizing theory: origins and orientations of commodity chain analysis', *Global Studies Journal* 1(3): 29–38.

Downing, J., Field, M., Ripley, M., and Sebstad, J. (2018) *Market Systems Resilience: A Framework for Measurement*, USAID, Washington, DC.

Downs, A. (1972) 'Up and down with ecology: the Issue attention cycle', *The Public Interest* 28: 38–51.

Dunn, E. and Arbuckle, G. (2001) 'Microcredit and microenterprise performance: impact evidence from Peru', *Small Enterprise Development* 12(4): 22–33.

Even, B. and Donovan, J. (2017) 'Value chain development in Vietnam: a look at approaches used and options for improved impacts', *Enterprise Development and Microfinance* 28(1-2): 29–43. <https://doi. org/10.3362/1755-1986.16-00034>

EVIDENSIA (no date) 'Informing action for a sustainable future' [website] <https://www.evidensia.eco/> [accessed 10 June 2020].

Farrington, J. (1994) 'Public sector agricultural extension: is there life after structural adjustment?' ODI Natural Resource Perspectives 2, ODI, London.

Frenz, A. (1990) 'Twinning' programmes for assistance to small enterprises: a review of GTZ experience', *Small Enterprise Development* 1(1): 32–7.

Gellert, P. (2003) 'Renegotiating a timber commodity chain: lessons from Indonesia on the political construction of commodity chains', *Sociological Forum* 18(1): 5–84. <https://doi.org/10.1023/A:1022602711962>

Gelli, A., Donovan, J., Margolies, A., Aberman, N., Santacroce, M., Chirwa, E., Henson, A., and Hawkes, C. (2019) 'Value chain to improve diets: diagnostics to support intervention design in Malawi', Global Food Security 25 <https://doi.org/10.1016/j.gfs.2019.09.006>.

Gereffi, G. (1999) 'International trade and industrial upgrading in the apparel commodity chain', *Journal of International Economics* 48: 37–70. <https:// doi.org/10.1016/S0022-1996(98)00075-0>

Gereffi, G., Humphrey, J., Kaplinsky, R., and Sturgeon, T. (2001) 'Introduction: globalisation, value chains and development', *IDS Bulletin* 32(3): 1–12.

Gibb, A.A. (1993) 'Key factors in the design of policy support for the small and medium enterprise (SME) development process: an overview', *Entrepreneurship & Regional Development* 5(1): 1–24. <https://doi.org/10.1080/08985629300000001>

Gibbon, P. and Ponte, S. (2005) *Trading Down: Africa, Value Chains, and the Global Economy*, Temple University Press, Philadelphia.

Gibson, A. (1997) 'Business development services: core principles and future challenges', *Small Enterprise Development* 8(3): 4–14. <https://doi.org/10.3362/0957-1329.1997.024>

Grierson, J. (2000) 'Vocational training for self-employment: learning from enterprise development best practice', *Small Enterprise Development* 11(3): 25–35. <https://doi.org/10.3362/0957-1329.2000.029>

Hamilton, S. and Fischer, E. (2003) 'Non-traditional agricultural exports in highland Guatemala: understanding or risk and perceptions of change', *Latin American Research Review* 38(3): 82–110. <https://www.jstor.org/stable/1555451>

Hawkes, C. and Ruel, M. (2011) 'Value chain for nutrition', prepared for the *IFPRI 2020 International Conference 'Leveraging Agriculture for Improving Nutrition and Health', 10–12 February 2011, New Delhi, India*.

Hellin, J., Lundy, M., and Meijer, M. (2009) 'Farmer organization, collective action and market access in Meso America', *Food Policy* 34(1): 16–22. <https://doi.org/10.1016/j.foodpol.2008.10.003>

Herr, M. and Muzira, T. (2009) *VC Development for Decent Work*, ILO, Geneva.

Hopkins, T. K., and Wallerstein, I. (1977) 'Patterns of development of the modern world-system', Review (Fernand Braudel Center), 1(2): 111–45.

Horton, D., Rotondo, E., Ybarnegaray, R.P., Hareau, G., Devaux, A., and Thiele, G. (2013) 'Lapses, infidelities and creative adaptations: lessons from evaluation of a participatory market development approach in the Andes', *Evaluation and Program Planning* 29: 28–41. <https://doi.org/10.1016/j.evalprogplan.2013.03.002>

Humphrey, J. and Schmitz, H. (2001) 'Governance in global value chains', *IDS Bulletin* 32(2): 19–29.

Humphrey, J. and Schmitz, H. (2004) 'Governance in global value chains', in H. Schmitz (ed.), *Local Enterprises in the Global Economy: Issues of Governance and Upgrading*, Chapter 4, Edward Elgar Press, Cheltenham, UK. <https://doi.org/10.4337/9781843769743.00011>

Johnson, S. and Kidder, T. (1999) 'Globalization and gender: dilemmas for microfinance organizations', *Small Enterprise Development* 10(3): 4–15. <https://doi.org/10.3362/0957-1329.1999.026>

Keeton, G.R. (1984) 'The basic needs approach: a missing ingredient in development theory?' *Development Southern Africa* 1(3–4): 276–93. <https://doi.org/10.1080/03768358408439092>

Kelly, E. and Marchese, K. (2015) 'Supply chains and value webs', *Appita Technology, Innovation, Manufacturing, Environment* 68(4): 282–5.

Kelly, S., Vergara, N., and Bammann, H. (2015) Inclusive Business Models: Guidelines for Improving Linkages between Producer Groups and Buyers of Agricultural Produce, FAO, Rome.

KOICA USAID (2014) 'Case study: USAID's partnership with Walmart and the implications for corporate engagement', *Journal of International Development Cooperation* 9(2): 156–76.

Lamboll, R., Martin, A., Sanni, L., Adebayo, K., Graffham, A., Kleih, U., Abayomi, L., and Westby, A. (2018) 'Shaping, adapting and reserving the right to play: responding to uncertainty in high quality cassava flour value chains in Nigeria', *Journal of Agribusiness in Developing and Emerging Economies* 8(1): 54–76. <https://doi.org/10.1108/JADEE-03-2017-0036>

Li, F. and Whalley, J. (2002) 'The deconstruction of the telecommunications industry: from value chains to value networks', *Telecommunications Policy* 9: 1–22. <https://doi.org/10.1016/S0308-5961(02)00056-3>

Liedholm, C. and Mead, D. (1987) *Small Scale Industries in Developing Countries: Empirical Evidence and Policy Implications*, International Development Paper 9, Michigan State University Department of Agricultural Economics, East Lansing, MI.

Lundy, M., Gottret, V., Ostertag, C., Best, R., and Ferris, S. (2007) *Participatory Market Chain Analysis for Smallholder Producers*, CIAT, Cali, Colombia.

Maertens, M. and Swinnen, J. (2015) *Agricultural Trade and Development: A Value Chain Perspective*, WTO Staff Working Paper, No. ERSD-2015-04, World Trade Organization, Geneva.

Maestre, M., Poole, N., and Henson, S. (2017) 'Assessing food value chain pathways, linkages and impacts for better nutrition of vulnerable groups', *Food Policy* 67: 31–9. <https://doi.org/10.1016/j.foodpol.2016.12.007>

Mahajan, V. and Dichter, T. (1990) 'A contingency approach to small business and microenterprise development', *Small Enterprise Development* 1(1): 4–16.

Mannon, S.E. (2005) 'Risk takers, risk makers: small farmers and non-traditional agro-exports in Kenya and Costa Rica', *Human Organization* 64(1): 16–27. <https://www.jstor.org/stable/44127001>

Mersland, R. and Strøm, R.Ø. (2010) 'Microfinance mission drift?' *World Development* 38(1): 28–36. <https://doi.org/10.1016/j.worlddev.2009.05.006>

Meyer, R. (1991) *Supporting Rural Non-farm Enterprises: What Can be Learned from Donor Programs?* Working Paper Series 91-08, Philippine Institute for Development Studies, Makati, Philippines.

Mitchell, J., Coles, C., and Keane, J. (2009) *Upgrading along Value Chains: Strategies for Poverty Reduction in Latin America*, COPLA Briefing Paper, Overseas Development Institute (ODI), London.

Morduch, J. (1999) 'The microfinance promise', *Journal of Economic Literature* 37(4): 1569–614.

Murray, D. (1991) 'Export agriculture, ecological disruption, and social inequity: some effects of pesticides in Southern Honduras', *Agriculture and Human Values* 8: 19–29. <https://doi.org/10.1007/BF01530651>

Murray, D. and Hoppin, P. (1992) 'Recurring contradictions in agrarian development: pesticide problems in Caribbean basin nontraditional agriculture', *World Development* 20(4): 597–608. <https://doi.org/10.1016/0305-750X(92)90047-Y>

Neilson, J. and Shonk, F. (2014) 'Chained to development: livelihoods and global value chains in the coffee-producing Toraja region of Indonesia',

Australian Geographer 45(3): 269–88. <https://doi.org/10.1080/00049182.2 014.929998>

Offenheiser, R.C. and Holcombe, S.H. (2003) 'Challenges and opportunities in implementing a rights-based approach to development: an Oxfam America perspective', *Nonprofit and Voluntary Sector Quarterly* 32(2): 268–301. <https://doi.org/10.1177/0899764003032002006>

Okello, J.J., Narrod, C.A., and Roy, D. (2011) 'Export standards, market institutions and smallholder farmer exclusion from fresh export vegetable high value chains: experiences from Ethiopia, Kenya and Zambia', *Journal of Agricultural Science* 3(4): 188–95. <DOI:10.5539/jas.v3n4p188>

Orr, A., Donovan, J., and Stoian, D. (2018) 'Smallholder value chains as complex adaptive systems: a conceptual framework', *Journal of Agribusiness in Developing an Emerging Economies* 8(1): 14–33. <https://doi.org/10.1108/JADEE-03-2017-0031>

Oya, C., Schaefer, F., and Skalidou, D. (2018) 'The effectiveness of agricultural certification in developing countries: a systematic review', *World Development* 112: 282–312. <https://doi.org/10.1016/j.worlddev.2018.08.001>

Peters, B.G. and Hogwood, B.W. (1985) 'In search of the issue-attention cycle', *The Journal of Politics* 47(1): 238–53.

Petersen, K. (2009) 'Revisiting Downs' issue-attention cycle: international terrorism and U.S. public opinion', *Journal of Strategic Security* 2(4): 1–16. <DOI: http://dx.doi.org/10.5038/1944-0472.2.4.1>

Pietrobelli, C. and Rabellotti, R. (2011) 'Global value chains meet innovation systems: are there learning opportunities for developing countries?' *World Development* 39(7): 1261–9. <https://doi.org/10.1016/j.worlddev.2010.05.013>

Ponte, S. (2002) 'The "Latte Revolution"? Regulation, markets, and consumption in the global coffee chain', *World Development* 30(7): 1099–122. <https://doi.org/10.1016/S0305-750X(02)00032-3>

Poole, N. and Donovan, J. (2014) 'Building cooperative capacity: the specialty coffee sector in Nicaragua', *Journal of Agribusiness in Developing and Emerging Economies* 4(2): 133–56. <https://doi.org/10.1108/JADEE-01-2013-0002>

Porter, M.E. (1985) *Competitive Advantage: Creating and Sustaining Superior Performance*, Free Press, New York.

Prigogine, I., Allen, P., and Schieve, W.C. (1982) 'The challenge of complexity: self-organization and dissipative structures', in W.C. Schieve and P.M. Allen (eds.), *Self-organization and Dissipative Structures: Applications in the Physical and Social Sciences*, pp. 3–39, University of Texas Press, Austin, TX.

Purcell, T., Gniel, S., and van Gent, R. (2008) *Making VC Work Better for the Poor: A Toolbook for Practitioners of Value Chain Analysis*, Making Markets Work Better for the Poor (M4P) Project, Department for International Development (DFID), London.

Rabe, H.J. (2004) *Armutsminderung durch den Privatsektor? Analysen, Berichte, Kontroversen*, Österreichische Forschungsstiftung für Entwicklungshilfe (ÖFSE) Edition 12, Südwind-Verlag, Wien.

Raikes, P. and Gibbon, P. (2000) 'Globalisation and African export crop agriculture', *Journal of Peasant Studies* 27(2): 50–93. <https://doi.org/10.1080/03066150008438732>

Raikes, P., Jenson, M.F., and Ponte, S. (2000) 'Global commodity chain analysis and the French Filière approach: comparison and critique', *Economy and Society* 29(3): 390–417. <https://doi.org/10.1080/03085140050084589>

Reardon, T., Timmer, C.P., and Berdegué, J.A. (2005) 'Supermarket expansion in Latin America and Asia', in *New Directions in Global Food Markets*, in A. Regmi and M. Gehlhar (eds.), *New Directions in Global Food Markets*, AIB-794 Economic Research Service, pp. 47–61, USDA, Washington, DC.

Riddell, R. (1999) 'The end of foreign aid to Africa? Concerns about donor policies', *African Affairs* 98: 309–35.

Rosset, P. (1991) 'Sustainability, economies of scale and social instability: Achilles heel of non-traditional export agriculture', *Agriculture and Human Values* 8: 30–7.

Rostow, W.W. (1959) *The Stages of Economic Growth and the Problems of Peaceful Co-existence*, Center for International Studies, Massachusetts Institute of Technology, Cambridge, MA.

Samater, I.M. (1984) 'From "growth" to "basic needs": the evolution of development theory', *Monthly Review* 36: 1–13 <https://doi.org/10.14452/MR-036-05-1984-09>.

Scheiterle, L., Ulmer, A., Birner, R., and Pyka, A. (2018) 'From commodity-based value chains to biomass-based value webs: the case of sugarcane in Brazil's bioeconomy', *Journal of Cleaner Production* 172: 3851–63. <https://doi.org/10.1016/j.jclepro.2017.05.150>

Schulpen, L. and Gibbon, P. (2002) 'Private sector development: policies, practices and problems', *World Development* 30(1): 1–15. <https://doi.org/10.1016/S0305-750X(01)00097-3>

Scott, A. (1999) 'Occupational health and safety in SMEs', *Small Enterprise Development* 9(3): 14–22.

Seibel, H.D. (2003) 'History matters in microfinance', *Small Enterprise Development* 14(2): 10–12.

Sheck, R., Donovan, J., and Stoian, D. (eds) (2013) *Assessing Impacts of Value Chain Development on Poverty. A Case-Study Companion to the 5Capitals Tool*, Technical Report 396, Rural Enterprise Development Collection 8, CATIE/ICRAF/Bioversity International, Turrialba, Costa Rica.

Shih, T.J., Wijaya, R., and Brossard, D. (2008) 'Media coverage of public health debates: linking framing and issue attention cycle toward an integrated theory of print news coverage of epidemics', Mass *Community and Society* 11: 141–60. <https://doi.org/10.1080/15205430701668121>

Shriver, J. and Abdalah, J.M.B. (2012) *Leveraging Municipal Government Support for Agricultural Value Chains in Nicaragua*, Catholic Relief Service (CRS), Baltimore, MD.

Simmons, E.B. (2002) 'Linking trade and sustainable development', *American University International Law Review* 18(6): 1271–302.

Sopov, M., Saavedra, Y., Sertse, Y., Vellema, W., and Verjans, H. (2014) *Is Inclusive Business for You: Managing and Upscaling an Inclusive Company: Lessons from the Field*, Centre for Development Innovation, Wageningen UR, Wageningen.

Springer-Heinze, A. (2008) *ValueLinks Manual*, GTZ, Eschborn, Germany.

Stamm, A. and Von Drachenfels, C. (2011) *Value Chain Development: Approaches and Activities by Seven UN Agencies and Opportunities for Interagency Cooperation*, International Labour Organization (ILO), Geneva, Switzerland.

Staritz, C. (2012) *Value Chains for Development: Potentials and Limitations of Global Value Chain Approaches in Donor Interventions*, Austrian Foundation for Development Research (ÖFSE), Vienna.

Stoian, D. and Donovan, J. (2013) 'An asset-based approach to achieving pro-poor value chain development: introduction to 5Capitals case studies', in R. Sheck, J. Donovan, and D. Stoian (eds), *Assessing Impacts of Value Chain Development on Poverty: A Case-Study Companion to the 5Capitals Tool*, pp. 7–14, Technical Report 396, Rural Enterprise Development Collection 8, CATIE/ICRAF/Bioversity International, Turrialba, Costa Rica.

Stoian, D., Donovan, J., Fisk, J., and Muldoon, M.F. (2012) 'Value chain development for rural poverty reduction: a reality check and a warning', *Enterprise Development and Microfinance* 23(1): 54–69. <https://doi.org/10.3362/1755-1986.2012.006>

Stoian, D., Donovan, J., Elias, M., and Blare, T. (2018) 'Fit for Purpose? Review of tools for gender-equitable value chain development', *Development in Practice* 24(4): 494–509. <https://doi.org/10.1080/09614524.2018.1447550>

Stoian, D., Monterroso, I., and Current, D. (2019) 'SDG 8: decent work and economic growth: potential impacts on forests and forest-dependent livelihoods', in P. Katila, C.J.P. Colfer, W. de Jong, G. Galloway, P. Pacheco, and G. Winkel (eds.), *Sustainable Development Goals: Their Impact on Forests and People*, pp. 237–78, Cambridge University Press, Cambridge, UK.

Sverrisson, A. (2003) 'Local and global commodity chains', *Linking Local and Global Economies* 1(2): 17–35. <DOI:10.4324/9780203987377.pt1>

Tallontire, A., Dolan, C., Smith, S., and Barrientos, S. (2005) 'Reaching the marginalized? Gender value chains and ethical trade in African horticulture', *Development in Practice* 15(3–4): 559–71. <https://doi.org/10.1080/09614520500075771>

Tanburn, J. (1999) 'How sustainable can business development service really be? Report on the Harare BDS workshop', *Small Enterprise Development* 10(1): 53–8.

Thiele, G., Devaux, A., Reinoso, I., Pico, H., Montesdeoca, F., Pumisacho, M., Andrade-Piedra, J., Velasco, C., Flores, P., Esprella, R., Thomann, A., Manrique, K. and Horton, D. (2011) 'Multi-stakeholders platforms for linking small farmers to value chains: evidence from the Andes', *International Journal of Agricultural Sustainability* 9(3): 423–33. <https://doi.org/10.1080/14735903.2011.589206>

Thornton, J.R., Agnello, R.J., and Link, C.R. (1978) 'Poverty and economic growth: Trickle down peters out', *Economic Inquiry* 16(3):385–94.

Tipps, D.C. (1973) 'Modernization theory and the comparative study of national societies: a critical perspective', *Comparative Studies in Society and History* 15(2): 199–226.

Tomecko, J. and Kolshorn, R. (1996) 'Promoting entrepreneurship: the CEFE method', *Small Enterprise Development* 7(4): 39–48.

Ton, G., Vellema, S., and De Ruyter De Wildt, M. (2011) 'Development impacts of value chain interventions: how to collect credible evidence and draw valid conclusions in impact evaluations?', *Journal on Chain and Network Science* 11(1): 69–84.

Torero, M. (2016) 'Evaluating inclusive value-chain development', in A. Devaux, M. Torero, J. Donovan, and D. Horton (eds), *Innovation for Inclusive Value-Chain Development: Successes and Challenges*, pp. 329–42, IFPRI, Washington, DC.

Vermeulen, S. (2015) *Climate Change Risk Assessments in Value Chain Projects*, IFAD, Rome.

Vermeulen, S., Woodhill, J. Proctor, F.J., and Delnoye, R. (2008) *Chain-wide Learning for Inclusive Agrifood Market Development*, IIED, London.

Von Braun, J., Hotchkiss, D., and Immink, M. (1989) *Non-traditional Export Crops in Guatemala: Effects on Production, Income and Nutrition*, Research Report 73, IFPRI, Washington, DC.

Weatherspoon, D.D. and Reardon, T. (2003) 'The rise of supermarkets in Africa: implications for agrifood systems and the rural poor', *Development Policy Review* 21(3): 333–55. <https://doi.org/10.1111/1467-7679.00214>

Webster, L. (1990) 'Fifteen years of World Bank lending to small and medium enterprises', *Small Enterprise Development* 1(1): 17–25.

Wolfensohn, J.D. (2000) 'How the World Bank is attacking poverty through small enterprise development and microfinance', *Small Enterprise Development* 11(1): 5–7.

About the authors

Dietmar Stoian, PhD (d.stoian@cgiar.org), Lead Scientist, Value Chains, Private Sector Engagement and Investments, World Agroforestry (ICRAF), Bonn, Germany.

Jason Donovan, PhD (j.donovan@cgiar.org), Senior Economist, Research Theme Leader for Markets and Value Chains, International Maize and Wheat Improvement Center (CIMMYT), Texcoco, Mexico

CHAPTER 2

Maize diversity, market access, and poverty reduction in the Western Highlands of Guatemala

Jon Hellin, Rachael Cox, and Santiago López-Ridaura

Abstract

The western highlands of Guatemala lie within the area where maize was first domesticated, and maize remains central to farmers' livelihood security. Over 50% of the population in the region are in poverty, and over 48% suffer from chronic malnutrition. Development efforts have focused on improved land management, crop diversification, and improved access to markets, especially for high-value vegetable crops such as snow peas. As a result of successful initiatives worldwide, more attention is being directed at the extent to which farmers can benefit from market opportunities for indigenous crops by receiving a price premium for providing the environmental service of conserving agricultural biodiversity. Such an approach bridges the gap between poverty alleviation and in situ conservation. We explored this potential development pathway through both qualitative and quantitative research. Focus groups were conducted in 5 communities in the maize-growing highlands of Guatemala, followed by a survey of 989 farm households in 59 locations. Our results show that most farmers in the western highlands of Guatemala are severely maize deficient; on average, farm households produce enough maize for only 6.9 months of consumption a year and are forced to purchase maize to meet basic consumption needs. The results are in sharp contrast to research conducted in highland communities in neighboring Mexico, where many farmers are able to sell their maize in relatively lucrative specialty maize markets. In the context of renewed interest in reducing poverty in Central America, our research suggests that rather than focus on market development for local maize varieties, development efforts should target other types of interventions.

Keywords: Guatemala; poverty reduction; maize; agricultural diversity; farmers' livelihoods; conservation through use

http://dx.doi.org/10.3362/9781788530576.002

Introduction

Poverty in the Guatemalan highlands

Rural poverty and food insecurity are endemic in Guatemala, and the over-whelming majority of the impoverished population lives in rural areas. Guatemala is known for its ethnic diversity. Indigenous groups typically have less access to education and suffer from higher rates of poverty and malnutrition; these communities make up 38% of the total population and live mainly in highland areas (United States Agency for International Development, 2010). Guatemala has the fourth highest level of child undernutrition in the world (World Food Programme, 2014).

The overwhelming majority of indigenous communities are engaged in smallholder agriculture, largely subsistence but with some market-oriented production. Over 90% of farmers in Guatemala farm on 20% of the country's arable land, contributing to the high levels of inequality in Guatemala. The mountainous landscape and underdeveloped infrastructure in the western highlands mean that rural communities tend to be isolated from the rest of the country. Furthermore, indigenous populations often farm marginal land that is very susceptible to soil and land degradation (Figure 2.1).

Poverty in the western highlands affects over 50% of the population while 48% suffer from chronic malnutrition. Poverty is also closely connected to Guatemala's 36-year civil war, which ended in the mid-1990s (Steinberg and

Figure 2.1 Maize farmer in the department of Huehuetenango. The farmer's plot is typical of those in the western highlands of Guatemala in terms of its small size, rocky soil, and steep slopes. (Photo by Jon Hellin)

Taylor, 2008). This was a particularly brutal war in which indigenous communities were targeted and tens of thousands of people were murdered; its legacy continues to impact the agroecological, social, and political landscape of the western highlands. A report commissioned by the United States Agency for International Development concluded that "historical patterns of structural exclusion, internal armed conflict, and unresolved social conflict reinforce and intensify social inequality, discrimination, and violence in interrelated and systemic ways. . . . Without means to address these patterns systemically, violent social conflict will likely continue to escalate, undermining overall development in the Western Highlands" (Democracy International, 2015: i).

Importance of maize

Maize is endemic to Mesoamerica (which includes the western highlands of Guatemala), and farmers have cultivated the crop for millennia. The ongoing evolution of maize diversity is closely linked with cultural traditions that include farmers' preferences, knowledge, and management practices (Pressoir and Berthaud, 2004). Many studies have discussed the role of maize in the spectrum of Mesoamerican farmers' livelihood activities (eg van Etten, 2006; Isakson, 2009; Keleman et al., 2013). In 2013 over 850,000 hectares of maize were harvested in Guatemala (FAOStat, 2013). Yields in Guatemala are low, at under 2 tons/ha for maize (World Food Programme, 2014).

Many of Guatemala's farmers practice a traditional system known as milpa, in which they intercrop maize with crops such as beans, chilies, and squash (Isakson, 2009). Even though many farmers also periodically work off-farm, the milpa remains an important cultural foundation in rural communities in Guatemala. Despite this, there are concerns that maize varieties have been and will continue to be lost in the face of livelihood, climatic, technological, and political changes. Steinberg and Taylor (2002), for example, argued that the political violence in Guatemala in the 1970s and 1980s led to a decline in maize diversity in the highlands because of the severe and often violent disruption of traditional agricultural practices.

There have also been accusations that commercial interests are seeking to introduce genetically modified crops (including maize) as part of the 2005 Dominican Republic, Central American United States Free Trade Agreement (Grandia, 2014). However, given the absence of seed companies operating in the western highlands and farmers' interest in only growing local maize varieties, it is not clear if genetically modified maize would indeed threaten traditional maize varieties.

Maize and farmers' livelihood security

Maize-producing households in the western highlands have to deal with trade-offs between growing maize and other livelihood options. The latter include shifting to alternative crops, working off-farm, and exiting agriculture completely (Isakson, 2009). These livelihood changes are already affecting maize diversity. Some farmers, especially in the department of San Marcos, have turned to the illegal production of poppy (Steinberg and Taylor, 2007). Since the 1980s, development organizations have promoted the cultivation and marketing of high-value vegetables, including broccoli, cauliflower, and snow peas, which have a market in the United States (Immink and Alarcón, 1993; Julian et al., 2000; Krznaric, 2006).

With an increasing shift toward export crops, maize and the milpa system have played less of a role in the landscape (Hamilton and Fischer, 2003), although many farmers in the Guatemalan highlands cultivate both maize and vegetable export crops. While large-scale producers tend to plant the majority of their land with export crops, smallholders who cultivate export crops often continue to grow maize as well (Isakson, 2009). This choice is linked to the cultural importance of the crop and to the desire to reduce the risk of crop loss or price reductions for the export crops.

Farmers' maintenance of maize landraces also creates the potential for new development initiatives, such as market access for these landraces. There is interest in the extent to which market opportunities for maize landraces can increase farmers' incomes while promoting in situ crop conservation. The maintenance of crop diversity through market opportunities is known as "conservation through use" (Keleman and Hellin, 2009). The interest in this approach is partly in response to concerns that asking poor farmers to conserve diversity for diversity's sake, without significant commercial or livelihood benefit, can help to perpetuate poverty.

Crop genetic diversity has 3 key types of value: private value to the farmer; value to the local public, such as the resistance to pests and diseases; and global value, such as the availability of diverse germplasm for future plant- breeding efforts (see Lipper and Cooper, 2009). Maintenance of crop diversity can be costly for farmers (Gruère et al., 2006; Bellon et al., 2015). In the western highlands, other crops, such as vegetables, offer better income opportunities than maize, so farmers need a cultural or economic incentive to maintain maize diversity (Bellon and Smale, 1998).

Over the past 25 years, there has been growing interest in strengthening the links between on-farm conservation, access to markets, and farmers' livelihood security. Since market-based trade by definition involves private-value goods, a market-based conservation strategy is targeted only to perpetuating activities or crops that offer private value to the farmer. An early proponent of these links observed:

> *Market options are among the least expensive conservation tools because they can rely on existing institutions and on farmer choice. . . . In areas of diversity, small amounts of traditional crops reach the market and generally receive premium prices. Income from producing traditional crops as specialty crops is an incentive to conserve them, and this incentive is available in most areas of diversity*

> *(Brush 1991: 163)*

There are many examples of price premiums being paid to farmers who provide the environmental service of conserving agricultural biodiversity. These include potatoes in the Andes (Devaux et al., 2009), minor millets in India (Gruère et al., 2009), laurel in Syria (Kruijssen et al., 2009), and maize in Mexico (Keleman and Hellin, 2009; Hellin et al., 2013; Keleman et al., 2013). A key research question is whether facilitating the emergence of niche markets for local maize varieties in the western highlands of Guatemala could contribute to poverty reduction (van Etten, 2006). Addressing this question is the focus of our research.

The rest of this chapter is structured as follows. In the methodology section we outline the mixed methods used in the study, consisting of focus group discussions with farmers and interviews with people selling maize in 2 urban markets (qualitative research) and a baseline survey (quantitative research). We then present the results of the research, which demonstrate that farm households do not produce enough maize to meet basic needs, let alone a surplus that could be sold. We discuss the results in terms of the potential to develop markets that would allow farmers to benefit from maintaining maize diversity, a form of payment for environmental services. We conclude that such potential is unlikely to be realized in the western highlands because of the maize deficit, caused in large by the small size and poor quality of the landholdings.

Methodology

The research was conducted as part of a research-for-development project in the western highlands of Guatemala. The main objectives of the project are to contribute to the reduction of poverty, food insecurity, and malnutrition, while increasing the sustainability and resilience of maize-based farming systems. The project is designed to decrease environmental degradation, improve the livelihoods of small-scale and resource-poor farmers, strengthen research and extension activities, and establish links with strategic partners including non-governmental organizations (NGOs), public agencies, and extension agents.

We adopted a mixed-methods approach that involved both quantitative and qualitative research—focus group discussions, semistructured interviews, and a survey. Such an approach had been successfully used by the first author while researching market opportunities for maize producers in Mexico (Hellin et al., 2010).

Throughout the qualitative research phase, we received logistical support from local NGOs in terms of the selection of communities and farmers. There is a slight danger that these NGOs may have inadvertently favored some communities and farmers over others, thus introducing some bias into the results. However, a single research method seldom sheds adequate light on a phenomenon. Using multiple methods can help facilitate deeper understanding, and for this reason, we complemented the qualitative research with quantitative research in the form of an extensive survey.

Qualitative research sheds light on the link between farmers' decisions and broader cultural and social pressures. It can be a fast and cost-efficient way to

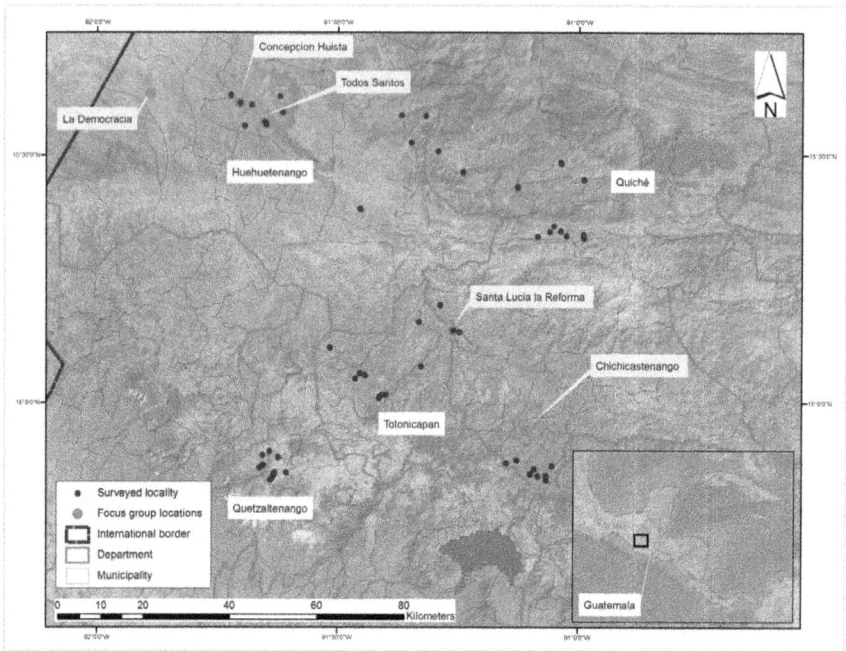

Figure 2.2 Map of the study area. (Cartography by Santiago López-Ridaura; data sources: Esri, Esri China [Hong Kong], Esri Japan, Esri Thailand, Garmin, GIS User Community, HERE, INCREMENT P, Intermap, MapmyIndia, METI, NRCAN, © OpenStreetMap contributors, USGS).

gather data. Interviews with groups of farmers often generate richer information than those with individual farmers because the former approach often allow for dynamic discussions that build on collective knowledge and experiences. We first conducted focus group meetings, 1 each in 5 representative maize-based farming communities in the western highlands in the departments of Huehuetenango, Quiché, and Totonicapán (Figure 2.2). This was followed by semistructured interviews with randomly selected maize sellers in markets in the towns of Huehuetenango and Chichicastenango.

In our study area, partner organizations identified 5 communities where farmers grow maize, typically in subsistence farming systems. A local extension worker, from the predominant partner organization active in each of the 5 communities, arranged for 10–20 farmers to participate in each focus group (Figure 2.3). Each group had approximately equal numbers of men and women and took place in the community hall. The same extension agent introduced the research team to the participating farmers. Each focus group was conducted by a member of the research team who is also a maize farmer in Mexico, using semistructured questions that had been designed based on the research team's knowledge of maize-based farming systems in the region.

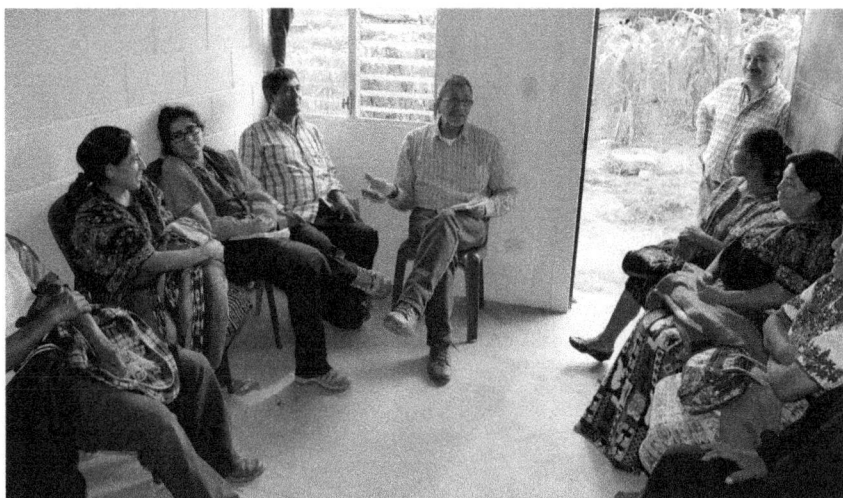

Figure 2.3 Focus group meeting in the department of Quiché. (Photo by Jon Hellin)

Topics included family size, landholding size, maize production, maize consumption, and how farmers cope with maize deficits.

A baseline survey complemented and helped to enrich the results from the qualitative research. The survey was designed to capture the diversity of maize-based farming systems in the western highlands in terms of farmers' resources, their main agricultural (crop and livestock) activities and practices, and their main sources of technical advice. It also included questions related to management of the milpa, types of maize planted, and postharvest practices. The survey instrument was pilot tested with 20 farmers; after adjustments, a team of 20 enumerators conducted the survey with 989 farm households in 59 maize-producing locations in the 3 aforementioned departments and in the department of Quetzaltenango (Figure 2.2). The following criteria were used to select the 59 locations:

1. They were within 16 municipalities targeted by the research-for-development project of which this study was a part.
2. Each was within 1 of the 4 meso-watersheds within the 16 municipalities.
3. They covered the different elevational levels at which maize is grown within those watersheds.
4. Reputable local partners of the research-for-development project (NGOs and state agencies) were available to facilitate the implementation of the survey.

At each surveyed location, small teams of enumerators walked radial transects, when possible, in order to implement the survey. Confidentiality was ensured by identifying participants with numbers rather than names. Of the

989 households surveyed, 226 were in Totonicapán, 350 in Quiché, 187 in Quetzaltenango, and 226 in Huehuetenango.

Results

In the western highlands, farmers tend to measure land area in *cuerdas* rather than hectares. The size of a *cuerda* varies but in many communities in the western highlands, 23 *cuerdas* are equivalent to 1 ha. Farmers who participated in the focus group meetings said that farmers had on average about 100 *cuerdas* (4.3 ha) in the 1980s but less than 10 *cuerdas* (0.4 ha) now. Often only a fraction of this meager land area is sown with maize; the remaining land is used to produce firewood, potatoes, broad beans, and broccoli.

The survey data showed that landholdings are very small in the western highlands and that at the same time, there is a large variability in maize farmers' average landholdings. In our study area, average arable land per farm household was 0.31 ha, but the median was 0.19 ha, suggesting a skewed distribution with a few farmers having relatively large landholdings and many having very small ones. There was some variation between departments: households in Huehuetenango had the largest average landholdings (average 0.39 ha, median 0.17 ha), followed by Quiché (average 0.22 ha, median 0.11), Quetzaltenango (average 0.13 ha, median 0.8 ha), and Totonicap'an (average 0.13 ha, median 0.8 ha) (Figure 2.4A). The average family size in the survey was 6 people per household and the average land availability per person ranged from 0.07 ha/person (median of 0.03) in Huehuetenango to 0.02 ha/person (median of 0.01) in Totonicapán (Figure 2.4B). In our study area, average land availability throughout the western highlands was 0.06 ha per person (median of 0.04). This figure coincides with a study by the World Bank (2006).

Farmers participating in the survey grow maize at elevations ranging from 1145 to 3557 meters above sea level (masl), with an average elevation of 2290 masl. The average elevation was the highest in the department of Quetzaltenango (2627 masl), followed by Huehuetenango (2230 masl), Quiché (2229 masl), and Totonicapán (2166 masl). Land above 2600 masl is known locally as *tierra fria* (cold land). In low temperatures, maize often requires atleast 10 months to mature; farmers often sow it in January and harvest it in November and December. In the lower-lying *tierra caliente* (hot land), there is a shorter growing season; maize is sown in April or May and harvested between October and December.

The maize crop throughout the highlands is rain-fed; very few farmers (including only 14% of the farm households surveyed) have access to irrigation. In many communities, farmers grow yellow, black, and white maize, and to a lesser extent red maize. Yellow maize is the most popular and is used to make tortillas (a thin, unleavened flat bread made from maize and a staple in almost every meal), tamales (meat wrapped in maize dough and steamed or baked in maize husks), and *atole* (a maize drink), which is often consumed at formal events.

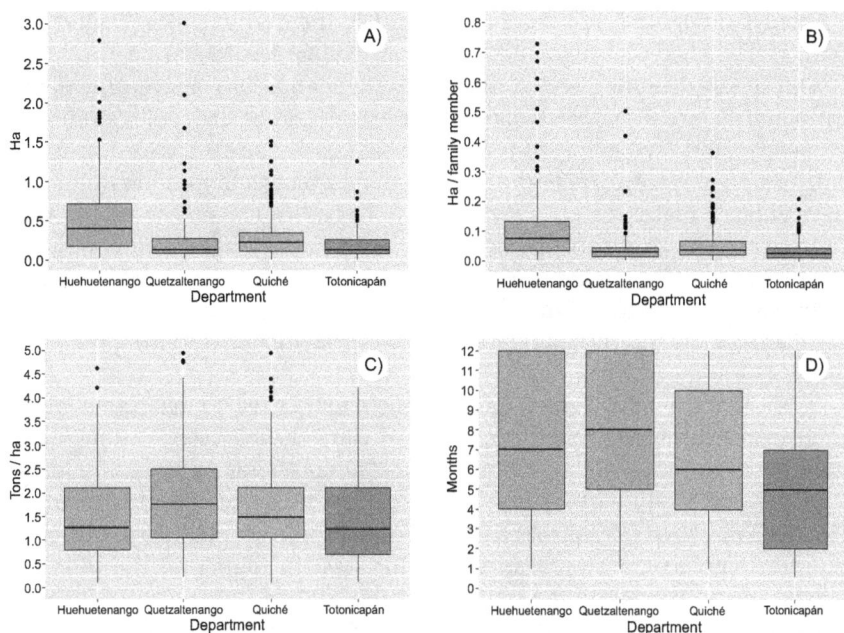

Figure 2.4 Average agronomic characteristics of the 989 surveyed farm households in 4 departments in the western highlands of Guatemala. (A) landholding area; (B) arable land per person; (C) maize yield, (D) months of maize self-sufficiency.

According to farmers interviewed, during the past 20 years, reduced rainfall and increased incidences of hail storms have caused considerable crop losses. Farmers also reported that *la canícula,* a short dry spell that occurs during the growing season, has been more protracted than in previous years and less predictable in its timing.

This has resulted in more pronounced crop losses. Maize yields are very low throughout the region. In the community of Todos Santos in the department of Huehuetenango, focus group participants reported that yellow, white, and red maize can yield 1.6 tons/ha and that black maize yields about 1.0 tons/ha but its value as a specialty and culturally important food crop often makes up for the lower yield. Isakson (2011) also reported that while black maize may have lower yields, it is still attractive to farmers because it is more resilient to environmental stresses and can grow in poorer soils where other types of maize often fail.

Average maize yield for farmers participating in the survey was 1.7 tons/ha (with a median of 1.5 tons/ha). Average yields per department showed great variability, with the highest maize yield found in Quetzaltenango (average 2.3 tons/ha, median 2.1 tons/ha), followed by Quiché and Huehuetenango (with averages of 1.7 tons/ha and 1.6 ton/ha respectively and both with a median of 1.0 tons/ha), and Totonicapán (average 1.5 tons/ha, median

1.2 tons/ha) (Figure 2.4C). As discussed earlier, the overwhelming majority of farmers in the western highlands grow maize on far less than 1 ha.

Our survey data suggest that the western highlands have a severe net deficit in maize (Figure 2.4D). Our data indicate that family size varies from 4 to 12 people, and 6 people consume about 1.2 kg of maize a day or just under 450 kg a year. Survey data also suggest that, on average, farm households produce enough maize for only 6.9 months of consumption per year and thus need to buy maize at some point. Maize self-sufficiency ranges from an average of 8.2 months (median = 8) in Quetzaltenango to 7.4 months (median = 7) in Huehuetenango, 6.9 months (median = 6) in Quiché, and 5.1 months (median = 5) in Totonicapán. Similar figures were obtained during the focus group meetings.

Even farmers who have a maize deficit may have to sell some maize immediately after the harvest in order to earn needed cash, although this was true for only 6% (57 of 989) of the farm households participating in the survey. Focus group participants in Concepción Huista in the department of Huehuetenango, reported that they had to sell some of their maize in a community some 30 km away. Farmers in the western highlands use the term *quintal* when referring to the weight of maize sold and consumed. Quintal is a historical unit of mass that is defined in various parts of the world as 100 lb or 100 kg. In Guatemala, 1 quintal is 100 lb, that is, the measurement used is the international avoirdupois pound, which is legally defined as 0.454 kg. In this chapter the authors use pounds and quintals.

In this community, farmers can sell local maize varieties for 160 quetzales (US$21.30) per quintal. Local maize varieties command a higher price than the "improved" white maize that is sold in the western highlands to make up for maize deficits. Improved maize consists of varieties that are the result of formal crop breeding programs, they are seen as improved as they are often higher yielding than farmers' local varieties. The improved maize comes from lowland commercial maize production areas in Guatemala and from neighboring Mexico and sells in the western highlands for 130 quetzales (US$17.30) per quintal.

For many farmers who are not self-sufficient in maize, the main time when they purchase maize is from June until they are able to harvest their maize toward the end of the year. In the city of Huehuetenango, we spoke to people selling maize and they said that it costs them 120 quetzales (US$16) to buy 1 quintal of maize at the frontier between Guatemala and Mexico. They can then sell the same maize for 125–130 quetzales (US$16.70–17.30) per quintal. Profit margins are meager, and many of those selling imported maize also sell agricultural inputs because these provide a higher profit margin.

In the western highlands, there are markets for maize landraces, but they are small and ad hoc in comparison with many parts of Mexico. In the town of Chichicastenango, we spoke to maize sellers in the local market. They sell local maize varieties for 5 quetzales (US$0.70) per pound and imported, commercially grown white maize for 1.5 quetzales (US$0.20) per pound.

This difference in price mirrors the results of research in neighboring Mexico, where Keleman and Hellin (2009) documented 2008 sale prices of 4 pesos (US$0.40) per pound for local maize varieties and 1 peso (US$0.10) per pound for commercial ones.

The difference in sale price is due to a culinary and cultural preference for native maize. This suggests a potentially lucrative market for those in a position to sell their local maize varieties, but with maize deficits in many parts of the western highlands, this is not an option for most farmers. Furthermore, the volumes of local maize varieties being sold are not very large. In Chichicastenango, we met a maize seller who sells local maize varieties at 200 quetzales (US$26.70) per quintal, but he only sells about 1 quintal every 20 days. It is bought by local producers of tortillas, who mix it with imported white maize and then sell the tortillas at a higher price, marketing it as made from local maize.

The maize that farmers in the western highlands buy when their own harvest is exhausted is often not a local variety but improved maize from commercial maize-growing regions in Guatemala and, increasingly, Mexico (Figure 2.5). Local traders whom we interviewed in June reported that the then price of 125 quetzales (US$16.70) per quintal of imported maize fluctuates; it goes up in August and then drops at harvest time. Those selling maize are Guatemalans who have tended to buy maize from Mexico, in some cases as far away as the northern Mexican state of Sinaloa. Maize from western Guatemala cannot compete with cheaper maize from the commercial maize-growing areas in Mexico and El Petén, a department in the north of Guatemala). Maize from El Petén is largely consumed in that region, and most of the maize purchased in the western highlands originates in Mexico.

Discussion: maize diversity, market access, and poverty reduction

In the western highlands of Guatemala, maize remains central to many farmers' livelihoods, although it is not a major element in the market economy. Farmers often grow maize for cultural and social purposes (Bellon, 2004), and this, together with the food security that it offers, explains its perseverance. This is not unique to Guatemala's western highlands; for example, researchers in Mexico have also documented the continued cultivation of maize for cultural reasons (Esteva and Marielle, 2003; Bellon and Hellin, 2011). Barkin (2002: 83) commented that, in the case of Mexico, maize cultivation is very closely linked to farmers' "collective search for mechanisms to reduce their vulnerability to many of the negative impacts of international economic integration. . . . implementing their own strategies as part of their search for alternatives to protect and reinforce their own social structures and lifestyles."

Farmers in the western highlands of Guatemala also mirror the behavior of many Mexican maize producers by continuing to grow maize while also engaging in off-farm labor. A recent study in the Guatemalan highlands found that even though off-farm activities and/or cultivating export crops

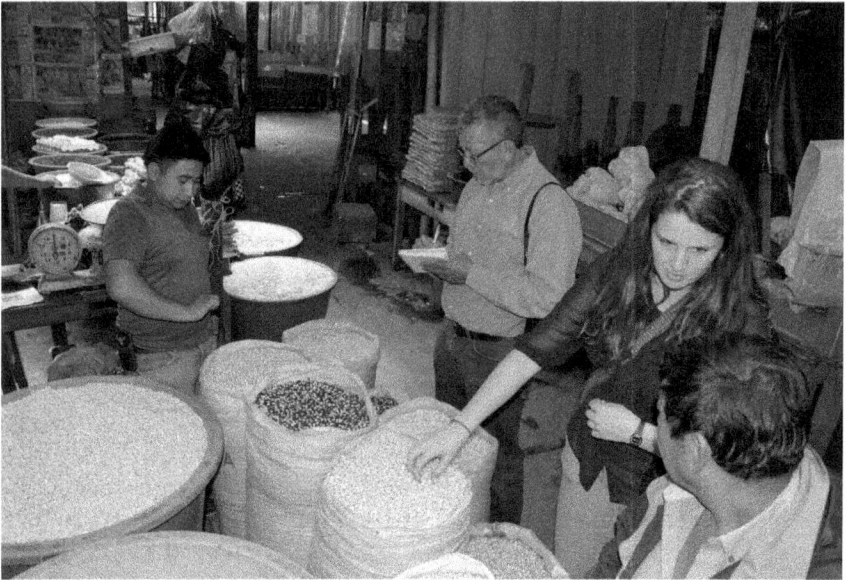

Figure 2.5 Native and improved maize varieties at the Chichicastenango market. (Photo by Jon Hellin)

may provide farmers with the majority of their income, they may still prioritize milpa agriculture over wage employment, and "even as peasant farmers engage in market forms of provisioning they are simultaneously instituting social protections to reinforce their subsistence-oriented agricultural practices and the attendant conservation of crop genetic diversity" (Isakson, 2009: 728).

Other studies have also documented that farmers' choices are often rational, even though they may not make sense from a purely economic perspective. Mayer (2002), for example, found that in the Peruvian Andes, farmers often treat subsistence and commercial activities as separate components of the household economy, despite the fact that off-farm income often subsidizes agricultural activities. Many participants in this study's focus groups reported working off-farm for part of the year.

The situation in the western highlands of Guatemala supports the "functional dualism" thesis, proposed by de Janvry et al., (1989) and expanded on by Blaikie (1989), that farmers in Latin American rely on income from part-time off-farm labor because their landholdings are too small to enable them to be self-sufficient. In the case of farmers surveyed in our study, arable land per household averaged 0.31 ha with a median of 0.19 ha—for most, too little for maize self-sufficiency. This in part reflects the historic discrimination against indigenous communities and long-standing legacy of social exclusion. The functional dualism thesis also suggests that even though farmers increasingly depend on off-farm labor, they are unable to find sufficient employment to enable them to exit agriculture entirely. Subsistence-oriented agriculture thus provides an important safety net, protecting farmers from low and irregular wages linked to off-farm labor.

The continued importance of maize to farmers' livelihoods in this region justifies maize-focused development initiatives. Van Etten (2006:707) studied maize diversity and farmers' livelihoods in the same region and concluded that

> *use-based opportunities to conserve maize biodiversity should be amplified. ... . regional or new products based on native maize biodiversity could be inserted in commercial contexts. These could be transformed into less perishable forms or convenience goods. Especially the rapidly growing acquisitive power of Guatemalan emigrant workers living in the US provides new channels for culturally specific products.*

Markets for traditional maize varieties exist in many parts of Mexico (eg Keleman and Hellin, 2009), but our results suggest that, in Guatemala's western highlands, the potential links between on-farm conservation of native maize, agricultural markets, and livelihood improvement are unlikely to be realized for most farmer, because there is such a maize deficit that farmers are unable to meet basic subsistence needs. Many farm households have to buy maize from outside the region to meet consumption requirements. In the case of the western highlands, the evidence suggests that the market cannot drive in situ maize conservation.

Conclusions

There is growing interest in the extent to which markets can contribute to in situ conservation of crop diversity and improved farmer livelihoods. Our results show that most farmers in the western highlands of Guatemala conserve local maize varieties for cultural and social purposes, and that this effort is economically supported by off-farm income-generating activities. Most of these farmers, rather than being net sellers of maize, are forced to purchase maize for several months of the year. This is in sharp contrast to highland communities in neighboring Mexico, where many farmers are able to sell their local maize in relatively lucrative specialty maize markets.

The research reported in this chapter is part of a larger research-for-development project that is also addressing issues of soil and water conservation and crop and farm diversification in the western highlands of Guatemala. In the context of renewed interest in reducing poverty in Central America, in part to reduce the flow of immigrants (especially young people) to the United States, the research reported here demonstrates that low maize production in the western highlands is caused by land shortages and marginal land quality. Short of wholesale land reform (something that is highly unlikely in the political context of Guatemala), our research suggests that rather than focus on market development for local maize varieties, development efforts target other types of interventions.

Acknowledgements

We would like to acknowledge support provided by United States Agency for International Development (USAID) through its Global Hunger and Food Security Initiative, Feed the Future. The authors are also very grateful for the invaluable comments provided by 2 anonymous reviewers.

Reprinted with the permission of BioOne. First published as Hellin, J., Cox, R., and López-Ridaura, S. (2017) 'Maize Diversity, Market Access, and Poverty Reduction in the Western Highlands of Guatemala,' Mountain Research and Development 37(2), 188-197, <https://doi.org/10.1659/MRD-JOURNAL-D-16-00065.1>

References

Barkin D. 2002. The reconstruction of a modern Mexican peasantry. *Journal of Peasant Studies* 30(1):73–90.

Bellon MR. 2004. Conceptualizing interventions to support on-farm genetic resource conservation. *World Development* 32(1):159–172.

Bellon MR, Gotor E, Caracciolo F. 2015. Conserving landraces and improving livelihoods: How to assess the success of on-farm conservation projects? *International Journal of Agricultural Sustainability* 13(2):167–182.

Bellon MR, Hellin J. 2011. Planting hybrids, keeping landraces: Agricultural modernization and tradition among small-scale maize farmers in Chiapas, Mexico. *World Development* 39(8):1434–1443.

Bellon MR, Smale M. 1998. *A Conceptual Framework for Valuing On-Farm Genetic Resources*. Economics Working Paper No. 98-05. Mexico City, Mexico: International Maize and Wheat Improvement Center (CIMMYT).

Blaikie P. 1989. Explanation and policy in land degradation and rehabilitation for developing countries. *Land Degradation and Rehabilitation* 1:23–37.

Brush SB. 1991. A farmer-based approach to conserving crop germplasm. *Economic Botany* 45(2):153–165.

de Janvry A, Sadoulet E, Young LW. 1989. Land and labour in Latin American agriculture from the 1950s to the 1980s. *Journal of Peasant Studies* 16(3):396–424.

Democracy International. 2015. *Legacies of Exclusion: Social Conflict and Violence in Communities and Homes in Guatemala's Western Highlands*. Washington, DC: United States Agency for International Development.

Devaux A, Horton D, Velasco C, Thiele G, López G, Bernet T, Reinoso I, Ordinola M. 2009. Collective action for smallholder market access. *Food Policy* 34(1):31–38.

Esteva G, Marielle C, editors. 2003. *Sin maíz no hay país*. Mexico City, Mexico: Consejo Nacional para la Cultura y las Artes.

FAOstat. 2013. *Guatemala Maize Area Harvested*. Rome, Italy: Food and Agriculture Organization of the United Nations. http://faostat.fao.org/site/567/ DesktopDefault.aspx?PageID=567#ancor; accessed on 28 July 2014.

Grandia L. 2014. Modified landscapes: Vulnerabilities to genetically modified corn in northern Guatemala. *Journal of Peasant Studies* 41(1):79–105.

Gruère G, Giuliani A, Smale M. 2006. *Marketing Underutilized Plant Species for the Benefit of the Poor: A Conceptual Framework.* EPT Discussion Paper 154. Washington, DC: International Food Policy Research Institute.

Gruère G, Nagarajanm L, King O. 2009. The role of collective action in the marketing of underutilized plant species: Lessons from a case study on minor millets in South India. *Food Policy* 34(1):39–45.

Hamilton S, Fischer EF. 2003. Non-traditional agricultural exports in high-land Guatemala: Understandings of risk and perceptions of change. *Latin American Research Review* 38(3):82–110.

Hellin J, Keleman A, Bellon MR, van Heerwaarden J. 2010. Mexico: Maize and Chiapas case study. *In:* Lipper L, Anderson L, Dalton TJ, editors. *Seed Trade in Rural Markets Implications for Crop Diversity and Agricultural Development.* London, United Kingdom: Food and Agriculture Organization and Earthscan, pp 151–186.

Hellin J, Keleman A, López D, Donnet L, Flores D. 2013. La importancia de los nichos de mercado: un estudio de caso del maíz azul y del maíz para pozole en México. *La Revista Fitotecnia Mexicana* 36(6):315–328.

Immink MDC, Alarcón JA. 1993. Household income, food availability, and commercial crop production by smallholder farmers in the western high-lands of Guatemala. *Economic Development and Cultural Change* 42:319–342.

Isakson RS. 2009. No hay ganancia en la milpa: The agrarian question, food sovereignty, and the on-farm conservation of agrobiodiversity in the Guatemalan highlands. *Journal of Peasant Studies* 36(4):725–759.

Isakson RS. 2011. Market provisioning and the conservation of crop biodi-versity: An analysis of peasant livelihoods and maize diversity in the Guatemalan highlands. *World Development* 39(8):1444–1459.

Julian JW, Sullivan GH, Sánchez GE. 2000. Future market development issues impacting Central America's nontraditional agricultural export sector: Guatemala case study. *American Journal of Agricultural Economics* 82:1177– 1183.

Keleman A, Hellin J. 2009. Specialty maize varieties in Mexico: A case study in market-driven agro-biodiversity conservation. *Journal of Latin American Geography* 8(2):147–174.

Keleman A, Hellin J, Flores D. 2013. Diverse varieties and diverse markets: Scale-related maize "profitability crossover" in the central Mexican high-lands. *Human Ecology* 41:683–705.

Kruijssen F, Keizer M, Giuliani A. 2009. Collective action for small-scale pro-ducers of agricultural biodiversity products. *Food Policy* 34(1):46–52.

Krznaric R. 2006. The limits on pro-poor agricultural trade in Guatemala—Land, labour and political power. *Journal of Human Development* 7(1):111– 135.

Lipper L, Cooper D. 2009. Managing plant genetic resources for sustainable use in food and agriculture: Balancing the benefits in the field. *In:* Kontoleon A, Pascual U, Smale M, editors. *Agrobiodiversity, Conservation and Economic Development.* New York, NY: Routledge, pp 27–39.

Mayer E. 2002. *The Articulated Peasant: Household Economies in the Andes.* Boulder, CO: Westview Press.

Pressoir G, Berthaud J. 2004. Patterns of population structure in maize landra-ces from the central valleys of Oaxaca in Mexico. *Heredity* 92:88–94.

Steinberg MK, Taylor M. 2002. The impact of political turmoil on maize culture and diversity in highland Guatemala. *Mountain Research and Development* 22(4):344–351.

Steinberg MK, Taylor M. 2007. Marginalizing a vulnerable cultural and environmental landscape. *Mountain Research and Development* 27(4):318–321.

Steinberg MK, Taylor M. 2008. Guatemala's Altos de Chiantla: Changes on the high frontier. *Mountain Research and Development* 28(3):255–262.

United States Agency for International Development. 2010. Strategic Review. Feed the Future. https://www.feedthefuture.gov/sites/default/files/resource/files/GuatemalaFeedtheFutureStrategicReview.pdf; accessed on 14 December 2016.

van Etten J. 2006. Molding maize: The shaping of a crop diversity landscape in the western highlands of Guatemala. *Journal of Historical Geography* 32:689–711.

World Bank. 2006. *Arable Land: Hectares per Person*. http://data.worldbank.org/indicator/AG.LND.ARBL.HA.PC; accessed on 24 August 2016.

World Food Programme. 2014. *Guatemala*. Rome, Italy: World Food Programme. www.wfp.org/countries/guatemala/overview; accessed on 28 July 2014.

About the authors

Jon Hellin, PhD (j.hellin@irri.org), Platform Leader, Sustainable Impact, International Rice Research Institute (IRRI), Los Baños, Philippines.

Rachael Cox (rachael@earthempower.com), EarthEmpower

Santiago López-Ridaura, PhD (S.L.Ridaura@cgiar.org), Sustainable Intensification Program, International Maize and Wheat Improvement Center (CIMMYT)

CHAPTER 3

What is cocoa sustainability? Mapping stakeholders' socio-economic, environmental, and commercial constellations of priorities

Judith Krauss

Abstract

Given growing concerns regarding the chocolate sector's long-term future, more private-sector, public-sector, and civil-society stakeholders have become involved in initiatives seeking to make cocoa more 'sustainable'. However, the commercial, socio-economic, and environmental priorities they associate with the omnipresent, yet polysemic term diverge considerably: while transforming the crop into a more viable livelihood for growers is essential for some, others prioritize the crop's links to global environmental challenges through agroforestry. A third dimension encompasses commercial concerns related to securing supply. The chapter explores how tensions and synergies manifest in these divergent understandings of what cocoa sustainability is and is to entail, which diverse civil-society, public-sector, and private-sector stakeholders bring to the table. It argues that priorities associated with 'cocoa sustainability' diverge, yielding synergies, tensions, and trade-offs. This chapter draws on the author's in-depth doctoral fieldwork in cocoa sustainability initiatives incorporating environmental measures, which encompassed semi-structured interviews, focus-group discussions, documentary analysis, and participant observation in Latin America and Europe. It proposes the 'constellations of priorities' model as an instrument to capture how the priorities driving cocoa stakeholders variously dovetail, intersect, and collide. Particularly against the backdrop of the sector's brewing crisis, the paper suggests that stakeholders systematically assess their and other actors' socio-economic, environmental, and commercial priorities as part of the equitable engagement required to transform the sector and attain genuine cocoa sustainability.

Keywords: cocoa sustainability, environment, trade-offs, development studies, standards

The cocoa sector is facing a crisis. Of late, concerns as to whether cocoa production will be able to satisfy rising demand in the long term have grown,

http://dx.doi.org/10.3362/9781788530576.003

particularly among private-sector actors. Given this projected shortfall, an increasing number of stakeholders, from private sector, public sector, and civil society alike, have begun engaging in far-reaching 'sustainability' initiatives (Glin et al., 2015; Tampe, 2016). Beyond the pre-existing notion of improved socio-environmental circumstances offering an opportunity to cater to consumers that are pressuring companies to show they care (Hughes, 2001), a second thrust now driving engagement with 'cocoa sustainability' emanates from a perceived business imperative to safeguard the industry's long-term viability (Barrientos, 2014). Consequently, the spectrum of stakeholders engaging with sustainability has widened beyond 100 per cent ethical manufacturers, encompassing varied constituencies with divergent understandings of what the omnipresent, but polysemic term means. Some associate primarily commercial priorities with the concept, aiming to safeguard supply in the quality they desire. For others, the socio-economic dimension and in particular livelihood improvement are paramount following decades of shrinking returns for growers. Others prioritize the opportunities for addressing global environmental challenges that cocoa agroforestry systems offer, including conserving biodiversity or combating climate change. In sum, the sector's predicament has introduced a sense of unprecedented urgency, widening the spectrum of stakeholders and priorities governing cocoa sustainability initiatives.

This paper looks into the question of how tensions and parallels are manifest in stakeholders' priorities within cocoa sustainability initiatives. It argues that this continuum of diverging understandings regarding what 'cocoa sustainability' is or is to entail offers a potential for tensions. Particularly against the backdrop of the variety of private-sector, public-sector, and civil-society stakeholders involved in the industry, it aims to unpack these divergences in priorities, addressing a knowledge gap. In terms of its relevance to broader debates, this paper makes a contribution firstly on the brewing crisis in the cocoa industry, discussing some observations and implications regarding the sector's long-term viability. Equally, the paper, based on in-depth fieldwork in Europe and Latin America, develops a framework for stakeholders to assess their own and other stakeholders' drivers in relation to cocoa sustainability. It proposes that the 'constellations of priorities' model and its visualization, developed through semi-structured interviews, documentary analysis, focus-group discussions and participant observation, could offer cocoa stakeholders a structure for conversations about synergies and tensions. More broadly, the paper problematizes the inflationary use of 'sustainability', painting over stakeholders' differing definitions and neglecting to engage with whether 'sustainability' also entails greater equity. Given the term's omnipresence, it argues its polysemy merits unpacking and systematic analysis in terms of underlying priorities to address and avoid tensions between stakeholders' differing objectives.

After some brief context on the current situation in the cocoa-chocolate sector, the paper introduces research design and methods followed by a discussion on the theoretical underpinnings of the 'constellation of priorities' model and its three socio-economic, commercial, and environmental dimensions. The paper goes on to demonstrate how, despite multiple overlaps among largely like-minded actors committed to socio-economically viable and carbon-neutral chocolate, stakeholders' priority constellations showed subtle divergences in a real-world case study. The final section concludes and emphasizes this paper's implications for wider debates especially in the cocoa sector.

The context of cocoa sustainability

A consensus emerged among chocolate-sector actors in the early 2010s that there was likely to be a gap between available cocoa supply and demand by 2020 (Thornton, 2010; ICCO, 2012a; Fountain and Hütz-Adams, 2015). Gross global production has averaged 3.76 million metric tonnes (mt) annually between 2004–05 and 2012–13 (ICCO, 2014). The 2014–15 and, according to forecasts, 2015–16 crop seasons have produced 4.24 and 3.99 mt cocoa, respectively (ICCO, 2015a, b, 2016a, b). Fears abounded that global production would not be able to match demand especially from emerging markets, estimated for 2020 between 4.5 million (Fairtrade Foundation, 2011) and 5 million (Hütz-Adams and Fountain, 2012). Irrespective of the precise size of projected shortages, the industry began to ask whether the sector's supply was viable in the long term.

The factors underlying cocoa stakeholders' fears emanate from the socio-economic, environmental, and commercial realms. Commercial concerns in part stem from the successive oligopolies (UNCTAD, 2008) within the cocoa marketplace. Firstly, over two-thirds of global cocoa production hails from Africa, the continent forecast to generate 74 per cent of total cocoa supplies for the 2015–16 cocoa year, with two West African countries, Côte d'Ivoire and Ghana, contributing *c.* 60 per cent of the worldwide crop between them (ICCO, 2016a). Beyond this geographical focus, further instances of concentration are observable in both trading and the brand manufacturer segment, dominated by only a handful of companies controlling half their respective marketplaces (UNCTAD, 2008; Candy Industry, 2010, 2017; Fountain and Hütz-Adams, 2015). Beyond these commercial qualms, socio-environmental challenges include the rising average age of cocoa growers in West Africa (ICCO, 2012b): as cocoa returns have been declining for decades, grower populations may shrink as the livelihood is unattractive for young generations (Hainmueller et al., 2011; Fountain and Hütz-Adams, 2015). Equally, there are questions on how to expand capacity-building and farmer organization opportunities across millions of smallholders in terms of logistics and scale (author interview with a private-sector representative, #142). Environmentally, as cocoa only grows within 20 degrees latitude either side of the equator, the surfaces conducive to cocoa cultivation are limited, meaning productivity-maximizing, yet degrading, practices cannot continue indefinitely. Equally, the effects and repercussions of climate change are difficult to forecast (Läderach et al., 2011; Ofori-Boateng and Insah, 2014).

In combination, these factors mean there is uncertainty over how the production of cocoa, and particularly cocoa matching the price and quality stakeholders require, can be safeguarded in the long term, prompting shifts towards 'sustainability' in the sector. As investors' and consumers' awareness of this quandary has exacerbated concerns, this paper argues that aspiring to engage with cocoa sustainability has morphed from nice-to-have to a commercial necessity. Projections of its key ingredient being in short supply have caught the sector's attention, triggering engagement across the niche, mainstream, and low-end market segments identified by Barrientos and Asenso-Okyere (2009). Virtually all major processors and brand-name manufacturers have responded by increasing the share of their 'sustainable' cocoa supplies, which is often understood to be commodities certified by Fairtrade, UTZ Certified, or Rainforest Alliance (Hütz-Adams and Fountain, 2012; Fountain and Hütz-Adams, 2015). Some stakeholders such as chocolate makers Mars, Ferrero, and Hershey have even pledged to have the entirety of their cocoa volumes certified by 2020 (Nieburg, 2012). Equally, despite all competitiveness in a concentrated marketplace, ever more multi-stakeholder partnerships have been emerging in cocoa (Bitzer et al., 2012). Fundamentally, however, the question also is to what extent do existing certification schemes or multi-stakeholder initiatives promote equity and remedy deep-seated deficiencies that have contributed to the sector's current predicament? Existing power asymmetries between global North and South and private-sector and other stakeholders are palpable in terms of limited opportunities for the global South, declining cocoa prices, and environmental degradation resulting from pressures to maximize productivity.

While this new sense of urgency presents a greater opportunity for civil-society and public-sector actors to find commercial partners for sustainability measures, this business imperative introduces different requirements in terms of initiatives' foci, set-up, and direction, requiring analysis. Also beyond cocoa, certification schemes, in some ways falling victim to their own success, increasingly have to reconcile diverse ethical and commercial stakeholder interests (Doherty et al., 2013), with different schemes pursuing a variety of priorities and principles (KPMG, 2013). The magnitude and scope of the cocoa industry's projected predicament require it to address the diverse socio-economic, environmental, and commercial issues discussed above, which, however, in itself furthers the potential for tensions: protecting long-term supply security as a driver is distinct from wishing to boost growers' socio-economic livelihoods, with addressing global environmental challenges an altogether different motivation. This considerable spectrum of priorities warrants unpacking: this paper thus constructs a framework to analyse different drivers in terms of tensions and congruence in stakeholders' understandings of what cocoa sustainability is and is to entail. This proposed framework, the 'constellations of priorities', is introduced after a brief discussion of research methods in the following paragraphs.

Research methods and design

The research encompassed voices from European and Latin American contexts all the way from cocoa production to chocolate consumption to conceptualize cocoa-related global production networks holistically (Henderson et al., 2002; Hess and Yeung, 2006). As researching production networks and value chains will require drawing on a variety of sources to unearth relevant information (Kaplinsky and Morris, 2000; Barrientos, 2002), four qualitative research methods were used to triangulate and confirm the data collected, encompassing semi-structured interviews, focus-group discussions, documentary analysis, and participant observation in Europe and Latin America. To capture consumers' perspectives, three focus-group discussions (Morgan, 1997; Bloor et al., 2001) were conducted with European chocolate consumers with an environmental, a social, and a business background, respectively. While non-representative, the perspectives nevertheless allowed testing what priorities European consumers associated with cocoa sustainability. Moreover, the study drew on 96 semi-structured interviews with cocoa producers, representatives of cooperatives, non-governmental organization (NGOs), development agencies, government, research, chocolate companies, and retailers (see Table 3.1).

Interviews elicit only what interlocutors are prepared to share (Laws et al., 2003), which could equally be said of focus-group discussion settings. Consequently, supplementing these methods with documentary analysis and observing events held irrespective of the researcher's presence was a triangulation strategy aimed at reducing researcher bias and broadening data sources. I analysed *c.* 400 documents, reports, and websites cognizant of their provenance and intended audiences (O'Laughlin, 2007), while also attending nine cocoa-related events for the purposes of participant observation (Jorgensen, 1989; Spradley, 1980). I used Nvivo 5 to code all the transcribed qualitative interviews, focus-group discussions, and notes (Mikkelsen, 2005), while remaining conscious of the need to manage the transition across different

Table 3.1 Breakdown of types of interlocutors interviewed

Interviews conducted	
Cocoa producers	21
Civil society	18
Cooperatives	7
Research	10
Government	11
Development agencies	11
Private sector	13
Certifiers	5
Total	96

sources of data and researcher roles in collecting information. To safeguard confidentiality and as a condition of ethical approval, all participants, organizations, and place names have been anonymized.

The 'constellations of priorities' model as a conceptual contribution

Theoretical underpinnings

Given priorities' relevance in determining cocoa sustainability initiatives' direction, set-up, and structure, it proved necessary to conceptualize stakeholders' diverse socio-economic, commercial, and environmental drivers that may variously intersect, dovetail, or collide. As Lukes (2005: 109) contends, stakeholders' interests will not be unitary, but manifold. In her 2009 study, Raynolds establishes a tripartite distinction between 'mission'-driven, 'quality'-driven, and 'market'-driven buyers of fair trade coffee supplies. She argues that while the buyers all purchased ethically traded coffee, their motivations differed considerably, entailing palpable consequences for their engagements. Mission-driven buyers follow an ethical philosophy, seeking to support its principles throughout their commercial operation. By contrast, quality-driven buyers are primarily after gourmet supplies. Market-driven buyers, finally, regard a fair trading seal as a business opportunity, pursuing mainstream business operations beyond their niche engagement. While Raynolds underlines that the buyer types inhabit a continuum rather than distinct categories, mission-driven buyers usually seek to establish a partnership-based setting, whereas market-driven stakeholders prioritize traceability. Raynolds's distinction also recalls another spectrum on which considerable divergences can occur, namely the continuum between stakeholders focusing on overhauling the system and those wishing to uphold, but tweak it (Renard, 2003).

While Raynolds's argument regarding the importance of drivers underlying sustainability engagements is well-taken, her tripartite distinction, while suitable for her research focus, proved nevertheless imperfect for this study for the following reasons. Firstly, regarding the 'quality-driven' category of buyers, convention theory would suggest that what different stakeholders take 'quality' to be will vary, underlining the need for systematic analysis: determinants of high 'quality' may range from market prices via brand considerations or standardization to social and environmental circumstances of production, requiring negotiation between different stakeholders (Fold, 2000; Renard, 2003; Cidell and Alberts, 2006). A second issue is that Raynolds's distinction looks exclusively at fair trading rather than other standards. Thirdly, it solely forefronts the 'buyer' stakeholder type. Raynolds's study (2009) observes that Gereffi et al.,'s (2005) fivefold categorization of value chains, establishing five governance types ranging from arm's-length markets to integrated hierarchical connections, is too narrow given the categorization's exclusive focus on lead firms. For the same reason, this paper seeks to develop a classification that is applicable throughout the production network and engages with the priorities of the diverse stakeholder types involved in cocoa sustainability initiatives, as mission-driven, market-driven,

and quality-driven are not ideal analytical lenses for non-governmental organizations, producers, or development agencies. Consequently, the objective
was to establish a framework able to capture tensions, synergies, and trade-offs
between diverse cocoa sustainability stakeholders' sets of priorities.

While convention theory and Raynolds's tripartite distinction served as
sources of inspiration, there was a need for a tailor-made model to capture
various stakeholders' drivers throughout cocoa sustainability initiatives.
Discussing that cocoa production may face competing demands from policy,
Franzen and Borgerhoff Mulder (2007: 3836) cite 'improving productivity,
reducing negative biodiversity impacts, and increasing the social and economic sustainability of production' as potential goals, highlighting that these
competing objectives can require trade-offs. Findings from interviews, participant observation, and documents suggested that, in more abstract terms,
stakeholder drivers could be analysed under three dimensions:

- socio-economic factors including, for example, grower livelihoods;
- environmental aspects on local and global scale (Bolwig et al., 2010);
- the commercial level, including safeguarding supply, which was a particular concern for stakeholders from the private sector.

Based on interview, documentary, and focus group data, these three dimensions proved valid starting points for delineating categories of drivers. Franzen
and Borgerhoff Mulder's paper (2007) distinguishes between economic vis-à-
vis ecological considerations, while the most common conceptualization of
the sustainable development triangle discerns social, economic, and environmental aspects. The socio-economic, commercial, and environmental delin-
eation chosen in this model deviates from both: firstly, the paper's chosen
distinction emphasizes the difference between private-sector stakeholders
pursuing their commercial interests, and socio-economic viability for producers. While both sets of drivers are based in economic-commercial interests,
there is a need to distinguish between buyers' interest in keeping cocoa prices
low, and producers' socio-economic interest in a living income, as they can be
diametrically opposed. Moreover, seeking to boost commercial productivity
by thinning out intercropped shade trees may contravene producers' desire
for diversified agroforestry systems that can improve food security and protect
environmental benefits. Both examples of incongruence and trade-offs thus
justify exploring these priorities in distinct domains. This observation recalls
the difficulties in reconciling commercial and social objectives in sustainability efforts (Mason and Doherty, 2015), with labels emanating from social
movements such as Fairtrade facing a particular challenge by operating within
a system that they aspire to change (Nelson, 2014).

Mapping different dimensions

In the 'constellations of priorities' model (see Figure 3.1), the commercial,
environmental, and socio-economic dimensions each encompass four axes
symbolizing priorities, many of which are interdependent and interconnected,

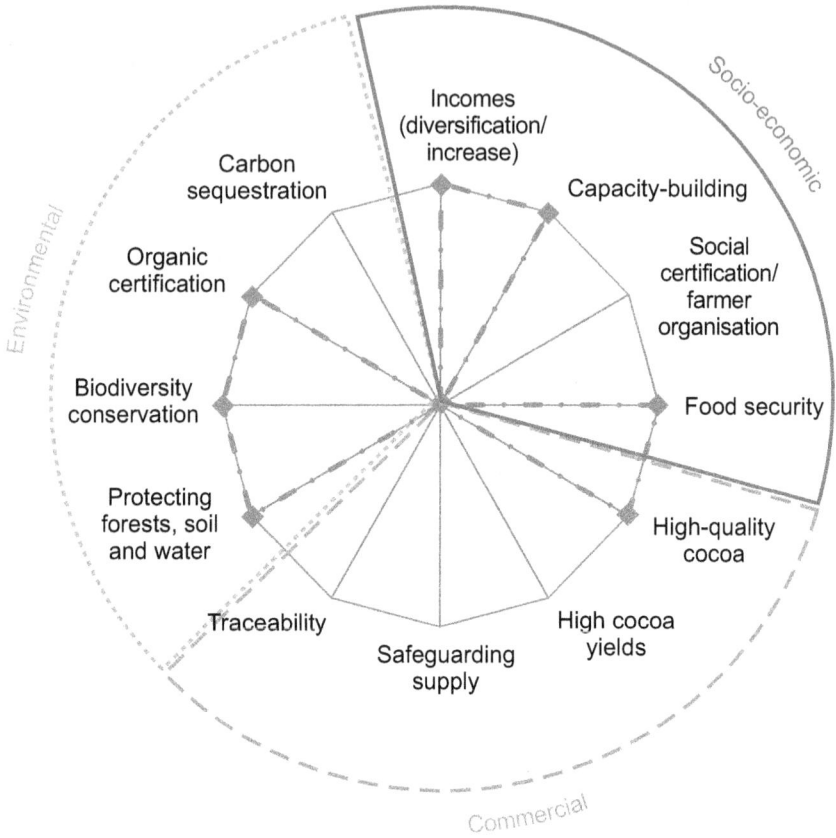

Figure 3.1 Constellation of priorities model: fictitious example.

but partly incompatible. The 12 axes, which do not aim to be exhaustive, partly derive from Franzen and Borgerhoff Mulder (2007), but are mostly based on data collected through this research, reflecting the drivers cited most frequently by interlocutors. My intention is to facilitate systematic (self-) assessments of the 'sustainability' priorities that cocoa stakeholders associate with the concept, although the model, with different axis designations, could be usable in other sectors. The spider-web diagrams shown in Figures 3.1–3.5 are only heuristic representations of complex situations, yet visualizations can help stakeholders identify starting points for necessary conversations at a glance. Beyond incongruence between stakeholder drivers, additional tensions may arise from actors' differing notions concerning time frames and spatial scales. The diagrams depict only the binary presence or absence of a driver at a specific time, no ranking or weighting. Moreover, lines between priorities in Figure 3.1 are meant only as a visual aid and do not indicate whether they are actually connected.

As Figure 3.1 visualizes, in the socio-economic domain, augmenting and diversifying grower revenues, for instance by way of diverse agroforestry systems, is a key concern (author interviews #142, private sector; #30 and #43, researchers; #69 and #74, development cooperation). Diversified systems spread risk and provide additional income sources (Somarriba et al., 2014), while also making a contribution to the food-security axis. The aspect of farmer organization is crucial for some social certifiers, but also for many development organizations who consider it an option to create long-term, self-sustaining support structures. Farmer organizations are often the vehicle for capacity-building, another axis in the diagram. Trade-offs between different socio-economic priorities may occur: diversified agroforestry increases food security but may reduce yields and thus cocoa-related incomes, while farmer organization and capacity-building ties up funds.

The environmental third of the diagram also encompasses four axes. The carbon sequestration axis represents the priority of afforesting or reforesting spaces in cocoa communities to offset greenhouse gases. A potential trade-off emerges with biodiversity, as tree selection in favour of fast-growing, non-native rather than endemic trees entails an implicit prioritization of reducing carbon (Haggar, 2013). Cocoa buyers interested in carbon neutrality pay additional premiums for carbon credits, linking to socio-economic income diversification. Organic certification is another axis: complying with the standard limits, for instance, usable inputs, but may also bring premium prices for cooperatives and growers (Pay, 2009). Conserving biodiversity is an axis for which cocoa agroforestry systems offer various opportunities (Tscharntke et al., 2015). The final priority is protecting forests, soils, and water, a key motivation for many cocoa producers given their dependence on their environment (author interviews #71, #75, #113, #138, cocoa producers; #30, researcher). For both conservation priorities, a potential trade-off emerges with productivity-maximizing approaches, which may clash particularly with protecting forests.

The commercial sphere occupies the model's final dimension. One commercial motivation is ensuring that cocoa quality lives up to buyers' requirements, with the socio-economic axis of capacity-building a crucial conduit. A further axis is increasing yields, an objective that is in growers' own interest, but may require trade-offs with plantations' long-term environmental viability. The priority may also lead to genetic concentration through hybrid varieties that maximize productivity, but replace higher-maintenance types that can garner higher prices because of their fine-flavour organoleptic parameters and preserve genetic diversity in the long term. Safeguarding supply is a key axis, which is due to gain in importance as shortage concerns intensify over time. However, trade-offs are likely with other axes such as preserving biodiversity or boosting food security. Finally, traceability is an increasing private-sector concern given tightening food safety regulations especially in the global North.

The following section will test this conceptual constellations of priorities model using the empirical case study of World Choc, analysing stakeholders' constellations of priorities before finally discussing synergies and tensions between different actors' drivers. Despite considerable synergistic elements between like-minded partners, there are subtle divergences which resonate with broader sectoral challenges and debates.

World Choc

Stakeholders and priorities

The 'World Choc' initiative encompasses one chocolate company, two NGOs, growers, and cooperatives in cocoa communities in one African and two Latin American countries, with the chocolate sold through the support of several retailers. The undertaking came about through a confluence of objectives by the three like-minded stakeholders discussed here. Children-for-children NGO Tree kids sought to find a commercial partner able to produce an ethically traded and carbon-neutral chocolate, their intention being to raise awareness and generate funds for their actual key pursuit, which is planting trees to mitigate climate change. Chocolate manufacturer Iller Chocolate, already offsetting chocolate production's carbon emissions in-chain through afforestation projects in cocoa communities, was able and willing to produce the chocolate bar. Environmental NGO Planet Concern, Iller's implementing partner working with cocoa communities, contributed expertise on intercropping cocoa with high-value timber with the dual purpose of sequestering carbon and diversifying growers' incomes. The product of their collaboration, 'World Choc', sells at a child-friendly price of €1, affordable even on limited allowances, and is a sweet milk chocolate amenable to Tree kids' young constituency. Bearing both a fair and a 'zero-climate' seal, the product is, according to the wrapper (bought in September 2013):

> just as we children want all products to be: climate-neutral and fair, because we do not want cocoa farmers' children to harvest cocoa beans for us, but them to go to school like us.

Beyond a certification premium, growers receive additional income from the high-value timber trees which are intercropped with cocoa in agroforestry systems (FHIA, 2007); these afforestation measures also help to offset all carbon emissions generated within the production network (Iller Chocolate, 2012; author interview #26, civil society; #30, researcher).

Given considerable parallels in terms of stakeholders' intentions, there are substantial parallels and thus synergies in terms of like-minded intentions driving the engagement. For instance, all three key stakeholders appear to view the venture as an opportunity to transform conventional wisdom and demonstrate the validity of alternative practices. Nevertheless, an in-depth analysis of different stakeholders' drivers using the constellations of priorities model highlights that there are subtle divergences resonating with a broader need for reflection in the sector.

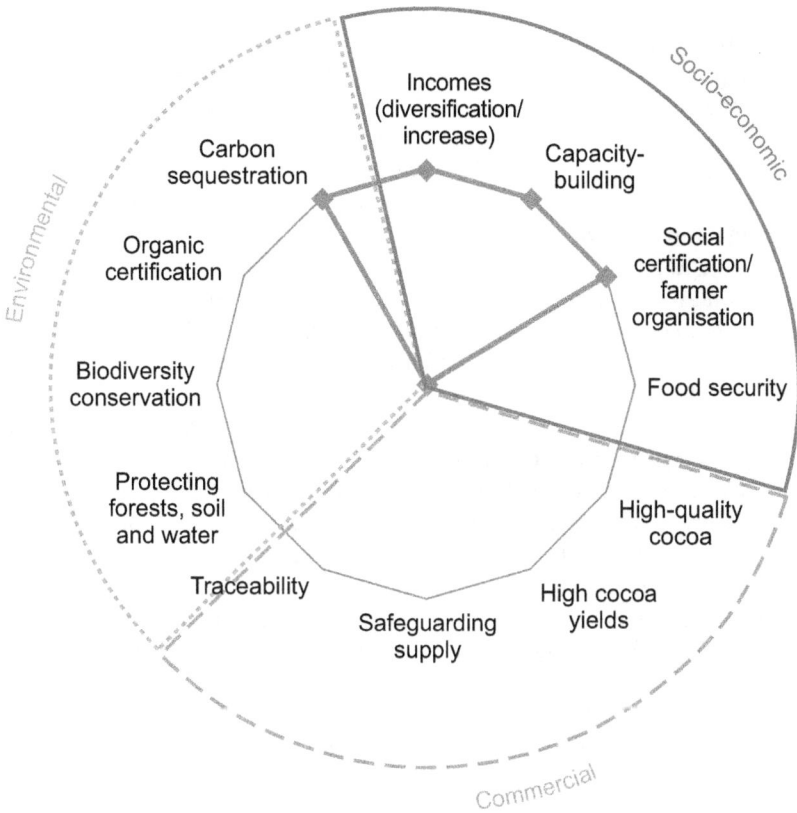

Figure 3.2 Constellation of priorities for NGO Tree Kids.

As Figure 3.2 illustrates, the key drivers for children-for-children's NGO Tree kids are an environmental aspect, carbon sequestration, and several socio-economic benefits. Their stated intention is that the chocolate bar be fair and ecological twice over (author interview #26, civil society); socio-economically, the 'double fair' adage alludes to growers receiving both the fair trading premium and extra payments for tree management, the objective being to 'tackle poverty at its root'. The NGO supports fair certification, viewing it as the only seal ensuring a better life for cocoa families, through farmer organization and better incomes. The additional premiums for carbon sequestration through tree management diversify income sources. At the same time, agroforestry and thus carbon credits are predicated on capacity-building for growers to support suitable cultivation and monitoring of timber trees' growth. The 'double ecological' representation stems from the argument that beyond Tree kids' own tree-planting efforts, Planet Concern also afforests for each chocolate bar sold. One could argue that their roots as a children's NGO become apparent in this 'twice over' adage and in the goal to 'tackle poverty at its root', given the simplifications inherent in such assessments. For instance, as the constellation of priorities model and the differentiated 'environmental' drivers show, equating tree-planting with an 'ecological' measure is a simplification as diverse stakeholders take diverse drivers to be 'ecological'. Similarly, various scholars in poverty research (e.g. Green and Hulme, 2005; Hickey and Bracking, 2005) would dispute the existence of a 'root' of poverty, emphasizing instead the presence of diverse power and social relations determining who can benefit from opportunities and investment.

Unlike the environmental and socio-economic domains, the commercial dimension encompassing traceability, supply security, high cocoa yields, and high-quality cocoa is not a priority for Tree kids, as Figure 3.2 visualizes. To the NGO, chocolate is a means to an end, the first of, as they hope, many products to hail from fair and climate-neutral production (author interview #26, civil society). To Tree kids, cocoa is interesting as a crop amenable to afforestation through its cultivability in agroforestry systems, as this link facilitates their primary goal of combating global warming. Moreover, the product lends itself to their campaign on account of its particular appeal to their predominantly young constituency, yet beyond this convenient link, there is no attachment per se to attaining high cocoa yields, safeguarding high-quality cocoa, or traceability. Their constellation of priorities places an accent on socio-economic priorities and planting trees for carbon sequestration, while the commercial dimension is a means to an end.

By comparison, for chocolate manufacturer Iller Chocolate, means and ends are reversed (see Figure 3.3), with their constellation prioritizing the long-term viability of their bread-and-butter business. As represented visually in Figure 3.3, Iller Chocolate places a considerable accent on the commercial domain, somewhat unsurprisingly. As a chocolate manufacturer, it is, by virtue of its own business and livelihood, naturally dependent on cocoa's continuing availability. Furthermore, its membership in a cooperative group, aims to offset all chocolate-related carbon emissions through afforestation in cocoa communities, and the intention to move towards 100 per cent fair-certified cocoa generates further commercial pressures in terms of compliance with standards and requirements (Iller Chocolate, 2012, 2013; Tree kids, 2013; author interview #30, researcher). Given its aspirations, there is an even greater necessity than for other chocolate-sector stakeholders to establish good relations with its growers and suppliers so as to increase independence from third-party traders and processors, and avoid risk from scandals. Iller's engagement is a conscious choice, partly to demonstrate to other cocoa stakeholders that certification in and of itself is not sufficient to attain 'sustainability', partly to make a business case in favour of cocoa cultivation to young farmers:

> [This is] to make a contribution towards solving the challenges in the cocoa sector, going one step further than fair certification by supporting cooperatives' afforestation projects. All types of certification are a basis towards a more holistic sustainability engagement. Sequestering carbon

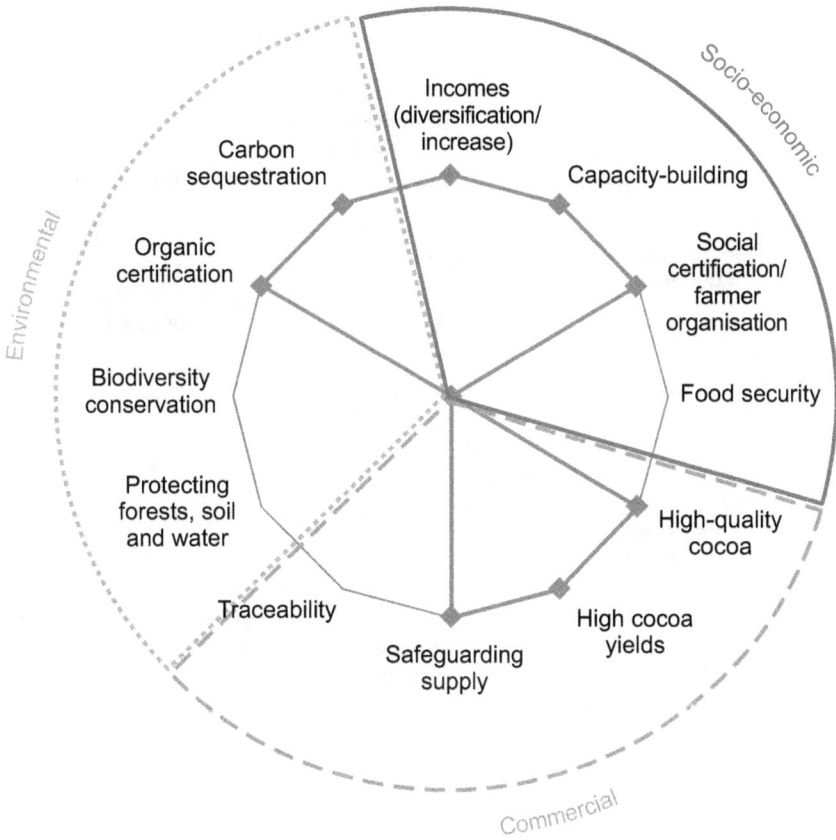

Figure 3.3 Constellation of priorities for company Iller Chocolate.

or climate neutrality is only one aspect of the plantations. The most important aspect is that small-scale farmers' income will multiply in the long term from the cultivation of precious timber. Growing cocoa in diversified systems is an attractive business case for the young generation (author interview #134, private sector).

This acknowledgement is noteworthy since it emphasizes that the prospect of supply shortages, and especially the underlying socio-economic factor of poor livelihoods, have shaped how Iller designed its engagement: at the same time, this logic also places the sustainability engagement in the wider context of challenges in the sector. Paying premiums for carbon sequestration in addition to good prices and premiums for fair certification is thus a means to the end of ensuring high-quality and long-term supply. This rationale is thus the inverse of Tree kids' viewpoint, for whom tree-planting is the end, and agroforestry with cocoa cultivation the means. This divergence in terms of underlying motivations is an interesting tension explored further below.

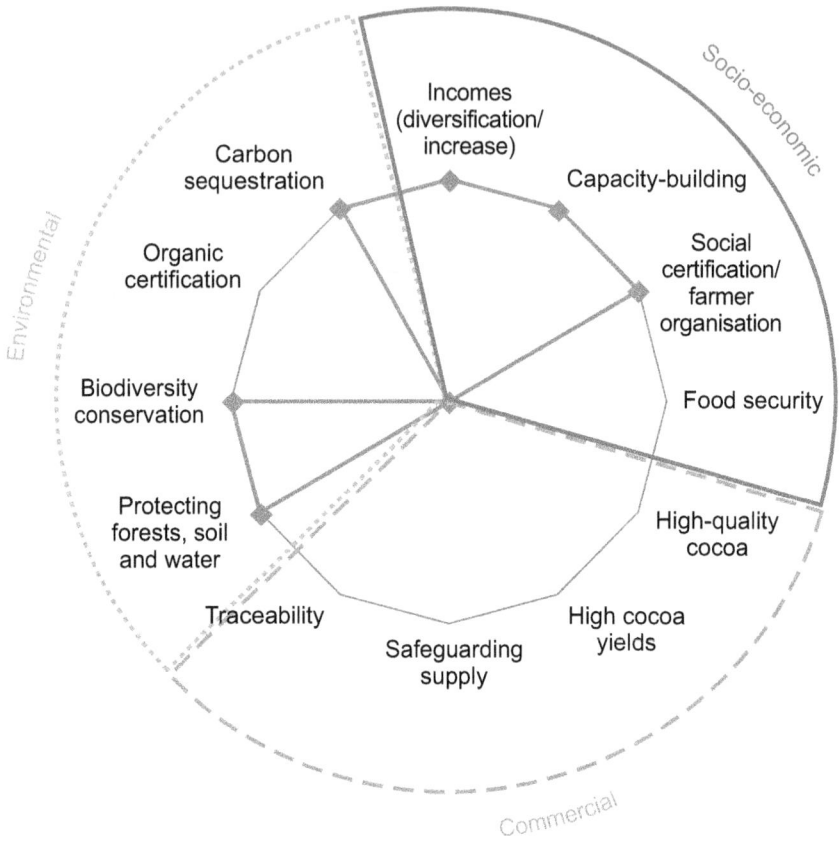

Figure 3.4 Constellation of priorities for NGO Planet Concern.

While both the chocolate manufacturer's and the NGO's vantage points are understandable, their framings of what nuances of sustainability take precedence, and the relationship of what is means, what is end, are reversed, creating incongruence in priority constellations that the initiative has to navigate.

As Figure 3.4 demonstrates, NGO Planet Concern contributes an organizational focus on environmental priorities given its expertise in conservation and carbon projects, yet also an emphasis on socio-economic measures to incentivize environmental awareness (Planet Concern, 2012, 2013a, b, 2014a, b, c, 2015a, b, c). Unlike companies that support unrelated causes from a philanthropic rationale (Utting, 2007) or purchase carbon credits in locations and sectors separate from their business interests (Peters-Stanley and Hamilton, 2012: 38), Planet Concern's work allows Iller's bread-and-butter business to entail greater benefits for cocoa communities. A key component of the intended fivefold increase in producer income is the precious timber planted and its sales revenue, with further income increases resulting from cocoa, yield improvements through capacity-building, and paid premiums for tree-planting and management. The underlying rationale is that the ecological objectives of carbon sequestration and conservation would be unattainable without creating livelihood opportunities for cocoa communities that are compatible with or stem from those environmental measures; however, this link also creates a tension that is explored further below. Again, commercial priorities are a factor only indirectly, given pressures affecting the funding chocolatier.

Discussion: congruence and divergence

Even in an initiative bringing together like-minded stakeholders, diverse priorities among World Choc actors have emerged in the analysis. Figure 3.5 visualizes considerable overlaps, but also certain divergences. Figure 3.5 shows that despite considerable parallels, there is a need to discuss divergences such as Iller Chocolate's commercial pressures, and the environmental drivers that NGO Planet Concern brings to the table. Whereas a private-sector stakeholder contributing commercial motivations may not be entirely surprising, there are implications of these motivations in terms of the degree to which differing priorities are commensurable, and the need to investigate how these priorities play out in terms of power asymmetries between different stakeholders located in global North and South. Equally, environmental priorities not shared by any other stakeholder raise questions.

Despite many parallels in priorities between World Choc's stakeholders, tensions emerge firstly between prioritizing different objectives in designing agroforestry systems. It becomes clear there is a delicate balance to strike in agroforestry designs between prioritizing high-value timber for income improvement, safeguarding a contribution to household food security by intercropping (e.g. fruit trees), boosting biodiversity through conducive habitats, increasing carbon sequestration through fast-growing trees, and safeguarding cocoa supplies. For instance, supply security concerns and resulting commercial pressures to safeguard cocoa yields create tensions with boosting high-value timber and thus generating carbon credits. 'Agroforestry', in much the same way as 'sustainability', thus will be subject to a diversity of priorities ranging from food security, augmenting cocoa supply, carbon sequestration to biodiversity conservation, requiring negotiation to navigate the divergences that emerge from incommensurabilities.

Another source of tension between diverging priorities arises through the choice of certification schemes. Even voluntary private standards are increasingly becoming de facto mandatory requirements for market access (Hoffmann and Grothaus, 2015). While certification schemes are often touted as facilitating more lucrative and stable engagements for smallholders, the combination of different seals can work to limit rather than enhance market access. For World Choc, the chocolate manufacturer partly requires cocoa communities to comply with four different seals, including carbon and forest certification.

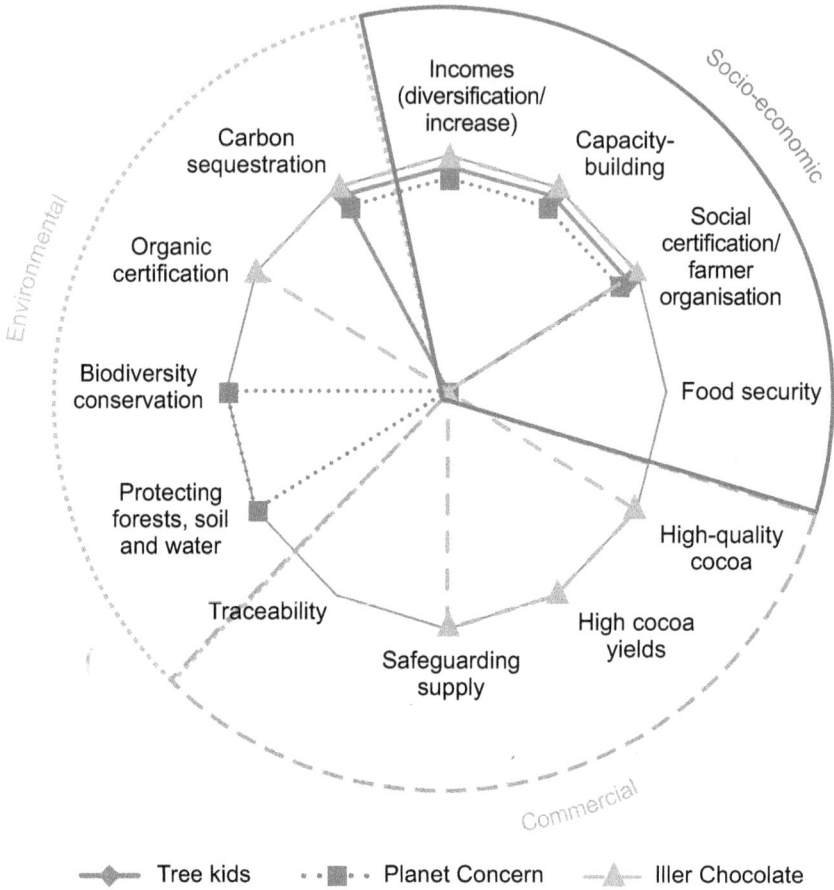

Figure 3.5 Constellation of priorities, divergences for World Choc.

This dynamic works to increase revenues for growers: as a rule, growers very much appreciate stable demand and higher prices (author interviews #71, #75, #103, #138, cocoa producers). However, the combination of seals also eliminates other sales options for cocoa communities as few buyers would pay premiums for all four standards. Further research would need to establish at what threshold losses become so prohibitive as to create de facto captive grower–buyer relationships. It is worth considering these interconnections' implications in terms of cementing rather than overcoming North–South power asymmetries in cocoa.

Another divergence of priorities in the case study emerges between what is end and what is means, an omnipresent dilemma in cocoa sustainability engagements. Between the two civil-society organizations and producers on the one hand, and private-sector retailers and chocolatier on the other hand, there are diverging viewpoints as to the relationship linking vehicle and objective between chocolate and socio-environmental measures. An element exacerbating this tension is the interdependence and inseparability of the three dimensions of commercial, socio-economic, and environmental priorities. Tree kids' primary driver of planting trees is predicated on Iller Chocolate and Planet Concern creating viable socio-economic opportunities in terms of cocoa prices, timber inter-cropping and carbon credits. In turn, all of this hinges on Iller's commercial ability to manufacture appealing chocolate and Iller's and Tree kids' capacity to mobilize and sell to Tree kids' tree-focused constituency. The premise of a children-for-children undertaking is an important factor in World Choc's sales success, succeeding where a carbon-neutral chocolate in a premium UK supermarket had previously failed (author interviews #33 and #134, private sector). This incongruence of purpose and divergence of drivers thus generates another difficult balance to strike between differing priorities.

Throughout the above-described divergences, the question of asymmetries in terms of power and ability to influence initiatives' direction emerges as relevant, both in the case study and across the sector. This initiative is something of a special case as the heavy reliance on Tree kids' constituency for sales and marketing bestows upon the children-for-children's NGO more influence than civil-society stakeholders can claim in most settings. However, even this deviation from the norm does not change the predominance of the global North, as the initiative does not establish value-adding processing or production stages or ownership shares among stakeholders in the global South. While pioneering and exemplary in terms of increasing and diversifying grower revenues as well as incorporating environmental considerations, the initiative still does not remedy North–South inequalities. However, these asymmetries have fanned the productivity-maximizing pressures on people and planet, furthering the socio-environmental challenges with which the cocoa sector is grappling. There is a wider question as to whether the sector's dilemma can be remedied without resolving fundamental imbalances between North and South and private-sector and other stakeholders. This paper proposes that another step towards these necessary transformations would be allowing growers and cooperatives an opportunity to contribute their own priorities in an equitable manner, raising the stature of socio-environmental drivers to preserve the land on and off which producers live while safeguarding cocoa livelihoods (author interviews #71, #75, #102, #103, #113, #138, cocoa producers).

In sum, while the initiative unites private-sector actors and NGOs who are largely like-minded in terms of delivering socio-economic benefits and offsetting carbon emissions, their constellations of priorities differ in the detail, raising wider questions for the cocoa sector. The balance to strike between carbon, cocoa, biodiversity and food security in agroforestry designs was one example of tensions. Another difficulty was the multitude of certification schemes, with disagreements as to means and end a key dilemma for World Choc and across the industry. Irrespective of the intention to work in partnership, the analysis showed the importance of knowing stakeholders' differing understandings of sustainability, rooted in their different organizational priorities. Equally, analysing how stakeholders' concomitant drivers govern behaviours proved crucial. This observation thus substantiates the paper's overall argument that unpacking diverging priorities systematically is essential to identify tensions, with the author proposing the 'constellation of priorities' as an instrument. The analysis also recalled in different ways the cocoa sector's pre-existing North–South power asymmetries, which this initiative, despite its pioneering efforts, does not alter.

In the broader cocoa conversation, this case study is noteworthy because private-sector, producer, and civil-society stakeholders aspire to engage with the socio-environmental transformations required to set the industry onto a more sustainable, supply-securing trajectory. In addressing socio-economic deficiencies through improved, stable, and diversified incomes, much to producers' appreciation, and ecological issues through carbon-sequestering cocoa agroforestry, the stakeholders seek to demonstrate their model's viability to chocolate competitors who are largely carrying on with business-as-usual, albeit with slightly tweaked practices. Nevertheless, asymmetrical power and decision-making relations persist even in this initiative, with all significant stakeholders and value-adding processes headquartered in the global North. While pioneering in many ways, the initiative does not alter this fundamental pre-existing injustice, which has contributed to cocoa's current socio-economic and environmental challenges. Supporting producers in terms of formulating their own priorities and increasing the share of chocolate bars' revenue benefiting the global South (e.g. through local value-adding processes) would thus be two recommendations to begin addressing power asymmetries.

Conclusion and broader implications

In sum, while 'sustainability' is often expected to be a force for good, rectifying socio-environmental issues and promoting genuine partnerships, sustainability initiatives investigated in cocoa (Krauss, 2016) often neglect to redress underlying power asymmetries particularly between Northern corporate actors and Southern stakeholders. Dynamics such as expecting multiple certification schemes or removing intermediaries from the production network, though increasing grower prices, also eliminate alternative sales outlets, thereby augmenting buyers' dominance. Based on my study, I would argue that equitable engagements between actors and their priorities in a spirit of fairness rather than charity can help to invite and heed especially Southern stakeholders' unique expertise to negotiate between diverse socio-economic, environmental, and commercial interests to attain sustainability in cocoa and beyond.

In conclusion, this paper has aimed to unpack stakeholders' priorities in cocoa sustainability. It argued that even within one initiative, the diverse actors involved and their differing understandings of sustainability in socio-economic, commercial, and environmental terms offer ample opportunity for tensions. It also argued that investigating these priorities and their implications can help negotiate viable balances between diverse interests. Following a discussion of the challenges facing cocoa-chocolate and the author's research methods, the paper presented a model, the constellations of priorities, which offers an opportunity for (self-)assessing stakeholders' priorities to enhance understanding and identify potentials for tension. The paper analysed a case study in terms of stakeholder priorities, identifying subtle divergences despite considerable synergies. The exploration confirmed the paper's argument of tensions emerging between differing understandings of cocoa sustainability, recommending the premise of engaging equitably with all stakeholder priorities as a vehicle to begin addressing underlying inequalities and negotiate genuine sustainability.

My study suggests that the magnitude of the industry's challenges requires transformational thinking to shift dominance, improve producer livelihoods, and safeguard production environments at scale. In my view, cocoa producers and cooperatives, considering the high stakes for their livelihoods involved, are in a unique position to help bridge existing disagreements on what is end and means, and help identify and negotiate trajectories that strike a balance between commercial, socio-economic, and environmental interests and are 'sustainable' in the long term. To this end, a meta-study chronicling stakeholders' constellations of priorities in various cocoa sustainability initiatives in the volume, mainstream, and niche market segments could prove instructive. A systematic, equitable exchange on and analysis of the commensurability of socio-economic, environmental, and commercial priorities across different actors and contexts could be an initial move towards negotiating between different stakeholders, especially from the global South, what genuine 'cocoa sustainability' is and is to entail.

In terms of recommendations relevant beyond cocoa, for private-sector actors, the analysis suggests that upholding socio-environmental priorities even in the face of commercial pressures is crucial for the long-term viability of supply. The discussion further suggests that a serious, equitable engagement with all stakeholders' priorities, including growers', could help initiatives bridge divergences on what is end and what is means, while also aiding a much-needed redressing of power asymmetries. For civil-society and similarly for public-sector stakeholders, the sector's challenges offer a window to question socio-economic and environmental conditions of production and trade in a manner that was hitherto unthinkable. However, for commercial pressures not to prompt untenable cultivation strategies prioritizing commercial 'sustainability', civil-society and public-sector actors are key in moderating these engagements as gatekeepers, through support, advocacy, and policy involvement, and are equally essential in using their clout to make less dominant voices heard.

Acknowledgements

The author is most grateful to everyone who contributed to the research in whatever way, and gratefully acknowledges support from the Sustainable Consumption Institute and ESRC grant ES/J500094/1.

References

Barrientos, S. (2002) 'Mapping codes through the value chain: from researcher to detective', in R. Jenkins, R. Pearson and G. Seyfang (eds), *Corporate Responsibility and Labour Rights. Codes of Conduct in the Global Economy*, pp. 61–76, London: Earthscan.

Barrientos, S. (2014) 'Gendered global production networks: analysis of cocoa–chocolate sourcing', *Regional Studies* 48(5): 791–803 <http://dx.doi.org/10.1080/00343404.2013.878799>.

Barrientos, S. and Asenso-Okyere, K. (2009) 'Cocoa value chain: challenges facing Ghana in a changing global confectionery market', *Journal für Entwicklungspolitik* XXV 2-2009: 88–107.

Bitzer, V., Glasbergen, P. and Leroy, P. (2012) 'Partnerships of a feather flock together? An analysis of the emergence of networks of partnerships in the global cocoa sector', *Global Networks* 12(3): 355–74.

Bloor, M., Frankland, J., Thomas, M. and Robson, K. (2001) *Focus Groups in Social Research*, London: Sage.

Bolwig, S., Ponte, S., du Toit, A., Riisgaard, L. and Halberg, N. (2010) 'Integrating poverty and environmental concerns into value-chain analysis: a conceptual framework', *Development Policy Review* 28(2): 173–94 <http://dx.doi.org/10.1111/j.1467-7679.2010.00480.x>.

Candy Industry (2010) 'What now, Candy World?' [online] <www.candyindustry.com/articles/83756-what-now-candy-world> [accessed 8 June 2017].

Candy Industry (2017) '2017 Global Top 100: Part 1 | Candy Industry' [online] <www.candyindustry.com/2017-Global-Top-100-Part-1> [accessed 5 February 2017].

Cidell, J.L. and Alberts, H.C. (2006) 'Constructing quality: the multinational histories of chocolate', *Geoforum* 37: 999–1007 <http://dx.doi.org/10.1016/j.geoforum.2006.02.006>.

Doherty, B., Davies, I.A. and Tranchell, S. (2013) 'Where now for fair trade?' *Business History* 55(2): 161–89 <http://dx.doi.org/10.1080/00076791.2012.692083>.

Fairtrade Foundation (2011) *Fairtrade and Cocoa: Commodity Briefing* [pdf] <https://www.fairtrade.net/fileadmin/user_upload/content/2009/resources/2011_Fairtrade_and_cocoa_briefing.pdf> [accessed 8 June 2017].

Fold, N. (2000) 'A matter of good taste? Quality and the construction of standards for chocolate products in the European Union', *Cahiers d'économie et sociologie rurales* 55–56: 91–110.

Fountain, A.C. and Hütz-Adams, F. (2015) *Cocoa Barometer 2015* [pdf] <www.cocoabarometer.org/Download_files/Cocoa%20Barometer%202015%20Print%20Friendly%20Version.pdf> [accessed 3 October 2015].

Franzen, M. and Borgerhoff Mulder, M. (2007) 'Ecological, economic and social perspectives on cocoa production worldwide', *Biodiversity Conservation* 16: 3835–49 <http://dx.doi.org/10.1007/s10531-007-9183-5>.

Fundación Hondureña de Investigación Agrícola (Honduran Foundation for Agricultural Research) (2007) *Uso de especies maderables tropicales latifoliadas como sombre del cacao* (Use of tropical broad-leaf timber species as shade trees for cocoa), Hoja técnica, Mayo 2007, La Lima, Cortés, Honduras: FHIA.

Gereffi, G., Humphrey, J. and Sturgeon, T. (2005) 'The governance of global value chains', *Review of International Political Economy* 12(1): 78–104 <http://dx.doi.org/10.1080/09692290500049805>.

Glin, L.C., Oosterveer, P. and Mol, A.P.J. (2015) 'Governing the organic cocoa network from Ghana: towards hybrid governance arrangements?' *Journal of Agrarian Change* 15(1): 43–64 <http://dx.doi.org/10.1111/joac.12059>.

Green, M. and Hulme, D. (2005) 'From correlates and characteristics to causes: thinking about poverty from a chronic poverty perspective', *World Development* 33(6): 867–79 <http://dx.doi.org/10.1016/j.worlddev.2004.09.013>.

Haggar, J. (2013) *Supporting Ecosystem Services in Fairtrade Value Chains* [pdf], NRI Working Paper Series, London: Twin Trading; Chatham, UK: Natural Resources Institute <www.nri.org/images/Programmes/climate_change/publications/Jeremy_Haggar_Report_Print_web.pdf> [accessed 8 June 2017].

Hainmueller, J., Hiscox, M.J. and Tampe, M. (2011) *Sustainable Development for Cocoa Farmers in Ghana. Baseline Survey: Preliminary Report* [pdf], Cambridge, MA: MIT and Harvard University <www.cocoaconnect.org/sites/default/files/publication/Hainmueller%20et%20al%20%282011%29%20baseline%20survey%2C%20preliminary%20report.pdf> [accessed 8 June 2017].

Henderson, J., Dicken, P., Hess, M., Coe, N.M. and Yeung, H.W.-c. (2002) 'Global production networks and the analysis of economic development', *Review of International Political Economy* 9(3): 436–64 <http://dx.doi.org/10.1080/09692290210150842>.

Hess, M. and Yeung, H.W.-c. (2006) 'Whither global production networks in economic geography? Past, present and future', *Environment and Planning A* 38(7): 1193–204 <http://dx.doi.org/10.1068/a38463>.

Hickey, S. and Bracking, S. (2005) 'Exploring the politics of chronic poverty: from representation to a politics of justice?' *World Development* 33(6): 851–65 <http://dx.doi.org/10.1016/j.worlddev.2004.09.012>.

Hoffmann, U. and Grothaus, F. (2015) *Assuring Coherence between the Market-Access and Livelihood Impact of Private Sustainability Standards* [pdf], UNFSS Discussion Paper 6 <https://unfss.files.wordpress.com/2013/02/unfss-discussion-paper-6-final-28may-2015.pdf> [accessed 11 January 2017].

Hughes, A. (2001) 'Global commodity networks, ethical trade and governmentality: organizing business responsibility in the Kenyan cut flower industry', *Transactions of the Institute of British Geographers* 26(4): 390–406 <http://dx.doi.org/10.1111/1475-5661.00031>.

Hütz-Adams, F. and Fountain, A.C. (2012) *Cocoa Barometer 2012* [pdf] <www.suedwind-institut.de/fileadmin/fuerSuedwind/Publikationen/2012/2012-44_Cocoa_Barometer_2012_Druckfreundlich.pdf> [accessed 23 January 2013].

International Cocoa Organization (ICCO) (2012a) *Monthly Review of the Cocoa Market Situation: May 2012* [pdf] <www.icco.org/about-us/

international-cocoa-agreements/doc_download/253-may-2012.html> [accessed 11 July 2012].

International Cocoa Organization (ICCO) (2012b) *Quarterly Bulletin of Cocoa Statistics XXXVIII*, No. 4; cocoa year 2011/12, London: ICCO.

International Cocoa Organization (ICCO) (2014) *Quarterly Bulletin of Cocoa Statistics, Vol. XL*, No. 3; cocoa year 2013/14, London: ICCO.

International Cocoa Organization (ICCO) (2015a) *Quarterly Bulletin of Cocoa Statistics, Vol. XLI* No. 1; cocoa year 2014/15, London: ICCO.

International Cocoa Organization (ICCO) (2015b) *Quarterly Bulletin of Cocoa Statistics, Vol. XLI* No. 3; cocoa year 2014/15, London: ICCO.

International Cocoa Organization (ICCO) (2016a) *Quarterly Bulletin of Cocoa Statistics, Vol. XLII, No. 1*; cocoa year 2015/16, London: ICCO.

International Cocoa Organization (ICCO) (2016b) *Quarterly Bulletin of Cocoa Statistics, Vol. XLII No. 3*; cocoa year 2015/16, London: ICCO.

Iller Chocolate (2012) *Nachhaltigkeitsbericht* [Sustainability Report; HTML] [accessed 01 October 2013].

Iller Chocolate (2013) *Klimaneutralität* [Climate neutrality; HTML] [accessed 01 October 2013].

Jorgensen, D.L. (1989) *Participant Observation: A Methodology for Human Studies*, Applied Social Research Methods Series 15, Newbury Park, CA: Sage.

Kaplinsky, R. and Morris, M. (2000) *A Handbook for Value Chain Research*, Brighton, UK: Institute for Development Studies, University of Sussex.

KPMG (2013) *Improving Smallholder Livelihoods: Effectiveness of Certification in Coffee, Cocoa and Cotton* [pdf] <http://www.sustaineo.org/tl_files/Sustaineo/Improving%20smallholder%20livelihoods%20-%20Effectiveness%20of%20certification%20in%20coffee,cocoa%20and%20cotton_study%20commissioned%20by%20SUSTAINEO.pdf> [accessed 22 May 2015].

Krauss, J.E. (2016) *Cocoa Sustainability Initiatives and the Environment: Mapping Stakeholder Priorities and Representations*, Doctoral thesis, University of Manchester.

Läderach, P., Eitzinger, A., Martínez, A. and Castro, N. (2011) *Predicting the Impact of Climate Change on the Cocoa-Growing Regions in Ghana and Côte d'Ivoire* [pdf], Centro Internacional de Agricultura Tropical (CIAT) <www.eenews.net/assets/2011/10/03/document_cw_01.pdf> [accessed 23 March 2013].

Laws, S., with Harper, C. and Marcus, R. (2003) *Research for Development: A Practical Guide*, London: Sage.

Lukes, S. (2005) *Power: A Radical View*, 2nd edition, Basingstoke, UK: Palgrave Macmillan.

Mason, C, and Doherty, B. (2015) 'A fair trade-off? Paradoxes in the governance of fair-trade social enterprises', *Journal of Business Ethics* 136(3): 451–69 <http://dx.doi.org/10.1007/s10551-014-2511-2>.

Mikkelsen, B. (2005) *Methods for Development Work and Research: A New Guide for Practitioners*, 2nd edition, London: Sage.

Morgan, D.L. (1997) *Focus Groups as Qualitative Research*, 2nd edition, London: Sage.

Nelson, V. (2014) 'Guest editorial: fairtrade impacts', *Food Chain* 4(1): 3–6 <http://dx.doi.org/10.3362/2046-1887.2014.001>.

Nieburg, O. (2012) 'Hershey stuns critics with commitment to source 100% certified cocoa by 2020' [online], Confectionery News <www.

confectionerynews.com/Commodities/Hershey-stuns-critics-with-commitment-to-source-100-certified-cocoa-by-2020> [accessed 14 April 2013].

Ofori-Boateng, K. and Insah, B. (2014) 'The impact of climate change on cocoa production in West Africa', *International Journal of Climate Change Strategies and Management* 6(3): 296–314 <http://dx.doi.org/10.1108/IJCCSM-01-2013-0007>.

O'Laughlin, B. (2007) 'Interpreting institutional discourses', in A. Thomas and G. Mohan (eds), *Research Skills for Policy and Development: How to Find Out Fast*, pp. 135–56, London: The Open University.

Pay, E. (2009) *The Market for Organic and Fair-Trade Cocoa* [pdf], Rome: FAO <www.fao.org/fileadmin/templates/organicexports/docs/Market_Organic_FT_Cocoa.pdf> [accessed 06 August 2012].

Peters-Stanley, M. and Hamilton, K. (2012) *Developing Dimension: State of the Voluntary Carbon Markets 2012* [pdf], Washington, DC: Forest Trends <www.forest-trends.org/publication_details.php?publicationID=3164> [accessed 05 August 2012].

Planet Concern (2012) *Project A - Progress report* [pdf] [accessed 30 September 2013].

Planet Concern (2013a) *Project A* [html] [accessed 28 September 2013].

Planet Concern (2013b) *Project B – Progress report* [pdf] [accessed 20 October 2014].

Planet Concern (2014a) *Project A - Progress report* [pdf] [accessed 20 October 2014].

Planet Concern (2014b) *Project C – Progress report* [pdf] [accessed 20 October 2014].

Planet Concern (2014c) *Project B – Progress report* [pdf] [accessed 18 January 2015].

Planet Concern (2015a) *Project B* [html] [accessed 18 January 2015].

Planet Concern (2015b) *Project A* [html] [accessed 18 January 2015].

Planet Concern (2015c) *Project C* [html] [accessed 18 January 2015].

Raynolds, L.T. (2009) 'Mainstreaming fair trade coffee: from partnership to traceability', *World Development* 37(6): 1083–93 <http://dx.doi.org/10.1016/j.worlddev.2008.10.001>.

Renard, M.C. (2003) 'Fair trade: quality, market and conventions', *Journal of Rural Studies* 19: 87–96 <http://dx.doi.org/10.1016/S0743-0167(02)00051-7>.

Somarriba, E., Suárez-Islas, A., Calero-Borge, W., Villota, A., Castillo, C., Vílchez, S., Deheuvels, O. and Cerda, R. (2014) 'Cocoa-timber agroforestry systems: Theobroma cacao-Cordia alliodora in Central America', *Agroforestry Systems* 88: 1001–19 <http://dx.doi.org/10.1007/s10457-014-9692-7>.

Spradley, J.P. (1980) *Participant Observation*, Fort Worth, TX: Harcourt Brace Jovanovich College Publishers.

Tampe, M. (2016) 'Leveraging the vertical: the contested dynamics of sustainability standards and labour in global production networks', *British Journal of Industrial Relations* <http://dx.doi.org/10.1111/bjir.12204>.

Thornton, P. (2010) *Cocoa Production 2020* [presentation], London: Armajaro Group.

Tree kids (2013) *FAQ – Schokolade* [FAQ – Chocolate; html] [accessed 25 February 2013].

Tscharntke, T., Milder, J.C., Schroth, G., Clough, Y., DeClerck, F., Waldron, A., Rice, R. and Ghazoul, J. (2015) 'Conserving biodiversity through certification of tropical agroforestry crops at local and landscape scales', *Conservation Letters* 8(1): 14–23 <http://dx.doi.org/10.1111/conl.12110>.

United Nations Conference on Trade and Development (UNCTAD) (2008) *Cocoa Study: Industry Structures and Competition* [pdf] <http://unctad.org/en/Docs/ditccom20081_en.pdf> [accessed 8 June 2017].

Utting, P. (2007) 'CSR and equality', *Third World Quarterly* 28(4): 697–712 <http://dx.doi.org/10.1080/01436590701336572>.

About the author

Judith Krauss (judith.krauss@manchester.ac.uk) is an Honorary Research Fellow at the Global Development Institute, University of Manchester, UK.

CHAPTER 4

Development impact bonds: Learning from the Asháninka cocoa and coffee case in Peru

John Belt, Andrey Kuleshov, and Eline Minneboo

Abstract

Impact bonds effectively allow the risk of implementing social development activities to be shared with private sector investors. Social or development impact bonds replace the upfront financing of charitable activities with a pay-for-success contract. Four actors together agree upon the outcomes and their indicators: outcome sponsor, investor, project implementers, and verifier. Under such a contract, a charitable donor or government ('outcome sponsor') takes the obligation to pay the 'investor' an amount determined by a set of objective indicators reflecting the outcome desired by the donor. The investor, expecting contract-based future payout, can recruit and pre-finance project implementers ('service provider') to achieve the agreed results. The achievements of the outcome indicators are assessed by an independent verifier to conclude the payout from donor to investor according to the contract. The structure allows charitable donors to transfer a significant share of risk to investors and/or financial markets. The Common Fund for Commodities (CFC), the Schmidt Family Foundation (SFF), Rainforest Foundation UK (RFUK), and the Royal Tropical Institute (KIT) were the first to apply the model in the agricultural sector in an emerging economy. The main objective of the impact bond was to increase productivity and market sales of cocoa and coffee produced by the Asháninka people, an indigenous community living in the Peruvian Amazon. This pilot provides valuable lessons learned to contribute to the development of the mechanism.

Keywords: impact bonds, social investing, public–private partnership, result-based finance

Impact bonds, shorthand for social impact bonds, social benefit bonds or development impact bonds, are a new social investment mechanism that is growing in popularity (Warner, 2013; CGD and Social Finance, 2013; Drew and Clist, 2015; Gustafsson-Wright and Gardiner, 2015; Gustafsson-Wright et al., 2015; Flynn and Young, 2016). Impact bonds bring together private investors, non-profit and private sector service delivery organizations, governments

http://dx.doi.org/10.3362/9781788530576.004

and donors to deliver results that society values (CGD and Social Finance, 2013). The current global social challenges are massive, including widespread poverty, unemployment, food shortages, lack of access to health services and education, and require large-scale and more effective ways of financing development programmes. Governments are looking for innovative models to finance their public agendas without substantially higher costs for society. Impact bonds seem an appropriate, innovative financial mechanism to use private funding to support public goals. Impact bonds mix result-based finance with impact financing and public–private collaboration (Gustafsson-Wright et al., 2015).

The prospects of impact bonds seem bright, but their application is still in its infancy. Impact bonds require a change in the financial structures of conventional donor and government agencies. Lessons can be drawn from the Asháninka Impact Bond in Peru, a pilot experiment by the Common Fund for Commodities (CFC), the Schmidt Family Foundation (SFF), Rainforest Foundation UK (RFUK), and the Royal Tropical Institute (KIT). The case presented here showcases the opportunities for impact bonds in the agricultural sector in an emerging economy.

In June 2016, CFC, the Ministry of Foreign Affairs of the Netherlands, and KIT organized the symposium 'Development impact bonds: game changer or hype?' to discuss with donor organizations, scientists and development practitioners the state of affairs and lessons learned so far. It was concluded that the mechanism is bold in its design by using private investment to support public objectives. Currently, many NGOs and governments experiment with result-based finance and explore new principles to finance their development agendas, and impact bonds could be of interest to them. This chapter will help to unravel various aspects of impact bonds by presenting a practical case from Peru.

Impact bonds: a new approach in development finance

Increasing global challenges, lower development budgets, and a rising pressure to show impact have started a process of questioning traditional development finance, providing a trigger for innovation to finance development. Result-based finance is one way to put more focus on outcomes instead of outputs. Impact bonds build on this principle of paying for outcomes.

Result-based financing and impact bonds replace the 'traditional' monitoring of process with evaluation of impact as the basis for providing development funds. There are advantages of impact monitoring as opposed to process monitoring:

- There is a lower administrative burden on the outcome sponsor who no longer needs to conduct costly monitoring and evaluation of activities.
- There is flexibility of implementation for the service provider because the contract does not need to list specific actions or a specific sequence of action. Instead, the obligations relate to achieving the outcomes.

- The sponsor is no longer compelled to make full payment for insufficient results on the grounds that activities were executed correctly but fell short of expectations due to external adverse events. The sponsor transfers these risks to other partners.
- Impact evaluation becomes an activity with significant material value; this will likely result in more credible impact assessments.

Basic structure of an impact bond

Compared with result-based financing, impact bonds include a third party, the investor, who pre-finances the necessary activities to achieve desired development outcomes. The investor is paid based on results achieved. Impact bonds generally involve four actors: investor, service provider, outcome sponsor, and verifier. The investor pre-finances the activities of a service provider, serving a particular societal outcome. An independent verifier assesses whether the outcomes are met according to the contractual arrangements. The outcome sponsor agrees to pay the investor once the agreed outcomes have been achieved. Impact bonds have variable returns, similar to equity investments, including interest on return (Gustafsson-Wright et al., 2015). The process to organize the design of an impact bond, including agreeing the outcomes and the specific contractual arrangements, can be complicated and time-consuming; therefore, an intermediary sometimes facilitates the process to create the structure for the development impact bond (DIB), including the legal and financial specifics (see Figure 4.1).

An impact bond adheres to four criteria. Firstly, measurable outcomes are to be defined that can be measured by the independent verifier. The simpler and clearer the outcomes are, the easier it is to measure success in an unambiguous manner (Gustafsson-Wright et al., 2015). Secondly, a reasonable time horizon to achieve the outcomes needs to be defined. Thirdly, there should be evidence that the outcomes can be achieved successfully. This will motivate the investor to provide the pre-financing and take the risk. Fourthly, the appropriate legal and political conditions need to be in place to support the impact bond. If governments are involved as outcome sponsors, the legal structure should generally allow them to pay for outcomes achieved beyond the fiscal year (Gustafsson-Wright et al., 2015).

Some recent impact bond examples

In 2010, the first ever social impact bond (SIB) was implemented in the UK. It aimed at reducing prison recidivism among short-term male prisoners. Since then, a considerable number of impact bonds have been operational; by January 2016, almost 60 impact bonds in total had been launched in 14 countries (see Figure 4.2). Out of these, 22 projects have reported performance data where 21 indicated positive social outcomes. Of these, 12 projects payments have been made, either to investors, or to be used for additional service

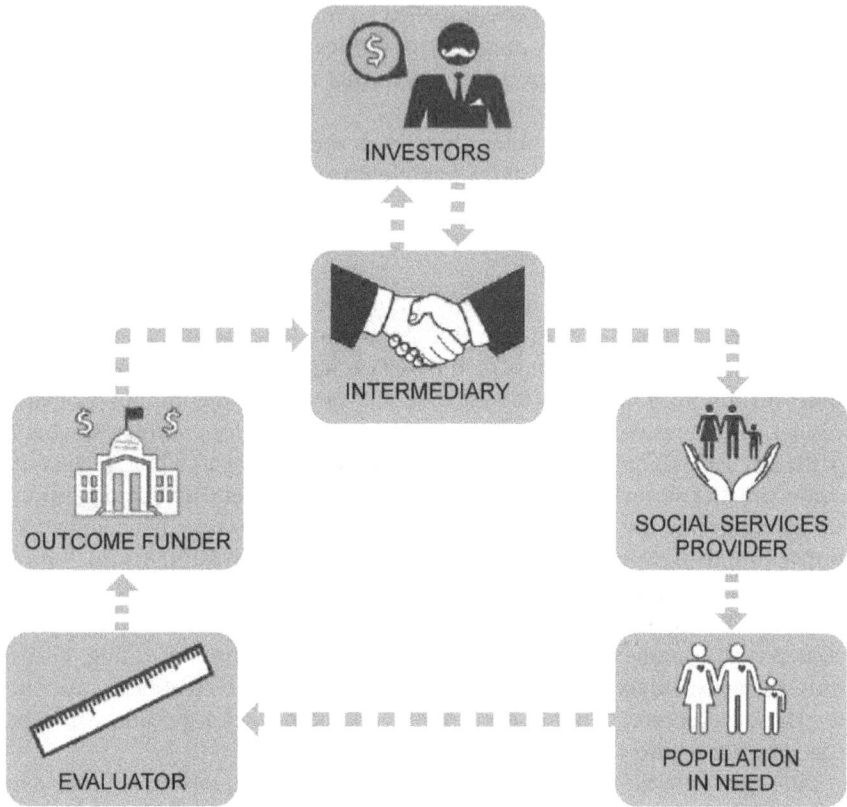

Figure 4.1 Impact bond mechanism.
Source: Gustafsson-Wright et al., (2015)

delivery, while in four projects the outcome sponsors fully repaid the investor capital (Dear et al., 2016). Most impact bonds are found in the UK – 31 in total – and all have a social focus including employment, homelessness, and child welfare (Dear et al., 2016). A SIB Innovation Fund set up by the UK Government was instrumental (Gustafsson-Wright et al., 2015).

The scale of these impact bonds differs widely. The smallest SIB, in Canada, targets 22 children and their mothers, while the largest one, in the USA, focuses on about 10,000 youth (Gustafsson-Wright et al., 2015). The investments also vary, whereby the smallest amount of upfront capital commitment is a SIB in Portugal, at $148,000, while the largest SIB is the Child-Parent Center Pay for Success Initiative in Chicago, USA, involving $16.9 m (Gustafsson-Wright et al., 2015). It must be noted that it is sometimes difficult to calculate the actual size of investment, since some projects include revolving funds, loans, or grants.

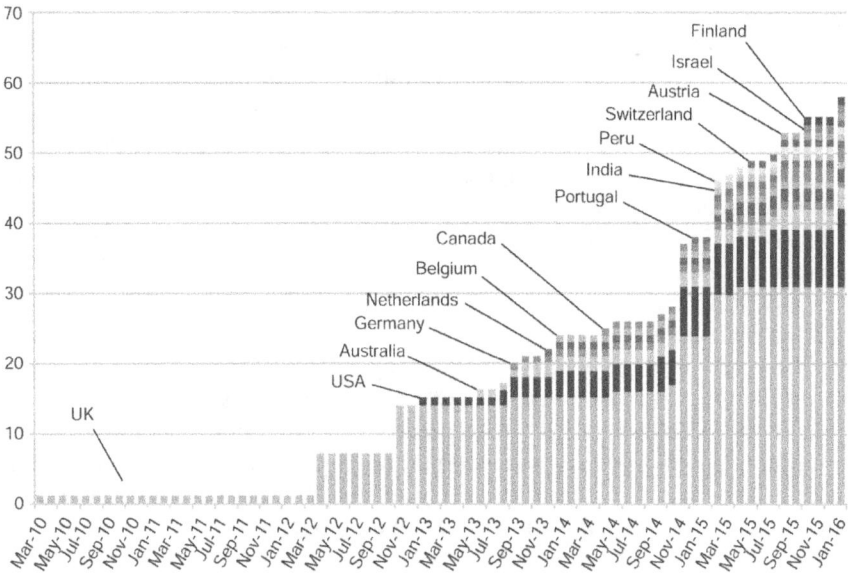

Figure 4.2 Impact bond contracts over time, 2010–2016.
Source: Gustafsson-Wright et al., (2015), Brookings Institution

Target indicators and DIB value to sponsor

A DIB contract must place a monetary value on a development outcome and it may be considered a major impediment for outcome sponsors if there is no clear basis for placing a value on a development result. Yet, finding a sound basis for setting the value of a development outcome depends on many assumptions and, at this stage, we see greatest potential in establishing a framework within which the outcome payer could be clear about the assumptions and methodology for converting these assumptions into a value. We can note the following possible options:

Replacement value
The value of the result can be evaluated as the cost that the outcome sponsor would need to incur if it wanted to produce the results itself. Results like operationalization of a production facility, construction of a warehouse, or installation of water pumps give a fairly precise approach to estimating their value. Outcome payers are likely to have all the necessary assumptions at hand, and it is immediately clear if financing via a DIB brings any benefits. At the same time, for a wide range of results, such as facilitating vertical diversification of smallholder producers, this approach is not directly applicable owing to the uncertainties of future developments in the value chain as the result of the project.

Activity-based approach

If the schedule of activities to be implemented towards the achievement of the result is known, it is technically not difficult to calculate the cost of implementing these activities. The total budget for activities, plus a certain level of profitability, provides a fair benchmark for projects focusing on issues such as education, vaccination campaigns, or quality certification for market access, among others. The negotiations between outcome sponsor and investor on the value of the DIB would be fairly simple in such cases. However, this approach faces a natural limitation because the investor would essentially need to take the risk of not reaching the intended results despite full and diligent implementation of activities ('effectiveness risk'). This risk would vary by sector, and the negotiation of profitability mark-up by the investor may be expected to fail if the expected effectiveness of proposed activities is insufficient in mitigating the effectiveness risk. At this stage it is not entirely clear where such a limit of activity-based approach would lie in practice because the limit will mainly be seen in the failure of negotiations of DIBs. It seems that identifying and examining such cases presents a separate research challenge to provide more insight into the practical applicability of an activity-based approach.

Financializing economic impact

This approach assumes that the outcome payer can agree on some measure of the economic impact of a project. The net economic value of a project could be calculated using assumptions as is commonly done in commercial projects. It is worth noting that a reasonable net present value of a project is a good indication of its commercial viability; the involvement of the outcome payer is only justified in projects where the economic value cannot be monetized, i.e. cannot be expected to generate a flow of revenues commensurate with economic impact. The outcome sponsor may wish to get involved in such projects because the use of normal forms of financing is not possible owing to lack of viable monetization. The determination of the value of such a DIB would best be based on objective economic indicators such as revenue, price premium for quality, or volume of transactions in a microfinance scheme, among others. The estimates of a net economic value are notoriously imprecise and, in the absence of some objective indicators, the negotiations of a DIB are also likely to fail. However, the list of specific activities to be financed under a DIB contract does not need to be negotiated and specified under such a contract, which opens considerable scope for the investor to monitor and mitigate the risk of delivering the intended result by adjusting the activities in the implementation process.

Financial analysis, risk evaluation, and pricing of a DIB by the investor

Approaching the matter of pricing a DIB contract from the standpoint of the investor, it is important to come to an estimate of the minimum required premium for the risk taking linked to a DIB contract. As mentioned above, the investor has to form an opinion about the 'effectiveness risk' referring to correct assessment of impact of activities to be financed on the indicators recorded in the contract.

At this stage it appears that investors are only willing to work with service providers with whom they have a prior relation and first-hand experience of their effectiveness in implementing planned activities. However, the possibility remains of making an incorrect assessment of the scope and magnitude of activities needed to achieve the target outcome indicators specified in the DIB contract, which may be called the 'process-outcome coordination risk'.

In this context, we would like to mention the 2013 Social Impact Bond with the Municipality of Rotterdam, Netherlands, where the ABN-AMRO Bank was the investor (ABN-AMRO, 2015). The bank valued the SIB payment in case of success by postulating a fixed mark-up rate to be added to the cost of agreed activities. The rate was not calculated but negotiated with the bond sponsor. We believe that this approach was largely the result of uncertainty about the effectiveness of envisioned activities. More precision will come in this risk assessment as experience accumulates.

The arrangements for settlement of a DIB contract are also a potential source of risk for the investor. The 'appropriation risk', referring to the risk of a public agency renouncing its obligations under a DIB contract due to failure to appropriate the required funds in the relevant year's budget, had been noted in the implementation of Rikers Island scheme by Goldman Sachs and MDRC (Rudd et al., 2013). Furthermore, in the discussions of the DIB concept with UN agencies and charitable organizations, it has become apparent to the authors that many see a challenge in convincing their respective governing bodies about signing a commitment to pay public or charity funds to a commercial organization. This relates closely to the reliability of the valuation of DIB contracts, underlining the importance of establishing an agreed valuation framework for DIBs.

Legal considerations

One of the likely impediments to the wider use of impact bonds is their legal structure, which presents considerable challenges because the basic setup involves at least four distinct parties. As main drivers of the model, the outcome sponsor and the investor need to agree on the critical legal issues. The contract specifies the indicators, the methodology of evaluating the outcome indicators, the time frame, and the schedule of payment. The agreement on these points is reached on the basis of a shared commitment to the objectives of a project; the DIB contract establishes a connection between development goals of the sponsor and financial returns of the investor. This contract makes development outcomes investable; the contract needs to be sufficiently precise in creating a clear mapping of development outcomes to undisputable indicators that can be assessed by the financial markets. The project itself can be defined in any mutually agreed form and the parties only need to express intention to support the goals of the project while agreeing that these goals are adequately represented by the indicators.

In principle, after the conclusion of such a bilateral impact bond contract, the sponsor and investor are free to take any steps necessary to arrange the implementation of development activities towards agreed indicators on the investor side, and verification of these indicators on the sponsor side. In ideal circumstances, this can be achieved by placing the two functions to open competitive bidding with reference to the DIB contract. Assuming that a private investor can achieve better implementation results in such a competitive setting than a not-for-profit organization, this creates a potential for efficiency gains compared with the 'traditional' aid scenario.

The investor would normally want to include a number of considerations in the contract commissioning the service provider to deliver development activities. Some of these identified in the context of the Asháninka project are as follows:

- The investor should impose an obligation on the service provider to make the project implementation sites accessible to the verifier and, possibly, the commissioner;
- The intellectual property rights need to be clearly specified, if any;
- There should be indemnity for the investor and commissioner for liability due to actions by the service provider;
- There should be a commitment to observe applicable international good practice standards and other restrictions such as international sanctions and anti-corruption laws.

Depending on the particular interests of the commissioner and/or investor, the parties may further agree to restrict the list of admissible activities to be financed from the proceeds of the impact bond. While this would probably be a limiting factor in the implementation, many charitable foundations that could potentially act as outcome sponsors have specific lists of permitted activities. We expect that further discussion may be in order to produce a 'good practice' list of standard conditions for a service contract based on a DIB.

The Asháninka Impact Bond

Sharing an interest in the DIB approach, CFC, RFUK, SFF, and KIT developed a partnership that allowed them to put a DIB in practice, thereby evaluating its effectiveness and efficiency while learning from the legal, administrative, and other operational implications for each of the implementing parties. They identified a longer running collaboration by RFUK in the Peruvian Amazon as ideal for their pilot. SFF took the role of the investor, pre-financing RFUK to cover the costs of implementing DIB project activities. RFUK was the service provider performing all activities, together with its partner organizations in Peru, required to achieve the results defined by the DIB. CFC was the outcome sponsor committed to pay the investor for the results achieved, up to a maximum of US$110,000. SFF and CFC agreed to engage KIT as the independent party to verify the accomplishment of the jointly agreed results. Details of the DIB setup were documented in a formal DIB agreement, which was undersigned by all the involved parties.

Target indicators

The overall objective of the DIB, as described in the DIB agreement, was to support the indigenous Asháninka people of Peru by assisting the members of their cooperative, the Kemito Ene Association, in establishing an environmentally sound production and marketing system for coffee and cocoa (CFC, 2014). The following outcomes were agreed among all the parties involved, formulated as specific, objectively verifiable outcome indicators (see Figure 4.3):

1. 60 per cent of the members of the Kemito Ene Association increase their supply to their association by at least 20 per cent, thereby improving their income.
2. At least 60 per cent of the members of the Kemito Ene Association improve their cocoa yield to 600 kg/ha or more.
3. The Kemito Ene Association buys and sells at least 35 tonnes of cocoa in the last year of the DIB project.

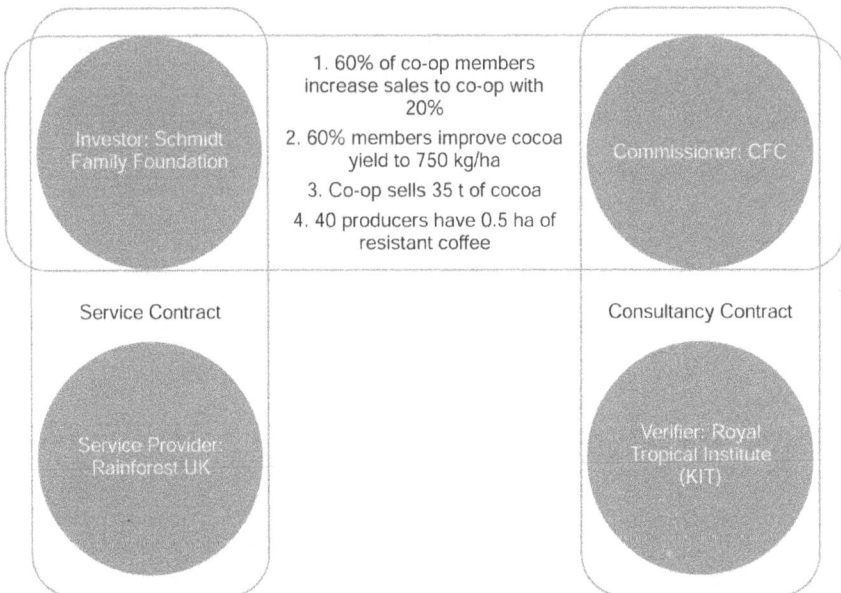

Figure 4.3 Asháninka DIB structure.

4. At the end of the DIB project, 40 members of the Kemito Ene Association have established at least 0.5 ha with a leaf rust-resistant coffee variety.

In the DIB agreement, the payment per level of achievement for each indicator was defined in detail (see Table 4.1).

The independent verifier collected the information on the extent to which the outcomes were achieved, assigning the range category for each of the different outcome indicators. To collect reliable information on the defined indicators, the following evaluation methods were applied:

*   review of project documentation of the service provider and its partners, including progress reports, field activity reports, and publications;

Table 4.1 Payment by level of achievement for each outcome indicator of the Asháninka DIB

	Target 100% achieved	Target 75% achieved	Target 50% achieved	Target not achieved
1	60% of the members of Kemito Ene Association increase their supply to their association by at least 20%	Between 59% and 41% of the members of Kemito Ene Association increase their supply to their association by at least 20%	Between 40% and 20% of the members of Kemito Ene Association increase their supply to their association by at least 20%	Below 20% of the members of Kemito Ene Association increase their supply to their association by at least 20%
2	At least 60% of the members of the Kemito Ene Association improve their cocoa yield to 600 kg/ha or more	Between 59% and 41% of the members of the Kemito Ene Association improve their cocoa yield to 600 kg/ha or more	Between 40% and 20% of the members of the Kemito Ene Association improve their cocoa yield to 600 kg/ha or more	Below 20% of the members of the Kemito Ene Association improve their cocoa yield to 600 kg/ha or more
3	The Kemito Ene Association buys and sells at least 35 tonnes of cocoa in the last year of the DIB project	The Kemito Ene Association buys and sells between 24 and 34 tonnes of cocoa in the last year of the DIB project	The Kemito Ene Association buys and sells between 12 and 23 tonnes of cocoa in the last year of the DIB project	The Kemito Ene Association buys and sells less than 12 tonnes of cocoa in the last year of the DIB project
4	At the end of the project, 40 producers have 0.5 ha of newly established coffee plots with leaf rustresistant varieties	Between 39 and 30 producers have 0.5 ha of newly established coffee plots with leaf rustresistant varieties	Between 29 and 19 producers have 0.5 ha of newly established coffee plots with leaf rustresistant varieties	Below 19 producers have 0.5 ha of newly established coffee plots with leaf rustresistant varieties

- on-site meetings and discussions with the service provider's project team, mainly focusing on information and data collection related to the defined outcomes;
- analyses of the data provided by the project staff;
- direct observations in the field through visiting project sites;
- focus group discussions with coffee and cocoa farmers at the two project sites, involving women and men;
- informal interviews with female and male farmers and other stakeholders during the field visits.

To verify the progress of the four outcomes, for each indicator the main sources of data were identified (see Table 4.2).

Pricing of the Asháninka DIB

It was agreed among the parties to assign the same weight to each of the four outcomes, implying that each represented a maximum of 25 per cent of the total DIB budget. When one performance indicator was achieved, the outcomes sponsor would reimburse the investor with the full amount for that specific outcome. When the target for an indicator was 75 per cent achieved, the outcome sponsor would reimburse the investor 75 per cent. When 50 per cent was achieved, the sponsor would reimburse 50 per cent. The outcome sponsor would not pay anything to the investor for targets which were not achieved.

While the indicators in the Asháninka project are consistent with calculating the monetary value of development outcomes ('financialization of economic impact' approach as indicated above), the actual negotiations were based on calculating the total cost of envisioned activities.

Table 4.2 Outcome indicators

Outcome indicator	Description	Data source
1	60% of the members of the Kemito Ene Association increase their supply to their association by at least 20%, thereby improving their income	Purchase records of the Kemito Ene specifying the amounts bought each year from each Kemito Ene member
2	At least 60% of the members of the Kemito Ene Association improve their cocoa yield to 600 kg/ha or more	Productivity figures for each farmer for each cocoa harvest reported by the project's field staff
3	The Kemito Ene Association buys and sells at least 35 tonnes of cocoa in the last year of the DIB project	Sales data of the Kemito Ene specifying for each year the amounts sold to its buyers
4	At the end of the project, 40 producers have 0.5 ha of newly established coffee plots with leaf rust-resistant varieties	Figures on number of hectares with newly established coffee plots for each coffee farmer reported by project's field staff

The estimate of the net economic impact was not included in the discussions, in the contract, or in the evaluation because of the lack of reliable data. To give a benchmark for evaluating the outcomes, estimates can be made retrospectively from the information available in the verification (KIT, 2015) by translating gains in yield, production, and turnover into US dollars at market prices for the farmers participating in the project (see Table 4.3).

The apparent bias of impact towards target three is balanced by the expectation that targets one, two and four will result in permanent gains, i.e. be cumulative into the future. With a 10-year horizon, the gross impact of the project amounts to $300,000, at 7 per cent discount rate, equivalent to circa 10 per cent gross rate of return. In retrospect, it is apparent that even the simplest estimate of this kind applied at the negotiation phase would yield useful insights into the relative value and payment commitment by the outcome sponsor for each of the target indicators.

Legal setup

The Asháninka DIB contract was initiated by RFUK and not by the CFC and SFF. This is not consistent with the ideal DIB model described above, particularly because the only choice for the investor is to accept or reject the DIB contract with a given specific service provider. KIT, acting as the verifier, was also closely involved in the project origination. Consequently, the impact bond contract was concluded in amended form reflecting this information: RFUK became the third signatory of the impact bond contract, and the CFC undertook the responsibility to appoint KIT as the verifier, with the terms of reference for appointment based on the agreed methodology for evaluation of the indicators.

The considerations mentioned above have been included in the Asháninka impact bond contract as follows:

- access to implementation sites by CFC, SFF, and KIT;
- indemnity for the CFC and SFF for liability due to actions by the service provider;

Table 4.3 Net economic impact

	Impact target (US$/year)	Impact actual (US$/year)	Expected after 5 years (US$/year)
Target 1	6,700	5,500	5,500
Target 2	18,000	6,000	6,000
Target 3	64,000	98,000	n/a
Target 4	Planting of leaf rust-resistant coffee does not generate impact in the first few years		23,000
Total	88,700	109,500	34,500

- commitment to observe applicable international good practice standards and other restrictions such as international sanctions and anti-corruption laws.

The remaining parameters of the contract have, essentially, been taken unmodified from the standard conditions used by the CFC and the SFF.

Discussion of the Asháninka DIB outcomes and results

The verifier evaluated the delivery of project outcome indicators by conducting a field mission envisioned in the verification contract between CFC and KIT, and in accordance with the terms of reference included in the DIB contract. The overall assessment is that the DIB has been a learning exercise for all the parties involved.

The verification report (KIT, 2015) concluded that some of the impact indicators were met, while others were not. The target for the first outcome was 75 per cent achieved, the target for the second outcome was not achieved, while the targets for outcomes three and four were both 100 per cent achieved.

A number of observations were recorded by the verifier concerning the experience of the various actors in project implementation under a DIB contract.

- The field team, including the local partner of RFUK and the Kemito Ene Association, was well prepared to describe the project objectives, the activities completed, the equipment bought, the collaborations set up, and so on. The team could also explain in detail why certain tasks were accomplished, and others not; why certain targets were met and others not.
- The field team did not fully realize that a DIB report mainly focuses on results and not on the way these outcomes have been achieved or explanations of why certain targets were met, or not. This was a major learning point.
- The large degree of freedom to design a project in such a way that outcomes are achieved was an eye-opener to them. This is obviously logical considering the team has been operating in conventional development projects, following strict rules by donors regarding project design, approach, priority themes, and reporting requirements including output-based monitoring and evaluation, among others.
- There was also insight that as project implementer you can have a direct influence in formulating results and setting targets, based on your knowledge and practical experience of the project area, incorporating learning from previous initiatives, responding to new insights and so on.
- Proposing outcomes and agreeing to a set of indicators, however, also means that you have the responsibility to take these seriously, to focus on reaching the mutually agreed targets.

- In conventional development projects, explaining why certain targets are not met, perhaps because they were unrealistic from the start, is allowed and perhaps even common practice in such a difficult context as development. DIBs, however, are different in this aspect; not reaching targets has a direct financial implication.
- The project team faced some limitations, particularly for the second impact indicator on cocoa productivity, in presenting the required data to substantiate the progress made in the impact indicator. The information became available, but only after the tedious work of reviewing numerous field reports and interviewing field staff; the team should have realized what kinds of data requirements were connected to the different impact indicators, and designed the project monitoring system around those data needs.
- The verifier could directly observe how this DIB led to a fundamental shift in looking at development projects among staff of the service provider and project team.

Each party will draw its own lessons from what it has learned by doing this DIB. A more entrepreneurial, performance-oriented perspective has the potential to help development projects to be more flexible, to respond more quickly to what works and what does not in achieving clearly defined results. The notion that the investor, motivated by getting its investment back and ideally obtaining a reasonable return on it, will assist the service provider to operate in a more entrepreneurial, result-oriented way, is potentially a very attractive proposition but in this DIB this relationship was still to emerge.

The impact bond in Peru is of a rather small scale, which is beneficial for learning and managing, though overhead costs can be substantial. An often heard claim about impact bonds is their ability to scale up easily compared with traditional non-governmental services, which are restrained by their financial means. Development impact bonds might be a promising tool to achieve scale, but more funding is required. Their scale is better measured in relative terms than in absolute numbers (Gustafsson-Wright et al., 2015). The DIB in Peru started on a small scale and the project can possibly scale up; however, it is too soon to tell. Time will also tell whether the project has led to sustainable impact, with the cocoa farmers managing to implement the activities as taught to keep up the improved results.

Conclusions

Impact bonds promise a radical change in the incentive structure in social and development finance, aligning public and charity finance with their intended results. However, is this innovative finance mechanism mature enough to deliver on the promising claims made?

The meaning of the DIB from a financial valuation standpoint amounts to connecting a development outcome with the value of financial reward commensurate with the achievement of the result. As indicated above, this creates a number of challenges which will potentially lead to failures in the negotiation of DIB contracts. One of the proposals made to address the issue would be to establish a non-profit agency service to independently provide the evaluation of a DIB contract and to provide an independent custody service to resolve the appropriation risk challenge.

The key advantages of impact bonds are in transferring the risk of ineffective use of public funds to the private investors and in governments or donors only paying in accordance with the achieved intended results. If the project does not obtain the intended result, the outcome payment is reduced and the investor may take a loss. This changes the mindset of donors and places the focus on measurable results instead of the usual monitoring of activities. For the private sector, impact bonds create a whole new set of investment instruments that are based on effective delivery of social outcomes. Essentially, impact bonds make social and development outcomes tradable in the financial markets by 'monetizing' them through the sponsor's commitment to the outcome. A set of challenges emerges in establishing the framework for effective and credible valuation of such instruments and their related risks.

Incomplete information about opportunities ('information friction') is obviously a serious impediment to impact bonds, where four or more independent players need to find a point of shared interest. Also, the legal structure is considerably more complicated, though not insurmountable as demonstrated in the case of the Asháninka project.

The facilitating role of KIT, the verifier, in reaching agreement on the indicators must be clearly recognized. It is not clear at this stage whether the role of the verifier in the conclusion of the impact bond contract always needs to be significant, or if it could be taken over by the bond arranger if present.

The development impact bond in Peru shows the opportunities for DIBs in emerging economies within the agricultural sector. From the Asháninka DIB, serving as a pilot for the participating organizations, interesting lessons emerge, including:

- the intensive preparation time and transaction costs required for designing the impact bond;
- the need for a clearly defined and easily measurable outcome matrix;
- a new demand for gathering monitoring data by project staff;
- a dramatic change in the donor–implementer relationship;
- the role of the investor vis-à-vis the implementer to safeguard their rate of return;
- the position of the community that ultimately reaps the benefit of the investment;
- the advantages of the model over conventional development projects and grants.

The successful completion of the Asháninka DIB contract demonstrates that the structure works as intended and the project results, as well its learning outcomes, have led the participants to open a discussion on a new DIB contract, thus expanding the impact of the pilot.

References

ABN-AMRO (2015) *Opportunities and Challenges in the Netherlands: Social Impact Bonds – October 2015* [pdf], The Netherlands: ABN-AMRO <https://www.abnamro.com/en/images/Documents/040_Sustainable_banking/ABN_AMRO_Rapport_Social_Impact_Bonds.pdf> [accessed 18 March 2017].

Center for Global Development and Social Finance (2013) *Investing in Social Outcomes: Development Impact Bonds: The Report of the Development Impact Bond Working Group*, Washington, DC: CGD; London: Social Finance.

Common Fund for Commodities (CFC) (2014) 'Autonomous, sustainable cocoa and coffee production by indigenous Asháninka communities', *Common Fund for Commodities Newsletter 4*, October 2014, Amsterdam: CFC.

Dear, A., Helbitz, A., Khare, R., Lotan, R., Newman, J., Crosby Sims, G. and Zaroulis, A. (2016) *Social Impact Bonds: The Early Years*, London: Social Finance UK.

Drew, R. and Clist, P. (2015) *Evaluating Development Impact Bonds: A Study for DFID*, London: UKaid/DFID.

Flynn, J. and Young, J. (2016) *Annotated Bibliography: Evaluating Impact Investing*. Evidence Report No 164, Policy Anticipation, Response and Evaluation, Brighton, UK: Institute of Development Studies.

Gustafsson-Wright, E. and Gardiner, S. (2015) *Policy Recommendations for the Applications of Impact Bonds: A Summary of Lessons Learned from the First Five Years of Experience Worldwide*, Washington, DC: Brookings Institution.

Gustafsson-Wright, E., Gardiner, S. and Putcha, V. (2015) *The Potential and Limitations of Impact Bonds: Lessons from the First Five Years of Experience Worldwide*, Washington, DC: Brookings Institution.

KIT (2015) *Autonomous and Sustainable Cocoa and Coffee Production by Indigenous Asháninka People of Peru: Field mission for the verification of impact indicators of the Development Impact Bond agreement* [pdf], Amsterdam: Royal Tropical Institute <http://common-fund.org/fileadmin/user_upload/Verification_Report.pdf> [accessed 18 March 2017].

Rudd, T., Nicoletti, E., Misner, K. and Bonsu, J. (2013) *Financing Promising Evidence-Based Programs: Early Lessons from the New York City Social Impact Bond* [pdf], New York: MDRC <www.mdrc.org/sites/default/files/Financing_Promising_evidence-Based_Programs_FR.pdf> [accessed 18 March 2017].

Warner, M.E. (2013) 'Private finance for public goods: social impact bonds', *Journal of Economic Policy Reform* 16: 303–19 <http://dx.doi.org/10.1080/17487870.2013.835727>.

About the authors

John Belt (jbelt@snv.org), Global Coordinator Inclusive Value Chains, SNV – the Netherlands Development Organisation.

Andrey Kuleshov (andrey.kuleshov@common-fund.org), Strategy and Development Advisor, Common Fund for Commodities (CFC), Amsterdam.

Eline Minneboo (Eline.minneboo@rvo.nl) Project Advisor, Netherlands Enterprise Agency.

CHAPTER 5

Stuck in a rut: Emerging cocoa cooperatives in Peru and the factors that influence their performance

Jason Donovan, Trent Blare, and Nigel Poole

Abstract

Agri-cooperatives play an important role in helping resource-poor farmers reach highvalue markets. In addition to linking smallholders to markets, cooperatives provide their members with various services, such as extension, credit, input subsidies, and social programmes. While the literature contains many examples of success, there has been limited discussion on the often long and turbulent process by which cooperatives develop over time and the viable options for shortcuts. This study examines four emerging cocoa cooperatives in Peru to determine their overall business viability, the key factors that advanced their development, and their capacity to address the needs of their members. Our findings suggest that strategies for supporting cooperative development have largely failed to address major internal weaknesses and the challenges posed in the external environment. The cooperatives have received time-bound, uncoordinated, and often small-scale, interventions, which have focused on infrastructure expansion and technical assistance. Important areas related to business management and governance structures, trust relationships with buyers, and sufficient working capital have largely been ignored. Shortcuts may be achieved through improvements in access to business development and financial services, deeper engagement by private sector to support the development process, and commitment by stakeholders to monitoring and critical reflection for strategy refinement.

Keywords: cooperatives; business performance; rural development; NGOs; cocoa

Introduction

Strong agri-cooperatives can play an important role in helping resource-poor farmers reach high-value markets, such as those for certified coffee and cocoa. These markets typically offer attractive prices and more secure buyer relationships, but require that small-holders commit to deliver pre-identified volumes on time and in the required form and quality. Cooperatives realize economies

http://dx.doi.org/10.3362/9781788530576.005

of scale in processing and marketing and provide advisory and other services to help their members respond to buyer demands. Such services include technical assistance, training, and input and credit provision. Cooperatives also manage relations with downstream buyers, certification agencies, governmental entities, NGOs, as well as with farmers, who must perceive benefits from their participation. Many NGOs and governments support cooperative development because of its potential to help achieve poverty reduction and encourage members' sense of empowerment through stronger links to markets. Cooperatives are also considered to be effective options for advancing conservation goals (Kruijssen, Keizer, and Giuliani, 2009), promoting products of cultural and economic importance (Devaux et al., 2009), and discouraging the production of illicit crops (Spellberg and Kaplan, 2010). Although cooperatives may not incorporate the poorest of rural populations (Bernard and Spielman, 2009), they often include households of limited means that struggle to meet their basic needs throughout the year.

In recent years, the literature on cooperative development in Latin America has debated the role of cooperatives in value chains (Beuchelt and Zeller, 2013; Poole and Donovan, 2014; Stattman and Mol, 2014) and in strengthening rural livelihoods (Bacon, 2015; Bebbington, 1996; Donovan and Poole, 2014; Valkila and Nygren, 2010). These studies present cases of one or more mature cooperatives engaged in an export market, which overcame adversity to evolve into a business organization able to offer attractive marketing terms and provide additional services to their members. Success is often attributed to external support, a strong market orientation, and the consolidation of democratic governance structures. Studies have also confirmed that cooperative development tends to involve considerable resources and development processes over prolonged periods, even under favourable external conditions (Donovan, Stoian, and Poole, 2008; Poole and de Frece, 2010). Frequently, the process is marked by periods of growth followed by crises due to incompetence, corruption, or bad luck, leading to prolonged periods of limited activity or dissolution (Kachule, Poole, and Dorward, 2005). Important questions remain about how to reduce the high costs and risks associated with building cooperatives into viable businesses. This implies an explicit strategy for supporting less-mature or emerging cooperatives, which have weaker member fidelity and governance structures, smaller market volumes, and fewer buyers, and may receive less support from governments and NGOs.

In Peru, government agencies and NGOs have considered cocoa cooperatives to be important partners in expanding the country's cocoa sector and have carried out numerous interventions and programmes in support of cooperative development (del Castillo, 2013). This study explores the circumstances facing four emerging cocoa cooperatives in San Martin, Peru – the largest cocoa producing department in the country. Despite having been organized for 10 years or longer, they have yet to reach a critical 'take-off' point: in respect of membership number, level of capital endowment, and buyer contacts they are still 'emerging', unlike the more consolidated group of cooperatives in Peru or elsewhere in Latin America. Section 'Cooperative assessment framework' provides a brief overview of debates surrounding organizational performance and introduces the frame-work for the assessment of the emerging cooperatives that was applied in this study. Section 'Case study background' provides an overview of the cocoa sector in Peru. Section 'Methodology' explains the methods used for data collection. Section 'Results' presents the results of the assessment. The paper ends with a discussion of the implications of the findings for the design of strategies to better support cooperatives, including potential shortcuts for achieving sustainable cooperative development.

Cooperative assessment framework

Researchers have long recognized the 'dual nature' of cooperatives – a result of being both a member-controlled organization and subject to economic constraints similar to those of other enterprises. However, developing-country cooperatives that are engaged in high-value markets, in addition to building appropriate governance structures, must often provide long-term support, such as technical assistance, technology development, and credit, to their members (Donovan et al., 2016). In many cases, cooperatives may represent the only source of support for resource-poor members looking to expand their production and respond to stringent quality requirements. The costs for service provision often are covered partially through subsidies provided by projects, government agencies, and, in some cases, down-stream buyers. In this way, cooperatives have taken on a role similar to that of NGOs. At the same time, cooperatives must build a successful business in an altogether difficult environment, from paying taxes and competing with local buyers for raw material, to engaging with various buyers, service providers, and support organizations. Below, we briefly review the discussion on performance assessment for businesses and NGOs and then present a framework for assessment of cooperatives.

Assessing cooperative performance

Researchers have applied financial-based metrics to study the performance of agri-cooperatives in North America and Europe, based on the underlying assumption that cooperatives are a variant of investor-owned firms. These studies assess performance (e.g. liquidity, solvency, and efficiency) based on financial ratios, where differences in ratios reflect differences in goals and related strategies (e.g. McKee, 2008). In the absence of good management and accounting data they have also applied nonfinancial measures to assess cooperative performance. In the early 1980s, Emerson and Boynton (1981) recommended the assessment of cooperatives based on household-level measures (prices received and access to services); investor-related measures (financial performance ratios and processing costs); and consumer/society-based measures (taxes paid, disposal techniques, and quality). Molnar et al., (2007) compared the performance of community-forest enterprises across countries based on production activities (e.g. volumes, sales, and employment), profitability, social, and environment benefits (e.g. improved forest management). Kachule et al., (2005) considered cooperative performance in terms of economic inclusion (ability to achieve scale, leverage of market power, and efficiency) and social inclusion (capacity building, democratic governance, and gender equity), and the influence of the business environment on performance. These are not easily measurable indicators. Various authors have also high-lighted the role that social capital plays in determining cooperative performance (Bernard and Spielman, 2009; Sexton and Islow, 1988). Where previous state intervention in cooperative organization has fostered a climate of mistrust among smallholders, Ruben and Heras (2012) boiled down cooperative performance to matters of bonding social capital (i.e. cooperatives' ability to establish and maintain trust, confidence, and commitment among members). In a similar vein, Uphoff and Wijayaratna (2000) identified bonding social capital as key to good performance and efficiency in farmer organizations in Sri Lanka. Arguably these performance dimensions are even less easy to measure.

Assessing NGO performance

The organizational theory literature contains a rich debate on NGO performance, although applications are limited in number. Lusthaus, Adrien, Anderson, Carden, and Montalván (2002) advocated a four-dimensional framework, focusing on organizational performance (effectiveness, efficiency, and relevance); external environment (political-legal context and markets); motivation (history, culture, and incentives); and capacity (leadership, structure, and human resources). Similarly, Lecy, Schmitz, and Swedlund (2012) conceptualized performance as revolving around NGOs' ability to achieve stated goals, mobilize resources, or garner favourable reputation, as considered by external informants and organizational stakeholders. Some have argued that NGO effectiveness is socially constructed, where the meaning of effectiveness changes over time and where different stakeholders judge effectiveness differently (Herman and Renz, 2008). The openness of organizational boundaries implies that NGO effectiveness depends on the effectiveness of other organizations and people and the ways in which they are interconnected (Scott, 2004). The use of such diffuse parameters may be a reason why economic sustainability has been elusive. Donors increasingly require NGOs to undertake assessment of their activities with quantifiable metrics. However, the dilemma facing NGOs is that current donor-imposed structures for performance impact monitoring and assessment have not encouraged organizational learning and capacity building (Newcomer et al., 2013; Stoian et al., 2012).

Framework for assessing cooperative capacity

No widely adopted framework has yet emerged which considers the unique features of cooperatives in developing countries, thereby limiting our ability to build on prior studies and highlight results that are complementary or contradictory. Our framework assumes that agri-cooperatives pursue three general objectives: (1) improve productive capacity and wellbeing among members, (2) build an economically viable and responsive enterprise; and (3) improve the broader environment in which members live (e.g. community development and environmental protection). While there is some overlap among the three objectives (e.g. meeting expectations at the household and community levels), each can be considered such a vital element of cooperative operations. Achieving these goals implies that cooperatives build their capacities across four domains (Figure 5.1): (1) physical capital, such as infrastructure, machinery, and tools used to collect, transform, and market agricultural products; (2) financial assets and flows, which include liquidity, the capacity to purchase raw material from members, and meet long-term investment needs; (3) trust and reciprocity in relations, including those with members, buyers, government agencies, certification agencies, and NGOs; and (4) internal governance and culture, which captures issues related to leadership, strategy, and member involvement in planning and oversight. These goals determine cooperative capacity, which is measured by effective response to the needs of its stakeholders, namely smallholder members; the internal management dimension; and the value chain, comprising of upstream suppliers and downstream buyers. Various external factors also influence the growth and development of cooperatives, including political level environment, international market trends, and local competition for raw material.

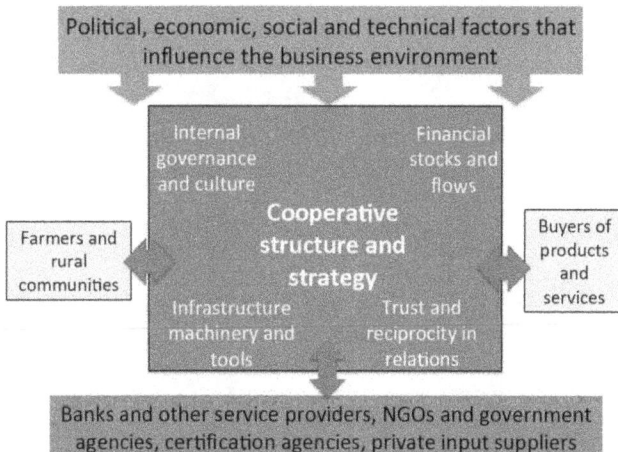

Figure 5.1 Framework for cooperative assessment.

Case study background

Only 20 years ago the Peruvian cocoa sector was in a state of near collapse. Over 50% of the national area under cocoa had been abandoned. Farmers faced serious disease problems (e.g. witches' broom, frosty pod, and black pod) and received limited state support. In addition, terrorism and social turmoil hindered investment in the sector. Peru had become a net importer of cocoa, unable to meet the needs of its relatively small domestic processing sector (Krauss and Soberanis, 2001). However, around 2005, prospects began to change thanks to improved political and economic conditions at home and political turmoil in Côte d'Ivoire – the world's largest cocoa producing nation. These conditions provided strong incentives for cocoa buyers to reconsider sourcing from Latin America. Meanwhile, there was a growing urgency within Peru and among bilateral donors in incentivizing producers to abandon coca production in favour of alternative crops, including cocoa (Chauvin, 2010). Large-scale interventions by the Peruvian government, the United Nations, and bilateral donors in the late 1990s and early 2000s became a major driver of cocoa expansion.

Between 2001 and 2013, cocoa production in Peru increased by over three fold, from 23,600 MT to 71,800 MT (Table 5.1). During the same period, the area of cocoa production expanded and productivity increased, largely due to the wide availability of the high-yielding, disease-resistant cocoa varieties.

Table 5.1 Cocoa in Peru, by volume and value, 2001–2013

Year	Production (mt)	Productivity (kg/ha)	Price (USD/ mt)	Total value (1000s USD)
2001	23,672	517	1088	25,764
2002	24,354	495	1779	43,327
2003	24,214	486	1753	42,449
2004	25,920	509	1551	40,195
2005	25,257	502	1538	38,847
2006	31,676	558	1594	50,493
2007	31,388	525	1952	61,275
2008	34,005	534	2581	87,759
2009	36,804	555	2889	106,317
2010	46,613	604	3133	146,038
2011	56,500	671	2978	168,269
2012	62,492	683	2392	149,470
2013	71,838	736	2690	193,244
% change 2013/2001	203.5	42.4	147.2	650.1

Source: MINAGRI, AGRODATAPERU

With prices more than doubling, the total value of production (in nominal USD) increased 7.5 times. Peru's recent rise in the global cocoa market is strongly linked to third-party certification systems, such as Fairtrade, UTZ Certified, and Rainforest Alliance. In 2011, Peru ranked as the second largest producer of certified cocoa in Latin America (following the Dominican Republic) (Finance Alliance for Sustainable Trade [FAST], 2012). In 2013, certified production accounted for nearly 35% of the nation's total production volume (Potts et al., 2014). As production expanded, so too did the number of cocoa cooperatives. In San Martin four cocoa cooperatives were founded in the 1990s by the United Nations Office on Drugs and Crime (UNODC) and hundreds more were created nationally by the USAID-led Peru Alternative Development (PDA) Program in the early 2000s. Many of these were relatively small in terms of membership and sales volume and relied highly on external support for carrying out basic operations (Cabieses, 2010; Tenorio, 2011).

Methodology

Four emerging cooperatives in San Martin were selected for this study (Figure 5.2). Each had existed for various years prior to data collection, but had exhibited relatively low membership levels and sales volumes. Interviews with key informants and cooperative representatives were used to select the cooperatives. All the cooperatives were initially organized with external support and had obtained thirdparty certification for cocoa. They also differed in important ways (Table 5.1) related to membership numbers, sales volume, and market orientation. The membership base of the cooperatives was similar. Most members were relative newcomers to cocoa production and maintained small cocoa plots of nearly three hectares, despite having much larger landholdings.

Data collection sought information on the context and cooperative capacity through structured and semi-structured interviews with cooperative leaders and with actors such as members, NGOs, and buyers who maintained direct relations with the cooperatives. The multi-dimensional approach allowed us to target specific questions to those with direct knowledge of the issue at hand and to triangulate information provided by other actors. A three-person research team collected data from each cooperative in 2015 on specific aspects of cooperative performance and the context:

1. evaluation of financial performance, through interviews with managers, key employees, and accountants;
2. governance structures, through focus group meetings with the board of directors, and semistructured interviews with managers, cooperative employees, buyers, support agencies, government officials, and second-tier organizations;
3. cooperative membership through structured interviews.

The member households were selected using a stratified random sampling method corresponding to the geographic distribution of the members and

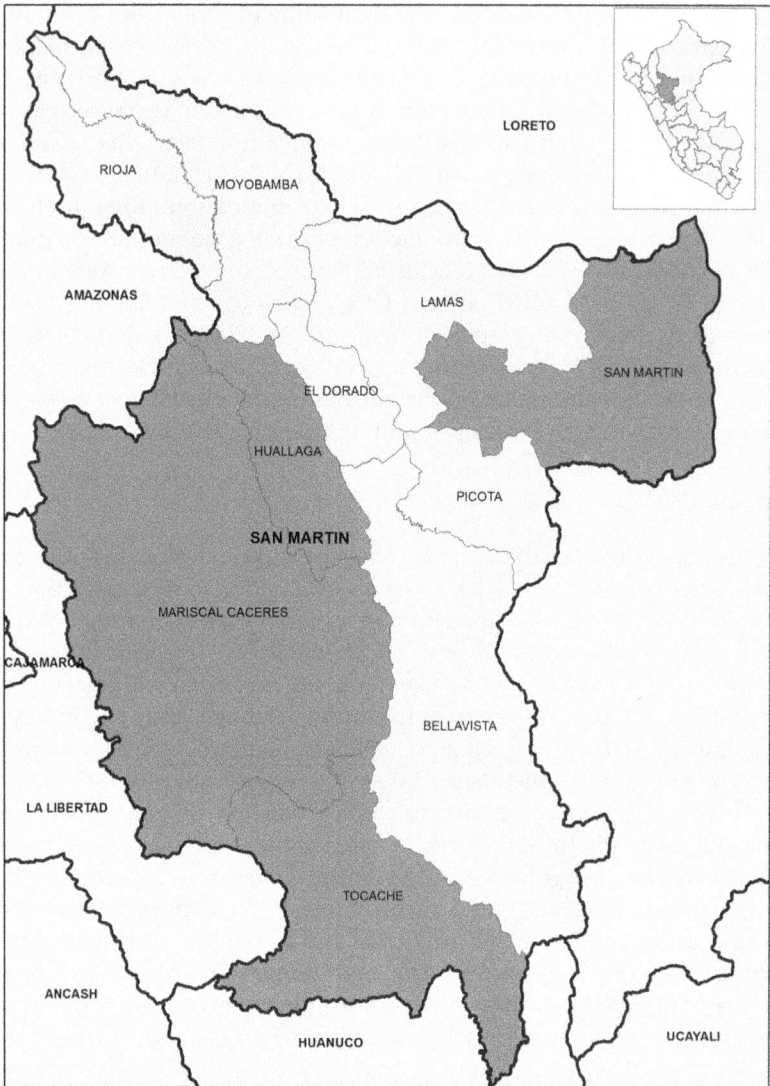

Figure 5.2 San Martin and its provinces, with sampled cooperatives located in shaded provinces.

weighted for gender to ensure women were deliberately selected. The interview data included socioeconomic characteristics, farming practices, and participation in, communication with, services offered by, and member satisfaction with the cooperative. In total, 130 members, roughly 26% women, were interviewed with a minimum of 30 interviews in each cooperative (Table 5.2).

Table 5.2 Characteristics of sampled cooperatives and their membership

Characteristic	Coop1	Coop2	Coop3	Coop4
Cooperative level				
Year established	2001	2008	2001	2007
Members (2014)	133	200	160	307
Major initial source of support	PDA	Church and municipal government	NGO	PDA
Direct export	No	Since 2013	No	Since 2014
Buyers of cocoa (2014)	Two national buyers (100%)	One international buyer (50%) one national buyer (50%)	One national buyer (100%)	One international buyer (40%) four national buyers (60%)
Cocoa marketed (MT)	2012: 223 2013: 200 2014: 200	2012:150 2013: 250 2014: 425	2012–13: No data 2014: 210	2012: 220 2013: 250 2014: 280
Certifications	UTZ 2015	Fairtrade 2013 UTZ 2014 Organic 2014	Rainforest 2014	Fairtrade 2014 Organic 2014 Rainforest 2014 UTZ 2014
Membership level (average 2014)				
Membership length (years)	8.9	3.8	4.4	5.3
Years producing cocoa	7.6	6.1	5.8	7.7
Farm size (Ha)	13.7	15.5	10.6	7.5
Land in cocoa production (Ha)	3.1	3.5	2.7	3.4
Cocoa productivity (kg/Ha)	565	672	687	631

Results

Coop1

Internal governance
Coop1's manager operates with little oversight from the board. The manager alone conducts the financial planning for the cooperative and has developed the strategic and operational plans, which the board approved without providing any inputs. To support the cooperative's transition to a viable enterprise, the regional government has paid the manager's salary, thus allowing for the manager to potentially have divided loyalties between the government and

members. Several members and the board of directors indicated during the interviews and focus group that they trust the manager's capacity to lead the cooperative, despite the manager having little formal training in business management. Much of the members' trust in the manager is based on interactions when the manager served as an agricultural extensionist in the community. The board of directors lacks the business acumen to evaluate the manager's recommendations and provide strategic guidance. The board members readily admitted that they do not understand the cooperative's financial statements.

Member relations
Coop1 membership is primarily comprised of indigenous tribes (90%) whose primary livelihood activity is fishing. Since the peak fishing time coincides with the cocoa harvest, they tend to have limited labour available for managing cocoa plantations, which has impacted the productivity of the farms. In Coop1, the members' cocoa plantations are the least productive of the four sampled cooperatives, with output at 565 MT of cocoa per hectare on average. Nearly all members stated that their engagement with Coop1 was motivated by the perceived benefits from the services Coop1 provides. In 2015, Coop1 offered technical assistance, organic certification, payment advances, and organic fertilizer. Members expressed a sense of loyalty to Coop1 because of their long history of interacting with the cooperative. The members on average had belonged to the Coop1 for nine years – roughly twice the average length of membership in the other cooperatives, extending back to when the farmers began growing cocoa. Coop1 provided 96% of the farmers with the resources to establish their cocoa plantations.

Infrastructure, machinery, and tools
In 2012, Coop1 constructed seven collection centres supplied by the smaller, neighbouring communities to dry and ferment cocoa. These investments have lowered transportation costs by providing centralized collection points and have allowed Coop1 to ensure high-quality product. PDA and the regional government provided nearly all the material at a cost of around 225,000 USD for construction. In addition, the regional and local government donated the land for the collection centres. The only property purchased by the cooperative with its own funds is its administrative office, which is valued at around 12,000 USD. In 2014, Coop1 received donations from the anti-drug agency of the Peruvian government to purchase chocolate-making equipment worth about 23,000 USD. The machinery is yet to be used. The rest of the operational equipment used by the cooperative, computers, electric scales, a motorcycle, and cocoa quality measuring tools were purchased using a loan of 4500 USD provided to the cooperative from its first buyer in 2011.

Buyer relations
Since Coop1 began selling cocoa it has sold to two large brokers and Coop2. Relations between Coop1 and one if its brokers terminated when Coop1

failed to fully repay the buyer-provided loan in 2011. The cooperative still sells cocoa to the remaining broker, although the broker has voiced frustration with Coop1 in failing to meet deadlines and delivery quotas. However, the buyer prefers to purchase cocoa from cooperatives, as the middlemen are even less trustworthy and supply poor quality cocoa. Coop1 does not have certification and has faced a disadvantage of competing with local intermediaries in the low margin commodity market. However, starting in late 2015, it was expected to be able to market UTZ certified cocoa, as the farmers will have completed the four-year transition period. In the focus group interviews, the board of directors of Coop1 expressed hope that their ability to obtain price premiums from certified cocoa would allow them to fully cover their costs and pay members higher prices.

Financial assets
The regional government pays the salary of the manager and accountant and PDA also pays for the extensionists, organic certification, and organic fertilizers provided to the farmers. External funding was so critical to Coop1's survival that it stopped buying cocoa for a period in 2013 when these funds were temporarily unavailable. Coop1 faces difficulties to service its outstanding debt of nearly 400,000 USD. Cocoa buyers provide Coop1 with much of its operational capital, which is repaid when the cooperative delivers cocoa to the buyer. In 2010, Coop1 received a loan from a long-time buyer, but chose to sell its cocoa to an intermediary that offered a higher price, never paying back the original loan of 195,000 USD. It has only been able to pay the interest on this original loan. Since then, Coop1 has taken out a loan in 2013 worth 125,000 USD from the other international buyer, which it has since repaid. In 2014, it received three loans totalling 189,000 USD. One worth 34,000 USD was provided by an NGO, another for 38,000 USD was from Coop2, and the third was given from a local lending agency for 117,000 USD. To help repay its delinquent loan to the international buyer, Coop1 was considering selling its administrative office that it owned, the rest of its infrastructure having been given in concession.

Coop2

Internal governance
Over the last three years, Coop2 has gone from near bankruptcy to exporting cocoa with plans to become profitable in a year or two. According to its members, board of directors, local governmental officials, the fortunes of Coop2 changed in 2012 when the cooperative hired a new manager who had experience working in one of the largest cocoa cooperatives in San Martín. Because of this history, the members of Coop2 trust the business judgement of the manager. Even though the cooperative has a capable board of directors, which included a retired teacher, a banker, and a former extension provider, almost all the recommendations made by the manager are accepted; and he makes

all the operating decisions. The board knows that the membership will back the manager in any disagreement. The manager feels like he has taken the role of 'training' the board members in their roles and how to run a cooperative. This reality of a mentor/mentee relationship has made the cooperative heavily dependent on the manager.

Member relations

Following a financial crisis (see discussion on financial assets), the manager insisted that the cooperative generate sizable revenue streams before investing in social programmes. However, this plan was not well received by members. Some believed that since the cooperative experienced improved financial conditions it should invest in services and pay dividends, even though Coop2 remained unable to recover costs without external subsidies. In fact, 47% of the membership in Coop2 thought it needed to provide more services, which was nearly double the response, 24% of the membership, in the other three cooperatives. The manager and president of the board of directors explained that one of their greatest challenges was helping the members understand the financial statements. Despite concerns over benefit distribution, none of the members interviewed in Coop2 planned to leave (between 10% and 20% of the members in the other cooperatives were planning on leaving). These members also sold over 70% of their harvest to the Coop2 in 2014. This fidelity can be attributed to the great turnaround the cooperative had made and the hope that Coop2 would become more profitable in the future. Several others expressed support for the cooperative because of its potential role in rural development.

Infrastructure, machinery, and tools

Coop2 lacked adequate infrastructure and equipment, limiting its potential to expand. While the other cocoa cooperatives in the area had new offices, storage facilities, and post-harvest equipment, fermenting and drying facilities, provided mainly by donors, Coop2 rented a cramped office and warehouse. The only infrastructure given to Coop2 by donors, PDA, and local governmental institutions, was five collection centres in the villages at a cost of nearly 65,000 USD. However, the fermentation bins built in these centres were poorly constructed and rotted within a few years of being built. Now, Coop2 is diverting a portion of its income to rebuild these centres. The administrative and warehouse building is small, which limits its ability to purchase larger volumes of cocoa. Since it rents the building, it has no incentive to expand and improve it. The only renovation the cooperative undertook was to replace a leaky roof. It lacks the assets it needs to transport the cocoa from the buying station to its warehouse. It only owns a cargo motorcycle and an off-road motorcycle, bought with its own funds at a cost of nearly 5000 USD. The municipal government provided the rest of the equipment, computers and other office machines and laboratory tools, at a cost of nearly 25,000 USD.

Buyer relations

The previous manager did not have well-established relationships with the buyers, which limited his ability to enter into contracts with the buyers. At one point Coop2 had its warehouse full but had failed to establish timely contracts with buyers to provide the money it needed to finance its loans. It nearly defaulted on its loans even though the value of the cocoa in store was more than enough to cover its payments. The cooperative now has developed strong relations with buyers and creditors, which has created the level of trust they need to work with Coop2. All the buyers interviewed explained the main motive for buying from Coop2 was that they trusted the manager. The largest buyer of the cooperative explained that even though the cooperative did not always meet contract deadlines the manager communicated well and could be counted on to eventually deliver the product. This difference in the relationship the cooperative had with its buyers was a principal factor in why the cooperative is now financially stable.

Financial assets

Coop2's inability to sell cocoa combined with highinterest loans from local credit institutions to secure working capital proved nearly fatal. Coop2's first loan in 2010 was from a local credit union for 40,000 USD. However, the cooperative defaulted on this loan in 2011. The former manager and president of the board of directors took out formal loans in their own name in 2011 of nearly 10,000 USD (3% monthly interest rate) to cover operating expenses. When the new manager took over, he secured informal loans, which added up to nearly 20,000 USD for 6 months (5% monthly interest rate). The manager also worked to have the 2010 loan refinanced; however, the 2011 loan taken out by the previous manager was no longer recognized by the cooperative. By 2013 access to finance improved when credit was obtained from three of the cooperative's largest buyers for a total of nearly 200,000 USD without interest, which was repaid in cocoa. By 2014, having paid back the buyerprovided loans, the cooperative gained access to international lenders, securing 100,000 USD with an 11% annual interest rate. Coop2 has also greatly increased the amount of cocoa it markets from 130 metric tons in 2012 to 425 metric tons in 2014. In fact, in 2014 it made a profit of 250,000 USD (from a loss of 10,000 USD in 2010), which was used to pay for organic certification and eliminate past debts.

Coop3

Internal governance

Coop3 stopped purchasing cocoa at the end of 2014. It started purchasing cocoa again in mid-2015 after replacing its management and leadership. The NGO that has supported the cooperative and its major buyer demanded the manager be changed as a condition of maintaining a relationship with the cooperative. The membership also chose a new board that no longer consisted exclusively of farmers but was made up mostly of teachers from the local school. The members hope that the new directors would be able to provide greater oversight and guidance to the manager. The board of directors basically manages the cooperative and has been integral in establishing operational procedures. The board has taken charge of external relations with funders, and participates in the strategic planning of the cooperative. The new manager is not from the community nor has worked there. Even though he understands the Peruvian cocoa industry, he lacks the social capital necessary to engage effectively with members: management-member relations are effectively governed not by the manager but by the board.

Member relations
The manager and board of directors admit that the cooperative needs to build trust first with its members and second with the buyers and the institutions that support it in order to become sustainable. Some of the members interviewed in remote communities were unaware that Coop3 remained active in the cocoa sector. Even with all the recent problems, 84% of the members interviewed still planned to participate and sell to the cooperative once it started buying again. The members felt that the cooperative paid higher prices, so it was in their interest to sell to it when they had the opportunity. There was a general expectation that the cooperative would be successful now that the cooperative had new leadership, even anticipating that the cooperative will soon be exporting. One common member comment was that '... with the new board of directors and manager, things are going to change'.

Infrastructure, machinery, and tools
Coop3 possessed facilities to process up to 50 metric tons of cocoa a month, more than twice the capacity it marketed in 2014. The local government gave the cooperative the building and land. The post-harvesting infrastructure in the headquarters and three collection facilities in the outlying communities were provide by grants from the local and national governments and PDA totalling 75,000 USD with an additional 5000 USD provided by its members. The scales and cargo motorcycle worth 3000 USD were provided by the national and local governments. PDA gave Coop3 11,000 USD worth of chocolatemaking equipment that it has used only infrequently.

Buyer relations
Since Coop3 has been selling cocoa in 2012, it has sold to six buyers. In 2014, it sold 200 metric tons of cocoa to a national buyer and 10 metric tons to a specialized organic trader. The cooperative is trying to re-establish relationships with some of its earlier buyers. However, buyers are waiting to see if Coop3's new management can be trusted in ensuring the cooperative meets its contractual arrangements with its current national buyer, who was the exclusive buyer of the 2015 crop. One of the largest Peruvian cocoa cooperatives, which in 2012 was the primary buyer from the cooperative, is assessing

Coop3's performance and quality control before entering into a renewed business relationship. Even with these challenges, Coop3 has maintained its current buyer, who not only pays a premium for certified cocoa but also pays for the certification.

Financial assets
The cooperative in late 2014 had defaulted on nearly 20,000 USD of debt, half of which dated back to 2012. At that time a neighbouring cooperative provided an interest free loan worth nearly 33,000 USD that was supposed to be repaid in cocoa. When the new management took over, 8000 USD of this debt still had not been paid and an additional loan of 10,000 USD with a monthly interest rate of 3% provided by a local credit union in early 2014 was in default. Each member in late 2014 was required to pay Coop3 nearly 150 USD to cover administrative costs. After discontinuing marketing in September 2014, this infusion of capital allowed the cooperative to once again begin to purchase cocoa by the end of March 2015. Even though Coop3 was able to make a margin on the cocoa it marketed, the former manager did not keep records of the administrative and marketing costs, so the actual profit or losses for the cooperative are unknown. The new management reported to have redoubled its efforts to maintain good records, as input for more effective marketing strategies and financial planning.

Coop4
Internal governance
Like Coop2, Coop4 stands out for achieving a degree of commercial success: it has been able to market a significant volume of cocoa although it has yet to become financially independent. Its former manager, who had previously worked for a PDA programme, played a leading role in the cooperative's organization and elaborated its strategic plan. He made nearly all decisions with little oversight from the board of directors. The new manager, who started work in 2013, does not have this history with Coop4. Thus, the board has adopted a more prominent role in decision making, especially in developing operational policy and financial decisions. The board members have had accounting training, which has allowed them understand the cooperative's finances, but have made little input on Coop4's strategic plan.

Relations with members
Although Coop4 did not receive noticeably higher prices from local buyers, there was a consensus that engagement with the cooperative forced other buyers to pay higher prices for their cocoa and apply fair trading practices (e.g. use of correct scales). Even with the intense competition, the members still sold 62% of their harvest to the cooperative. One of the founding members clearly demonstrated this loyalty to support Coop4: 'We need the cooperative so that we can receive fair prices. Its competition ensures that the middlemen cannot cheat us'. To become financially self-sustaining (see discussion on financial

assets), Coop4 must increase cocoa sales by adding members or capturing more cocoa from its current members. They hope to double the amount of cocoa marketed in 2015 to 500 MT and then to 1000 MT by the end of 2019. However, being able to commercialize this amount of cocoa will likely be a challenge considering that Coop4 faces a very competitive environment. Every major cocoa broker in Peru has a buying station in the community where it operates. The competition is so fierce that major buyers offer Coop4 members above market prices in an attempt to gain their business.

Infrastructure, machinery, and tools
In 2012, Coop4 built new offices and storage facilities and purchased processing equipment and vehicles. PDA and local and national government paid 170,000 USD for the buildings and the cooperative provided the additional 90,000 USD. Coop4 took out a loan from a local credit union to finance the project. Additionally, between 2009 and 2013 PDA and regional government paid over 100,000 USD for 2 trucks, 3 cargo motorcycles, and 3 off-road motorcycles. Coop4 contributed around 10,000 USD to supplement the grants in purchasing this equipment. An additional 10,000 USD was donated by PDA to purchase computer equipment. Like many cooperatives in the region Coop4 has been given chocolatemaking equipment. While much of this equipment has fallen into disuse because of the difficulty in making chocolates and the lack of markets and expertise, Coop4 has seen this equipment as providing a real opportunity to sell into a value added market. It received a grant from PDA to hire a chocolatier to train members in making the product.

Relations with buyers
This intensively competitive environment may be a factor in Coop4's poor relationship with buyers. At times, Coop4 has not met its contractual obligations, especially deadlines, and does not communicate well with the buyers. The awkward sales relationship is demonstrated by the fact that even though one buyer explained that it would no longer purchase from Coop4 the manager still said that the cooperative was actively selling cocoa to this trader. The change of management may have also strained these relations, as the former manager made contracts the new manager found disadvantageous. Furthermore, the leadership of the cooperative believes that it can now directly export cocoa and no longer needs to be dependent on the large buyers. So, they have little interest in maintaining and building these relationships.

Financial assets
The large amount of support it has received from PDA and the Peruvian government has helped the cooperative maintain financial stability. Nearly all of the staff, except for the accountant, were paid from grants. To cover all these administrative costs, the management estimated that it would need to market 520 MT of cocoa, much more than the 280 MT marketed in 2014. The leadership is hopeful that it can meet this target by 2017. Coop4 like the

other cooperatives has faced challenges in servicing its debts. Its original loan with a regional credit union to purchase land and help construct its main buildings totalled 115,000 USD with a 2% monthly interest rate. In 2013, Coop4 borrowed an additional 18,000 USD from a different credit union with a 2.2% monthly interest rate for working capital. In 2014, a large national coffee and cocoa cooperative lent Coop4 100,000 USD and in 2015 130,000 USD for working capital that would be paid off with cocoa sold to the larger cooperative. In 2014, Coop4 was unable to pay off its original loan for its land and buildings and has been working to refinance the loan. Because of the high interest rates, the debt has increased from 115,000 USD in 2012 to 130,000 USD by mid 2015.

Looking across the cooperatives
Figure 5.3 presents the primary motivation reported by members for joining their cooperative. In some cases, the primary motivation strongly reflected the influence of the external organizations that led the process that established the cooperative. For example, Coop1 – where members showed a strong interest in access to production inputs – was started by PDA with the intent to expand smallholder cocoa production. Similarly, organizers of Coop4 explicitly aimed to provide cocoa growers with an alternative to unproductive trading relationships with local buyers, thus the relatively strong interest in better prices. Interestingly, Coop4 is the only case where access to better prices did not feature as the most important reason for cooperative participation, likely reflecting the strong influence of NGOs in promoting cocoa expansion over business development. Furthermore, the cooperatives are likely to face difficulties to change expectations in the near future: the inability of the cooperatives to purchase their members' cocoa ranked as the most important reason for members of Coops 2–4 and the second most important reason for members of Coop1 (Figure 5.4) to sell cocoa outside their cooperative.

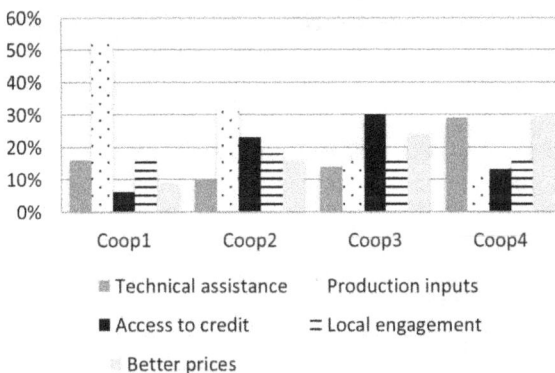

Figure 5.3 Primary motivation of members to join cooperative.

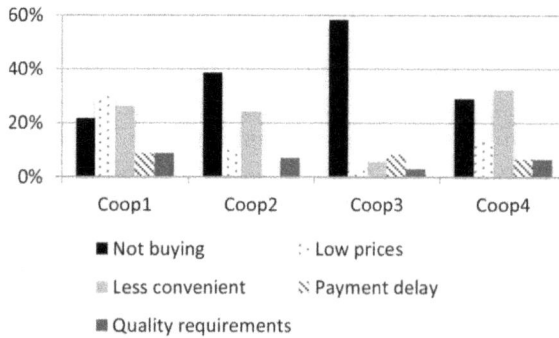

Figure 5.4 Primary motivation of members to sell their cocoa outside the cooperative (2014).

Table 5.3 compares outcomes for each cooperative across the five parameters. The cooperatives had most advanced in their expansion of infrastructure, equipment, and tools. This could be expected given that external interventions prioritized their support to cooperatives in physical capital. The parameter where the cooperatives least advanced was in the consolidation of buyer relations. Major issues existed related to noncompliance with contracts and weak trust between buyers and cooperative managers – issues that, left unaddressed, are likely to severely impede the development process. Mixed outcomes resulted for the remaining three parameters. The governance structures varied considerably in practice. The board itself took critical decisions in Coop3 while managers with limited member involvement administered the other three cooperatives. Evidence suggested that limited business skills, specifically in Coop1 and Coop4, contributed to weak partnerships with buyers. Overall, the cooperatives were able to retain members, particularly by offering their members access to services, and in some cases, higher prices than those paid by the intermediaries, and more transparent purchasing practices. However, the cooperatives' dependence on external funding sources will likely challenge their capacity to meet demands over time, at least for services such as technical assistance. Across the cooperatives financial capacities appeared frail. On one hand, they secured funds through buyers and lenders. Contracts with buyers, expanding cocoa production, and overall favourable world cocoa have encouraged lenders to provide credit to the cooperatives, which is used to purchase members' cocoa. On the other hand, the level of credit for operations was insufficient and the cooperatives lacked their own capital, leaving them with limited capacity to purchase members' cocoa.

Discussion and conclusion

Mature cocoa cooperatives have emerged that are able to provide a range of services for their members, with important implications on rural livelihoods and rural landscapes. They have positioned themselves in global value chains, able to interact over time with international buyers eager for access to certified and otherwise high-value cocoa and other commodities. Extensive support from NGOs and donors, and in some cases international buyers, has played an important part in the success of these cooperatives. As noted by Bebbington, Quisbert, and Trujillo (1996) in their study of the cocoa cooperative 'El Ceibo', 'the achievements of Ceibo have not come cheaply, and remind us that building capacity in a campesino [sic] organization require significant and sustained investment of resources' (p. 203). Similarly, the Ghanaian cocoa cooperative Kuapa Kokoo was an early participant in certified cocoa markets and received significant support from NGOs and international cocoa buyers over many years (Nelson, Opoku, Martin, Bugri, and Posthumus, 2013). Both these cases depict a pattern whereby development organizations and buyers picked a favoured cooperative supported 'their organization' over time, through thick and thin. The pattern is not unique to cocoa, and has endured despite the risks, as even well-established cooperatives face critical operating vulnerabilities (e.g. departure of key staff, and limitations to broaden their impact by incorporating new members and gaining critical mass in terms of marketed volumes (Poole and Donovan, 2014). However, such an approach falls short in a context characterized by expanding cocoa production and buyer presence and the emergence of dozens, if not hundreds, of small cooperatives looking to expand membership and participate in markets for products that are certified or otherwise of high quality. This study examined four emerging cooperatives in the rapidly expanding Peruvian cocoa sector in an effort to understand the circumstances that have shaped their development and gain insights into options for improved strategies for supporting cooperative development. Each cooperative had a set of strengths and weaknesses, and the precise analysis differed from one organization to another – with none of them exactly alike. In general, however, the cases analysed here fell way short of meeting performance objectives. These findings reinforce the significance of key elements of cooperative structure and strategy depicted in Figure 5.1 of human, social, physical, and financial enterprise assets: a common performance failing is the difficulties of financial management, which are handled differently by each of the cooperatives. Working capital and access to affordable finance affects capacity to provide advance payments to members and provide services to members over the long term, and thus impacts on stakeholder relationships, particularly members and buyers. It is evident also that the expectations of members vary between the different cooperatives, but whatever part other objectives play in members' participation, the cocoa price matters. Secondly, governance models are a significant performance dimension, in particular the different levels of respective skills and the power relationships between the boards of directors, the management, and the membership. The consolidation of governance allows for building good relationships with external buyers in competitive product and finance markets. Finally, trust and good communication are key factors in building bonding social capital. In the face of intense competition from independent cocoa buyers, cooperatives will grow and

Table 5.3 Summary of viability assessment across cooperatives (+++ = strong capacity; ++ emerging capacity; + weak capacity)

Cooperative	Governance	Member relations	Infrastructure, equipment, and tools	Buyer relations	Financial assets
Coop1	Assessment: + • Lack of business training or experience of leadership • Externally paid manager (regional government) makes all major decisions • Board has little knowledge of operations	Assessment: ++ • Expectation of future benefits motivates participation and sales • Weak sense of ownership of the cooperative	Assessment: +++ • Adequate buildings to store and process cocoa • Lack of transport for cocoa purchases from members • Access to office space, but lack of title prohibits ability to use buildings as loan guarantee • Underutilized equipment for production of processed cocoa	Assessment: + • Failure to fulfil contract requirements particularly timely delivery at times never fulfilling contracts	Assessment: ++ • Access to credit through international provider, but difficulty with repayment • In default on a loan backed by a major buyer
Coop2	Assessment: ++ • Externally paid manager, selected and paid by projects • Deference to the managers' decisions • Board of directors knowledgeable on daily operations, but limited impact on strategy	Assessment: ++ • Members are content with the cooperative having seen its financial turn around • Expectations of more benefits as cooperative becomes profitable	Assessment: + • Rents a main building that does not have adequate space • Rural buying stations were built by donors using substandard wood • Limited transportation and processing capability	Assessment: +++ • Trust the cooperative because of its manager who has established a relationship with the buyers due to his history working in the industry	Assessment: ++ • Manager has been able to obtain credit buyers and in international markets • Still lacks sufficient working capital

Coop3	Assessment: ++ • Externally paid manager (buyer) unfamiliar with the cooperative/unable to make strategic decision • Board effectively manages the cooperative while nearly hired manager learns his position	Assessment: ++ • Even though the cooperative had stopped buying for some time, most members are hopeful for the future and appreciate the extension services they receive	Assessment: +++ • Secure access to office space, excess capacity in warehouse, and post-harvesting space • Underutilized equipment for production of processed cocoa • Limited transportation capability	Assessment: + • Commercial relations with only buyer; with history of incomplete contracts • Buyer purchases conditioned on hiring buyer selected manager	Assessment: + • No access to working capital (credit) due to default and weak administration • Dependent on current buyer and an NGO to provide funds • Income from carbon credits are restricted
Coop4	Assessment: ++ • Board understands the operations • Newly hired, externally paid manager (project) has limited experience with the board • Still developing strategic plan	Assessment: ++ • View cooperative as necessary to control prices and ensure fair practices • Side selling because of lack of price difference	Assessment: +++ • New and more than adequate buildings, processing, and transport equipment • Only cooperative fully utilizing its chocolate-making equipment	Assessment: + • Extensive competition in the area has made the cooperative sceptical of buyers • Failed to meet contract commitments	Assessment: ++ • Extensive support from donors • Difficulty in paying loans with high interest rates

consolidate their operations by providing members with attractive prices and useful services. Engagement by cocoa cooperatives in multiple certification systems (e.g. Fairtrade, Rainforest Alliance, and UTZ Certified) reflects, in part, interest in diversifying their buyer portfolio and providing more attractive terms to members.

In all cases, external organizations, mainly local and regional governments and PDA-supported NGOs, played a major role in the formation of the cooperatives. However, they failed to fully address the critical needs of obtaining access to financial assets, building healthy commercial relationship, and improved governance structures. External support targeted a few needs: infrastructure development and covering costs for administration, technical assistance, and the provision of inputs to members. Buyers had supported the cooperatives by facilitating access to credit (either directly or by providing collateral); however, the cooperatives likely represented a high level of risk for deeper and broader support.

Services provision

The coops remain weak business organizations, but dependency relationships are not entirely asymmetrical. The public objective of licit agriculture such as cocoa production requires viable commercial production; and the international market needs assured supplies of high-quality product, particularly as climate change is likely to affect global production. But real challenges remain in order to wean the coops off government and NGO supports which underwrite underperformance. Value chain partners need a stronger commitment to build the 'soft' assets associated with human skills of management and governance. Soft asset formation may continue to be necessary for years after the technical assistance, infrastructure, and financial support have been scaled down. A sectorial dialogue is necessary to ensure that the design and delivery of these services are aligned and harmonized between government policy, the approaches of development agencies, NGOs, research and training centres, and most of all, closer collaboration, communication and coordination in the value chain among cooperatives, buyers, and processors. Among promising – and replicable – initiatives interlinking smallholders and collective organizations with commercial input suppliers, credit provision, output marketing, and even management services are the multistakeholder partnership approach supported by the UN World Food Programme,[1] and the scheme for inclusive value chain model of Standard Bank Group (Stanbic) in Africa.[2]

Governance

Well-qualified leadership is not only necessary to make critical decisions and develop a coherent strategy. The abilities of manager and directors are also important to build good relations with members and with buyers. These cases bring to light the overall lack of business leadership in rural areas and the tendency for leaders to acquire their skills through lengthy learning-by-doing processes, at times supported by training and technical assistance interventions. All the buyers commented that a key factor in choosing to do business with a cooperative is their confidence in the manager and to a lesser extent with the board of directors. This relationship with the leadership is so important that it has critically affected the survival of all the cooperatives included in this study. In Peru as in many other markets, there is a relatively small group of businesses that export cocoa. Buyers for these businesses share information on cooperative performance among themselves and are likely to 'blacklist' cooperatives and their managers who have shown to be unreliable business partners. Several cocoa buyers mentioned they would reconsider purchasing cocoa from Coop2 if it changed managers. Coop3's buyer would only continue purchasing from the cooperative once the buyer installed its own manager. The leaders of Coop1 and Coop4 have failed to establish and maintain good business relationships, which has greatly limited their ability to market cocoa. In countries like Peru that have weak institutions, especially weak courts to enforce contract laws, the need for strong relationships between the buyer and the cooperative is even more critical (Hoskisson, Eden, Lau, and Wright, 2000).

Finance

One characteristic shared by relatively large, successful exporting cooperatives, irrespective of the principal crop, is the amount of outside support, especially financial support, received during the incubation stage that allowed them to grow and compete. Clearly, these emerging cooperatives were unable to either offer extension services or pay for a large staff when they were first formed. The challenge lies in determining how long funding should be provided and how best to target resources. While cooperatives are likely to welcome donations and subsidies for the expansion of physical capital, including large-scale processing equipment, such investments should be made with caution unless based on sound financial planning (e.g. investment capacity for repair and expansion) and marketing strategies. The provision of chocolate-making equipment to emerging cooperatives in remote areas makes little sense in a context where the recipient cooperatives are struggling to consolidate basic business operations. Most importantly the cooperatives will not grow their membership or consolidate their administration unless they have affordable access to working capital. An effective and trusted leadership is more likely to gain access to affordable credit. However, even the most trusted manager faces challenges finding credit to make purchases because of thin credit markets in these remote settings. A coordinated effort between private industry and the government loan guarantees – as in the Stanbic case cited above – is needed to foment and subsidize these credit markets.

This study, carried out in a context where cocoa cooperatives participate in a rapidly growing cocoa sector with considerable competition among local buyers, highlights the need for local stakeholders to investment in the formation of bonding social capital from the beginning of the cooperative development process. The challenges presented here are relevant in other contexts where efforts in cooperative building are expected to contribute to revitalizing the cocoa sector, for example Papua New Guiana (Garnevska, Joseph, and Kingi, 2014) and Ghana (Donovan, Stoian, Foundjem, and Degrande, 2016). Cooperatives need strong partners along the way who understand their needs and circumstances. Government agencies and NGOs will continue to play a key role; however, there is need for deeper engagement to design monitoring systems with feedback loops for joint reflection and learning. Greater coordination with the private sector is needed to better understand the options for coordinated interventions and joint risk-sharing. For emerging cooperatives, value chain partnerships for building governance and leadership capacities will be critical. A future research and development challenge is to better understand and manage the economic incentives that drive the relationships between buyers and cooperative suppliers in value chains such as cocoa in Peru, in such a way that commercial partners rather than external donors are willing to commit the financial resources that hitherto come from donors and the public sector. Finally, new forms of collaboration, such as cooperative–cooperative business schools, may also work for newly formed cooperatives if more mature cooperatives are willing to share experiences and skills.

Notes

1. https://www.growafrica.com/groups/patient-procurementplatform
2. http://www.inclusivebusinesshub.org/project/project-profile-stanbic-agricultural-banking-in-nigeria/

Acknowledgements

We would like to thank Franziska Salzer, Ever Equsquiza, and Alfonso Tenorio for their valuable contributions to data collection.

This study was supported by the CGIAR Research Program on Policies, Institutions and Markets (PIM) and the CGIAR Research Program on Forests, Trees and Agroforestry (FTA). We thank the donors who support PIM and FTA through their contributions to the CGIAR Fund.

Reprinted with the permission of Taylor & Francis. First published as: Donovan, J. Blare, T. and Poole, N. (2017) 'Stuck in a rut: emerging cocoa cooperatives in Peru and the factors that influence their performance', International Journal of Agricultural Sustainability, 15:2, 169-184, DOI: 10.1080/14735903.2017.1286831

Funding

The CGIAR Global Research Program Forests, Trees and Agroforestry (FTA) and CGIAR Global Research Program on Policies, Markets, and Institutions (PIM) provided funding for this research.

References

Bacon, C. (2015). Food sovereignty, food security and fair trade: The case of an influential Nicaraguan smallholder cooperative. *Third World Quarterly, 36*(3), 469–488.

Bebbington, A. (1996). Organizations and intensifications: Campesino federations, rural livelihoods and agricultural technology in the Andes and Amazonia. *World Development, 24*(7), 1161–1177.

Bebbington, A., Quisbert, J., & Trujillo, G. (1996). Technology and rural development strategies in a small farmer organization: Lessons from Bolivia for rural policy and practice. *Public Administration and Development, 16*(3), 195–213.

Bernard, T., & Spielman, D. J. 2009. Reaching the rural poor through rural producer organizations? A study of agricultural marketing cooperatives in Ethiopia. *Food Policy, 34*(1), 60–69.

Beuchelt, T., & Zeller, M. (2013). The role of cooperative business models for the success of smallholder coffee certification in Nicaragua: A comparison of conventional, organic and organic-fairtrade certified cooperatives. *Renewable Agriculture and Food Systems, 28*(3), 195–211.

Cabieses, H. (2010). The 'miracle of San Martín' and symptoms of 'alternative development' in Peru (Drug Policy Briefing No. 34). Transnational Institute. Retrieved from https://www.tni.org/en/briefing/miracle-san-martin-and-symptomsalternative-development-peru.

Chauvin, L. (2010, January 31). *Drug Lords vs. Chocolate: From Coca to Cacao in Peru*, TIME. Retrieved from http://content.time.com/time/world/article/0,8599,1957708,00.html.

del Castillo, L. (2013). Las cooperativas: La apuesta del gobierno para la inclusión del productor agrario. *La Revista Agrícola*. Retrieved August 15, 2016, from http://www.larevistaagraria.org/sites/default/files//revista/LRA147/Las%20cooperativas%20la%20apuesta%20del%20gobierno%20para%20la%20inclusión%20del%20productor%20agrario.pdf

Devaux, A., Horton, D., Velasco, C., Thiele, G., Lopez, G., Bernet, T., ... Ordinola, M. (2009). Collective action for market chain innovation in the Andes. *Food Policy, 34*(1), 31–38.

Donovan, J., & Poole, N. (2014). Partnerships in fairtrade coffee: A close-up look at how buyers and NGOs build supply capacity in Nicaragua. *Food Chain, 4*(1), 34–48.

Donovan, J., Stoian, S., Foundjem, D., & Blare, T. (2016). *Advisory services by cooperatives engaged in high value markets* (GFRAS Good Practice Note Number 23). Geneva: Global Forum for Rural Advisory Services (GFRAS). Retrieved from http://www.g-fras.org/fr/good-practice-notes/19-agri-cooperatives.html

Donovan, J., Stoian, D., Foundjem, D., & Degrande, A. (2016). Fairtrade cocoa in Ghana: Taking stock and looking ahead. *Sweet Vision, 61*, 14–17.

Donovan, J., Stoian, D., & Poole, N. (2008). *Global review of rural community enterprises: The long and winding road to creating viable businesses, and potential shortcuts* (Technical Series 29/Rural Enterprise Development Collection 2). Turrialba: CATIE.

Emerson, M. B., & Boynton, R. D. (1981). Comparative performance of cooperative and private cheese plants in Wisconsin. *North Central*

Journal of Agricultural Economics, *3*(2), 157–164. https://www.jstor.org/stable/1349130?seq=1#page_scan_tab_contents.

Finance Alliance for Sustainable Trade. (2012). *Market research for sustainable investments: A brief overview of the sustainable cocoa sector in Latin America and the Caribbean*. Montreal: Author.

Garnevska, E., Joseph, H., & Kingi, T. (2014). Development and challenges of cocoa cooperatives in Papua New Guinea: Case of Manus province. *Asia Pacific Business Review*, *20*(3), 419–438.

Herman, R., & Renz, D. (2008). Advancing non-profit organizational effectiveness research and theory: Nine theses. *Nonprofit Management and Leadership*, *18*(4), 399–415.

Hoskisson, R. E., Eden, L., Lau, C. M., & Wright, M. (2000). Strategy in emerging economies. *Academy of Management Journal*, *43*(3), 249–267.

Kachule, R., Poole, N., & Dorward, A. (2005). *Farmer organisations in Malawi: The organization study* (Final report for "Farmer Organisations for Market Access," DFID Crop Post Harvest Research Programme, R2875). London: Imperial College London.

Krauss, U., & Soberanis, W. (2001). Rehabilitation of diseased cocoa fields in Peru through shade regulation and timing of biocontrol measures. *Agroforestry Systems*, *53*(2), 179–184.

Kruijssen, F., Keizer, M., & Giuliani, A. (2009). Collective action for small-scale producers of agricultural biodiversity products. *Food Policy*, *34*(1), 46–52.

Lecy, J., Schmitz, H. P., & Swedlund, H. (2012). Non-Governmental and not-for-profit organizational effectiveness: A modern synthesis. *VOLUNTAS: International Journal of Voluntary and Nonprofit Organizations*, *23*(2), 434–457.

Lusthaus, C., Adrien, M. H., Anderson, G., Carden, F., & Montalván, G. P. (2002). *Organizational assessment. A framework for improving performance.* Washington, DC: IDRC/IADB.

McKee, G. (2008). The financial performance of North Dakota grain marketing and farm supply cooperatives. *Journal of Cooperatives*, *31*, 15–34.

Molnar, A., Liddle, M., Bracer, C., Khare, A., White, A., & Bull, J. (2007). *Community based forest enterprises: Their status and potential in tropical countries* (ITTO Technical Series #28). Yokohama: International Tropical Timber Organization.

Nelson, V., Opoku, K., Martin, A., Bugri, J., & Posthumus, H. (2013). *Assessing the poverty impact of sustainability standards: Fairtrade in Ghanaian cocoa.* Greenwich: Natural Resources Institute, University of Greenwich.

Newcomer, K., El Baradei, L., & Garcia, S. (2013). Expectations and capacity of performance measurement in NGOs in the development context. *Public Administration and Development*, *33*(1), 62–79.

Poole, N., & Donovan, J. (2014). Building cooperative capacity: The specialty coffee sector in Nicaragua. *Journal of Agribusiness in Developing and Emerging Economies*, *4*(2), 133–156.

Poole, N., & de Frece, A. (2010). *A review of existing organisational forms of smallholder farmers' associations and their contractual relationships with other market participants in the East and Southern African ACP Region* (EU-AAACP Paper Series No. 11). Rome: Food and Agriculture Organization of the United Nations.

Potts, J., Lynch, M., Wilkings, A., Huppé, G., Cunningham, M., & Voora, V. (2014). *The state of sustainability initiatives review 2014: Standards and the green economy*. Winnipeg: International Institute for Sustainable Development (IISD).

Ruben, R., & Heras, J. (2012). Social capital, governance and performance of Ethiopian coffee cooperatives. *Annals of Public and Cooperative Economics*, *83*(4), 463–484.

Scott, W. R. (2004). Reflections on a half-century of organizational sociology. *Annual Review of Sociology*, *30*, 1–21.

Sexton, R., & Islow, J. (1988). *Factors critical to the success or failure of emerging agricultural cooperatives* (Information Series 11921). Davis: University of California, Davis, Giannini Foundation.

Spellberg, J., & Kaplan, M. (2010). A rural economic development plan to help the USA win its war on cocaine. *Development in Practice*, *20*(6), 690–705.

Stattman S., & Mol, A. (2014). Social sustainability of Brazilian biodiesel: The role of agricultural cooperatives. *Geoforum*, *54*, 282–294.

Stoian, D., Donovan, J., Fisk, J. & Muldoon, M. (2012). Value chain development for rural poverty reduction: A reality check and a warning. *Enterprise Development and Microfinance*, *23*(1), 54–60.

Tenorio, A. (2011). *El Cocoa en la Región San Martín*. Tarapoto: CAPIRONA.

Uphoff, N., & Wijayaratna, C. (2000). Demonstrated benefits from social capital: The productivity of farmer organizations in Gal Oya, Sri Lanka. *World Development*, *28*(22), 1875–1890.

Valkila, J., & Nygren, A. (2010). Impacts of fair trade certification on coffee farmers, cooperatives, and laborers in Nicaragua. *Agriculture and Human Values*, *27*(3), 321–333.

About the authors

Jason Donovan, PhD (j.donovan@cgiar.org), Senior Economist, Research Theme Leader for Markets and Value Chains, International Maize and Wheat Improvement Center (CIMMYT), Texcoco, Mexico.

Nigel Poole (np10@soas.ac.uk) Emeritus Professor of International Development, SOAS University of London, London, UK.

Trent Blare (tblare@ufl.edu), University of Florida Institute of Food and Agricultural Sciences, Tropical Research and Education Center.

PART II

Design and Implementation of VCD

CHAPTER 6

Fit for purpose? A review of guides for gender-equitable value chain development

Dietmar Stoian, Jason Donovan, Marlène Elias and Trent Blare

Abstract

This chapter presents a review of seven guides for gender-equitable value chain development (VCD). The guides advocate persuasively the integration of gender into VCD programming and raise important issues for designing more inclusive interventions. However, gaps persist in their coverage of gender-based constraints in collective enterprises, the influence of norms on gender relations, and processes to transform inequitable relations through VCD. Guidance for field implementation and links to complementary value chain tools are also limited. The chapter identifies opportunities for conceptual and methodological innovation to address the varying roles, needs, and aspirations of women and men in VCD.

Keywords: gender and diversity, labour and livelihoods – poverty reduction, economics, globalisation (incl. trade; private sector), aid – development policies, methods

Introduction

Over the past few years, organisations engaged in the development of agricultural value chains have increasingly labelled their interventions as "inclusive". This conveys an explicit interest to carry out development programmes that *"include and substantially benefit large numbers of poor people – often smallholders, but also artisans or small-scale retailers or customers"* (Harper, Belt, and Roy 2015). Such value chain development (VCD) often aims to improve access by smallholders and small and medium enterprises (SMEs), including cooperatives and producer associations, to information, inputs, and services. Emphasis is placed on developing more equitable business relationships between different actors along the nodes of a value chain, with expectations that beneficial outcomes accrue to small-holders and SMEs but also to their business partners further downstream in the chain. Interventions typically focus on facilitating stronger links between these actors and expanding the provision of affordable and effective services from within and outside of the chain (Kaplinsky 2016).

http://dx.doi.org/10.3362/9781788530576.006

However, it is increasingly recognised that inequalities also occur within a given node of a value chain, based on gender, age, ethnicity, and other factors of social differentiation (Coles and Mitchell 2011). Failure to address these inequalities is problematic from a gender and a broader equality perspective, and may effectively undermine the potential of VCD to contribute to both economic and social progress (Bamber and Staritz 2016). This potential has been highlighted in approaches to women's economic empowerment, with authors advocating the adequate application of a gender lens in value chain analysis and associated development programming (KIT, Agri-ProFocus, and IIRR 2012; Rubin and Manfre 2014; Quisumbing et al., 2015). Gender-based constraints and opportunities for strengthening women's participation in value chains figure prominently in these publications, often with a strong focus on women's capacity to enhance income and make decisions on its use.

To facilitate the operationalisation of gender equity in VCD programming, several international organisations have elaborated guides and tools that support practitioners in the design, implementation, and assessment of gender-equitable VCD. Despite their growing number, the guides have yet to be examined regarding their use of concepts related to gender and value chains, and their potential to effectively transform inequitable gender relations through VCD even if applied by non-gender specialists. This chapter reviews seven guides for gender-equitable VCD that were published by development organisations with a recognised capacity to influence VCD programming and policy. Our objective is twofold: first, to help practitioners select the guides that best suit their needs; and second, to provide donors, researchers, and development organisations with critical reflection on ways forward for advancing gender equity through VCD. We begin by reviewing the literature on gender in value chains. The subsequent section presents a framework and methodology for the guide review, with the criteria and parameters that guided our assessment. We then present results, with emphasis on the strengths and weaknesses that the guides show against the criteria and parameters. In the final section, we identify opportunities and needs for conceptual and methodological innovation to promote the design, implementation, and assessment of interventions which include the goal of equitable engagement of women and men in value chains.

Gender in value chains: reviewing the literature

The literature recognises that value chains are embedded in socio-cultural contexts in which informal gender norms and values, beliefs, and power relations operate across scales – from the household and community levels to the national and global economy. These social norms, relations, and institutions shape women's and men's often unequal ability to participate in and benefit from VCD (Rubin and Manfre 2014). Globally, gender norms attribute to women the responsibility for the majority of non-remunerated activities that maintain the household – the "reproductive" realm. These activities prop up "production" and form an integral, often invisible, part of value chains. The need to engage in these activities, combined with the difficulty to command the labour of other household members, can pose important labour constraints for women, and reduce their time and energy to generate income through value chains.

Women also tend to have more limited control over assets than men, reducing their decision-making power and capacity to engage in more profitable nodes of value chains (Quisumbing et al., 2015). Examining changes in asset endowments resulting from VCD, and how income translates (or not) into livelihood benefits, is therefore critical, not only at household level but also among individual household members (Coles and Mitchell 2011). Women may not participate in certain value chain activities, yet benefit from their spouse's economic gains. For example, value chain income may be spent on improved housing, better food, and enhanced health services. The reverse is also true, as women's participation in value chains may fail to deliver expected gains if they do not maintain control over their income. Differences in the intra-household distribution of benefits derived from VCD can both be a result of and a contribution to inequitable access to assets between male and female household members. Such gendered asset gaps are widespread and have a bearing on women's and men's ability to negotiate among themselves and with external actors. They also influence how barriers to entry to a given value chain may be overcome and, hence, determine the terms under which women can participate in VCD (Quisumbing et al., 2015).

Gender inequality is also inscribed in laws, regulations, and other formal institutions that, along with the availability and orientation of technical, business, and financial services, influence the differentiated opportunities for women and men to engage in value chains. VCD interventions in the enabling environment may often be non-gender-specific as they address blockages that apply to all value chain actors. In contrast, gender-sensitive interventions may focus on levelling the playing field by reforming laws, policies, and other institutions that constrain women, such as land and property ownership statutes, labour codes, and other forms of governance that may discriminate against them (Coles and Mitchell 2011). Gender-sensitive policies or services may also include tailoring of financial products to the needs of women in diverse types of households to facilitate their participation in value chains (Oduol et al., 2017).

Due to deep-seated gender inequalities in informal and formal institutions, women and men commonly engage under different terms in value chains, with regard to different activities in the same value chain or across different value chains altogether. Value chain analysis with a gender lens has therefore focused on sex-segmentation across the nodes of a value chain and on women's and men's overall returns to labour (Ingram et al., 2014). However, women's roles in value chains often lack visibility due to their concentration in home-based work, the informal sector, and part-time employment (Shackleton et al., 2011). Women's participation is also more likely in certain nodes of the chain, and segregation into low-technology occupations may limit their opportunities to generate new skills and capabilities (SOFA Team and Doss, 2011). Some authors have examined value chains in which women dominate the production stage and the extent to which corporate social responsibility or ethical trade schemes foster their participation in trainings and membership in cooperatives and other types of collective enterprises. They have also looked into the effects on women's returns on labour, working conditions, and access to markets, but generally found that gender sensitivity of such schemes needs to be greatly enhanced to achieve the desired ends (Barrientos, Dolan, and Tallontire, 2003; Elias and Carney, 2004; KIT, Agri-ProFocus, and IIRR, 2012).

Women's engagement in agricultural cooperatives and producer associations has shown promise for enhancing their benefits from value chains (Ferguson and Kepe, 2011). Membership – and particularly leadership roles – in these collective enterprises can improve access to knowledge, information, services (e.g. training, credit), and other benefits. It increases women's ability to manage their work, earn and make decisions on income, and influence business operations (Lyon et al., 2010). Yet, women often face significant challenges to become members and participate in the governance of cooperatives (Manchon and Macleod, 2010). Without such membership, they are likely to be deprived of management functions in the enterprises or in other nodes of the chain (Coles and Mitchell, 2011). VCD with explicit gender equality goals may focus on strengthening women's own enterprises, particularly for products traditionally produced by women (e.g. Elias and Arora-Jonsson, 2017), or women's active participation in mixed-sex cooperatives (Quisumbing et al., 2015).

This literature review shows that VCD can reproduce but also reform existing gender relations. From a development perspective, there is an underlying assumption that careful design and implementation of VCD can provide opportunities to enhance gender equity (Coles and Mitchell, 2011; Quisumbing et al., 2015). In many cases, women's economic empowerment can be expected to be an explicit goal of gender-equitable VCD. However, the pathways linking interventions and desired outcomes may be less clear. Focus areas for empowerment may be women's membership in collective enterprises, enhanced income and self-confidence through individual or collective commercial activities, improved intra-household (gender and other) relations, and the ability to make or influence strategic decisions within the household, community, and beyond (Shackleton et al., 2011; Ingram et al., 2014; Rubin and Manfre, 2014).

Framework and methodology

The literature review pointed to key themes to be considered when seeking to enhance gender equity through value chain development. We combined these themes in a framework that guided our assessment of gender-equitable VCD guides (Figure 6.1).

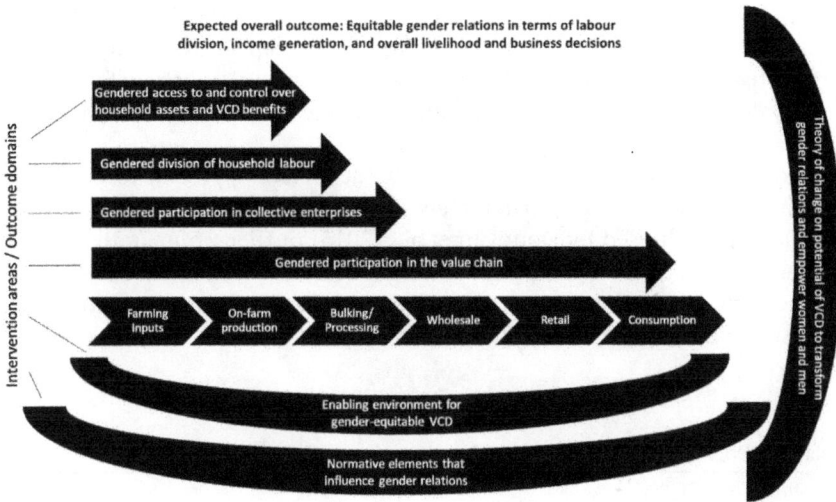

Figure 6.1 Framework for assessing guides for gender-equitable value chain development.

The framework presents seven assessment criteria derived from the litera-ture on gender in value chains. The first criterion addresses the guides' theory of change for empowering women, men, and households through VCD. Each guide suggests how behaviour change is expected to happen through inter-ventions and their implications for chain stakeholders. Such a theory may be explicitly stated in a guide or deduced from the recommended activities and the expected outcomes and impacts. As women's empowerment is not a linear process and may prompt backlash against them, we also considered whether the guides explicitly mention the assumptions, risks, and potential repercus-sions that accompany the change process. The second criterion focuses on the guides' attention to the normative elements that influence opportuni-ties and constraints in value chains as well as preferences and aspirations of women and men in relation to chain engagement. The third criterion covers the instruments and methodological recommendations for analysis of the enabling environment and its implication for gender-equitable VCD. This criterion seeks to understand how the guides orientate users in understanding the laws, regulations, and other formal institutions that, along with support services, influence the differentiated opportunities for women and men to engage in value chains.

The following two criteria address the issue of sex-segmentation and dif-ferent levels of women's and men's participation across chain nodes and in collective enterprises. The sixth criterion examines how the guides cover the gendered division of household labour across market and non-market live-lihood activities. In particular, we considered how such arrangements condition the roles of different household members in value chains and the trade-offs that often exist between these activities. With the final criterion we look into the guides' focus on women's and men's (separate or joint) access to productive assets as well as the intra-household distribution of benefits derived from value chain participation, including income and decision-making on its use.

Along with the assessment criteria, the deductive approach to our study required the definition of parameters for detailed assessment, following a similar approach used by Donovan et al., (2015) in their comparative review of generic guides for VCD programming. For each assessment criterion we defined one to four parameters, for a total of 17 parameters across the seven assessment criteria (Table 6.1).

Table 6.1 Criteria and parameters for review of guides

General criteria	Parameters
(1) Theory of change on potential of VCD to transform gender relations and empower women and men	• Assumptions about strengthened capacities and access to information and decision-making • Building of self-confidence with effects on intra-household relations (increased equity, but also potential backlash or repercussions) • Enhanced ability to influence strategic decisions within the household, enterprise, community and beyond • Individual versus household-level outcomes
(2) Normative elements that influence gender relations	• Gender norms and values • Social acceptability of value chain activities • Preferences and aspirations
(3) Enabling environment for gender-equitable VCD	• Gender-responsiveness of laws, policies, formal rules, and regulations in relation to VCD • Service offer of support organisations with focus on genderequitable VCD
(4) Gendered participation in the value chain	• Roles of women and men along value chain nodes
(5) Gendered participation in collective enterprises	• Position of women and men in the enterprise (e.g. management, administrative staff, permanent or temporary labour) • Influence on strategic business decisions
(6) Gendered division of household labour	• Division of labour in market and non-market-oriented activities (gender roles, time and labour constraints, drudgery) • Trade-offs across activity realms
(7) Gendered access to and control over household assets and VCD benefits	• Access to and control over productive assets (separate versus joint assets) • Intra-household distribution of VCD benefits/income • Influence on strategic livelihood decisions

Table 6.2 Reviewed guides on gender-equitable value chain development

Guide	Year	Authors	International organisation
Making the strongest links: a practical guide to mainstreaming gender analysis in value chain development	2007	Linda Mayoux, Grania Mackie	International Labour Organization (ILO)
Promoting gender equitable opportunities in agricultural value chains: a handbook	2009	Deborah Rubin, Cristina Manfre, Kara Nichols Barrett	United States Agency for International Development (USAID)
Improving opportunities for women in smallholder-based supply chains: business case and practical guidance for international food companies	2010	Man-Kwun Chan	Bill and Melinda Gates Foundation (BMGF)
Gender mainstreaming in value chain development: practical guidelines and tools	2010	Jacqueline Terrillon	Netherlands Development Organisation (SNV)
Gender in value chains: practical toolkit to integrate a gender perspective in agricultural value chain development	2013	Angelica Senders, Anna Lentink, Mieke Vanderschaeghe, Jacqueline Terrillon	Agri-ProFocus
Measuring women's economic empowerment in private sector development: guidelines for practitioners	2014	Erin Markel	Donor Committee for
Developing gender-sensitive value chains: a guiding framework	2016	FAO	Food and Agricultural Organization of the United Nations (FAO)

Given the objective of this study, we selected methodological guides for gender-equitable VCD that: (1) principally target development practitioners engaged in VCD programme design, implementation, and assessment; (2) include a set of specific methodological steps and practical tools for collecting and analysing gender-sensitive data; and (3) are published by an influential international development or funding organisation, thus offering the prospect of wide-scale circulation. The seven guides selected according to these criteria are presented in Table 6.2.

Where relevant, we reference how each of the guides addresses a given criterion. In case of uneven coverage across the guides, we focus on the most illustrative examples. The guides are presented according to the level of attention given to each criterion, beginning with those where coverage is more extensive.

Findings: what the guides cover

Theory of change about potential of VCD to transform gender relations and empower women and men

Few guides specify the mechanisms by which VCD is expected to transform gender relations at the individual, household, enterprise, or chain levels. Anticipated impact pathways can be deduced from the envisaged outputs, outcomes, and impacts resulting from implementation and the recommendations for addressing gender-based constraints. Most guides foresee the elaboration of action plans or actionable strategies that specify interventions to overcome these constraints, enhance women's engagement in a given value chain, and promote equitable VCD outcomes.

SNV expects a strategic plan for addressing gender issues in VCD across seven areas (effective public policy management, market intelligence, multi-stakeholder processes, value chain financing, group consolidation, strengthening value chain service providers, and impact on micro level). For each of them, a possible formulation of *"gender equality objectives"* and *"targeted performances"* is derived from indicative *"key gender equality issues"* (2010, 27–39).

USAID envisions a *"framework"* and a *"process"* for integrating gender issues into agricultural value chains. Gender-based constraints are anticipated to be removed by taking stock of them and identifying corrective actions. These actions are expected to be mutually supportive and transformative – a *"win-win"* based on synergies between gender relations and VCD. Gender integration approaches and resulting outcomes are projected to move along a continuum from *"gender exploitative"* to *"gender accommodating"* and *"gender transformative"* (2009, 101–104).

BMGF seeks to stimulate policies and practical action of food sourcing companies to improve women's opportunities as part of their ongoing sourcing from smallholders and associated support programmes (2010, 10). Unlike the other guides, which largely focus on analysing and over-coming gender-based constraints, BMGF makes a business case and provides companies with practical guidance for improving opportunities for women in their supply chains.

ILO envisages an action plan for external agencies to support gender equity in the value chain, with a focus on identifying a *"basket of win-win strategies"* for short-term improvements; for more contentious issues where gender-specific conflicts of interest between stakeholders require careful negotiation they suggest a long-term view and strategy (2007, 63).

AgriProFocus (2013) anticipates a *"picture of the value chain"* that illustrates men's and women's roles in terms of positions and power. Along with the identification of constraints and opportunities for women's upgraded involvement in the value chain, this picture serves as an input for practitioners to enhance their interventions.

DCED leads to a *"strategic results framework"* that integrates the women's economic empowerment theory of change into strategies for private sector development, and to programme-specific *"results chains"* (2014, 10–13).

The general focus is on defining indicators and collecting data for a gender-responsive system for results measurement (2014, 13–34), without specific guidance for developing an actionable strategy.

FAO puts forth a *"gender-sensitive value chain framework"* (2016, 23–29), with gender-sensitive value chain analysis as a first step toward implementation. Beyond this analysis no directions are given for interpreting the findings and translating them into action points.

Several guides direct the user in designing interventions based on the findings of gender-sensitive value chain analysis (ILO, BMGF, AgriProFocus and, to a lesser extent, USAID). However, only DCED points to potential trade-offs between increased value chain engagement of women and their other livelihood activities, as well as limited choices in the most vulnerable households where trade-offs and risks tend to be highest. Most guides (USAID, SNV, AgriProFocus, DCED and FAO) identify women's lack of self-esteem and confidence in their own skills as a factor limiting their pursuit of non-traditional roles in value chains. SNV and AgriProFocus consider the importance of developing human agency, self-assertiveness, and confidence among women as critical elements of both empowerment and organisational strengthening.

Normative elements that influence gender relations

Most guides address the normative elements that influence men's and women's ability to participate in value chains. They present a list of indicators or questions that cover gender norms, values, and beliefs in relation to value chains and market activities. Three guides provide more detailed guidance in this respect: SNV, USAID, and FAO. The SNV guide includes a list of questions to encourage discussion among women and men stakeholders on the implications of the cultural setting, values, and norms on gender relations. Brief examples are provided to demonstrate the influence of stereo-types and presumptions about what men and women can and should do. Users may, however, require additional guidance on how to contextualise such testimonies and how to translate the findings into intervention goals and activities, including constructive dialogues with men for achieving envisaged behaviour changes.

As an input to *"gender-based constraint statements"*, USAID (2009, 82) suggests four questions to guide data collection in relation to *"perceptions and beliefs"*. One example is *"Are there aspects of production that men/women are discouraged from doing?"* Tool users are expected to present their findings during stakeholder workshops to determine normative gender-based constraints. AgriProFocus derives insights into such constraints based on the questions, tables, and examples from USAID. FAO cautions that, as a result of prevailing sociocultural norms, women may lack the self-confidence to exercise agency as value chain participants. "Understanding and addressing this challenge requires taking into account the fact that social dynamics are often complex and require a holistic approach. Norms and values affect and are likely to be internalised by all of a given society's members, including those who are excluded or disadvantaged." (2016, 21)

Analysis of gender norms focuses essentially on women, with regard to their sexual and reproductive roles, work, mobility, and gender-based violence (2016, 39). Similar to the other guides, emphasis is placed on the analysis of gender norms, with scarce guidance on how to translate the findings into practical action.

The other guides also address gender norms, though in less detail. DCED considers *"gender norms, and men's and women's attitudes toward gender roles"* as one of seven areas where household-level outcomes and women's economic empowerment are measured. The underlying assumption is that *"positive changes in norms and behaviours can bring about long-term changes in women's economic empowerment"* (2014, 21). The guide limits its directions to measurement and attribution, leaving it to the user to determine how normative and behavioural changes can be induced. ILO identifies indicators at individual, household, community, national, and international levels. Some indicators are focused on gender norms (*"cultural constraints and stereotypes"* and *"gender blind/ discriminatory concepts of 'ownership'*, *"worker"* production/reproduction, market/ non-market"* (2007, 56)). BMGF makes occasional reference to gender norms, for example, when pointing at cultural norms that restrict women's interactions with men on business matters. It argues how companies sourcing from smallholders may challenge traditional gender norms concerning land and crop ownership (2010, 20), but it lacks guidance on how to assess the influence of norms on gendered constraints and opportunities within the value chain.

Enabling environment for gender-equitable VCD

Three guides (USAID, SNV, ILO) stand out for their attention to the enabling environment for achieving gender-equitable VCD. Focus and scope of assessing the enabling environment vary, without clear distinction between formal and informal institutional aspects. USAID concentrates on the business environment and provides guidance on how to analyse gender aspects associated with transaction costs (registration and licensing fees), discrimination laws, and information access (2009, 45). The guide also suggests critical themes to be considered when developing strategies to enhance the enabling environment (2009, 46), particularly as regards policies and procedures that adversely affect men or women, and for improved public–private sector coordination to foster women's entrepreneurship (2009, 47). SNV recommends to collect data on the regulatory environment using a *"macro-meso-micro grid"* that covers the cultural context and regulatory environment as well as the delivery of *"pro-poor development services"* (2010, 12). The analysis of the formal institutional environment with a gender lens is to draw on databases of legislation, pertinent research findings, and project and government reports (2010, 14–15). ILO recommends analysing both enterprises and the enabling environment to identify inequality along the chain and its underlying causes (2007, 63–64). It focuses on macro-level factors like enterprise regulation, inflation, infrastructure, and property legislation, as these are considered to be often more significant in influencing the income levels and women's vulnerability than targeted enterprise projects or programmes. Examples of favourable macro-level policies in support of women homeworkers are also included (2007, 65).

The other guides pay less attention to how the enabling environment shapes gender outcomes. AgriProFocus covers access to finance (2013, 26) and gendered influence on enabling factors (2013, 51–52) to determine how women and men leaders can influence policy-making and legislation to promote their economic rights and gender equality. While it clearly recognises the influence of the business environment on value chains (2013, 10), it provides little guidance on how to analyse and advance intervention strategies. BMGF does not consider macro-level analysis, but advocates *"engaging national governments to improve relevant regulations and policies"* (2012, 63). DCED does not recommend indicators beyond the household level, safe for those cases where a programme combining private sector development and women's economic empowerment seeks to have direct influence on them (2014, 22). FAO makes a reference to the national and global enabling environments, including societal and natural elements shaping these (2016, 16), but provides no guidance for analysis or actions to be taken.

Gendered participation in the value chain

Most guides address gendered value-chain participation by suggesting questions to be considered and presenting simple designs for data collection and analysis, often linked to value chain mapping. They recommend the collection of sex-disaggregated data on gender roles in production and marketing, although recommended analysis is almost exclusively focused on women. No distinction is made between domestic and global value chains, despite the fact that extending such analysis to the downstream segments of global value chains is costly and of little use when VCD interventions focus on the upstream and midstream segments of a given chain.

Four guides (FAO, AgriProFocus, SNV, ILO) provide in-depth coverage of gendered participation in value chains. FAO proposes gender-sensitive value chain mapping as a first step towards making women's work and participation in the value chain visible, including identification of gender-based constraints at each node of the chain (2016, 26–27). AgriProFocus suggests value chain mapping (2014, 54–57), including reflection on differences in women's and men's activities in each node as well as women's constraints and opportunities to participate in each of them. Similar to FAO, the guide emphasises women's under-recognised contribution to on-farm production. Participatory workshops are the recommended method for data collection and analysis. SNV suggests participatory chain mapping (2010, 17–19), with sex-disaggregated estimates of the number of persons involved and the relative share of value contributed and received by actors at each node. This is accompanied by a list of questions that cover the gendered division of labour, roles in different nodes of the chain, and the value given to women's roles in paid and unpaid work. ILO recommends the use of secondary sources or workshops to collect sex-disaggregated data on workers and their skills composition along the nodes of a chain (2007, 50). This is supplemented by questions to stakeholders on gender discrimination in tasks, markets, and production processes, as well as gendered differences in skills, resources, and time availability.

The other guides limit their coverage to the number of workers along the chain nodes and the major roles within each of them (USAID), or they recommend sex-disaggregated outcome and performance indicators without regard to the varied roles of women and men along the nodes of a value chain (DCED, BMGF).

Gendered participation in collective enterprises

The guides provide limited orientation for analysing how collective enterprises help smallholders engage with other value chain actors, or with input and service providers operating from outside of the chain. They also pay scarce attention to the roles that women and men play in collective enterprises and options for facilitating change in associated power relations. However, some guides do recognise possible constraints to women's participation in such enterprises. USAID, for example, cautions that membership criteria may discourage women's participation when insisting on single membership for an entire family or when requiring proof of legal land ownership (2009, 26). Some general guidance on collecting data and analysing barriers at the level of collective enterprises is provided by DCED, BMGF, AgriProFocus, and SNV.

At the enterprise level, DCED recommends sex-disaggregated data collection on ownership, number and position of employees, and participation in training, among others (2014, 24). BMGF explains why women tend to be underrepresented as members and leaders in collective enterprises and provides guidance on what large-scale buyers and processors can do to increase women's participation via their engagement with collective enterprises. Suggestions include quotas for representation on committees and boards, along with focused support to women assuming leadership positions (2014, 25–26). AgriProFocus provides guidance on how to design workshops that facilitate women's participation in producer associations. It recommends targeting women in capacity building to support their active participation (2013, 28) and negotiation of equal access to productive resources (2013, 30). SNV encourages stakeholders to discuss the participation of women in producer associations as well as their voice in governance, access to benefits, and opportunities to be elected to governing bodies (2010, 24).

Gendered division of household labour

Save for BMGF, the guides address the gendered division of labour within households. DCED points to the *division of labour, time, responsibilities* as a category for which indicators are proposed. It introduces the concept of time poverty and recommends time-use surveys *"to examine gendered divisions of labour and potential trade-offs between time spent on market, non-market, and leisure activities"* (2014, 20). AgriProFocus poses questions on the division of labour between women and men in the household and along chain nodes (2013, 50), including guidance for activity mapping, identification of associated gender-based constraints and opportunities, and the design of actions to ameliorate these (2013, 63). Importantly, DCED and AgriProFocus reference the potential for trade-offs between women's reproductive activities and those directly oriented to value chains.

SNV points to the need to collect gender-disaggregated data on labour division at household (2010, 16) and chain (2010, 19) levels, and on how public policy influences this division (2010, 27). It guides users in applying their findings to formulate *"gender equality objectives"* and *"performances"* – measured as gender-equitable outcomes – in multi-stakeholder processes (2010, 31) and at the micro-level (2010, 38). USAID recommends interviewing men and women farmers and key informants to collect data on the gendered division of labour, including production, marketing, and selling (2009, 74). A hypothetical case study is used to facilitate tool application. However, the way it is presented may actually reinforce existing gender stereotypes by stating that *"women and girls do most of the household work"* while *"on the farm, men typically provide labour for field preparation"* (2009, 79). ILO presents questions on the gendered division of labour, in regard to *"individual differences in skills, resources, time between men and women"* and *"gender constraints at household/ family/kinship level"* (2007, 57). FAO stresses the importance of the topic as the *"division of labour in many agrifood contexts is both gendered and unequal, a reality that frequently results in women's activities being overlooked or underestimated in conventional 'gender-blind' VC analyses"* (2016, 27). Both the ILO and FAO guides rely on the user to define data collection methods and derive meaning from the data collected.

Gendered access to and control over household assets and benefits

All the guides consider access to productive assets among household members, along with the intra-household distribution of benefits derived from using these assets. Overall, however, they offer insufficient guidance for asset analysis. While most focus on land, labour, and equipment, AgriProFocus and USAID take a broader view by accounting for human, social, natural, physical, and financial capitals. AgriProFocus draws on the frameworks and methods regarding access to assets and intra-household allocation of benefits presented in the SNV and USAID guides, distinguishing between intangible (e.g. education and social relationships) and tangible (e.g. land, livestock, and machinery) assets. USAID proposes access to assets as one of the four areas of gender assessment, including examples of how issues such as *"women typically need to have husbands co-sign loans"* (2009, 80) translate into gender-based constraints. SNV poses questions to facilitate tool users' engagement with local stakeholders, including *"What is women's and men's access to resources in order to perform tasks?"* and *"Do women and men benefit equally at the household level?"* (2010, 22). DCED includes *"decision making regarding income, productive assets, investments, and expenditures"* as a category for which indicators are to be defined (2014, 19). The guide focuses on women's decision-making power on income and expenditures, rather than looking across a portfolio of assets. ILO identifies indicators such as income, individual and household asset endowments, and control over income flows (2007, 56) and suggests participatory workshops and key informant interviews for data collection. FAO proposes *"access to and control over productive resources"* and *"access to and control over benefits"* as key areas for which gender-sensitive indicators should be applied (2016, 27), without specifying the methods. Except for AgriProFocus, SNV, and USAID, there is limited guidance on how to collect and analyse this sensitive information.

Summary assessment

All the guides seek to shed light on opportunities for gender-equitable VCD involving smallholder farmers. Most focus on women's empowerment, while only some address gender relations in value chains and the context in which they operate. The guides vary in their focus across different levels of chain actors and with regard to the attention paid to the environment in which VCD takes place. Table 6.3 reveals the emphasis for analysis and action placed by the guides across the following levels: (1) individuals, (2) households, (3) collective enterprises, (4) value chain, and (5) business and regulatory environment.

Table 6.3 shows that the guides, except BMGF, prioritise analysis and proposed action at the household level, while focusing in at the individual level for a better understanding of gender differences and inequalities between female and male household members. In addition, several guides examine gender issues along the nodes of the chain, although little attention is paid to the role of women and men in collective enterprises. Similarly, only SNV and USAID suggest in-depth analysis of policies, laws, and formal regulations affecting gender equity as part of the business and regulatory environment. In general, there is significant variation in the extent to which the guides cover the topics addressed by our assessment criteria (Table 6.4).

As Table 6.4 illustrates, the guides advocate stronger coverage of four out of the seven criteria that underlie our assessment: (1) gendered participation in the value chain; (2) enabling environment for gender-equitable VCD; (3) gendered division of household labour; and (4) gendered access to and control over household assets and VCD benefits. Even in these cases, only two to four guides – usually including SNV, AgriProFocus, USAID, and DCED – pay more attention to these. The other topics receive markedly less attention, namely the theory of change on the potential of VCD to transform gender relations and empower women and men, the normative elements that influence gender relations, and gendered participation in collective enterprises.

Table 6.3 Focus of the guides across different levels of the value chain

	ILO	USAID	BMGF	SNV	AgriProFocus	DCED	FAO
Individual	++	+++	+	+++	++	++	+++
Household	++	+++	+	++	+++	++	++
Collective enterprise	+	+	+	+	++	+	+
Value chain	+++	++	++	++	+++	+	+
Business/regulatory environment	+	++	+	+++	+	+	+

Note: strong focus (+++), some focus (++), limited focus (+)

Table 6.4 Coverage of the guides across the assessment criteria

	ILO	USAID	BMGF	SNV	AgriProFocus	DCED	FAO
Theory of change on potential of VCD to transform gender relations and empower women and men	+	++	++	++	+	+	+
Normative elements that influence gender relations	+	++	+	++	+	+	++
Enabling environment for gender-equitable VCD	++	+++	+	+++	+	+	+
Gendered participation in the value chain	++	+	+	++	+++	+	+++
Gendered participation in collective enterprises	+	+	+	+	+	++	+
Gendered division of household labour	+	+	+	++	+++	+++	+
Gendered access to and control over household assets and VCD benefits	+	++	+	++	+++	++	+

Note: strong (+++), some (++), limited /none (+)

Taking stock and looking ahead

The seven guides are grounded in theories and concepts of gender studies, particularly as regards women's empowerment, and advocate persuasively for the integration of gender into VCD. They make an important step forward in sensitising development programming on the importance of incorporating gender into the design of value chain interventions. Emphasis is placed on understanding and strengthening women's ability to benefit from value chain engagement. With farming households as the entry point for analysis, the guides focus in to help understand gender-based constraints and opportunities at the individual level, and contextualise these with a broader view on the different nodes of a chain and the business and regulatory environment in which it operates. Most guides seek to advance gender equality in terms of labour division within the chain and decision-making and distribution of benefits derived from it. To some extent, they also advocate gender-equitable access to livelihood and business assets and shared engagement in non-market livelihood activities (e.g. agricultural production for household consumption and reproductive activities).

At the same time, our review uncovers some blind spots in the conceptual and methodological underpinning for advancing gender-equitable VCD. Conceptually, the guides tend to treat economic growth and gender equality as mutually supportive goals, which VCD initiatives can help achieve if adequately designed. Theories of change on the transformative potential of VCD, as reflected in the outputs and outcomes expected from guide implementation, are premised on the notion that women and men make decisions individually, with little attention given to areas of jointness and negotiations within the household. Deeper engagement in value chains, particularly of women, would consequently be based on individual considerations, rather than household-level coordination and shared, often complementary responsibilities. Most of the guides thus envision transformation through development of women's capacities and skills, strengthening women's participation in collective enterprises, and associated changes in the enabling environment. Chant and Sweetman (2012) caution, however, that conflating the empowerment of women as individuals with the goal of removing the structural discrimination which women face recreates the very problems gender development seeks to transform. Few of the guides point to the importance of strengthening women's bargaining position within the household to enhance their capacity to make strategic household and life decisions, and to effectively negotiate the new roles or opportunities they assume within a value chain. In general, the guides underestimate the potential trade-offs between these new roles and engagement in other, non-market-oriented livelihood activities. Repercussions on women's and men's overall workload and leisure time, and trade-offs between market-oriented production and food security, go largely unaddressed. So too do the complex processes of redirecting labour and other household resources across the portfolio of livelihood activities, with varied involvement of women and men in each of them. Yet, these require specific consideration in view of their effects on individual and household well-being (Rubin and Manfre, 2014).

A deeper reflection on the effects of VCD on women's and men's well-being and household-level livelihood outcomes also requires a better understanding of masculinities. This includes attention to the potential challenges to men's idealised roles as business and community leaders and household providers as gender relations are renegotiated. In many cases, unlocking women's ability to increase their participation in market-oriented activities will hinge on men assuming a greater share of other livelihood activities, including care responsibilities within the household. Shifts in gender relations can cause anguish and backlash, including situations where men try to assert their masculinity in violent ways. Such shifts must therefore be carefully managed to support both women and men in the change process (Diallo and Voia, 2016). While in some contexts men may deliberately want to be "left out" of women-focused rural development initiatives, excluding them upfront increases the likelihood of men's disapproval or frustration with the initiative, and of women ending up with greater workloads and responsibilities.

Laudably, all the guides recommend the collection of sex-disaggregated data on gender roles. However, guidance for analysis of such data is limited and, where provided, the analytical focus tends to be on women only. Without a dual view on women and men, however, there is a risk that targeted outcomes may empower women economically but compromise their personal wellbeing and quality of life. Practitioners need clarity about how to address these complex and sensitive processes during the VCD design phase and once the interventions are underway. In particular, they would appreciate design and implementation options that stimulate a fruitful dialogue and reflection on gender norms and ways to overcome gender-based constraints. Such discussion would also help to deepen the understanding of the conditions under which women's and men's empowerment are mutually reinforcing, and those when they are at odds.

At the micro level, an opportunity exists for deeper coverage of how household and individual asset endowments, livelihood strategies, aspirations, and vulnerability influence smallholders' priorities and their options for value chain engagement. From a food security perspective, households highly constrained in land and other critical assets often orientate farm production towards their own consumption rather than the market, given the uncertainty of output prices and the cost of purchased food (see Graef et al., 2016). In contrast, households with assets above a minimum threshold stand a greater chance to assume risks and use their assets for market participation and, thus, are more likely to engage in value chains over the long term (Stoian et al., 2012). Differentiation also exists within the household, often with a strong gender dimension. For example, male members may prioritise income generation while female members may primarily seek to ensure household food security. Decisions on the use of income, however, may depend on "spousal dominance" rather than gender per se, as shown for decisions on education expenditures among ethnic groups in Indonesia exhibiting either male or female dominance (Fernandez and Kambhampati, 2017). Moreover, in terms of labour division, decision-making and asset control, households are more than the sum of individual aspirations and realisations. Guides for gender-equitable VCD will therefore benefit from greater attention to intra-household negotiations, including decisions taken jointly by men and women, with regard to the distribution of income and access to resources and the implications they hold for the design of gender-equitable VCD.

Another aspect that merits stronger attention are the contributions of VCD to positive (or negative) feedback loops of asset-building (or erosion) within the household. None of the guides considers the interplay between expenditures – based, for example, on increased income derived from VCD – and the building of different types of assets (e.g. spending of income on farm investments, nutrition and health, and education to increase natural and human capital), or their erosion (e.g. using income to buy alcohol, drugs, and other items that compromise health and household well-being). It would also be important to distinguish between assets managed predominantly by men or women, and those that are jointly managed. The latter would be particularly relevant for understanding how individual and collective outcomes can best be achieved (see Meinzen-Dick et al., 2011). In addition to differentiating between male, female, and jointly controlled household assets, the guides could better account for the complementary sets of knowledge and skills needed for building and using these. Bringing these aspects to light requires analysis that looks for both trade-offs and synergies across gendered realms of activities, assets, and benefits.

Future guidance on gender-equitable VCD also requires stronger focus on the roles of men and women in collective enterprises. Strengthening the capacity of these enterprises to address discriminatory gender norms and to provide entry points for more meaningful participation by women needs to figure prominently in initiatives for gender-equitable VCD. In support of these goals, research can show how gender relations within collective enterprises impact their business performance. In the case of microfinance institutions, for example, female chief executive officers and female board chairs were found to be positively related to their performance, though this result was not driven by improved governance (Strøm, D'Espallier, and Mersland, 2014). In a global context, it has been demonstrated that women entrepreneurs make important contributions to enterprise performance, and that the diversity and complexity of women's entrepreneurial leadership is both economically and contextually embedded (Henry et al., 2015). An enhanced understanding of the context-specific conditions that allow women to assume leadership roles in collective enterprises is critical, as is active enabling of such leadership to translate into benefits for enterprises, households, and individuals. As a first step, guides for gender-equitable VCD can draw on the VCD literature, particularly generic guides for value chain analysis and development that address leadership and management aspects at enterprise level (e.g. Bernet, Thiele, and Zschocke 2006; Lundy et al., 2007; Purcell, Gniel, and van Gent 2008; Donovan and Stoian, 2012). These aspects can then be brought under a gender lens to identify entry points for enhanced gender equality at enterprise level, as well as related benefits for business performance and well-being among members.

Methodologically, our review highlights the potential for future guides to offer more integrated and practical guidance for the design, implementation, and assessment of gender-equitable VCD. Arguably, the perceived ease of use will be a key criterion when practitioners decide which guide to select. Most guides provide general guidance on methods for analysis and development of gender-responsive intervention strategies. This may be appreciated by research and development organisations with high capacity to customise methodology and tools according to their needs and local conditions. However, development practitioners with limited research capacity and less exposure to international debates on gender likely will be challenged to specify their approach, to select the appropriate instruments, and to adapt them to a given context. Virtually all the guides omit details on implementation requirements in terms of skills, time, and budget. The extensive checklists of topics featured in most guides, with numerous considerations and questions, will pose a challenge for even the more experienced implementers. Importantly, the lack of guidance on how to interpret potentially ambiguous findings increases the risk that gender stereotypes are perpetuated rather than tackling them through differentiated analysis and action.

Finally, guides for gender-equitable VCD need to provide clear links with other value chain tools. None of the guides reviewed here claims to cover all relevant aspects of VCD. At the same time, they fall short in making reference to well-established tools covering complementary aspects of VCD. This prompts the question: to what extent are they fit for purpose as a standalone tool? In the previous sections we suggested opportunities for making explicit reference to widely adopted guides for value chain analysis and development. The task ahead is to enable practitioners to assemble an appropriate set of tools including, but not limited to, those that apply a gender lens. A recent review of VCD approaches and tools used by practitioners in Nicaragua and Vietnam brought to light that the agencies leading VCD typically rely on a single tool (Donovan, Stoian, and Poe, 2017). As most VCD interventions seek to promote multiple goals, including gender equality, practitioners will appreciate suggestions for combining a guide for gender-equitable VCD with other tools for VCD programming. Alternatively, there might be an opportunity for developing an integrated tool for VCD that adopts a gender lens for all relevant aspects, from programming and execution to monitoring and evaluation. In their current form, the practical use of the guides for gender-equitable VCD seems to lie principally in their capacity to sensitise development practitioners on the importance of, and to introduce the basics for, considering gender dimensions in VCD. They can also be used for upgrading existing systems for monitoring and evaluation of VCD initiatives to elucidate gender-differentiated effects, but they do not serve as standalone guides for effective design, implementation, and assessment of gender-equitable VCD.

Looking forward, this review points to important opportunities for a deeper integration of gender into VCD through conceptual and methodological innovation in practitioner-oriented guides. Particularly important will be the elaboration of new tools that cover to a fuller extent the capacity of households, and of women and men therein, to deepen their engagement in value chains. Such tools will employ the notion of jointness inherent in household activities, decision-making, and access to productive assets. They will also address the complementarities and frictions between women's and men's individual aspirations, capacities and benefits; and they will allow to better understand the actual and potential effects of women's and men's (separate and collective) empowerment on overall outcomes at the household and enterprise levels. Doubtless, any deeper consideration of the gender dimension in VCD adds complexity. This, in turn, requires more detailed guidance for practitioners on how to plan for gender-equitable VCD, considering the skills needed, the time required, and the additional costs incurred. Finally, a deeper understanding of the circumstances and needs of individuals, households, enterprises and other value chain actors and the complex dynamics of their interactions requires a structured process of monitoring, evaluation, and learning – another aspect to be included in future guidance on gender-equitable VCD. The refinement of guides over time will be accelerated by the availability of research findings that shed light on context-specific options for negotiating change in household and business relations, the critical factors behind the change, and resulting implications for promoting gender equality through VCD. Researchers and practitioners will benefit from deeper collaboration among themselves and joint learning with chain stakeholders to better address the "how" and "what now" questions, which have largely been absent in discussions on gender-equitable VCD.

Acknowledgements

This study was supported by the CGIAR Research Program on Policies, Institutions and Markets (PIM) and the CGIAR Research Program on Forests, Trees and Agroforestry (FTA). We thank the donors who support PIM and FTA through their contributions to the CGIAR Fund. We are also grateful to the anonymous reviewers who offered constructive suggestions to improve this chapter.

This is an open access article. It was originally published as Stoian, D., Donovan, J., Elias, M., and Blare, T. (2018) 'Fit for purpose? A review of tools for gender-equitable value chain development', *Development in Practice*, 28:4, 494-509 <https://doi.org/10.1080/09614524.2018.1447550>.

References

Bamber, P., and C. Staritz. 2016. *The Gender Dimensions of Global Value Chains.* Geneva: International Centre for Trade and Sustainable Development.
Barrientos, S., C. Dolan, and A. Tallontire. 2003. "A Gendered Value Chain Approach to Codes of Conduct in African Horticulture." *World Development* 31 (9): 1511–1526.
Bernet, T., G. Thiele, and T. Zschocke. 2006. *Participatory Market Chain Approach (PMCA) – User Guide.* Lima: International Potato Center (CIP) – Papa Andina.
Chan, M. K. 2010. "Improving Opportunities for Women in Smallholder-based Supply Chains: Business case and practical guidance for international food companies." Accessed 12 May, 2018. http://agriprofocus.com/upload/ Bill_and_Melinda_Gates_Improving_opportunities_for_women_in_small_ scale_supply_chains_-guide1428576461.pdf.

Chant, S., and C. Sweetman. 2012. "Fixing Women or Fixing the World? 'Smart Economics', Efficiency Approaches, and Gender Equality in Development." *Gender & Development* 20 (3): 517–529.

Coles, C., and J. Mitchell. 2011. *Gender and Agricultural Value Chains: A Review of Current Knowledge and Practice and Their Policy Implications*. Rome: Food and Agriculture Organization of the United Nations. Accessed 12 May, 2018. www.fao.org/3/a-am310e.pdf.

Diallo, S. A., and M. Voia. 2016. "The Threat of Domestic Violence and Women Empowerment: The Case of West Africa." *African Development Review* 28 (1): 92–103.

Donovan, J., S. Franzel, M. Cunha, A. Gyau, and D. Mithöfer. 2015. "Guides for Value Chain Development: A Comparative Review." *Journal of Agribusiness in Developing and Emerging Economies* 5 (1): 2–23.

Donovan, J., and D. Stoian. 2012. *5Capitals: A Tool for Assessing the Poverty Impacts of Value Chain Development*. Turrialba: Tropical Agricultural Research and Higher Education Center.

Donovan, J., D. Stoian, and K. Poe. 2017. "Value Chain Development in Nicaragua: Prevailing Approaches and Tools and Persistent Gaps." *Enterprise Development and Microfinance* 28 (1–2): 10–27.

Elias, M., and J. Carney. 2004. "The Female Commodity Chain of Shea Butter: Burkinabe Producers, Western Green Consumers and Fair Trade." *Cahiers de Geographie du Quebec* 48 (133): 71–88.

FAO. 2016. *Developing Gender-Sensitive Value Chains – A Guiding Framework*. Rome: Food and Agriculture Organization of the United Nations.

Ferguson, H., and T. Kepe. 2011. "Agricultural Cooperatives and Social Empowerment of Women: A Ugandan Case Study." *Development in Practice* 21 (3): 421–429.

Fernandez, A., and U. S. Kambhampati. 2017. "Shared Agency: The Dominant Spouse's Impact on Education Expenditure." *World Development* 96: 182–197.

Graef, F., G. Uckert, J. Schindler, H. J. König, H. A. Mbwana, A. Fasse, L. Mwinuka, et al., 2016. "Expert-based ex-Ante Assessments of Potential Social, Ecological, and Economic Impacts of Upgrading Strategies for Improving Food Security in Rural Tanzania Using the ScalA-FS Approach." *Food Security* 9 (6): 1–16.

Harper, M., J. Belt, and R. Roy. 2015. *Commercial and Inclusive Value Chains: Doing Good and Doing Well*. Rugby: Practical Action.

Henry, C., L. Foss, A. Fayolle, E. Walker, and S. Duffy. 2015. "Entrepreneurial Leadership and Gender: Exploring Theory and Practice in Global Contexts." *Journal of Small Business Management* 53 (3): 581–586.

Ingram, V., J. Schure, J. C. Tieguhong, O. Ndoye, A. Awono, and D. M. Iponga. 2014. "Gender Implications of Forest Product Value Chains in the Congo Basin." *Forests, Trees and Livelihoods* 23 (1–2): 67–86.

Kaplinsky, R. 2016. *Inclusive and Sustainable Growth: The SDG Value Chains Nexus*. Geneva: International Centre for Trade and Sustainable Development.

KIT, Agri-ProFocus, and IIRR. 2012. *Challenging Chains to Change: Gender Equity in Agricultural Value Chain Development*. Amsterdam: KIT Publishers.

Lundy, M., M. V. Gottret, C. Ostertag, R. Best, and S. Ferris. 2007. *Participatory Market Chain Analysis for Smallholder Producers*. Cali: International Center for Tropical Agriculture (CIAT).

Lyon, S., J. A. Bezaury, and T. Mutersbaugh. 2010. "Gender Equity in Fairtrade–Organic Coffee Producer Organizations: Cases from Mesoamerica." *Geoforum* 41 (1): 93–103.

Manchon, B., and M. Macleod. 2010. "Challenging Gender Inequality in Farmers' Organisations in Nicaragua." *Gender and Development* 18 (3): 373–386.

Markel, E. 2014. *Measuring Women's Economic Empowerment in Private Sector Development – Guidelines for Practitioners*. Cambridge: Donor Committee for Enterprise Development (DCED).

Mayoux, L., and G. Mackie. 2007. *Making the Strongest Links: A Practical Guide to Mainstreaming Gender Analysis in Value Chain Development*. Addis Ababa: International Labour Organization (ILO).

Meinzen-Dick, R., N. Johnson, A. Quisumbing, J. Njuki, J. Behrman, D. Rubin, A. Peterman, and E. Waitanji. 2011. "Gender, Assets, and Agricultural Development Programs: A Conceptual Framework." CAPRi Working Paper 99. Washington, DC: International Food Policy Research Institute (IFPRI).

Oduol, J. B. A., D. Mithöfer, F. Place, E. Nang'ole, J. Olwande, L. Kirimi, and M. Mathenge. 2017. "Women's Participation in High Value Agricultural Commodity Chains in Kenya: Strategies for Closing the Gender Gap." *Journal of Rural Studies* 50 (2017): 228–239.

Purcell, T., S. Gniel, and R. van Gent. 2008. *Making Value Chains Work Better for the Poor: A Toolbook for Practitioners of Value Chain Analysis*. London: Department for International Development.

Quisumbing, A. R., D. Rubin, C. Manfre, E. Waithanji, M. van den Bold, D. Olney, N. Johnson, and R. Meinzen-Dick. 2015. "Gender, Assets, and Market-Oriented Agriculture: Learning From High-Value Crop and Livestock Projects in Africa and Asia." *Agriculture and Human Values* 32 (4): 705–725.

Rubin, D., and C. Manfre. 2014. "Promoting Gender-Equitable Agricultural Value Chains: Issues, Opportunities, and Next Steps." In *Gender in Agriculture: Closing the Knowledge Gap*, edited by A. R. Quisumbing, R. Meinzen-Dick, T. L. Raney, A. Croppenstedt, J. H. Behrman, and A. Peterman, 287–313. Rome: FAO and Springer Science + Business Media B.V.

Rubin, D., C. Manfre, and K. Nichols Barrett. 2009. *Promoting Gender Equitable Opportunities in Agricultural Value Chains: a Handbook*. Washington, DC: US Agency for International Development.

Senders, A., A. Lentink, M. Vanderschaeghe, and J. Terrillon. 2013. *Gender in Value Chains. Practical Toolkit to Integrate a Gender Perspective in Agricultural Value Chain Development*. Arnhem: Agri-ProFocus.

Shackleton, S., F. Paumgarten, H. Kassa, M. Husselman, and M. Zida. 2011. "Opportunities for Enhancing Poor Women's Socioeconomic Empowerment in the Value Chains of Three African Non-Timber Forest Products (NTFPs)." *International Forestry Review* 13 (2): 136–151.

SOFA Team and C. Doss 2011. "The Role of Women in Agriculture." ESA Working Paper 11–02. Rome: FAO.

Stoian, D., J. Donovan, J. Fisk, and M. Muldoon. 2012. "Value Chain Development for Rural Poverty Reduction: A Reality Check and a Warning." *Enterprise Development and Microfinance* 23 (1): 54–69.

Strøm, R. O., B. D'Espallier, and R. Mersland. 2014. "Female Leadership, Performance, and Governance in Microfinance Institutions." *Journal of Banking and Finance* 42: 60–75.

Terrillon, J. 2010. *Gender Mainstreaming in Value Chain Development: Practical Guidelines and Tools*. The Hague: Corporate Network Agriculture SNV.

About the authors

Dietmar Stoian, PhD (d.stoian@cgiar.org), Lead Scientist, Value Chains, Private Sector Engagement and Investments, World Agroforestry (ICRAF), Bonn, Germany.

Jason Donovan, PhD (j.donovan@cgiar.org), Senior Economist, Research Theme Leader for Markets and Value Chains, International Maize and Wheat Improvement Center (CIMMYT), Texcoco, Mexico.

Marlène Elias (marlene.elias@cgiar.org), Senior Scientist at the Alliance of Bioversity International and CIAT, Rome, Italy.

Trent Blare (tblare@ufl.edu), University of Florida Institute of Food and Agricultural Sciences, Tropical Research and Education Center.

CHAPTER 7

Building frontline market facilitators' capacity: The case of the 'Integrating Very Poor Producers into Value Chains Field Guide'

Dan Norell

Abstract

Utilizing the case of the Integrating Very Poor Producers into Value Chains Field Guide, *the chapter provides its strengths (extensive tools and worksheets, case studies from recovery and development settings) and limitations (very brief overview of market systems, only focuses on the implementation phase of market development, only focuses on integrating the very poor into markets). The knowledge assessment results of two workshops lead the author to question how much is learned in workshop settings. The online survey showed that the most used section of the Field Guide was 'Linking Very Poor Producers with Buyers & Suppliers'. The 70 per cent experiential, 20 per cent from others, and 10 per cent formal ratios regarding learning led the author to recommend more on-the-job learning. Extensive feedback from the users provided lessons on improved tool design and capacity building for tool users. The chapter concludes with a number of recommendations: frontline workers need written guides; translate guides; include a monitoring and evaluation system; get organizational commitment to build frontline market facilitators' capacity; more research into the different methods of building capacity (workshops; written guides; a monitoring and evaluation system; and online and in person training events are likely the most effective combination).*

Keywords: value chain development, public–private partnerships, market development, market systems development, enterprise development

Development organizations often produce materials such as operational guides and training manuals, yet it is unclear if these products are being utilized by their intended audience, especially frontline field staff. The *Integrating Very Poor Producers into Value Chains Field Guide* (Field Guide) developed by World Vision under the FHI 360 FIELD Leader with Associates with USAID funding, is one such operational guide. This Field Guide, accompanying Pocket Guide and introductory video were created as resources

http://dx.doi.org/10.3362/9781788530576.007

for frontline market facilitation staff to better implement market development programmes (Norell and Brand, 2013; www.microlinks.org/library/integrating-very-poor-producers-value-chains-field-guide).

Often guides are not written for the frontline staff of development organizations. Rather 'Guides are written for researchers and experienced NGO and government staff' (Donovan et al., 2013: 14).

Documented dissemination and training is often included with the development of a document, but how the document is utilized by staff is not as easy to ascertain. Once documents such as this Field Guide are distributed and field staff trained, how can organizations increase the usage of manuals by frontline market facilitation staff to achieve more effective and higher quality programme outcomes? More importantly, how have individuals altered their projects or behaviours as a result of using the Field Guide?

To address these questions, we will examine the case of utilizing the *Integrating Very Poor Producers into Value Chains Field Guide* and examine to what extent practitioner usage is increased as a result of reading the Field Guide and attending a workshop. Through an exploration of several approaches including the consideration of this case, we plan to present lessons learned that will aid the economic development sector in the creation and dissemination of guides and manuals.

Behaviour change is a subject that is well researched within the development field as it relates to global health initiatives. However, there is limited information regarding behaviour change as it relates to work undertaken by market development frontline field staff. This chapter seeks to examine this broader area of research of market facilitator usage within the specific context of the case example of dissemination of the *Integrating Very Poor Producers into Value Chains Field Guide*.

Several approaches to building frontline market facilitators' capacity

A number of organizations have developed different approaches to building the capacity of market facilitators:

The Growing Organizational Value Chain Excellence (GROOVE) Network. CARE, CHF International (now called Global Communities), Conservation International, and Practical Action established the GROOVE Market Facilitation Mentoring Program (GROOVE network, 2014). This programme seeks to increase staff capacity as market facilitators and value chain programme managers to design, implement, and monitor market-based approaches through a nine-month training programme. The core work of the programme is done through the utilization of a mentor/ mentee relationship. Learnings from the GROOVE Market Facilitation Mentoring Program suggest significant benefits to mentees in terms of being able to share their challenges with facilitating market linkages and obtain advice and support as they attempt new approaches. The challenges with the Market Facilitation Mentoring Program included the potential tension between the mentor and the supervisor of the mentee, and the competition between mentoring activities and tasks required to do their jobs.

Engineers without Borders (EWB) Canada developed the *Practitioner's Guide to Market Facilitation: Facilitation as Behavior Change* tool (Engineers without Borders, 2012). This tool was developed to broaden the thinking of field staff and managers in market facilitation projects. The four-quadrant framework is meant to expand thinking around these barriers and challenge the assumption that capacity building is the right intervention in all cases. It was discovered that much of EWB field work was heavily concentrated on capacity building. The staff adopted a mind-set that the gap they were addressing had to do with a lack of relevant knowledge and skills. The Practitioner's Guide intends to assist project staff to think about systemic change differently from the way they would encourage one particular actor. In an example in the Practitioner's Guide, the systemic change desired is to strengthen the market for quality maize. At the trader level, this could mean adopting quality differentiated pricing. It is important that project staff keep the desired systemic change in mind as a compass to direct these actor-level changes. Through continuous exposure to the model, EWB found that frontline workers were better able to think holistically about business problems and identify issues related to conviction, role modelling, and reinforcing mechanisms, allowing them to be more adaptable facilitators.

Practical Action's *Participatory Market Systems Development* programme (Practical Action, 2014) seeks to incorporate the very poor into value chains. This programme oversees the facilitation of marginalized farmers in low-income countries to gain access to more functional markets, so they are able to sell their products and increase their income. To achieve these ends, this programme includes a number of tools and processes, including:

- *Preliminary market mapping.*
- *Hooks.* Issues that will attract and engage market actors.
- *Market opportunity groups.* Groups that represent and empower target producers.
- *Interest forums.* To convene and engage stakeholders to work together to improve the market system.
- *Participatory market mapping workshops.* To bring together market system actors around joint analysis, relationship, trust-building, and negotiation.
- *Moving from analysis to action.* Concrete actions are agreed upon by market stakeholders to improve the market system.

The Participatory Market Chain Approach (PMCA) is an approach to market development that was developed by the International Potato Center.

The PMCA engages smallholder farmers, market agents and agricultural service providers in a facilitated process that builds trust among these diverse groups and promotes collective action, which in turn leads to innovations that benefit smallholders as well as other chain actors (Horton et al., 2013).

Based on the work of the organizations described above and others, it is clear that success in market development is based on a number of good practice steps to building the capacity of field staff. First, field staff can benefit from formal or informal mentoring experiences where the staff person can share their challenges in facilitating market linkages and attain advice and support as they attempt new approaches. Second, continuous exposure to the way of working helps field workers to think about systemic solutions to business problems and identify issues related to reinforcing mechanisms. Third, to change market systems, market facilitators need to bring market system actors together to analyse the market system and negotiate actions to improve it. Fourth, adherence to guides often leads to better programme results (Horton et al., 2013: 30).

A case example from the *Integrating Very Poor Producers into Value Chains Field Guide*

World Vision has implemented a number of guides and field-based training initiatives, including the one examined in this case study, the *Integrating Very Poor Producers into Value Chains Field Guide* (Field Guide) (Norell and Brand, 2013) and the accompanying condensed Pocket Guide. The Field Guide has several sections:

I.   Understanding Very Poor Producers
II. The Market Systems Approach
III. Linking Very Poor Producers to Buyers & Sellers
IV. Linking Very Poor Producers to Other Producers

The annexes include six case studies

1. Livelihoods for Very Poor Girls and Young Women: Kenya Value Girls Program – The 'Girl Effect' – Cardno Emerging Markets
2. Agricultural Productivity Context: Promoting Agriculture, Governance and the Environment (PAGE) project – World Vision Sierra Leone
3. Food Security Context: Market Linkages with Export Firms – Haiti Multi-Year Assistance Program – World Vision Haiti
4. Food Security Context: Graduation from Food Aid – Productive Safety Net Program Plus – CARE Ethiopia
5. Post-Conflict Context: Working with Producer Groups – ProRENDA Project – World Vision Angola
6. Recovery Context: Working with Producer Groups – Cyclone Livelihoods Recovery project – World Vision Bangladesh

The Field Guide provides accessible information for field staff to use to implement market development programmes. World Vision has held field-based trainings on Field Guide utilization in Bangladesh, Ethiopia, Haiti, Tanzania,

Malawi, and Ghana. Training sessions have also been held in the Washington, DC area both within World Vision and with the broader development community, including a one-day training at two of the annual SEEP conferences. The SEEP Network also hosted three webinars on the Field Guide: 1) overview; 2) supplier–producer–buyer market linkages (http://vimeo.com/60278784); and 3) producer–producer linkages (http://vimeo.com/66860108). Alongside the content presented, webinar participants were encouraged to engage in a chat format through which they had the opportunity to ask questions of other participants and of presenters regarding their experiences and thoughts.

The Field Guide fills a gap in the literature by providing very practical tools for frontline community-level market facilitators. Its strengths include the following:

- The 24 tools and worksheets provide the frontline market facilitator with two-page, fill-in-the-blank worksheets that guide their facilitation of improved commercial relationships between producers and input suppliers and output market buyers.
- The six case studies provide practical field examples of how to integrate very poor producers into markets in recovery and development settings.

The limitations of the Field Guide include:

- only a very brief section on market systems;
- a focus only on the implementation phase of market development;
- a focus on integrating very poor producers into markets rather than trying to work with the entire market system.

Methodology

In 2013, the Economic Development Senior Technical Advisor at World Vision Inc. in Washington, DC, Dan Norell, co-facilitated economic development workshops in Ghana for West Africa and Malawi for Southern Africa. These workshops, similar to previous workshops conducted in Bangladesh, Ethiopia, Tanzania, and Haiti, were positioned to provide field workers with an overview of value chain approaches and tools by training in the *Integrating Very Poor Producers into Value Chains Field Guide*. The workshop sessions included understanding the context of very poor producers; linking very poor producers to buyers and suppliers by building trust and facilitating win–win relationships; factors impacting producer-to-producer linkages including the lack of participation in value chains by women, the lack of confidence and trust between producers and buyers/suppliers, and the limited ability of the very poor to take on risk.

Both regional workshops lasted three days and were attended by 110 field practitioners, including government officials, representatives of national and international NGOs, and representatives of the private sector involved in public–private partnerships.

Table 7.1 Knowledge assessment results

West Africa Regional Workshop in Ghana	
Average pre-test scores	11.4 correct /20 questions
Average post-test scores	12.3 correct /20 questions
Total average score improvement after workshop	7.9%
Southern Africa Regional Workshop in Malawi	
Average pre-test scores	7.37 correct /11 questions
Average post-test scores	8.12 correct /11 questions
Total average score improvement after workshop	10.2%

Workshop facilitators gave pre- and post-tests to workshop participants to assess their market development knowledge on the first and last days of the workshop. The first knowledge assessment consisted of 20 questions distributed to NGO, government, and private sector workshop participants at the first day of the West Africa Regional Workshop held in Accra, Ghana. The same assessment was distributed at the end of the three-day workshop, and the results were compiled, with each participant's responses analysed. If a participant responded to one assessment, but not the other, their responses were not included in the final analysis. The length of time it took workshop participants to complete the assessment (40 minutes) was deemed too long for the workshop context. The assessment was reduced to 11 questions (20 minutes) for the Southern Africa Regional Workshop held in Malawi.

Discussion of the results

The results suggest that both West Africa and Southern Africa workshop participants saw an increase in average test scores after the workshop. Southern Africa Regional workshop participants experienced higher improvement scores of 10.2 per cent compared with 7.9 per cent in West Africa (see Table 7.1). Although both workshop scores improved, the percentage increment is relatively low. This may have been a result of methodological challenges. First, although there was a total of 110 participants at the West and Southern Africa Regional workshops, only 62 participants (56 per cent) engaged in both the pre- and post-knowledge assessment. Some participants only participated in one or the other test because of coming in late to the workshop or leaving the workshop early. Also, there were some tests that were incomplete and could not be accurately scored. The results may have been different if more participants took both assessments.

Second, the pre-test results may have been influenced, as World Vision staff received two days of training on value chain development prior to taking the pre-test. This may have given World Vision practitioners a higher pre-test score, explaining the relatively low improvement scores between the pre-test and the post-test.

Third, West africa regional workshop participants had a longer knowledge assessment test, possibly adversely affecting participants' performance. There may also have been professional cultural barriers in both workshops that come into play with test-taking. Most workshops do not administer pre- and post-tests to adult NGO, government, private sector, and farmer workshop participants. Although verbal translations of the pre- and post-tests were given to workshop participants, the questionnaire was in English. Therefore, non-English speakers, particularly the French speakers in the West Africa workshop, may have struggled with the language barrier.

In a careful analysis of the test results of each workshop participant who had a worse score from the pre-test to post-test, several patterns emerged. For persons with prior knowledge in value chain development, it seemed that they scored better with the morning pre-test than the late Friday afternoon post-test. Since this was the last activity at the workshop on Friday afternoon, many workshop participants may have hurried through the written test to be able to begin their travel home, get to their emails, or to see their families.

It is important to consider whether or not the workshops were effective, although the workshop evaluations from the participants indicated a high level of appreciation. The West Africa Regional Workshop evaluations had an average score of 4 out of 5. The Southern Africa Regional Workshop participants gave the workshop for content a score of 4.67, for presenters 4.6, and relevance 4.74 out of 5. The follow-up survey described below indicates a lot of usage of the Field Guide. Given the relatively minor increases in the pre- and post-test scores, there are questions about the effectiveness of workshops in general to impart new knowledge, build the capacity of frontline field staff, and improve the performance of market development programmes.

Knowledge assessment analysis

Through the pre-test and post-test knowledge assessment, gaps in the current knowledge of workshop participants may be detected. It is important to address such gaps in order to maximize the utilization of operational guides. Table 7.2 gives an example of one such gap in knowledge.

The results of the knowledge assessment imply that there is a common gap among frontline staff. Having identified the gap through the assessment, it is essential to go back and correct any aspects of misinformation, as these field staff will be the ones passing on this information to their colleagues.

The *Integrating Very Poor Producers into Value Chains Field Guide* dedicates a section (page 76) to the importance of increasing a family's ability to take on risk; one such way is through the diversification of income. The importance of the diversification of income sources was also discussed at the USAID Microenterprise and Private Enterprise Promotion (MPEP) Seminar *What Will It Take to Transform African Agriculture?* (USAID, 2013), where it was emphasized by Professor Thom Jayne of Michigan State University that, 'Small farmers need to increase their sources of income to increase income and reduce risks'.

Table 7.2 Gap in knowledge

Knowledge assessment question	Number of participants answered incorrectly	Is this addressed in the Field Guide?
True/False: Taking on multiple sources of low-income activities increases a producer's or household's risk compared to seeking higher income activity Answer: *False*	65%	Section IV: linking very poor producers to other producers: *What can I do to assist very poor producers to be comfortable taking on more risk?* (p. 73)

Market facilitators need to encourage profitable on- and off-farm economic activities. It is important that market development programme managers reinforce with the frontline market facilitators the need for targeted households to diversify sources of income.

Online user survey analysis

Approximately two months after each workshop, an online follow-up survey was sent to workshop participants on their usage and understanding of the Field Guide. The survey questions asked whether or not workshop participants had used the Field Guide, had shared it with other colleagues, and what parts of the Field Guide they used the most. Out of 110 workshop participants, 66 participants, or 60 per cent, completed the online user survey sent after the workshop. Farmers who attended the workshop but did not have access to the internet were contacted via phone. This feedback is important to understand the effectiveness of an organization's operational guides. As previously mentioned, formal training workshops do not necessarily lead to behaviour changes, thus it is vital to understand whether participants change their behaviour after a workshop. Through the survey responses, it became clear that most participants felt they gained positively from the workshops. The utilization survey response was that 63 per cent of participants referred back to the content of the Field Guide after the workshop, while 81 per cent of participants shared the Field Guide with their colleagues. Participants mentioned that they used the worksheets and case studies in the Field Guide to facilitate workshops for frontline market facilitators. Twenty-four per cent of participants stated that they use the Field Guide at least once a month, while other participants who had not yet used the Field Guide mentioned that they were intending to incorporate it into the following quarter.

Table 7.3 shows the percentage of workshop participants who had used the Field Guide.

Some of the quotations from those who listed 'other' stated:

It will be used in the next workshop.

I have been using the Field Guide when we have needed any information related to value chain approach.

Table 7.3 Field Guide usage frequency

I use the Field Guide	Percentage
once a month	24
I have not used it yet	18
once a week	12
every day	8
other	37

I have not directly used it in the field, but knowledge of it is essential for project coordination.

Although 69 per cent of participants were representatives of international NGOs, farmers who were leaders in their producer groups were invited to the workshops as Subject Matter Experts. The farmers also had positive feedback on the Field Guide and the workshop. A Malawian farmer who attended the workshop said:

After the workshop, I revised the key areas of interest, especially value [chain] approach. It gave me an understanding on how the different actors are coordinated in the chain and how farmers can benefit; I also learned the importance of being in groups. I went back to brief my committee members. This gave us the urge to re-organize our team according to the different value chains. We have also taken steps to encourage the very poor to join savings groups to access loans to finance the value chains. As a group we have endorsed decisions that do not discriminate [against] the very poor. For example, we buy inputs in bulk as a group.

Another Malawian farmer who attended the workshop also discussed his most important learnings: '[I learnt] about the value chain approach and the importance of understanding different situations of producers in order to find tailor-made solutions for their challenges'.

Table 7.4 concerns those who had not used the Field Guide and lists some of the reasons workshop respondents gave for not using the Field Guide.

Some of the quotations from the 38 per cent who stated 'other' included: Would like a translation to Market Facilitator languages

I am developing my functional area strategy within which this will be used

I have integrated it into next year's budget when we will start implementing it

A Ghana workshop participant stated, '… knowledge of value chains is essential for my role'. This concept was also apparent through another participant in Ghana as she stated, 'Parts were used to enrich my presentations on

Table 7.4 Reasons for not using the Field Guide

If you have not used the Field Guide, what are the reasons for not using it?	Percentage
It would take some planning to use and integrate. I have not had the time to do so	20
My role would be to show or encourage others to use it which I have not yet had the time or opportunity to do	21
It is not directly relevant to my job activities and so I have not had the opportunity to use it	7
I have not had time to read it, look at it, or use it	3
The English is too difficult	3
other	38

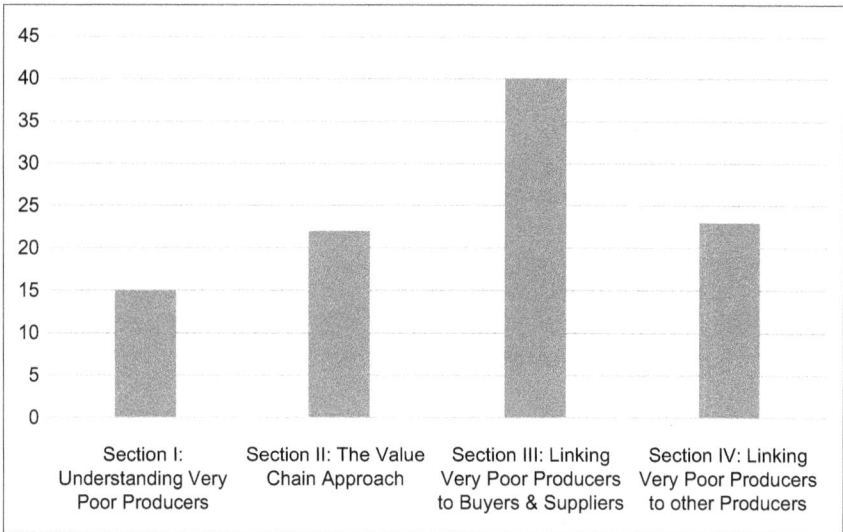

Figure 7.1 Most used sections of the Field Guide.

value chain workshops'. The respondents were also asked what the most used section of the Field Guide was (see Figure 7.1).

Discussion of results

Although there was a great deal of positive feedback from the online user survey, there were also some recommendations that organizations should take into account when developing and rolling out operational guides such as the *Integrating Very Poor Producers into Value Chains Field Guide*. Twenty-seven per cent of participants stated that they would not require any further support to use the Field Guide, and 53 per cent of participants suggested that further assistance in terms of extra support from a mentor, support meetings, webinars, or ongoing workshops would help them use the Field Guide more effectively. Thus, organizations may need to include mentoring, additional webinars, and ongoing workshops so that field staff may better understand operational guides such as the Field Guide.

There has also been additional dissemination of the Field Guide. Since the Field Guide was posted on the USAID Microlinks website in October 2012, it has been:

- accessed 2,600 times ...
- by 2,106 unique users ...
- in more than 50 countries (top 10: US, India, Ethiopia, Kenya, Bangladesh, Canada, UK, Philippines, Vietnam, Pakistan);
- accessed by users spending an average of more than 5 minutes on the landing page, which means it is likely they watched the video and downloaded the PDF of the Field Guide (the site average is only 2 minutes).

According to a knowledge management specialist, the Field Guide is the most accessed library resource on Microlinks. Also, over 800 physical copies of the Field Guide have been distributed at workshops and other venues.

The challenge of workshop learning is that there is a limited amount of knowledge that is retained for on-the-job usage. The 70:20:10 model asserts that employees acquire their knowledge in three ways (see Figure 7.2):

- 70 per cent acquired informally: on the job including stimulation such as stretch projects, delegation, and job rotation
- 20 per cent acquired from others: through mentoring, coaching, daily contact with managers and colleagues, and communities of practice
- 10 per cent acquired through formal learning: courses, training, and workshops

While the Field Guide provides 22 tools and worksheets for market facilitators from the Women's Participation Improvement Tool to the

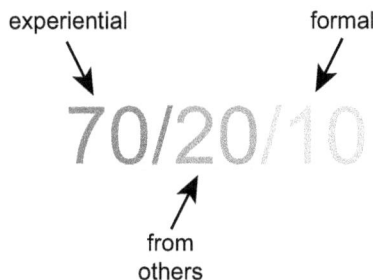

Figure 7.2 How people acquire learning.
Source: Cross, 2012

supplier–Producer–Buyer Trust Building Tool, organizations utilizing written operational guides need to foster the 70 per cent experiential learning.

Organizations can benefit from operational guides such as the Field Guide through on-the-job learning by:

(a) emphasizing the high-value learning activities **within employees' existing work;**
(b) **Boosting the relevance of what employees learn** from their activities;
(c) Equipping employees with **simple, scalable tools and support** that enable them to **move from action to reflection to application** (Corporate Executive Board, 2008).

Respondents reported that Section III: Linking Very Poor Producers to Buyers & Suppliers was the most used section (40 per cent). This likely reflects the need for market facilitators to use the tools in this section to work to build win–win relationships between producers and the input suppliers and the output market buyers.

Regarding sharing the Field Guide with others, survey respondents stated that they had used the Field Guide for:

1. Capacity building (training staff, savers in savings groups, government staff)
2. Project design (concept papers, multiyear planning)
   • project planning (revise detailed implementation plans)
3. Project implementation
   • building stronger supplier–producer and producer–buyer market linkages;
     • presented the Field Guide ideas on supplier–producer–buyer linkages to companies;
     • arranged for a buyer for female Shea butter producers;
     • linked farmer group to a seed company;
     • used concepts to guide 'project staff who thought the best way to support poor producers was to eliminate the "middle men" in all scenarios';
   • building stronger producer-to-producer relationships;
     • meetings with fish producers and cassava producers, training lead farmers on how best to manage producer-to-producer relationships

In terms of feedback from the respondents on portions of the Field Guide and Pocket Guide that were too difficult to understand, they stated: 'the concept of value chain development should be more clearly defined in the Field Guide rather than being referred to another source'.

Regarding recommended changes to the Field Guide that would make it more useful or easier to use, the respondents suggested:

• *Case examples.* 'More success stories and practical examples [from] around the globe'; 'The examples should include other products other than agriculture, e.g. handicraft, domestic products';

- *Project design.* Logframes and budgets;
- *Financial services.* 'Need a clear link between value chain and savings';
- *Value chain analysis.* 'Issues of Value Chain Selection and Mapping do not come out clearly in the Guide. If this could be incorporated in the guide [it] could be rich in content';
- *Conceptual model(s).* 'Add more flesh to the concept of value chain (in depth on value chain) so that it can be especially easier for the village agents to articulate and facilitate';
- *Translations.* 'Translated into our local languages so that it can be easily used by;
- the local marketing facilitators who mostly use the local language';
- *More visual.* 'DVD should be attached to the Field Guide'.

Lessons on improved tool design and capacity building for tool users

1. *In terms of capacity building, tools need to be easy to use and easy to teach others.* It was positive that trainees of a three-day course were able, in turn, to train NGO staff, government staff, and beneficiaries. This shows that the training was effective enough to be able to be shared with others.
2. *With project design tools need to be able to contribute to a clear description at the activity level of a logframe.* While the Field Guide was clearly designed for the implementation phase of the project cycle, workshop participants were able to use it in the planning and design phase as well. To further build the capacity of tool users with project design, development organizations need to have feedback from the monitoring and evaluation components of a project to continually improve project design.
3. *Regarding building stronger supplier–producer and producer–buyer market linkages, tool users need clear guidance on how to build trust in commercial relationships where there has often been mistrust in the past.* It was quite gratifying to learn that the Supplier–Producer–Buyer section of the Field Guide was the most used section (40 per cent). The Field Guide and training on the Field Guide empowered users to present the possibilities of improved market linkages with farmers to companies, facilitate market linkages, arrange for buyers, help producers to have a point person for marketing, and provide training on marketing.

   Producer–buyer relationships have been fraught with mistrust. The farmers often believe that the buyers use different size cans to take advantage of the farmer (Norell and Brand, 2013: 38). Any market development set of tools needs to ensure improved checks and balances between farmers and buyers.
4. *Regarding technical terminology, any suite of tools needs to use plain language that is understandable to NGO workers, government extension agents, buyers, suppliers, and, most of all, producers.* The co-authors wrote the Field Guide with frontline, community-based NGO workers as the primary users. Still there were users who wanted clearer language and simpler terminology.

5. *Tools need to be translated into local languages for frontline staff to use.* While the entire Field Guide is in English, the shorter Pocket Guide has also been translated into Spanish, French, and Portuguese.
6. *Tools need to use a lot of case studies to illustrate the point the author is trying to make.* The Field Guide has six case studies in the annexes. Based on the feedback, it seems that it would have been helpful to have more sections of the case studies inserted throughout the main body of the Field Guide to better illustrate the programme guidance in each section.
7. *Any comprehensive market development suite of tools should have financial services included.* The content of the Field Guide was focused on the implementation phase and did not include linkage to financial services. In earlier drafts of the Field Guide there were sections on financial services, but the authors felt that they could not do justice to linkage to financial services and still keep the Field Guide to a manageable length.
8. *Any comprehensive market development guide should include value chain selection and mapping.* In order to focus on the implementation phase of the project cycle, the authors of the Field Guide did not include value chain selection and mapping. However, some of the survey respondents clearly wanted value chain selection and mapping to be part of the Field Guide.
9. *Any comprehensive market development guide needs to include a section on conceptual models.* Since the primary audience was to be frontline workers, the authors of the Field Guide decided to have only a very brief section on the market system approach.

The authors felt that Field Guide users could get a much more thorough grounding in the conceptual approach from either their own organization or from market development guides that included more of a conceptual framework and the entire project cycle. The importance of a conceptual model and development approach is outlined in 'Lapses, infidelities and creative adaptions: Lessons from evaluation of a participatory market development approach in the Andes' (Horton et al., 2013). The authors stress the importance of following a market development model.

10. In the more visual world of today, any suite of tools should be accompanied with visual resources.
11. A suite of tools should also have visuals that illustrate the concepts. The Field Guide could have included one-page posters that could be photocopied and used for training or posters on a wall. *Tool designers need to develop feedback loops to get feedback from frontline staff.*

In the development of the Field Guide, the developers were careful to get feedback from staff on the concepts, tools, and worksheets that would be most relevant. Tool designers may also want to consider online platforms for feedback, but realizing that frontline market facilitators do have limitations of connectivity.

Recommendations on the dissemination of guides

Based on the experience of the dissemination of the Field Guide, the following recommendations are made:

1. *Provide written operational guides that can be shared with frontline workers.* With the utilization surveys, the workshop participants report a fairly high utilization rate of 63 per cent and sharing rate of 81 per cent. This is a positive development in the dissemination of the Field Guide. With 2,106 unique users from more than 50 countries, the Field Guide has been made available throughout the global development community.

   Operational guides need to be user friendly for frontline staff who have limited time, internet connectivity, and sometimes only a few hours of electricity in a work day. They need to be able to photocopy one or two pages to take to a meeting with an input supplier, output market buyer, or producer group leadership.

2. *Provide written translated operational guides in major languages and, where feasible, local languages.* While the accompanying Pocket Guide is available in English, Spanish, French, and Portuguese, the full Field Guide is currently only available in English. The lack of translations for the Field Guide limits the effectiveness of knowledge transfer to frontline market facilitators. In the utilization survey, respondents pointed out the limitation of a document only in English.

3. *Any capacity-building effort such as the development of manuals and implementing workshops needs to be accompanied by measurement of individual and programme performance through a monitoring and evaluation system.* Another limitation of the capacity-building efforts associated with the dissemination of the Field Guide is that there was no measure of the individual or programme performance levels. A well-designed and implemented monitoring and evaluation system holds staff accountable for improving their individual capacity and also programmatic results.

   Any learning system (written manual, workshop, online learning) needs to be accompanied by the organizational commitment to understand and measure improved capacity and performance of frontline market facilitators.

   As one experienced manager of a development organization stated, 'The only time I changed my behaviour and adapted new techniques was because the donor or my manager required it' (Practitioner interview, May 2013).

4. *Given the importance of on-the-job learning, any operational guide will optimally be included as part of an online learning programme that also includes face-to-face meetings.* Online learning programmes provide a new way for operational guides, such as the Field Guide, to be utilized by frontline staff. World Vision is implementing an online learning programme for frontline market facilitators that includes the Field Guide as part of the resource materials. The online course allows participants to learn about

market development principles and apply them to their frontline market facilitation job with the support of their peers and mentors from other market facilitation projects around the world.

5. *More research is needed on how to better build the skills of market facilitators, comparing the relative effectiveness of webinars, regional workshops, technical training events, distribution of hard copies of operational guides, and incorporating the operational guide within the market development model of the development organization.* With this case example of the Field Guide, the promoters used a combination of internet downloads, SEEP Network webinars, regional workshops, technical training events at the SEEP Annual Conference, physical distribution, and incorporation of the operational guide within a market development project model. As mentioned above, World Vision intends to roll out an online certification series of modules for frontline market facilitators.

6. *Workshops combined with a written operational guide, a comprehensive monitoring and evaluation system, and online and/or in-person training series are likely to be most effective for building organizational commitment to and skills in a market development approach.* Workshops can build enthusiasm within and across organizations for effective market development. A written operational guide, such as the Field Guide, provides just-in-time information for frontline market facilitators to successfully conduct a meeting with suppliers and producers or buyers and producers. The written guide should also be complemented with DVDs, posters, and videos. Online and/or in-person training series are likely to be most effective for building the capacity of frontline market facilitators.

Acknowledgment

The author thanks those who provided research and contributed to this chapter, including Sara DuBois, Stephen Gannon, Samantha Hinkle, Joanna Patouris, and Hanna Woodburn.

References

Cross, J. (2012) 'Why corporate training is broken and how to fix it', *Inside Learning Technologies & Skills* November 2012 [online] <http://viewer.zmags.com/publication/847ec6ea#/847ec6ea/1> [accessed 15 May 2014].

Donovan, J., Cunha, M., Franzel, S., Gyau, A. and Mithofter, D. (2013) *Guides for Value Chain Development: A Comparative Review*, Wageningen, the Netherlands: Technical Center for Agricultural and Rural Cooperation (CTA).

Engineers without Borders (2012) 'A practitioner's guide to market facilitation: facilitation as behavior change' [website] USAID's Microlinks <www.microlinks.org/library/practitionersguide-market-facilitation-facilitation-behavior-change> [accessed 3 October 2013].

Growing Organizational Value Chain Excellence (GROOVE) network (2014) *Market Facilitation Mentoring Program: Administrator's Guide* [pdf] USAID Microlinks <www.microlinks.org/sites/microlinks/files/resource/files/GROOVE-AdminGuide-508_0.pdf> [accessed 3 October 2013].

Horton, D., Rotondo, E., Ybarnegaray, R., Hareau, G., Devaux, A. and Thiele, G. (2013) 'Lapses, infidelities, and creative adaptations: lessons from evaluation of a participatory market development approach in the Andes', *Evaluation and Program Planning* 39: 28–41 <http:// dx.doi.org/10.1016/j.evalprogplan.2013.03.002>.

Norell, D. and Brand, M. (2013) *Integrating Very Poor Producers into Value Chains Field Guide* [online] USAID Microlinks <http://microlinks.kdid.org/library/integrating-very-poorproducers-value-chains-field-guide> [accessed 19 May 2014].

Practical Action (2014) 'Participatory market systems development' [website] <http://practicalaction.org/participatory-market-systems-development> [accessed 3 October 2013].

The Corporate Executive Board Company (2008) *Unlocking the Value of On-the-Job Learning* [pdf] <http://greatmanager.ucsf.edu/files/On_the_Job_Learning.pdf> [accessed 3 October 2013].

USAID (2013) 'What will it take to transform African agriculture: 2013–2030' [website] MPEP seminar series <http://microlinks.kdid.org/sites/microlinks/files/resource/files/MPEP%20Seminar%204_FINAL.pdf?file=http://microlinks.kdid.org/sites/microlinks/files/resource/files/MPEP%20Seminar%204_FINAL.pdf&nid=6695> [accessed 24 April 2014].

World Vision (2013) 'Local value chain development' [website] <http://lvcd.wordpress.com> [accessed 3 October 2013].

About the author

Dan Norell (dnorell@worldvision.org), Senior Technical Advisor, Economic Development on the Food Security & Livelihoods Team, World Vision, Washington, D.C. Dan will become an independent consultant in economic development in January 2021.

CHAPTER 8

Value chain development in Nicaragua: Prevailing approaches and tools used for design and implementation

Jason Donovan, Dietmar Stoian, and Keith Poe

Abstract

This chapter draws on four contrasting cases of value chain development (VCD) in Nicaragua to assess approaches and tools used in design and implementation. We interviewed 28 representatives from the international NGOs leading the interventions, the local NGOs that participated in implementation, principal buyers, and cooperatives. Despite the complexity of market systems, results showed a relatively basic approach to VCD, reflected in: 1) reliance on a single tool for design and implementation; 2) expected outcomes based on technical assistance and training for smallholders and cooperatives; 3) local NGOs and cooperatives with key roles in implementation; and 4) limited engagement with other chain actors, service providers, and researchers. We conclude with a call for a broader approach to VCD, based on a combination of tools to account for multiple, context-specific needs of diverse stakeholders, deeper collaboration between key actors within and outside the value chain, and evidence-based reflection and learning.

Keywords: business services, agriculture, smallholders, NGOs, rural development, methodologies and tools, impact

Value Chain Development (VCD) is defined here as the process by which government agencies, NGOs, and private companies engage with smallholders and their businesses (e.g. co-ops and producer associations) to reduce poverty, increase the efficiency of value chains, and enhance their environmental and social performance. VCD has emerged as a major area of rural development programming (Seville et al., 2011; Devaux et al., 2016). Interest in VCD mainly stems from an increased commitment to poverty reduction (Humphrey and Navas-Alemán, 2010) and the awareness that commercial success in relatively complex agrifood value chains requires intense collaboration among chain actors, including producers, processors, and retailers (Hobbs et al., 2000; Humphrey and Memedovic, 2006). The rapid growth in demand for products in which smallholders are considered to have a comparative

http://dx.doi.org/10.3362/9781788530576.008

advantage – e.g. horticultural products that require high labour inputs – can provide a strong incentive for private sector collaboration in VCD processes, for example to reduce risks associated with raw material sourcing and to comply with corporate social responsibility or similar standards. By focusing on the nature and quality of interactions and institutional arrangements between chain actors, VCD offers an opportunity to address common problems and design interventions with potential to generate win–win outcomes. Improved relations among chain actors are expected to yield tangible benefits in terms of overall chain performance and, under certain conditions, poverty reduction (Cattaneo et al., 2010).

In addition to the interactions and arrangements between chain actors, VCD processes typically involve external organizations, often NGOs, which support VCD in pursuit of broader development goals, in many cases with financial support from various sources (e.g. bilateral donors, government agencies, and large-scale businesses). NGOs engage with chain actors to determine the scope and modalities of external support, including the sharing of information, resources, benefits, and risks. The design of VCD approaches that effectively respond to the needs and realities of poor chain actors and build a solid basis for long-term chain growth and consolidation is no small task. The effectiveness of external support depends, in part, on the capacity of external organizations to anticipate the responses of smallholder households who typically face trade-offs when committing their own resources to VCD at the expense of other livelihood activities (Stoian et al., 2012). Gender relations, organizational and management capacities of cooperatives, availability of complementary technical, business, and financial services, and overall market conditions also shape the design of interventions and their ultimate outcomes. Moreover, the needs of chain actors may change during VCD implementation in response to market trends, changes in the regulatory framework, specific conditions of given chain actors, and new insights gained during the VCD process.

These complex factors, both internal and external to a given value chain, need to be understood and adequately addressed when embarking on a VCD initiative. A decade ago, this journal featured considerable debate on options for the design of market-oriented interventions with smallholders that preceded a broader value chain discourse. Chapters by Lusby and Derks (2006), Albu and Griffith (2006), and Meyer-Stamer (2006), for example, presented a logical case for the design of VCD interventions based on extensive field experience in given countries and with actors engaged in a particular value chain. During the early discussion on VCD, these chapters provided useful insights into how VCD could advance rural development goals. After roughly a decade of continued proliferation of VCD, however, there is a need for cross-cutting analysis on what approaches and tools are used for VCD design and implementation and what gaps exist in terms of tool coverage and implementation strategies. This paper seeks to contribute to such analysis by drawing on four contrasting cases of VCD initiatives from Nicaragua, a country where VCD approaches have featured prominently in efforts to address rural poverty.

Methodology

We analysed secondary information and conducted key informant interviews in Managua, where NGOs and government agencies engaged in VCD are headquartered, to gain an overview of the various interventions in VCD under implementation or recently completed. We then selected four cases – dairy, cocoa, coffee, and horticulture – based on the following criteria: 1) current phase of intervention was near completion or recently completed (last 12 months); 2) interventions implied a range of services provided directly to one or more chain actors; and 3) key stakeholders were willing to participate in interviews and share documentation. These cases cover diverse conditions in terms of product (perishable vs. non-perishable), target market (national vs. export), and need for labour and other inputs. Each case involved a selected number of small-holders, a cooperative, principal buyers, and a partnership between an international NGO and various local NGOs. None of the cases involved VCD led by government agencies – a possible limitation of this study. In two of the cases (dairy, horticulture), the VCD initiative began as an NGO-led project in collaboration with local actors, while in the other two (cocoa, coffee), a large-scale buyer initiated the VCD process in collaboration with local organizations, joined later on by an international NGO.

Primary data was collected in 2016 through 28 structured interviews with representatives of the NGOs leading the VCD interventions, principal buyers, and the cooperatives as representatives of the smallholders engaged in each chain. For each case, we identified the key elements of the NGO-led intervention, such as facilitation of information or inputs, training, and technical, business, or financial assistance to smallholders, their business organizations, and other value chain actors (Table 8.1). Within each lead NGO, interviews involved the intervention (project) leader and two or three other key staff. Areas covered in the interview included: 1) key elements of the VCD approach; 2) tools applied in VCD design and implementation; 3) key partners for implementation; 4) major achievements; 5) principal challenges faced; and 6) perceptions of needs for improved VCD design, implementation, and assessment. Interviews with cooperative representatives focused on achievements and bottlenecks during the VCD process, relations with principal buyers and service providers, including the lead NGO, and needs for future support. Eight cooperatives (two per case) were sampled, and the lead NGOs were consulted with regard to their selection to ensure that variation in terms of capacity and experience in the VCD process was captured. Finally, interviews with the principal buyers covered the strengths and limitations of their relations with the cooperatives and the lead NGO, their achievements in the VCD process, and bottlenecks for deeper collaboration. In most cases, there was only one principal buyer. In the dairy case, there were two buyers, but only one was available for participation in this study.

Results

Lead NGOs

As shown in Table 8.1, all lead NGOs were international organizations that have been active in Nicaragua since the 1990s, if not earlier. In all cases, the NGOs were well connected to national-level rural development circles and enjoyed strong contacts with bilateral donors, government agencies, and large-scale businesses. Their activities in VCD were more recent, beginning between 2005 and 2008. This period coincides with the signing (2004) and ratification (2005–2007) of the Free Trade Agreement between the United States, Central America, and the Dominican Republic (DR-CAFTA) – a time when many bilateral donors allocated resources to promoting increased trade capacity of Central American countries, including Nicaragua. At the time of data collection, the budget managed by the NGOs for the selected VCD initiatives ranged from about US$2 m to $10 m, over a period of four or five years. Each lead NGO had mobilized funding for its VCD work from a bilateral donor (only in one case co-investments were made by a major buyer), and all of them expected less funding for VCD-related work in the near future – perhaps more a reflection of overall donor retrenchment in Nicaragua than of waning donor interest in VCD.

Table 8.2 presents the key features of VCD design. Two of the lead NGOs used the Link methodology (Lundy et al., 2012) for designing their intervention, while the others relied on the inclusive Business methodology elaborated by SNV (2008) or a unique methodological approach they designed for their intervention. There were no reports of other guides, methodologies, or tools used for VCD interventions, for example for addressing gender equity, impact assessment, the business environment, cooperative development, monitoring and evaluation, or joint learning. The actual selection of the chain for intervention considered the NGOs' experience in a given chain (and interest in building a reputation for work in certain chains), along with the anticipated income generation potential for small-holders. In some cases, criteria were established for smallholder participation (e.g. 10 dairy cows per household) in the intervention, while in none of the cases were explicit steps taken to identify the poorest segments of the rural population and encourage their participation. Monitoring and evaluation was carried out in response to donor requirements. In all cases, the VCD initiative in question was a follow-up on previous, similarly designed interventions. Initiatives aimed to reach 1,250 to 5,500 smallholder households, organized into 6–25 cooperatives. Three of the cases were fully funded by bilateral donors. The other case (coffee) was financed through a partnership between the Dutch Government and a large-scale coffee buyer. In general, direct private sector investment in supporting

Table 8.1 Overview of VCD cases selected for research

Case	Start year	Local chain actors	External service provider(s)	Brief description
Cocoa	1990	Initially 1 co-op, later grew to 6; 1 international buyer	Lead NGO: established locally in 1998, designed and monitored project Local NGOs: implementation of activities with households and co-ops	Cocoa buyer collaborated several years with local NGO to restart cocoa production (1990–2005). The collaboration evolved into a business endeavour in 2005 with project funds that supported the purchase of a warehouse, support to the co-op, and technical assistance. Collaboration with the lead NGO followed in 2009.
Coffee	2008	11 co-ops; 1 international buyer	Lead NGO: established locally in 1991, responsible for design, implementation, and monitoring	First phase of VCD began in 2008 to improve productivity of coffee plantations between the lead NGO and a major coffee buyer. A second, more intensive phase began in 2013 in response to the spread of coffee rust disease. Buyer provided 50% of project investment, with the aim to ensure supply of coffee through smallholder renovation of coffee plantations.
Horticulture	2005	17 co-ops; 6 large processors; 2 major buyers	Lead NGO: established locally in 1946, designed and monitored project Local NGOs: implementation of activities with smallholders	The lead NGO aimed to help smallholders improve productivity and quality of horticulture supplied to demanding supermarkets in major cities. NGO support has focused strongly on facilitating the links with local supermarkets, building co-op capacity, and facilitating technical assistance to smallholders.
Dairy	2013	25 co-ops, 4 large buyers	Lead NGO: established locally in 1976, responsible for design, implementation, and monitoring	Lead NGO efforts sought to increase income and productivity from small-scale dairy operations to supply the growing national demand for higher quality dairy products. The lead NGO had previous experience in smallholder livestock production from previous projects.

Table 8.2 Design features of the VCD interventions

Case	Methodology used	Source of funding for interventions	Target beneficiaries	Major lines of action (in order of budget allocation)	Gender focus
Cocoa	Link	100% bilateral donor	1,250 smallholders 6 co-ops	Smallholders: technical assistance to increase yields Co-ops: financial and administrative management, legal assistance	None
Coffee	Inclusive Business	50% bilateral donor 50% private sector	3,441 smallholders 11 co-ops	Smallholders: technical assistance to increase yields; credit for some growers (provided by principal buyer) Co-ops: financial and administrative management, marketing	Component was added during implementation (family gardens with some 900 women)
Horticulture	Link	90% bilateral donor 10% own sources	1,500 smallholders 23 co-ops	Cc-ops: Strengthening organizational capacity, legal support for business formalization, infrastructure expansion Smallholders: Technical assistance for production, infrastructure expansion	Target of 30% women participants (not met)
Dairy	Self-designed	100% bilateral	5,500 smallholders 25 co-ops	Smallholders: upgrading smallholder production capacities Cc-ops: improved management, buyer relations, infrastructure expansion, links with rural credit provider	None

smallholder participation in relation to the VCD initiative was limited during the interventions assessed for this study.

Overall, the lead NGOs, in collaboration with cooperative partners, provided most of the inputs to the design process. Principal buyers primarily provided feedback and inputs to intervention design and coordinated with NGO partners during the implementation process. Smallholders, in turn, provided inputs to VCD design during workshops in an initial planning stage. Regardless of the target chain and the methodology used, the overall intervention design was quite similar. Specific lines of activity included support for building cooperative capacity, technical assistance and training for strengthening smallholders' capacity in primary production, and, in some cases, support for small-scale processing (dairy and horticulture). In the coffee, cocoa, and dairy cases, activities focused on smallholders essentially aimed at higher yields (e.g. 20 per cent increase for cocoa, 50 per cent for dairy). In the case of horticulture, ambitious objectives were set which centred on boosting production of produce to meet volume requirements of supermarkets. Across all the cases, activities at cooperative level focused on building the capacities of recently organized cooperatives to provide services for members – as part of the NGOs' phasing out strategies. NGOs reported no specific assessment or dedicated activity to understand and address potential gender inequalities. In one case (horticulture), the initiative envisaged 30 per cent of the participants to be women but the target was not met. The interventions focused on different target groups, none of them including explicitly the poorest households in rural areas and, in some cases, involving relatively well-off households (e.g. households with 10 cows for dairy production).

Partnerships for implementation
The lead NGOs identified implementation partners and the relevance and capacity of these partners for achieving VCD objectives (Table 8.3). All lead NGOs regarded the partnership with the major buyer as critical. In the cocoa and coffee cases, a division of labour emerged whereby the NGO focused on smallholder production and cooperative development, and the major buyer engaged the lead NGO on commercial matters (contracts, pre-financing). In the dairy and horticulture cases, the lead NGOs played a strong initial role in establishing the links between the cooperatives and the major buyer, but later shied away from deep engagement with buyers as the interventions evolved. Lead NGO engagement with smallholders tended to be indirect – in all but one case (dairy), the lead NGOs contracted a local NGO to provide technical assistance to smallholders, and monitored as well as evaluated progress during the intervention via local NGO staff, village-level promoters, and cooperative leaders. Across all cases, the lead NGO forged strong partnerships with local NGOs and cooperatives for implementation of activities. Cooperatives usually received services directly from the lead NGOs (e.g. developing business management capacities and skills). Cooperatives were also hired by lead NGOs to provide advisory services to their members. Involvement of local or national

government agencies in project design and implementation was relatively limited. The exception was the dairy case, where the lead NGO engaged with municipal governments for services provision to smallholders (ear tags for cattle) and co-investment in infrastructure. All lead NGOs recognized the importance of smallholder access to financial services, but they had difficulties in building effective partnerships with specialized service providers – either because this fell outside the scope of the intervention or because financial services providers were reluctant to engage (e.g. 'micro-finance institutions only provide services to producers who have paperwork in order'). Partnerships with a research organization were limited to the dairy case (tracking of cattle diseases), and no partnerships were identified with the media, national or departmental government agencies, or specialized providers of business or financial services despite some efforts to establish such links.

VCD implementation
Lead NGOs provided their perceptions of the major obstacles they faced for achieving the intervention-linked goals with smallholders and cooperatives. When referring to households, the responses highlighted the challenge of encouraging resource-poor farmers to intensify their engagement with the major buyer in the value chain. Examples of obstacles reported include: 'farmers rely on traditional information and farming systems – many are aware of the need to update, but do not see the need to implement the full set of agronomical management steps required' (cocoa case); 'the mindset of the producers, no funds for purchase of inputs' (dairy); and 'reach quality standards required by formal buyers – to shift the traditional producer's mindset of subsistence' (horticulture case). In the case of cooperatives, responses highlighted the limited capacity of cooperatives to consolidate their governance structures (including mechanisms against mismanagement) and to meet the needs of their buyers owing to lack of access to raw materials (side-selling by members). For example, 'cooperative members are still tied into the informal market and network of middlemen. It was hard to get them selling to [an internationally owned supermarket], but it will be easy to get thrown out of the chain if they do fail to deliver on time.' the main buyer for horticulture echoed this by stating, 'We will just import directly from neighbouring countries if the local product does not meet deadlines and quality standards'.

Lead NGOs reported how they engaged with smallholders, cooperatives, and major buyers during the implementation process. They communicated most frequently with cooperatives for the purpose of assessing progress and adjusting activities. In some cases, the NGOs described examples of how intensive engagement with cooperatives led to adjustments in activities and priorities (e.g. building of cooperative collection centre and new efforts to expand access to finance). Engagement with smallholders tended to be less frequent and indirect, mainly through partner cooperatives and local NGOs. In the case of horticulture, the lead NGO noted that smallholder engagement was more intensive during an initial phase of activity, but as cooperatives

Table 8.3 Partnership approach by lead NGOs

Case	Smallholders	Cooperatives	Buyers and other chain actors	Barriers to forming deeper partnerships (reported by lead NGO)
Cocoa	Services to smallholders provided by local NGOs and co-ops; feedback loops established through network of project-supported local promoters	Lead NGO engaged co-op leadership for intervention design; co-ops provided information upon request; technical assistance carried out by local NGOs	Lead NGO focused mainly on training for improved primary production and supporting the co-op; limited communication and coordination by the NGO with other chain actors (and vice versa)	Young co-ops dependent on NGO support for survival; only one major buyer within the country; lead NGO with limited staff dedicated to the project
Coffee	Technical assistance and other services to smallholders provided by co-ops engaged with project; some feedback received through project-supported co-ops	Lead NGO provided technical assistance for strengthening co-op management (e.g. leadership, planning, quality control, marketing) and service capacity	Frequent engagement between lead NGO and high-level staff from buyer's company; limited coordination on the ground; separation of tasks between buyer (pre-financing) and lead NGO (cooperative development)	Sole buyer set business terms, preventing co-ops from selling to other large buyers
Horticulture	Strong links with producers during initial phase of activity; intensity declined as co-ops became stronger and were able to channel more resources to members	Lead NGO implemented project through local partners that coordinated meetings, oversaw quality and delivery issues, and provided financial advice to co-ops	Initially, strong and direct link to establish relationship; as project progressed, interactions with buyers based on a 'light-touch' approach	Co-ops rather recently founded with high need for strengthening their capacity; producers with need for guidance on quality and logistical issues to fully engage with large buyer
Dairy	Lead NGO provided technical assistance, access to inputs, and training to smallholders either directly or through co-ops	Lead NGO delivered training and support in setting up accounting and management systems; some training on institutional strengthening and governance	Made initial contacts and stepped back from the negotiations, although became involved for training purposes; linkages with input suppliers and MFI (not formalized)	Dairy sector relatively weak, without national guidelines or policy framework; all large buyers purchase milk from smallholders without formal contracts

grew in capacity (and began to receive greater amounts of project resources), coordination with smallholders was transferred to cooperatives. Initial efforts to establish feedback loops and learning cycles between the lead NGOs and key value chain actors were not followed through, leaving insights up to each partner rather than striving for joint learning. In one case, both the major buyer and the NGO had implemented separate systems for monitoring outcomes by smallholders. Efforts to engage in joint monitoring and learning, where reported, usually involved the lead NGO and the main implementing partners (local NGOs or cooperatives) and focused essentially on outputs. As a general practice, local NGOs and cooperatives reported to the lead NGO on intervention specific activities and achievements.

When asked to assess their capacity to address different elements of the VCD implementation process (Table 8.4), lead NGOs considered as a particular strength their capacity to understand the needs of cooperatives. This reflects the general approach to design and implement VCD initiatives in close cooperation with cooperatives – in some cases NGOs had worked with the cooperatives for several years (e.g. cocoa). Competences were also considered relatively strong with regard to assessing market trends, business context, and impact, along with monitoring and learning. These strengths are fundamental for the lead NGOs to engage with donors and implement large-scale projects on their behalf. The extent to which lead NGO capacities in monitoring project outcomes (donor-driven) led to improved learning within the value chain (e.g. options for adaptive management for improved processes and outcomes) is not addressed here. Among the capacities considered weakest, lead NGOs pointed at difficulties to access tools and methodologies for intervention design and assessing consumer demand and retail sourcing. Two lead NGOs mentioned the lack of tools for addressing gender: 'Gender is a very complex issue, we do not have a specific tool designed which addresses specific gender approaches'. The perceived need to assess VCD outcomes in terms of gender equity seemed to be the driving force behind this assessment.

When asked about the most critical aspect of VCD where lead NGOs needed support in terms of new tools, methods, or technical assistance, they provided the following responses:

> We know the field and farmers, but we don't understand the final market. There is a need to better understand prices and trends in the international cocoa market. If we didn't sell to [international cocoa buyer], we wouldn't know to whom to sell the cocoa (cocoa case).

> We are keenly aware of each step in the value chain. Our needs are mainly in the emotional and social intelligence side of understanding needs of producers and also with the staff. Another area is gender, since we do not typically run gender projects, but try to incorporate gender aspects into our projects, as flawed as these efforts may be (coffee case).

Table 8.4 Self-assessment by lead NGOs of their capacity to address different elements of VCD

	Capacity (1-5, where 1 = very limited capacity and 5 = very strong capacity)				
	Cocoa	Coffee	Horticulture	Dairy	Average
Understanding needs of cooperatives and producer associations in complex business environments	4	5	5	5	4.8
Assessment of business context incl. market trends and their implications for the design and implementation of VCD	4	5	5	4	4.5
Impact assessment, monitoring, and joint learning /innovation as related to VCD	4	5	5	4	4.5
Capacity to collaborate with and coordinate among stakeholders from multiple sectors (government, NGOs, private, media)	5	3	4	5	4.3
Qualified staff within your organization to get the job done	4	3	5	4	4.0
Gender roles, in terms of ability of women to participate in the chain or equitable distribution of benefits from VCD interventions	3	5	4	4	4.0
Assessment of the value chain dynamics (actor relations, market opportunities, bottlenecks)	3	3	5	5	4.0
Assessment of risks related to VCD for poor actors in the chain, including potential trade-offs between market and non-market activities	2	4	4	5	3.4
Demand assessment, including consumer demand and retail sourcing	2		4	5	3.0
Access to methodologies and tools for intervention design which address the needs of women and men actors	2	4		4	2.8

Improved knowledge of the market and consumer behaviour. Also in understanding pricing and demand in other markets (horticulture case).

We lack the ability to stay ahead of appropriate and up-to-date practices and technologies. We are unable to learn from others ... Our reality of project cycles does not allow us time to critically evaluate with whom we work. The challenge is how to choose the right person and the producer groups. How do you do that without rushing and being constrained by the project cycle? (dairy case)

Cooperatives

The cooperatives varied significantly in terms of their consolidation, with the oldest established in 1995 (cocoa) and the youngest in 2010 (dairy). Their membership was small to medium, ranging from 18 (dairy) to 259 (cocoa) members. The cooperatives were engaged in the sale of semi-processed products to downstream buyers and processors, save for those that delivered fresh produce to supermarkets. In all cases, cooperatives specialized in a single type of product.

Engagement with VCD intervention
Major investments in the value chain focused on the expansion of machinery and infrastructure, including collection and processing centres (cocoa), a fleet of vehicles for transport of raw material (coffee), and a packaging and washing centre (horticulture). Most of these investments were co-financed by the VCD initiative. Major self-reported accomplishments from engagement with buyers and NGOs related to higher income generation through access to certification (cocoa and coffee) and meeting strict quality requirements (dairy and horticulture). At the same time, most cooperatives identified as principal constraints or risks the lack of reliable supply (inability to meet buyers' demands), dependence on a single buyer (cocoa), and the absence of buyer contracts (dairy and horticulture). In the case of cocoa, cooperative representatives noted 'there is only one major cocoa buyer in the country and members have limited capacity to invest in cocoa production – we are dependent on third parties for working capacity and covering our expenses, such as technical assistance to members'. In the case of horticulture, representatives mentioned, 'The large buyers do not sign contracts with us. Outbreaks of diseases and members' limited grasp of cooperatives continue to be difficult to manage'. Leaders of one of the dairy cooperatives added, 'We have to depend on the buyers' laboratory for analysis. There is no third-party certification. The large buyers do not sign contracts with us'. In addition to support from the NGOs engaged in the respective VCD initiative, the cooperatives reported minimal collaboration with external support organizations (e.g. government agencies, other NGOs, other cooperatives) or researchers.

Table 8.5 reports the cooperatives' prioritization of needs with regard to business development and value chain engagement. The self-assessment shows how cooperative representatives see the organization based on their experiences, including interactions with buyers, NGOs, and other cooperatives. The most urgent needs included diversification of buyers/markets, enhanced logistics and processing, food safety, and traceability. The involvement of women

Table 8.5 Needs assessment among cooperatives (n = 8) with regard to support for more effective value chain engagement

	Number of coopemtives reporting					
	No need	Very low need	low need	Occasional need	Moderate need	Urgent need
Designing improved communication systems	5	1			1	1
Greater involvement of women, youth as farmers	3	2	2		1	
Greater involvement of women, youth in cooperative management	2	3	2		1	
Cooperative business administration and financial management	4	1	1	1	1	
Stronger participation of members in cooperative governance	6	1		1		
Risk management and mitigation	7				1	
Logistics and export processes	5				1	2
Processing, food safety, traceability	6					2
Managing certification processes	5			1	1	1
Designing more efficient and effective techn ica l assistance	5	1	1		1	
Strategies and procedures for engaging with new or existing buyers	3		1	1		3

and youth in farming and cooperative management was identified by most cooperatives, but generally with a low level of priority.

Principal buyers

The principal buyers had long-standing operations in Nicaragua, ranging from 17 to 25 years of presence in the country. All except one (dairy) were multinational companies headquartered in Europe or the United States, with multi-million (US$) annual turnover in Nicaragua.

Engagement with VCD intervention
Overall, buyers tended to limit their direct engagement with smallholders engaged in the VCD initiatives to the purchase of raw or semi-processed products. Only the cocoa buyer offered annual loans and contracts to cooperatives,

which included year-end bonuses for investments in infrastructure (as part of normal business partnership, independent of VCD intervention). In 2008, theft and mismanagement by cooperatives left this buyer with roughly US$70,000 in unpaid loans, which the cooperatives managed to repay over a 10-year period. In the case of coffee, training and seedlings were made available to some smallholder growers to help them recover from coffee rust (as part of the VCD intervention), along with price incentives for high-quality coffee. Coordination with lead NGOs was light in many cases, limited to senior staff when 'they come looking for support' (cocoa buyer) or when there was a felt need for a coordination meeting. The dairy case provided an example of collaboration at field level, where the representatives of the principal buyer and NGO staff collaborated in the design and implementation of training events. Cooperatives had yet to facilitate links between their partner cooperatives and smallholders and other service providers, including those that provide specialized technical, business development, and financial services.

The buyers expressed appreciation for NGO-led efforts to build productive and cooperative management capacities. In addition, a complementary approach emerged between the two actors as buyers engaged with cooperatives on commercial options and NGOs attempted to respond to the needs of smallholders and cooperatives (in terms of business administration and infrastructure development). Major lessons learned by the principal buyers through their engagement in VCD included:

> Efforts to support small cooperatives require a long-term approach, and with patience, outsiders are able to contribute. There is a need to focus more on building entrepreneurial spirit in cooperatives and move away from providing assistance (cocoa case).

> It is critical to identify the producers who have potential, as well as the best organized cooperatives (coffee case).

> We know the farmers have been milking cows for generations, so to improve pasture quality and herd management, we coordinate with cooperatives on a weekly basis to ensure high-quality milk (dairy case).

> The fresh vegetables market in Nicaragua is still very basic; growers face low productivity, few value-adding options, and high levels of disease. There is no culture of greenhouse management. Growers still require extensive support (horticulture case).

Although buyers recognized the need for support to smallholders and cooperatives, they themselves appear reluctant to engage deeply with lead NGOs, cooperatives, and smallholders. According to one buyer representative, 'We still do not understand the NGO model, but the bigger issue is that NGOs do not understand our business model'. Another buyer representative added, 'we need more [name of intervention] to support producers, as engaging with smallholders with technical services or other support is not our business'.

Discussion and conclusions

Despite the complexity of market systems, results showed a relatively basic approach to VCD, reflected in: 1) reliance on a single tool for design and implementation; 2) expected outcomes based on technical assistance and training for smallholders and cooperatives; 3) local NGOs and cooperatives with key roles in implementation; and 4) limited engagement with other chain actors, service providers, and researchers. Below we discuss each of these points in turn.

Reliance on a single tool for design and implementation

Across the cases, the NGOs leading VCD relied on a single tool for their initiatives, either a guide designed in-house or a third-party tool they were familiar with through previous exposure (e.g. training by those who designed the tool). This merits concern as no one tool has been published that covers the full range of development-relevant issues embedded in VCD processes, nor its different stages (design, implementation, assessment, adjustments). Guides for value chain analysis and development typically focus on given aspects (e.g. business relations, labour issues, participatory processes), without covering a broad range of associated issues, such as gender equity, monitoring and evaluation, gaps in service delivery, and differentiation of smallholder households (Donovan et al., 2015). The tools used for the studied VCD initiatives are no exception, as they focus on specific issues such as business relations between small-scale suppliers and major corporations and multinational companies (Link methodology) or new business opportunities that involve companies and benefit low-income communities (inclusive Business methodology). Complementary tools are available, for example, those focusing on gender equity, but these, in turn, do not address all relevant aspects from a broader VCD perspective either (see, for example, Terrillon, 2010; Senders et al., 2013). Reliance on a single tool for VCD therefore holds the risk of important blind spots with regard to the multiple needs of smallholders and other resource-poor value chain actors. Interviews with buyers and representatives of cooperatives and NGOs, for example, brought to light several issues not addressed in the respective guides that required specific attention in the VCD initiatives (e.g. weak cooperative governance structures and management models, specific needs of women and the youth, and limits of smallholders to intensify production for sale). Such diverse needs are best addressed through the design of context-specific VCD initiatives that draw on a mix of tools and allow for client-specific needs at household and cooperative levels.

Expected outcomes based on technical assistance and training

The interventions were based, in part, on an assumption that technical assistance and training in response to market opportunities in the value chain would lead to significant and positive changes among smallholder households (e.g. improved farming practices, greater output) and cooperatives (e.g. increased performance and capacity to deliver services to members). However, resource-poor smallholders face a number of limitations and risks when intensifying their allocation of labour and other resources to a given value chain in view of their diversified livelihood strategies (Stoian et al., 2012). The ultimate impact of VCD will depend on the capacity of these households to address a broad set of issues such as food insecurity, varying availability of household labour, gender inequalities, and limited access to critical inputs and services. Similarly, to achieve shortcuts to cooperative development, cooperatives need access to an array of specialized technical, business, and financial services beyond those that could be provided by any one NGO in the framework of a single project. Lead NGOs can play an important role in bringing to light the needs and circumstances of smallholders and cooperatives and helping to facilitate engagement by other service providers. This implies a long-term commitment to development of the value chain beyond the cycle of a given project, which might be envisaged but not always possible owing to funding constraints. Long-term commitment, in turn, requires coordination among NGOs, cooperatives, and their members to prioritize needs and related investments in the short, mid, and long term. This is particularly important given that, as the results showed here, perceptions of need and priorities for investment tend to vary significantly between NGOs, cooperatives, and other value chain stakeholders.

Local NGOs and cooperatives with key roles in implementation

Another important issue in VCD implementation is the relationship between the international NGOs leading the VCD initiatives and the local NGOs executing them. The former played a critical role in developing the approach to VCD, from selecting the tool for design and implementation to engaging with funding agencies and the principal buyers to get activities running. However, their presence on the ground during implementation was fairly limited. It is acknowledged that international NGOs face relatively high costs to maintain a critical number of specialized staff for VCD implementation and monitoring in the country and, consequently, seek to become cost-competitive by outsourcing execution of activities to local NGOs and, where appropriate, cooperatives. While such delegation has the potential to build local capacities and facilitates phasing out, it often requires upfront investments to ensure that local actors are adequately prepared. Our study did not look into the extent to which this level of preparedness existed among local NGOs and cooperatives prior to the VCD initiatives but, based on our own experiences, we would expect that in many cases, local execution partners require in-depth and in-breadth development of capacities for successful VCD at the onset of a given initiative. In the cases reviewed here, coordination between the lead NGO and local NGOs centred mainly on monitoring and donor reporting, without close collaboration on a day-to-day basis to discuss opportunities and bottlenecks and identify options for moving forward. While efficient in terms of resource use, such a division of labour and delegation of responsibility limit the pursuit of a broader approach to VCD that spans cross-cutting aspects, capitalizes on insights from both international and local VCD work, responds to opportunities and bottlenecks as they emerge, and generates lessons for adapting the current VCD approach and the design of future interventions.

Limited engagement with other chain actors, service providers, and researchers

Interactions between the NGOs and principal buyers varied from case to case, but in general there was a clear separation of tasks. Engagement between lead NGOs and major buyers was usually limited to initial coordination for project design and periodic feedback during implementation. Buyers appeared reluctant to engage in joint strategy formulation and decision-making, facilitate access to financial services, or experiment with new business relations (e.g. embedding finance and technical assistance in purchase contracts). More active involvement of principal buyers would be needed to achieve impact at scale. Emphasis should be on: 1) identification of short-term benefits and clear prospects for further benefits over the mid to long term as part of the VCD design phase; 2) support strategies for cooperatives that address bottlenecks prioritized by the buyers (e.g. requirements in relation to volumes, quality, and timely delivery); and 3) continuous monitoring of key performance indicators to measure progress and as an input for joint reflection on collaboration needs and investment priorities.

Looking ahead, various opportunities emerge from this research to advance how VCD is designed and implemented. More debate within and among NGOs and other stakeholders engaged in VCD will help to understand the opportunities for a broader and more adaptive approach to VCD, one that employs feedback loops in implementation (non-linear design) and utilizes an integrated set of tools based on diverse stakeholder needs and conditions. As the external business environment can become less favourable over an intervention period, it is critically important for integrated VCD approaches to allow for alternative options if assumptions about demand trends, the regulatory framework, and the behaviour of chain actors and service providers turn out not to stand up to expectations. Where the right tool for a given element of a VCD approach is unavailable, NGOs can work with specific partners, such as research institutions, to advance existing and develop additional tools. Such interactions can also help to develop viable mechanisms for critical reflection, joint learning, and continuous improvement.

Models for designing and implementing VCD initiatives with varying roles and responsibilities of international leads, local partners, and other stakeholders also require us to revisit underlying assumptions about respective strengths and weaknesses. International–local hierarchies and the notion of a governmental or non-governmental lead agent promoting VCD based on externally sourced funding may need to give way to more horizontal, integrated, and collaborative approaches where different service providers and value chain actors play complementary roles, pool human and financial resources, and draw on diverse, mutually reinforcing methodologies and tools. 'Communities of practice' of NGOs and other lead agents in VCD across a portfolio of value chains in a given country, and across countries, would strengthen evidence-based improvements in VCD design and implementation. Funding agencies, committed buyers, national and local government agencies, and cooperative leaders could also contribute to and benefit from these collaborative frameworks. Participation of cooperative leaders in such endeavours is critical to ensure mutual understanding and mediation between external agents, who tend to focus on mid- to long-term development goals, and the former, who need to address pressing, often short-term needs.

Lastly, the findings suggest an opportunity for greater involvement of researchers in the design and implementation of VCD. They can make important contributions to facilitate broader, more integrated approaches to VCD by designing tools with practitioners that address the most glaring gaps in the overall VCD tool kit, particularly as regards the operationalization of ways to enhance gender equity, integrated service delivery by cooperatives and external providers, and management of production and commercial risks. A sound combination of VCD methodologies and tools and their adaptation to local contexts would also account for better anticipation of trends and risks, as well as bailout options with possible shifts from one value chain into another. Such a broader approach to VCD would have a stronger focus on a given geography as a biophysical, socio-economic, and institutional space; be mindful of diverse market- and non-market-oriented livelihood activities of smallholders across this space; and support them and other value chain actors in searching out options across a portfolio of value chains to maximize synergies and minimize risks.

Acknowledgment

This work was undertaken as part of the CGIAR Research Program on Policies, Institutions and Markets (PIM). The authors thank PIM for funding the study and all donors who support PIM through their contributions to the CGIAR Fund.

References

Albu, M. and Griffith, A. (2006) 'Mapping the market: participatory market chain development in practice', *Small Enterprise Development* 17(2): 12–22 <http://dx.doi.org/ 10.3362/0957-1329.2006.016>.

Cattaneo, O., Gereffi, G. and Staritz, C. (eds.) (2010) *Global Value Chains in a Postcrisis World: A Development Perspective*, Washington, DC: World Bank Publications.

Devaux, A., Torero, M., Donovan, J. and Horton, D. (eds.) (2016) *Innovation for Inclusive Value Chain Development: Successes and Challenges*, Washington, DC: IFPRI.

Donovan, J., Franzel, S., Cunha, M., Gyau, A. and Mithofer, D. (2015) 'Guides for value chain development: a comparative review', *Journal of Agribusiness in Developing and Emerging Economies* 5(1): 1–22 <http://dx.doi.org/10.1108/JADEE-07-2013-0025>.

Hobbs, J., Cooney, A. and Fulton, M. (2000) *Value Chains in the Agri-Food Sector: What Are They? How Do They Work? Are They For Me?* Saskatoon, Canada: Department of Agricultural Economics, University of Saskatchewan.

Humphrey, J. and Memedovic, O. (2006) *Global Value Chains in the Agrifood Sector*, Vienna: United Nations Industrial Development Organization.

Humphrey, J. and Navas-Alemán, L. (2010) *Value Chains, Donor Interventions, and Poverty Reduction: A Review of Donor Practice*, IDS Research Report 63, Brighton, UK: IDS.

Lundy, M., Becx, G., Zamierowski, N., Amrein, A., Jairo, J., Mosquera, E. and Rodríguez, F. (2012) *LINK Methodology: A Participatory Guide to Business Models that Link Smallholders to Markets*, CIAT Publication No. 380, Cali, Colombia: CIAT.

Lusby, F. and Derks, E. (2006) 'Shea kernels from Mali: a value chain case study', *Small Enterprise Development* 17(2): 36–46 <http://dx.doi.org/10.3362/0957-1329.2006.018>.

Meyer-Stamer, J. (2006) 'Marking market systems work? For the poor?' *Small Enterprise Development* 17(4): 21–32 <http://dx.doi.org/10.3362/0957-1329.2006.041>.

Senders, A., Lentink, A., Facet, T., Vanderschaeghe, M. and Terrillon, J. (2013) *Gender in Value Chains: Practical Toolkit to Integrate a Gender Perspective in Agricultural Value Chain Development*, Arnhem, the Netherlands: Agri-ProFocus.

Seville, D., Duxton, A. and Vorley, B. (2011) *Under what Conditions are Value Chains Effective Tools for Pro-poor Development?* London: International Institute for Environment and Development and Hartland, VT: Sustainable Food Lab.

SNV (2008) *Inclusive Business: Profitable Business for Successful Development*, SNV and World Business Council for Sustainable Development, The Hague, Netherlands: SNV.

Stoian, D., Donovan, J., Fisk, J. and Muldoon, M. (2012) 'Value chain development for rural poverty reduction: a reality check and a warning', *Enterprise Development and Microfinance* 23(1): 54–69 <http://dx.doi.org/10.2499/9780896292130_02>.

Terrillon, J. (2010) *Gender Mainstreaming in Value Chain Development: Practical Guidelines and Tools*, The Hague, The Netherlands: Corporate Network Agriculture SNV.

About the authors

Jason Donovan, PhD (j.donovan@cgiar.org), Senior Economist, Research Theme Leader for Markets and Value Chains, International Maize and Wheat Improvement Center (CIMMYT), Texcoco, Mexico

Dietmar Stoian, PhD (d.stoian@cgiar.org), Lead Scientist, Value Chains, Private Sector Engagement and Investments, World Agroforestry (ICRAF), Bonn, Germany.

Keith Poe (keithericpoe@gmail.com), consultant, Managua, Nicaragua.

CHAPTER 9

Value chain development in Vietnam: a look at approaches used and options for improved impact

Brice Even and Jason Donovan

Abstract

Despite the widespread use of value chain development (VCD) approaches to poverty reduction, there has been limited debate on how VCD is implemented in the field, from the approaches, methods, and tools used, to the investments and partnerships made. The chapter presents five case studies: tea, dairy, horticulture, cinnamon, and fish in Vietnam. For each case, we conducted interviews with development agencies, producer organizations, and principal buyers. The cases examined how VCD interventions were designed, the role of different stakeholders in the implementation process, and the challenges faced by practitioners and chain actors to achieve impact at scale. Results suggest that VCD interventions tended to focus on supporting smallholder participation in high-value, fast-growing markets, but based on a narrow set of activities, mainly around upgrading smallholder production capacities and establishing producer associations. Overall, collaboration with downstream buyers and service providers was muted and, in a few cases, non-existent. Opportunities for increased impact exist based on increased collaboration between practitioners and researchers to employ VCD tools in specific contexts, as well as to design new tools for addressing specific needs and facilitate joint learning on the implementation process and related outcomes. The findings also suggest a need for dedicated approaches to supporting producer organizations, given their central role in the implementation of VCD interventions.

Keywords: agriculture, smallholders, producer organizations, NGO

Value Chain Development (VCD) is defined by the World Bank as 'an effort to strengthen mutually beneficial linkages among firms so that they work together to take the advantage of market opportunities, that is, to create and build trust among value chain participants' (Webber and Labaste, 2010). In developing countries, VCD often brings together businesses engaged in the chain (e.g. retailers, processors, cooperatives), input and service providers (e.g. financial institutions), and at times, development agencies interested in poverty reduction. Many governments, donors, and NGOs consider VCD

http://dx.doi.org/10.3362/9781788530576.009

processes, given their potential to advance both economic growth and poverty reduction, as a key component of their rural development strategies (Seville et al., 2011; Devoux et al., 2016; Humphrey and Navas-Alemán, 2010). These processes recognize the role of formal and informal institutions in shaping how value chains operate and the resulting implications for smallholders and other chain actors (Gibbon, 2001). VCD may engage stakeholders at different levels, from working with smallholders to strengthen their capacity for chain engagement, to working with businesses along the chain to improve their coordination and collaboration, to working with government agencies and private businesses to improve the business environment (Humphrey, 2005; Stoian et al., 2012).

Several methodologies and tools have been published to facilitate the design of VCD initiatives. The guides differ in terms of approaches, objectives, and targeted users, and propose different approaches to the design, implementation, and monitoring of VCD interventions. Donovan et al., (2015) identified their strengths and weaknesses and provided recommendations for guide selection according to the context of the intervention and the development goals of the implementing organization. Yet, despite the importance of VCD to rural development programming, little is known about, on the one hand, how these guides are actually used by stakeholders (e.g. NGOs, government agencies, private businesses) and, on the other, the outcomes and impacts of VCD intervention. Stoian et al., (2012) highlighted the challenge to design VCD interventions that deliver impacts on rural poverty, and the need for interventions to better consider the capacities of rural households and potential trade-offs they face to invest in chain-oriented activities. This study examines the design and implementation of five VCD interventions in Vietnam. Specifically, it looks at the tools used, the activities carried out, the various businesses and organizations engaged in the process, and the strengths and limitations of actors involved. The Vietnam context for VCD, where the government plays a strong hand in the design and implementation of VCD interventions, provides a unique perspective for this study.

Methodology

Each case encompasses a specific VCD intervention carried out by a selected implementing organization (IO), defined here as the organization responsible for the design and implementation of a VCD intervention. The VCD intervention is likely to include a set of specific actions aimed at actors along the chain, such as providing training or technical or financial assistance to smallholders, their business organizations, and other value chain actors. Our cases met the following criteria: 1) the IO had been actively engaged in providing services to smallholders and businesses where the objective was to improve market smallholder access, chain linkages, and/ or the overall business environment; 2) the intervention was close to completion or had been recently completed; and 3) relevant members of the IO were willing to participate in interviews and share documentation. Case selection also aimed to achieve a mix in terms of product focus (e.g. perishable versus non-perishable for export) and final market destination (e.g. national versus export). In most of the cases, there was a major buyer that interacted with the IO and purchased from a group of smallholders, some of whom also received services from the IO. In addition, the cases included cooperatives or other forms of smallholder business organization that engaged with the IO, buyer, and smallholders.

To obtain a richer understanding of the range of experiences and perceptions on the VCD process, data collection covered three key stakeholders in each intervention: IOs, producer organizations, and buyers. Within each IO, interviews included the intervention (project) leader and other key staff identified by the IO when necessary. In all cases but one, interviews were also carried out with a major buyer that interacted with the IO and purchased from a group of smallholders, some of whom also received services from the IO. Subjects covered in the interviews included: tools applied in VCD design and implementation, key partners for implementation, major achievements and obstacles, and perceptions of needs for improved design and implementation. Interviews with the cooperatives covered themes such as achievements and bottlenecks during the VCD process, relations with buyers and service providers, including the IO, and perceptions on needs for future support. Five producer organizations were selected for data collection; the selection was carried out in collaboration with the IO with the aim of achieving a diversity of capacity and experience in the VCD process. Finally, interviews with major buyers covered the strengths and limitations of their relations with producer organizations and the IO, their achievements in the VCD process, and bottlenecks for deeper collaboration.

Results

Profile of interventions

Overview of the cases.
Table 9.1 provides a synopsis of the five cases and the business environment in which the chain actors operate. NGOs implemented three interventions while government agencies implemented the remaining interventions. Across all cases but one, producer organizations were recently created and had a limited number of members. Private buyers were diverse in terms of operation (processors, exporters, and retailers), size (from 18 to nearly 1,000 employees), and targeted markets (local, national, and international markets). Among the VCD interventions, only one targeted a chain that was part of on-farm traditional consumption (horticulture). Other interventions addressed typical cash crops of limited importance for local diets (tea, cinnamon) and products whose high market prices were likely to discourage farmers from consuming them on-farm (milk, catfish). Budgets of the considered interventions ranged from US$300,000 to $4 m, over three to six years. Three interventions (tea,

Table 9.1 Overview of the market context and VCD-participating producer organizations

Case [IO]	VCD stakeholders	VCD interventions	Business environment
Tea [international NGO]	6 processing companies; 200 farmer groups [7,000 targeted producers]	Intervention aimed to improve market access through increased quality of tea and improved chain links. Producers were organized into informal groups and received technical support on production and post-harvest management while local tea processors received financial and technical support. Processors were actively involved in the delivery of intervention activities.	Tea processing and exporting is done by state-owned and private enterprises. About 60–80% of the tea production is exported. Vietnamese tea is known on international markets for its low quality (pesticide residues) and low price. Government and enterprise strategies are mostly based on improving tea quality.
Dairy [international NGO]	1 cooperative [2,800 targeted producers]	Intervention grew out of an NGO's interest in supporting smallholder dairy farmers. The NGO supported a milk cooperative created 10 years earlier and previously supported by several development organizations. Cooperative members received technical and financial assistance, while the cooperative management team received organizational support. Local government authorities were closely associated with the intervention's implementation.	Since the 1990s, the milk sector in Vietnam has seen a steady increase in demand. Domestic production satisfies only about 20–25% of the national demand. While production is still scattered – most of the producers have 1–5 cows – the processing sector is monopolized by a few large-scale companies, usually buying fresh milk directly from producers through collection points.
Horticulture [government agency]	2 retailing companies; 3 farmers' groups embedded in 1 cooperative [60 targeted producers]	The initiative addressed the lack of affordable, off-season supply of quality fresh vegetables in Hanoi, and was designed by a pool of national research institutions and an international development agency. Existing farmers' groups were trained and merged into a formal cooperative. Commercial relationships were facilitated with retailers. Local government agencies were closely associated with the implementation of the intervention.	Consumption of fresh vegetables is high in Vietnam. Overuse of chemicals is a growing issue, and demand for safe vegetables is increasing, in urban but also in rural areas. Retailing system is evolving to adapt to the demand shift, pulling the production sector toward a change of practices. The government is also promoting safer agricultural practices.

(Continued)

Table 9.1 (continued)

Case [IO]	VCD stakeholders	VCD interventions	Business environment
Cinnamon [international NGO]	3 private processing companies; 70 farmers' groups [4,000 targeted producers]	Intervention was part of the same umbrella programme of the tea intervention. Producers were organized into informal farmers' groups and received technical support. Local processors and local service providers received technical support from the IO and were also in charge of implementing some of the intervention's activities. The IO worked closely with local government agencies to implement ground activities but also to improve the business environment.	Cinnamon is usually harvested when households need cash. Links along the chain are weak. Producers struggle to access information and market, while processors can hardly ensure consistent supply and lack of capacity to reach remunerative high-end markets.
Fish [government agency]	1 trading company; 1 association [130 targeted producers]	Intervention fell under guidance of the Ministry of Agriculture and Rural Development (MARD). A farmers' association was created. Producers received technical training and were supported to obtain quality certification. A local trading company was involved in the implementation of the intervention's activities. The IO also worked closely with other local and national government agencies.	Fisheries and aquaculture are a key economic sector with nearly $6.5 bn (2015) in export sales and domestic consumption at 35 kg per capita per year. There are about 500,000 aquaculture farms employing more than 1.6 million people. Government agencies and NGOs are working to promote closer chain coordination between farmers and processors.

cinnamon, horticulture) were funded by bilateral donors, with minor in-kind contributions from the private sector (staff time and small equipment). One intervention (dairy) was half-funded by the implementing NGO (through its own funds) and half by provincial authorities, while another (fish) was completely funded by the Vietnamese government.

Intervention design and selection of the chains
The design of three VCD interventions (horticulture, tea, cinnamon) was inspired by the making markets Work for the poor (m4p) (DFiD, 2005) approach, but IOs reported not having used the specific tools included in the toolkit to design the intervention. One IO (dairy) used the Valuelink guide (Springer-Heinze, 2008) for conducting the value chain analysis while another one (fish) did not use any of the existing methodologies and relied on guidelines provided by the central government. Several factors may explain the avoidance or incomplete use of existing approaches and tools. IOs outlined that tools do not fit with their needs in the specific context of their interventions, and that they needed to design ad hoc tools to address bottlenecks identified on the ground. IOs also reported that available resources (budget, staff time) were barely adequate at the design stage to allow a comprehensive use of the tools proposed by VCD methodologies. Language may also have been a barrier as most of the VCD guides are only available in English while few IO staff have sufficient English language skills.

The main criteria reported for value chain selection were favourable market conditions. Indeed, all the targeted chains either benefited from an increasing domestic demand (milk, fish, and horticulture) or were considered key elements of smallholders' livelihoods strategies. Three IOs also identified the willingness of donors and opportunity for funding, as well as overall impact potential of the intervention, as other important factors for selecting the chains. IOs were mainly responsible for intervention design. Consultations were organized with value chain stakeholders (except for the fish case), including smallholders and buyers (processors and retailers).

Inclusion of the very poor and women
Four of the interventions had clear objectives to advance gender equity. In the milk and cinnamon cases, IOs ensured that women's participation rate in the intervention's activities was over 50 per cent. Specific trainings were designed for women on nutrition, family planning, as well as business planning, and staff were trained on gender issues. In the case of tea and vegetables, there were no such measures, but as these crops were mainly grown by women, positive impacts on women were expected. In the tea case, 60 per cent of the targeted farmers were women, and the horticulture intervention 'was designed to address women: one hundred percent of the targeted farmers were women'. However, beyond these basic practices, there were little or no specific measures to ensure women's participation in VCD processes.

Participation of the very poor in the value chain interventions seemed limited. Three interventions (tea, cinnamon, and milk) were explicitly targeting poor ethnic minorities. In the case of tea and cinnamon, IOs recognized that the VCD crops were mainly grown by poor households, and assumed that an intervention in these chains would necessarily impact them positively. IOs also assumed that targeting northern mountainous provinces, among the poorest of Vietnam, would ensure participation of the very poor in the development of the value chain. IOs relied on local partners, namely authorities at the communal level (cinnamon) and processing companies (tea) to select the targeted farmers, and had limited control over the final selection of participating households. In the milk case, farming households were chosen according to socio-economic criteria (including income and landholdings) with the support of provincial authorities. The horticulture and fish cases, implemented by government agencies, did not give priority to poverty reduction but rather to meeting market demand. Farmers participated on a voluntary basis, according to their willingness to join a group of producers and to adopt improved farming practices. In the fish case, a minimum area of fishing pond was required to be part of the intervention. While there was insufficient data available to verify this, it is likely that the project in large part worked with better-off households in these two cases.

Major intervention activities
The interventions focused their activities on supporting smallholders; in particular by enhancing their productive capacities to respond to the needs of buyers, both in terms of production volumes and quality of outputs. Considerable effort was put into technical support and training. Across all interventions, quality enhancement was considered a critical way to access new markets (more formal) and to ensure higher prices for producers (although only in the tea, cinnamon, and horticulture cases had buyers actually offered a premium price based on quality criteria). The interventions had specific objectives regarding food safety and the related on-farm practices, in particular proper use of chemicals. For instance, the horticulture intervention specifically responded to the increasing demand for safe vegetables – referring to crops produced under VietGAP (Vietnamese Good Agricultural Practices) or the like, in particular practices avoiding overuse of agrochemicals – in northern urban areas of Vietnam, namely Hanoi. Discussions with private retailers happened later on, to design training activities in line with their specific needs. Eventually, the adoption of improved horticultural practices enabled producers to sign contracts with two retailing companies, offering premium prices for produce conforming to required quality standards. In the cases of tea and cinnamon, most of the training activities were designed and implemented directly by processors. Although no contracts were signed, the initiative helped foster commercial relationships between producers and buyers, as producers were offered higher prices when meeting quality expectations.

In the design of VCD interventions, IOs placed a particular focus on producer organizations and cooperatives. Beyond building their planning, business, marketing, and organizational capacities, the IOs supported the creation and the formalization of these producer organizations. Only the milk case had an existing formally organized cooperative. For the other cases, IOs supported the creation of structures for organizing smallholders into groups. For the tea and cinnamon cases, IOs created several dozen informal groups. This enabled VCD interventions to reach thousands of producers, but expectations were low regarding sustainability of these groups after the interventions end. It seems that the creation of these groups mostly served the achievement of the project's outputs (i.e. delivery of training to smallholders) rather than longer-term objectives of outcomes and impact (i.e. supporting the establishment of strong and autonomous farmers' organizations). In the two other cases, IOs focused on a smaller number of farmers and supported the establishment of formal producer organizations. In the horticulture case, two informal groups were merged into a formal cooperative while in the fish case, a formal association was created.

Significant work was done by IOs to foster links within the chains. Although IOs did not directly engage with the configuration of business relationships between producer organizations and buyers, they facilitated dialogue and encouraged more dynamic interactions between them. None of the IOs claimed to use a specific tool or method. In the horticulture case, the IO introduced farmers' groups to retailers in Hanoi and helped set up the commercial relationship. This led to the signature of a supply contract between the retailers and the newly created cooperative, guaranteeing minimum purchasing prices and volumes. In the tea and cinnamon cases, IOs considered buyers (processing companies) as the main entry point for upgrading value chains, and therefore placed the lead firms at the core of their intervention. Training was organized for their staff, notably on marketing, business planning, and quality management. Then IOs channelled smallholders' training activities through these processing companies. This was considered essential to ensure that smallholder production complied with buyers' requirements, and therefore sustain the links between smallholders and buyers.

IOs also worked to improve the overall business environment in which the chains operated, in particular trying to influence local and national regulations by working closely with authorities and fostering public–private dialogue. In the horticulture case, a certification trademark owned by the District People's Committee was registered at the national level under the National Office of Intellectual Property. The trademark enabled farmers' produce to be recognized as safe vegetables and therefore to access more remunerative markets. In the cinnamon case, several provincial regulations were issued regarding production and post-harvest processes, aimed at formalizing quality standards and providing a clear legal framework for producers and processors. In the tea and cinnamon cases, IOs organized public–private policy dialogues at the national level; however, there was no evidence of concrete outcomes benefitting smallholders.

Partnerships for implementation

As shown in Figure 9.1, some IOs relied heavily on partnerships with medium- or large-scale buyers (including processors, wholesalers, and retailers) for project implementation. In the tea case, five processors were chosen as partners and were placed at the core of the intervention. Receiving capacity building and financial support from the iO, these local processors then acted as the main project implementers at the provincial level, interacting directly with smallholders and producer organizations. The cinnamon intervention adopted a similar strategy. However, it did not just rely on local private processing companies but also on local service providers. In the horticulture case, the iO involved private retailers after the beginning of the intervention. Retailers were not consulted at the design stage of the intervention and had no responsibility for implementing intervention activities. Retailers reported that 'they were only asked to provide support for quality control and to buy the produce from farmers' and that 'project design would have been much better if the iO had contacted them at the design stage, to better take into account the market's requirements'. In the milk and fish cases, IOs did not collaborate with the private sector. In the fish case, private buyers were of small scale as well as scattered, and the iO did not have the capacity to reach and include them in the intervention's activities. On the other hand, in the milk case, the large-scale company buying raw milk from the cooperative was approached by the iO, but refused to be part of the intervention.

Government agencies operating at the provincial level also played a major role in the VCD interventions. In all but one case, government agencies participated in intervention design and provided support to smallholders (e.g. technical assistance, land access, certification processes). The fish and horticulture cases were implemented by government agencies, a provincial quality assurance department (fish case) and a national research organization (horticulture case). In both these cases, government agencies established partnerships with other government agencies for providing trainings to chain actors and

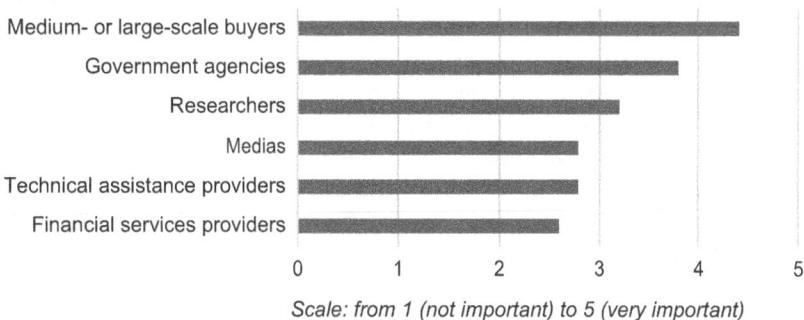

Scale: from 1 (not important) to 5 (very important)

Figure 9.1 Perceptions of IOs regarding the importance of value chain actors in achieving VCD outcomes.

supporting certification processes or issuance of regulations. The cinnamon, tea, and milk interventions, implemented by international NGOs, also established close partnerships with government agencies and local authorities from the start. In two cases, government agencies interacted directly with producer organizations, superseding INGOs, whose staff numbers were limited, and taking advantage of their local presence to run daily activities on the ground.

Partnerships with research organizations were minimal. Except for the horticulture intervention, designed and implemented by a consortium of national and international research organizations, and the cinnamon intervention, in which national research institutes contributed to design and delivered trainings, engagement with researchers was not contemplated in the intervention design. Although financial service providers were considered important for achieving the expected outcomes of the initiatives, IOs did not engage them in design or implementation. Mistrust between the private sector and INGOs as well as between the private sector and government may have also played a role in the general limited set of partnerships identified in the cases. IOs mentioned that it is 'difficult to achieve involvement of both the public and private sector, as they have different mindsets and different approaches' and that 'the involvement of the government discouraged private actors to join the project'. Another iO reported that 'partnerships with private actors are tricky and challenging, as they want to get quick benefits. If there are no short-term results, they might leave the partnership'.

Engagement of chain actors in VCD

Engagement by producer organizations
In most cases, producer organizations were organized at the beginning of the intervention (except for the dairy case, where the cooperative was established in 2004). The newly formed organizations were small, with 46 members on average (303 producer organizations covered by the five interventions). The largest had 2,800 members (dairy cooperative) and the second largest had 130 members (fish association). All the other organizations had fewer than 50 members. Among these 303 groups, only two were formal cooperatives engaged in commercial relationships with buyers (a processor for the dairy cooperative and retailers for the horticulture cooperative). For the other cases, producer organizations sometimes facilitated transactions (e.g. organizing delivery of raw material, quality control before delivery, price negotiation), but did not purchase raw material from their members.

Consequently, with the exception of the dairy cooperative, the producer organizations had no income and were unable to invest in supporting their members or advancing their own growth and development. The dairy cooperative supported its members for on-farm investment (e.g. animal shed, milking machines) through advances and partial subsidies (up to 30 per cent). The horticulture cooperative, having no capital yet, was not able to support its members, but its formal status enabled it to buy a truck (pre-funded by one of the retail partners); the cooperative leader also provided the poorest members with cash advances to purchase inputs. In the tea and cinnamon cases, the main role of the informal groups was to channel interventions' activities (mostly trainings) and to initiate collective action. Some of the informal groups managed to set up basic control quality systems to better match buyers' requirements. The horticulture and fish organizations also engaged in the certification process with the support of the IOs and local authorities. Overall, although most of these groups did not directly engage in commercial relationships, it appears that they contributed in upgrading produce quality and level of trust within the chains.

When asked about the main constraints they faced, producer organization representatives pointed out their commercial vulnerability and the need to diversify their portfolio of buyers (especially for those engaged in commercial relationships, where there was a need to avoid dependency on only one buyer), as well as the necessity to increase their capacity in terms of business management, financial negotiations, business planning, and marketing. Lack of financial capital and logistic capacities were also mentioned as important constraints for more engagement in value chains.

Another critical issue is the sustainability of these producer organizations over time. Despite the efforts deployed by IOs in organizing farmers, their overall level of development and the autonomy of the organizations remained weak. This is especially true for the informal groups created within the framework of the tea and cinnamon interventions. In comparison to producer organizations supported by the milk, fish, and horticulture initiatives, these groups appeared to be more isolated and had fewer available resources. There is a high risk that these organizations disaggregate after the withdrawal of the IO.

Engagement by buyers
Buyers involved in the cases showed a high diversity in terms of size, strategy, and type of business. In the dairy case, one internationally owned buyer purchased milk from the cooperative and provided technical assistance to cooperative members (e.g. animal health, quality control). However, the IO reported that the buyer had no interest in being part of the VCD intervention. In the other cases, buyers were mostly medium-scale companies (tea, cinnamon, and horticulture) and small-scale enterprises or individual traders (fish and cinnamon). Except for the dairy and horticulture cases, companies bought directly from individual producers, or from intermediaries. Prices were either negotiated, in the case of horticulture (although the cooperative complained that effective paid prices were lower than those agreed in the contract), or decided by the buyers based on prevailing market prices, sometimes with premiums according to quality (tea, cinnamon). IOs had little or no control on commercial relationships between individuals or producer organizations as well as buyers, and private actors were said to be reluctant to have a third party looking at their business arrangements with suppliers.

Buyers invested in chains to support smallholders and cooperatives in diverse ways. Three buyers (milk, tea, and fish) provided technical assistance, especially in terms of agricultural practices and quality standards. Three buyers (tea, horticulture, and fish) also reported providing cash advances to cooperatives or directly to producers. For instance, a retailer provided the horticulture cooperative with a truck, which is being repaid in instalments deducted from the vegetable sales of the cooperative, while a tea processing company provided smallholders with high-quality fertilizers and pesticides, along with training on proper use of these chemicals. While three companies mentioned being involved in quality certification processes (mostly around safe labels), only one of these companies (cinnamon) was planning to support the certification costs. None of the companies provided farmers with the formal guarantee of buying their production. Overall engagement of private sector buyers in building links with smallholders is not only limited, but also relatively recent in Vietnam – now increasing in prevalence as the economy formalizes and privatizes. Furthermore, while initiatives were successful in upgrading linkages between smallholder producers and buyers, businesses were reluctant to engage further with producer organizations beyond technical assistance and, to a lesser extent, the provision of inputs and equipment. This indicates that businesses engaged with producer organizations to increase product quality, but refrained from providing other kinds of support. Although businesses claimed the need to organize farmers, capacity building of these newly created organizations (e.g. in terms of governance, organization capacity, financial management, and production planning) was left to the IOs.

When asked what the main constraints and risks were preventing deeper engagement in the VCD processes, buyers mentioned that side-selling discouraged them from investing in smallholders, and pointed to low volumes provided by the producers in regards to their needs. Buyers also mentioned bad perceptions about NGOs and the public sector. In some cases the over-representation of the public sector in intervention design and implementation repelled buyers from getting involved. However, the two companies that were involved with interventions led by INGOS reported that it was their first experience working with NGOs, and that it had been positive overall: 'we realized that NGOs can bring more than just money' (tea). Their perception of NGOs had positively evolved, leading to the recognition that 'both kinds of organizations have complementary strengths' (cinnamon).

Major perceived obstacles

When asked about major obstacles to achieving greater impact at scale (see Figure 9.2), IOs emphasized the lack of trust between chain actors, especially between producer organizations and buyers (i.e. processing and retailing companies). IOs mentioned for instance that 'the most critical issue is between cooperatives and [buyers from] the private sector. Private sector does not trust farmers and cooperatives' (horticulture case). Private sector engagement

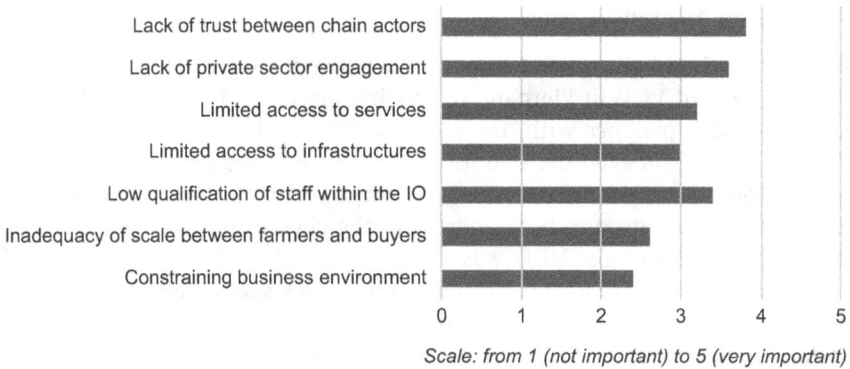

Figure 9.2 Perceptions of IOs regarding major obstacles to achieving greater impact at scale.

toward smallholders was seen as critical, for instance the 'milk sector is characterized by a willingness of private actors to vertically integrate the value chain rather than working with smallholders' and 'volumes of cinnamon produced by smallholder farmers discourage companies to invest in value chain development'. Access to infrastructures and services, in particular to financial services, were also highlighted by IOs as critical constraints. Smallholders were not able to provide the necessary collateral for accessing loans while producer organizations neither have the required legal status to contract loans from banking institutions (in the case of informal groups and associations) nor capital to provide the required collateral. However, although it was considered critical by the IOs, none of them engaged in supporting producer organizations to access financial services.

IOs also mentioned the lack of qualification within their own organizations as an issue for achieving greater impacts, and reported that 'government and NGO staff do not have a business mindset and struggle to support producer organizations', notably in terms of business planning, business management, and marketing. In some cases, it also impeded them from appealing to and convincing private sector representatives to engage with them in supporting smallholder farmers; IOs expressed the need to strengthen their capacity to influence the private sector and foster their participation in inclusive business mechanisms. IOs and buyers also mentioned discordance between the scale of smallholder farming and the demand from downstream segments of the chain as a reason for failure in VCD. This perception reveals the structural gaps between the scattered farming production system (average farm size of 0.5 ha in Vietnam), struggling to constantly supply quality produce, and the buyers, whose demand is growing and who face difficulties in handling a myriad of suppliers. It also reveals a certain negative perception of smallholder farming by other stakeholders, suggesting that small-scale farming is not compatible with the development of more structured and efficient value chains.

Discussion and conclusions

Our results highlight several important challenges faced by IOs to design and implement VCD in Vietnam. In the first place, IOs had a limited awareness of, and experience with, the range of VCD tools available. This is true for the NGOs, and even more so for the government agencies. Practitioners' perception of the potential and of the scope of the existing tools remains narrow, and they need to be supported in the choice and use of these tools. Intervention design for VCD was relatively simple (relying on superficial assessments of local market conditions and chain stakeholders), and most of the intervention activities focused their support on farmers and their organizations in complying with buyers' requirements in terms of quantity and quality. Although there are some cases where new tailor-made tools were needed (e.g. regarding the inclusion of pro-poor, women, or ethnic minorities in VCD processes, or regarding the understanding and analysis of informal market systems), there are also issues for which the right tools already exist, but are unknown by practitioners. Translation of the VCD guides into local languages may increase adoption of the tools by IOs, combined with structured engagement among donors, tool designers, and local implementers to raise awareness of the strengths as well as limitations of each guide or tool. Structured engagement would also support practitioners in selecting and using the most appropriate set of guides and tools during the implementation process.

IOs also faced a lack of resources or technical support to undertake deeper analysis of the chain and business environment before implementation. Projects dedicated limited funds for investigation in the framework of their VCD programmes, either prior to or after the allocation of the grants. Value chain analyses carried out before obtaining funds from the donors tended to be superficial and incomplete, highlighting only a part of the bottlenecks and leverage points that could be addressed by the interventions. From the donor side, options for enabling deeper analysis and critical reflection in general could be to encourage the involvement of research organizations and the private sector at the earliest stage of intervention design, as well as to make funds available for deeper mapping and assessment of value chains and more intensive stakeholder engagement. Another option would be to authorize more flexibility in project implementation planning, allowing for feedback loops and adjustments of activities according to progress achieved on the ground and the knowledge acquired throughout the intervention's implementation. This would also require stronger and innovative monitoring and evaluation frameworks (in addition to the outputs' monitoring of the intervention) in which researchers could have a role (notably in terms of data collection and data management) and longer project time frames – allowing measurements of outcomes and impacts in the long term.

VCD interventions tended to work with better off rather than poor and vulnerable farmers. There was a clear distinction between interventions led by

NGOs and those led by governmental organizations, in terms of approaches, objectives, and activities. For instance, while NGO motivation was guided by poverty reduction, the government-led initiatives tried to respond to domestic market trends and end-consumer demand, especially those from urban areas, and were not designed with a specific aim of reaching the most vulnerable. In the cases examined here, NGOs were willing to include the very poor, and therefore selected value chains considered as pro-poor, such as tea and cinnamon. On the other hand, government organizations selected their beneficiaries according to farmers' willingness and their potential contribution to the success of the intervention for local urban populations, and naturally ended up working with better-off populations who were better informed and had higher potential for achieving the expectations of the intervention. In the tea and cinnamon cases, farmers were selected within the existing supply networks of the private partners, allowing a connection between smallholders and those engaged in the value chain. Although the IOs kept the right to examine the compliance of the beneficiary selection with their own criteria, it reduced their ability to include very poor and vulnerable populations. This was in part because private buyers tended to collaborate with the better-off – those having better access to inputs, infrastructure and services, as well as owning larger production areas, enabling them to provide bigger volumes and higher quality. This suggests a need for specific tools to address specific opportunities, constraints, and trade-offs related to the inclusion of the very poor into VCD.

Our results highlight the importance of producer organizations for fostering vertical linkages within the chains, and achieving fruitful collaboration with downstream buyers. Most of the producer organizations in our case were recently established and are still not formally registered as cooperatives. Many of these structures were created by the IOs for the needs of the projects, and have limited capacity to deliver services to their members. Producer organizations channelled the activities of the VCD interventions, mainly technical assistance, but cannot yet propose additional services to their members, resulting in a high level of dependency on outside assistance projects. While the organizations may have contributed to providing markets with quality products, most of them were unable to handle business issues (i.e. purchasing from producers and selling to buyers). Only a few of them had actually engaged in commercial relationships. Others had little or no revenue streams beyond membership fees, which limited their ability to invest, to be active actors of the chain development, and to sustain over time. This also affected their credibility toward buyers who therefore still tend to deal with middlemen or to integrate the raw material collection function within their operations. Research has pointed to the long and winding path by which producer organizations evolve into viable organizations owing to, among other features, the disabling business environment in which they operate (Donovan et al., 2008). This suggests that preliminary work needs to be done by IOs and partners to facilitate the development of producer organizations or to find alternative forms for organizing support services for smallholders. VCD guidelines would need to better inform these prerequisites, as well as provide ways to assess the readiness of producer organizations for VCD engagement. It also highlights the contradiction between the willingness of donors and governments to support interventions that address a large number of poor and unorganized smallholders, the limited timespan allowed for interventions, and the expected sustainability of these large-scale projects once the intervention ends. As previously suggested by Wertheim-Heck et al., (2010), it seems that starting VCD interventions with a core group of producers – rather than thousands of producers – whose success will later on attract more stakeholders, is a way to cope with producers' low level of organization and to ease the reorientation of the intervention according to progress and achievements. Longer interventions' time frames could also help to avoid the problem of stages being skipped and would enable interventions adequately correspond to VCD dynamics and the required capacity building, long-term engagement, and trust building among actors.

Strong involvement of buyers is crucial for the success of VCD processes. In three cases (horticulture, tea, and cinnamon), businesses offered price incentives to smallholders and their organizations according to the quality of the delivered products, and in two cases (tea and cinnamon), businesses took advantage of IO-provided financial support to deliver technical assistance to their smallholder suppliers. In some instances, buyers invested with their own funds in VCD (e.g. covering cost of certification, cash advances for inputs and equipment). In the other cases, IOs did not establish cooperation with buyers (fish and dairy). Buyers were reluctant (mostly because of side-selling risks) to engage further in supporting producers organizations in the long term or in setting up mechanisms that would allow for sharing risks with smallholders and their organizations.

More broadly, our results suggest a need for more diversified partnerships for VCD design and implementation. IOs typically engaged with government agencies (i.e. authorities at the district and provincial levels, and decentralized technical departments of the ministries and the central government), but less attention was placed on other actors such as private service providers, financial institutions, and buyers from the private sector. In some cases, the strong focus on the public sector may have repelled private sector actors from becoming involved. There are several opportunities to enhance buyer engagement in VCD processes. Firstly, it seems important to strengthen producer organizations, to facilitate their consolidation into reliable business partners for downstream buyers. Secondly, efforts should be made to involve buyers from the design stage of the intervention, to ensure that the intervention responds to needs, but also to stipulate favourable terms (for smallholders) as a precondition of private sector involvement in the interventions. Thirdly, IOs should be strengthened on a wide range of skills, including facilitation, business analysis, and business planning, for them to better understand and interact with the private sector.

Finally, the results suggest that benefits may be achieved from deeper collaboration between researchers and practitioners (e.g. though structured joint learning processes). Such collaboration may allow practitioners to better address the multi-dimensionality and complexity inherent in VCD processes, and applied researchers to better understand the options for improved tool design and expansion of the current set of guides and tools available that lead to greater impact at scale. By better understanding the needs and circumstances of rural households, VCD interventions could be tailored to different types of households, and embrace activities around a set of value chains, thus helping to reduce the potential trade-offs from VCD interventions that seek specialization by smallholders in a particular chain. Ensuring that research outputs can be understood and used by development practitioners – in an efficient and profitable way for smallholder farmers – should become a priority.

Acknowledgement

This study was funded by the CGIAR Research Program on Policies, Markets, and Institutions (PIM).

References

Devoux, A., Torero, M., Donovan, J. and Horton, D. (eds.) (2016) *Innovation for Inclusive Value Chain Development: Successes and Challenges*, Washington, DC: IFPRI.

DFID (2005) 'Making Market Systems Work Better for the Poor (M4P). An introduction to the concept', discussion paper prepared for the ADB-DFID 'learning event', ADB Headquarters, Manila.

Donovan, J., Stoian, D. and Poole, N. (2008) *Global Review of Rural Community Enterprises: The Long and Winding Road to Creating Viable Businesses, and Potential Shortcuts*, Technical Series 29/Rural Enterprise Development Collection 2, Turrialba, Costa Rica: CATIE.

Donovan, J., Franzel, S., Cunha, M., Gyau, A. and Mithöfer, D. (2015) 'Guides for value chain development: a comparative review', *Journal of Agribusiness in Developing and Emerging Economies* 5(1): 1–22 <http://dx.doi.org/10.1108/JaDee-07-2013-0025>.

Gibbon, P. (2001) 'Upgrading primary production: a global commodity chain approach', *World Development* 29(2): 345–63 <http://dx.doi.org/10.1016/S0305-750X(00)00093-0>.

Humphrey, J. (2005) *Shaping Value Chains for Development: Global Value Chains in Agribusiness*, Eschborn, Germany: GTZ.

Humphrey, J. and Navas-Alemán, L. (2010) *Value Chains, Donor Interventions and Poverty Reduction: A Review of Donor Practice*, IDS Research Report 63, Brighton, UK: IDS.

Seville, D., Buxton, A. and Vorley, B. (2011) *Under What Conditions Are Value Chains Effective Tools for Pro-Poor Development?* [pdf], Sustainable Food Laboratory and International Institute for Environment and Development <http://pubs.iied.org/pdfs/16029IIED.pdf> [accessed 9 February 2017].

Springer-Heinze, A. (2008) *ValueLinks Manual: The Methodology of Value Chain Promotion*, Eschborn, Germany: GTZ.

Stoian, D., Donovan, J., Fisk, J. and Muldoon, M. (2012) 'Value chain development for rural poverty reduction: a reality check and a warning', *Enterprise Development and Microfinance* 23(1): 54–69 <http://dx.doi.org/10.3362/1755-1986.2012.006>.

Webber, C.M. and Labaste, P. (2010) *Building Competitiveness in Africa's Agriculture: A Guide to Value Chain Concepts and Applications*, Washington, DC: World Bank.

Wertheim-Heck, S., Quaedackers, P., Anh, N.T. and van Wijk, S. (2010) 'Value chain development of avocado in Vietnam', *Urban Agriculture Magazine – From Seed to Table* 24: 35–8.

About the authors

Brice Even (b.even@cgiar.org), Sustainable Food System Specialist, The Alliance of Bioversity International and the International Center for Tropical Agriculture (CIAT), Hanoi, Vietnam.

Jason Donovan, PhD (j.donovan@cgiar.org), Senior Economist, Research Theme Leader for Markets and Value Chains, International Maize and Wheat Improvement Center (CIMMYT), Texcoco, Mexico.

CHAPTER 10

Making markets work for women: How push and pull strategies can support women's economic empowerment

Christine Faveri, Kerry Jane Wilson,
and Perveen Shaikh

Abstract

In many countries, the inability of women to negotiate pervasive social, legal, and cultural barriers inhibits their participation in the productive sphere, particularly their entry into market systems as producers and entrepreneurs. The paper draws on case studies from projects implemented by the Mennonite Economic Development Associates (MEDA) in Ghana, the Entrepreneurship and Community Development Institute (ECDI) in Pakistan, and Zardozi in Afghanistan to show how practitioners can maximize 'push' and 'pull' strategies to increase the scale, impact, and sustainability of women's economic empowerment programming. Despite differences in country contexts, value chains, and sectors, the authors illustrate the importance of 'push' strategies in helping women to overcome the persistent gender-based discrimination that undermines women's understanding of markets, access to networks, self-confidence, and business success. They also show how deliberate 'pull' strategies that use commercially based incentives can increase women's incomes and business sustainability. The authors conclude that a blend of push and pull strategies will provide the most reach and impact for women's economic empowerment projects, ensuring income growth and gender equality dividends for families and communities.

Keywords: women's economic empowerment, market systems development, Ghana, Afghanistan, Pakistan

Gender inequality has been defined as a binding constraint that affects inclusive market system development around the world (De Santos, 2013). For several years, the United Nations has underscored the multiplier effect that investing in women and girls can have on productivity, efficiency, and sustained economic growth. The private sector is increasingly recognizing that equitable inclusion of women in formal employment can increase GDP significantly in many regions of the world (Goldman Sachs and JBWere, 2009).

http://dx.doi.org/10.3362/9781788530576.010

In turn, there is evidence that reducing poverty can increase women's economic empowerment. However, women's access to economic resources cannot be considered an end in itself. For women to be economically empowered, they must have the ability and choice to make and act on economic decisions (Golla et al., 2011). Academics and policymakers concerned about women's economic empowerment and inclusive gender equitable growth, have learned that effective and sustainable development programming must be grounded in a strong understanding of the specific and localized environments in which programmes operate. Women's economic empowerment alone may not lead to gender equality (Jones, 2012). A multiplicity of context-specific variables will determine the transformative potential of paid work (Kabeer et al., 2011).

Feminist theory and practice have underscored the importance of recognizing the social, class, and gender-specific rules and norms that order and shape relations between women and men, and between women themselves, in both the public and the private sphere. Market systems thinking is now acknowledging how gender analysis can help to identify the change points in a system that will facilitate a positive shift in women's ability to act and interact with complex market systems and subsystems (Markel and Jones, 2014).

Practitioners can use such learning to develop strategies to help women to move into markets ('push' strategies) and to encourage market actors to use commercial incentives to engage women producers and actors ('pull' strategies).

This chapter looks at how push and pull strategies have been used by three non-governmental organizations in different country contexts to facilitate market systems changes benefiting women: in the tailoring and embroidery sector in Afghanistan; hand-embellished fabrics in Pakistan; and the soybean value chain in northern Ghana. It shows how 'push' strategies will remain essential where women are severely culturally isolated but that the push-to-pull ratio can increase as certain pre-requisites are in place: women's business skills, networks, trust between market actors, and a proven business case for working with women. Finally, the authors show how 'push' and 'pull' can optimize scale, reach, and impact in terms of women's economic empowerment.

Using push and pull to support women's economic empowerment in Afghanistan, Pakistan and Ghana

Facilitating inclusive market systems development requires a number of strategies and interventions to catalyse system-level changes. USAID has referred to some of these strategies as 'push' and 'pull' strategies, particularly when describing market systems development programming (Seep Network, 2014):

- *Push strategies* are designed to help very poor individuals and households build up a minimum level of assets (e.g. human, financial, social, cultural) that increases their capability to engage with other market actors (both public and private) and transition out of a cycle of extreme poverty. Interventions may build household assets; improve linkages to social protection; build livelihood and 'market readiness' skills; improve 'soft' skills such as confidence, negotiating, or relationship building; address chronic or temporary deficiencies in consumption; or strengthen household capacity to manage risk.

- Pull strategies leverage commercial incentives to facilitate the more gainful participation of the poor in economic opportunities so they can continue to improve their well-being beyond a project's life through sustained engagement in market systems – be it as a producer, labourer, employee, or business owner. Interventions may create less risky entry points or lower barriers to market entry.

In all parts of the world, gender inequality complicates access to finance, mobility, literacy, negotiation power, business registration, confidence, and trust between market actors. This is particularly true in religious or culturally conservative communities in countries such as Afghanistan and Pakistan where women's interactions are strictly moderated by family members; there is an insecure/conflict environment; and there are gendered rules and norms of the institutions with which women engage. However, even in middle-income countries, like Ghana, women's involvement in the economic sphere can be invisible and therefore go unsupported in economic development initiatives. For example, in northern Ghana, women in rural areas are primary contributors to the local economy as unpaid subsistence farm labour, but are rarely regarded as farmers.

A contextual understanding of how women and men interact in their communities; the roles that women play in the productive and reproductive sphere; and the social and cultural barriers and opportunities to women's full participation in market systems are critical to designing strategies that will maximize outcomes for women.

Zardozi: Markets for Afghan Women

Zardozi is a registered Afghan non-governmental organization (NGO) that has provided marketing support services to home-bound Afghan women embroiderers since 1984. In 2008, Zardozi shifted from a direct service delivery model to one of market facilitation to help raise incomes for poor, uneducated women through a commercially sustainable system which links female producers working in the informal economy to local markets. Zardozi works in four urban and semi-urban areas of Afghanistan: Kabul, Mazar, Herat, and Jalalabad.

Zardozi's Markets for Afghan Artisans project, jointly funded by the united Kingdom's Department for International Development and Oxfam Novib (2009– 2015), was designed to overcome the shortcomings of traditional economic development projects for women in Afghanistan that have focused on vocational training without solid market analysis and the expansion of women in the formal sector. Through market research, Zardozi discovered that traditional business lines for women, such as tailoring and embroidery, were still able to absorb a significant amount of new business and thus began their work by focusing on connecting women already active in these sectors to new market opportunities.

In Afghanistan, supporting women to succeed in the informal sector is important given cultural and security constraints on women's mobility. Zardozi typically works with women in two major categories: those who are permitted by their families to engage in market activities with men; and those who have permission to operate a business only within the confines of their home or community.

Zardozi models itself as a business support network for women, providing them with membership in a credible organization that backs their businesses, new and advanced skills training, market research and information, and linkages with buyers. They work with skilled women who are committed to starting a business and focus on helping them to build their markets and social networks. In Afghanistan, this is critically important as men's business support networks are embedded in trust-based extended family relations. Business networks facilitate access to credit, inputs, buyers, and distribution channels for goods. Because women are not valued or perceived as potential business partners, they are routinely excluded.

Zardozi's use of push and pull strategies in Afghanistan

Many of the strategies that Zardozi employs to reach and support women can be termed 'push' strategies. For NGOs operating in Afghanistan, this is a critical first step in reaching and mobilizing Afghan women, many of whom are extremely poor, illiterate, and isolated. Zardozi's clients take tremendous risks to cross cultural barriers to earn an income.

A traditional 'push' strategy implemented by Zardozi has been the provision of basic business and skills training to women working in the informal garment sector. The entry point is training around new designs for sewing and beadwork products – socially and culturally acceptable activities that women can undertake in their homes. The 'push' from Zardozi comes in the provision of basic equipment (cutting table, scissors, or sewing machine) and product samples as required. What are atypical, in Afghanistan, are Zardozi's next steps. After the initial training, women are provided with intensive business training and then linked directly to a market or buyer, ideally within 6 weeks. A full cycle of the programme would see a woman mentored through the production of at least one order for a product.

Once women are successful in understanding the process and committed to continuing their businesses, Zardozi encourages them to join their network. This is a membership based organization where they can receive ongoing business services (design, marketing, quality control, branding, and packaging) for a small fee. The services are delivered through Zardozi's Community

Business Centres (CBCs) (67 in total) located in women's houses. Set up as women-only safe spaces, the CBCs are located within walking distance of 30 to 35 group members and are connected to one of four registered Nisfe Jahan or guilds that function as a community-level business association for women. The Nisfe Jahan is now registered with the Ministry of Justice. There are four branches (Herat, Mazar, Jalalabad, and Kabul) in the process of federating and establishing links with other similar associations such as Afghan Women's Business Federation, Afghan Women's Business Council, and Afghan Women's Network. Through the CBC, Zardozi facilitates linkages for women with local banks and promotes participation in local savings groups and traditional rotating savings and Credit Associations, where available. The CBCs encourage women to engage in flexible diverse business opportunities, e.g. moving from sewing to also raising chickens to sell eggs. They also provide social/peer support, build confidence and aspiration for business, allow women to cope with change, and stay connected to an informal market place that has very few opportunities for women.

In Afghanistan, 'pull' strategies to stimulate women's economic empowerment are more limited and challenging to employ. Due to years of war and insecurity, the market remains largely informal and national level production is limited. There are few business role models and fewer women-owned businesses. Zardozi's 'pull' strategies, therefore, focus on making introductions and building relationships with informal traders and shopkeepers to facilitate orders for their clients. The gender-related barriers that women face in terms of interacting with male staff members, shopkeepers, and business-owners have limited Zardozi's ability to step away and let market linkages take over. Women need ongoing support and confidence building, not only in terms of engaging in paid work, but also in order-management, branding, marketing, and negotiation in an extremely male-dominated environment. As such, Zardozi plays a key role in managing risk for both the women and the private sector buyers.

Despite these challenges, Zardozi is making headway and remains a unique model in the Afghan context. In just three years, they have facilitated opportunities for approximately 6,000 women. Their members have measured an average fourfold increase in income in traditional value chains ranging from US$16 per month (23 per cent of clients) to over $300 per month (the most entrepreneurial 14 per cent). For example, some women have expanded into new and lucrative markets such as the private school uniform market in Herat where uniforms were purchased previously from iran. Zardozi helped to identify and connect women to this new market using wholesale fabrics imported from Pakistan. The connection has resulted in the sustained local procurement of uniforms from Zardozi clients with women managing their own orders and relationships with the schools.

The majority of Zardozi's clients (62 per cent) earn between $18 and $62 per month. These women are the most risk averse and focus on raising just enough money to support their family. For the most part, women report being able to reinvest their earnings in their businesses while balancing demands on their income related to children, healthcare, and household expenses. Qualitative surveys also show improvements in women's healthcare and family nutrition; an increase in investments in girls' education; and a new confidence in women to confront gender stereotypes in the communities in which they live. Women mention a change in their status within the family and the community and more agency and control over their incomes. Zardozi's clients have become more mobile as the family sees the benefits of their businesses and that no harm comes to them despite pushing the cultural boundaries of operating in a public space.

Long-term, sustainable economic empowerment for women in Afghanistan will take time and require more effort, and engaging and convincing men and families about the value of women's economic empowerment is critical for Zardozi's clients and for the future of the country. Women's lack of self-confidence and opposition from family members are significant barriers to women's business expansion. Efforts to address this, for example through awareness-raising and celebrations of women's successes, have gone some way to reversing family opposition. Zardozi has found that tackling gender biases through concrete demonstrations of women's economic contributions to their families and communities is an important strategy for building women's social capital in Afghanistan.

ECDI: Entrepreneurship and Community Development Institute in Pakistan

The Entrepreneurship and Community Development Institute (ECDI) has been working for over two decades to support women and the poor to attain their socio-economic potential. In the past, ECDI focused on building the capacity of individual women entrepreneurs and micro, small, and medium enterprises through training and provision of business development services. However, in recent years, ECDI chose to move from a service provision model to the development of pro-poor markets by stimulating competitiveness among key market players. Value chain analyses showed that social and cultural barriers resulting in women's isolation from the public sphere, prohibited women producers of hand-embellished fabrics from earning fair wages from their labour. ECDI became a key partner in the Entrepreneurs project, funded by the United States Agency for International Development (2009– 2014), which sought to increase women's incomes and access to the high-value hand-embellished fabric market that exists for Pakistani work nationally and abroad. ECDI's client base for the project was home-bound rural and peri-urban women working on embellished fabrics on a piecework basis. Like Zardozi, ECDI chose to work with women producers and small enterprises as a critical route to increasing women's economic and social capital. In rural Sindh, Rural South Punjab, Balochistan, and Swat, hand embellishment is the primary livelihood for women; however, poor women, particularly in rural areas, earn very little and sometimes no return on their labour. Constrained by lack of mobility, violence, ethnic and religious strife, power shortages, and a deteriorating law and order situation, accessing buyers is difficult. Furthermore, home-bound women have limited access to market information, lack quality inputs, and suffer from an absence of credit facilities to improve and expand their production.

ECDI's use of push and pull strategies in Sindh, Pakistan

ECDI was one of the pioneers of an innovative 'push' strategy in Pakistan called the Female Sales Agent model. The model focused on building the capacity and confidence of local women producers, who had a relatively greater degree of mobility within the community, and worked through these Sales Agents to reach other home-bound women. ECDI began with extensive social mobilization of families and communities to create buy-in for women's participation in the project, then identified a cadre of women that could be trained as Sales Agents in business and product marketing. The Female Sales Agents received training in a variety of areas including design, marketing, basic accounting, quality assurance, negotiation skills, and conflict resolution. They also acted as the liaison between the market and other women home-based producers. They brought new product designs, production techniques, and resources to the women; and carried finished products to market; ensuring payment for the home-bound women. Female Sales Agents earned no wages from the project.

The project also set up 15 Common Facility Centres (CFC) as hubs for business training and marketing. Unlike Zardozi, the Entrepreneur's CFCs were legally registered small businesses operated by a group of women entrepreneurs. Each CFC is now equipped with resource materials, sample catalogues, sample books, training manuals, and other relevant materials. They serve to aggregate women's products and act as informal 'buying houses'. They also have become community centres for the women to meet and work on orders together. As both a 'push' and 'pull' strategy, the CFCs have provided women with important connections to microfinance institutions for loan products and have enabled buyers, marketing, and design teams to interact with large swathes of producers who were previously inaccessible to them. By the close of the project, some CFCs were being supported by private sector companies (such as Asassah, Texlynx, and Indus Heritage Trust) to ensure a continued stream of hand-embellished fabric for their garments.

One 'pull' strategy that ECDI was able to employ has been to help women pitch their handiwork and designs to private sector buyers, thus brokering trust in the market place. Mainstream stores and brands were keen to get into the hand-embroidered product market after seeing the success of home-based boutiques and high-end designers. Through their years of working with women in hand-embellished fabrics, ECDI was able to approach business owners directly with a solid business case. This strategy was well received in Pakistan where the larger companies in the garment and textile sector tend to be male-owned and wary of working with women directly. Connecting private sector actors directly with the women producers built the women's capacity to understand and meet private sector standards around quality and timeliness. ECDI also encouraged the private sector to create incentives versus penalties to help women improve their products and was successful in negotiating bonuses for women who delivered quality products on time.

Under the Entrepreneur's project, ECDI helped to create self-employment opportunities for 7,000 women embellishers and 120 Female Sales Agents. Across the entire project (a total of four value chains), women reported an average increase of 93 per cent in net sales and a 19 per cent average increase in project-related income from 7 per cent to 26 per cent at the household level from 2010 to 2014 (Innovative Development Strategies, 2014). In addition, an independent assessment by Innovative Development Strategies showed that project participants experienced better overall enterprise management with the greatest increase in marketing skills (35 per cent), preservation of outputs (31 per cent), quality control (28 per cent), and linkages to domestic producers (26 per cent). Focus group discussions pointed to a positive change in community attitudes toward women and women's entrepreneurship and a self-reported change in women's status within the household including greater decision-making power, confidence, and independence.

ECDI have continued to help their clients secure contracts and have facilitated linkages between their clients and 17 high-end designer labels in Pakistan and exports to Canada, Italy, and England. They have found that moving into larger and more sophisticated orders will require more oversight from them, a trend that will likely continue given the literacy and confidence challenges facing their women clients. And while some of the educated Female Sales Agents have started using social media and SMS to connect with the market directly, the majority of ECDI's clients continue to remain worlds apart from the growing middle class market in Pakistan that they serve.

MEDA: Mennonite Economic Development Associates in northern Ghana

Mennonite Economic Development Associates (MEDA) has been working for over 60 years to facilitate business solutions to poverty. Statistical data for Ghana shows that women account for approximately 50 per cent of the agricultural labour force and produce around 70 per cent of Ghana's food crops (Ghana Ministry of Food and Agriculture, 2004). Many farmers in northern Ghana are poor. They often own less than 2 acres of land and struggle to produce enough crop in a single rainy season to feed their families for the year. In particular, women farmers are frequently overlooked and under-served. Women have limited knowledge of market players; do not receive technical training from extension agents; and tend to sell produce in small quantities in informal local markets. They are last in line for land preparation services, have limited access to labour-saving technologies and rarely access loans to cover production costs.

However, across the north of the country, women play a significant role in the provision of food and nutrition within families. Although access to land is controlled by men and men control cash crops, women cultivate kitchen gardens and often small plots of marginal land for additional food crops. Surplus produce often is sold to the local market to generate income which is reinvested back in to the household.

In 2012, MEDA undertook a gender and market analysis of the soybean sector in Ghana as part of the design of the Greater Rural Opportunities (GROW) Project, funded by the Department of Foreign Affairs, Trade and Development Canada (2012–18). The analysis showed that soybean has strong potential as a revenue-generating crop for women in the north and that it could contribute significantly to household diets due to its high nutritional content. The GROW project seeks to work with women soybean farmers to strengthen production and market linkages, increase access to appropriate financial services, and support women farmers to expand the production of nutrition foods and increase nutritional awareness.

MEDA's use of push-pull strategies in Ghana

MEDA adapted a number of successful 'push' strategies to help increase the productivity and profits of women soybean farmers. They began by bringing communities together to talk about gender equality and the roles women and men have been assigned at work and at home. Men and traditional leaders were asked to endorse women's participation in the project and encouraged to think about how they could support the women in their family to be successful farmers, for example through the provision of land to the women. MEDA has found that the identification of male champions, particularly husbands and chiefs that control productive resources in rural communities, is an important strategy for facilitating women's economic empowerment in Ghana.

MEDA also adapted the successful Female Sales Agent model from Pakistan to the GROW project creating a cohort of Women lead farmers to train, mentor, and guide other women farmers in their communities in soybean production. The Nucleus Farmer model, currently promoted in northern Ghana, creates Nucleus Farmers with land holdings of 5–50 acres (predominately men) and provides them with tools to disseminate inputs, services, financing, and product aggregation to hundreds or a thousand farmers. By contrast, the GROW project's Women Lead Farmers are trained as entrepreneurs to provide products and services to 20–30 other women smallholder farmers in their own communities. After basic training in improved agronomic practices, business, and negotiation skills, the Lead Farmers provide direct extension services, support, and assistance to women in their groups. Like Zardozi and ECDI, MEDA actively connects Women Lead Farmers directly to market actors such as financial service providers, input suppliers, tractor operators, threshing machine service providers, and soybean buyers to facilitate linkages to help 'pull' women's products into market. Through field visits, the women learn about soybean demand, quality, pricing, and market behaviour. They also work within their groups to expand dry season economic activities where market opportunities exist.

In the first three years of the project, MEDA has seen the Women Lead Farmers take on new and different market roles, becoming active agents of change in the market system. Women have become distributors of inputs and extension services to other farmers (male and female) as well as soybean aggregators. The project is supporting some women to become soybean processors, producing value-added products such as soy-milk and tofu to sell in the local retail market. In addition, the project is piloting initiatives with government, private sector businesses, and NGOs to test the efficacy of using the Lead Farmers to disseminate timely market information using information communications technology (e.g. SMS and voicemail messages) and extension advice in local dialects to illiterate farmers through mechanisms such as 'Talking Books'. The Talking Book, an innovative low-cost audio computer, was designed by Literacy Bridge and is being piloted through the MEDA GROW project.

One difference in MEDA's experience was the way in which MEDA consciously worked on identifying potential 'pull' strategies early in the design of the project to leverage commercial/market actors to help overcome the barriers that face women farmers in the north. At the outset of the project, MEDA pitched the business case for working with women to a range of input suppliers, service providers, financial institutions, and soybean processors, encouraging them to tap into the vast new network of women farmers that the project would create as new customers, suppliers, and producers.

MEDA also brought several large soy processing companies to meet the women farmers prior to the first harvest. After seeing the volume of soybeans that were being produced by the women, two companies approached MEDA to negotiate purchases with the women farmers directly. Women's groups were able to secure a competitive market price for their harvested beans and a commitment from the buyers to cover the costs of collection and transport to processing plants in the south. Through this process, community members learned about the value of the women's crop; became energized by the bargaining and competition between firms for their beans; and learned more about how processing companies viewed the women as a key production source to meet Ghana's large unmet soybean demand.

Another 'pull' strategy that the GROW project used was to work with a financial institution to help women farmers access production loans. Sissala Rural Bank lacked the capital to provide small production loans to women farmers so MEDA engineered a three-way partnership arrangement between the bank and a local NGO, whereby MEDA financed a $50,000 loan to the bank which it committed to using for women farmers. The local NGO provided on-the-ground follow-up with the borrowers, facilitated the sales of beans promptly after harvest to ensure repayment and followed-up with any delayed payment. The first year of the project saw a 54 per cent increase in women's access to finance both through voluntary savings and loan associations (VSLAs) and formal loans from Sissala Bank. The GROW team is now working to help the women form VSLA groups that will invest their savings in agricultural production.

As the project enters its third year, over 11,000 women farmers have been registered, 40 per cent have planted soybeans, and 515 Lead Farmers are actively working in their communities. The number of women who are producing and selling soybean increased by 44 per cent at the end of the first year, reflecting significantly more connections to processors and other buyers than existed before. Other early impact indicators show that 71 per cent of women reported having access to timely market information, including on such topics as pricing (70 per cent) and potential buyers (20 per cent). Of those female farmers that received market information, 50 per cent of them indicated they were able to negotiate with different buyers to agree on terms of sales such as transportation, pricing, storage, and payments.

Aside from increasing soybean production, women are diversifying their dry-season activities with new crops that will further enhance household income and nutrition. Moving forward, MEDA is devoting resources towards addressing other bottlenecks in the soybean value chain to increase the reach and sustainability of the project. For example, GROW will be working with seed growers to ensure enough available seeds at planting season, linking them to the Women Lead Farmers and Sales Agents, and working with technology suppliers to help improve the availability of hand-held planters to provide more low-cost technology options for women farmers.

MEDA has learned that discussions with private sector actors around the business case for working with women helps market actors view women farmers as clients or suppliers in their own right. Once the case is made, women have a much easier time integrating into the market and the potential for sustainability increases. Christian Bellow, Operations Manager for Golden Web Soybean Processing Company said, 'Next year we don't need MEDA to be there. We can buy directly from the women. It is self-sustaining. That's what we are looking for.'

Conclusions

In the authors' experience, the key to designing inclusive market systems development programming lies first in understanding the complexities of the programming environment from a gender, social, and market systems perspective. Each of the three organizations set out to design women's economic empowerment projects that directly addressed the gender discrimination and market challenges that women faced and did so in a way that was culturally sensitive and appropriate. The starting point was to demonstrate to women and their families that they could expand their informal, home-based work as a business; and then to develop the business case for other market actors to help them succeed.

Using a combination of 'push' and 'pull' strategies is critical, particularly when working with poor and marginalized women. 'Push' strategies will help to 'level the playing field', increase women's skills and confidence, and expand women's understanding of the market systems in which they work. All three organizations created networks and spaces for women to connect – for social support, learning, consciousness-raising, and negotiating. Zardozi's Community Business Centres and ECDI's Common Facility Centres provided culturally acceptable, women-only spaces for the project to offer business services and support to more women than could be reached in their individual homes. ECDI's Female Sales Agent model in Pakistan and MEDA's Women lead farmers model in Ghana are further adaptations that have expanded the reach and scale of women's networks through empowering women in their own communities to assume positions as teachers, leaders, role models, negotiators, and agents of change. It is worth noting that the Female Sales Agents and Lead Farmers are not remunerated by the projects. The women earn income from market-based sales of their products alongside the women in their groups. As such, this innovative model is replicable, scalable, and also sustainable.

'Pull' strategies that bring recognition of women's role in the value chain and market system are easier to employ in countries like Ghana where social and cultural norms and customs are less prohibitive of direct interactions between women and men. However, in all of the case studies, there was some degree of 'pull' (see Figure 10.1). Whether this was facilitating introductions for women garment makers to new markets in Afghanistan or facilitating discussions around design, quality, and timeliness of delivery with buyers and women embroiders in Pakistan, the connections created a spark of awareness about the potential market that existed and the role of women within it. In Ghana, 'pull' strategies such as facilitating women's access to formal credit and demonstrating the business case for engaging women as input suppliers and

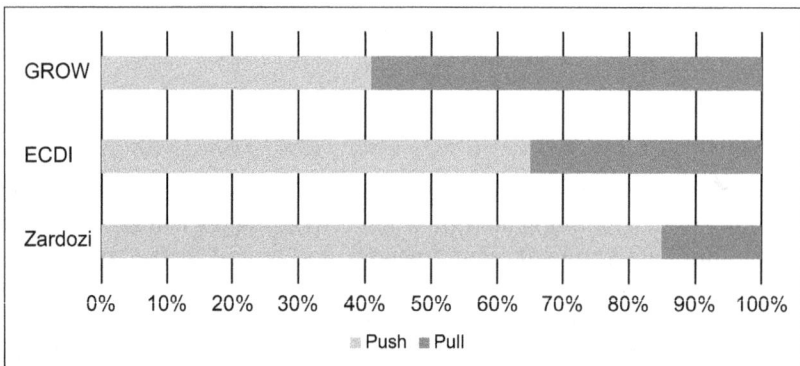

Figure 10.1 Comparison of case studies using push-pull approaches with women.

seed processors in their own communities are examples of how 'pull' can be used to expand private sector reach and women's roles in market systems. As demonstrated by the case studies above, 'push' and 'pull' strategies can increase women's economic empowerment and generate dynamic shifts in gender relations and market systems. They also create potential for lasting change.

Making markets work for women is not easy. For many, facilitation, in market systems development terms, is new. NGOs struggle to catalyse change within market systems without becoming part of the system itself. Continual capacity building within organizations is key but, ultimately, experience is the most effective teacher. No two communities will be the same and adapting and employing successful models will garner new learning. And as Zardozi, ECDI, and MEDA have learned, celebrating women's successes is key. When community members see buyers that are eager to do business directly with women, they begin to internalize the importance of women's economic empowerment and the transformative potential that it can bring.

References

De Santos, A. (2013) *Women's Entrepreneurship Diagnostic*, Washington, DC: USAID.

Ghana Ministry of Food and Agriculture (2004) *Gender and Agricultural Development Strategy*, Accra, Ghana: Ministry of Food and Agriculture.

Goldman Sachs and JBWere Investment Research (2009) *Australia's Hidden Resource: The Economic Case for Increasing Female Participation*, Sydney, Australia: Goldman Sachs and JBWere Investment Research.

Golla, A., Malhotra, A., Nanda, P., and Mehra, R. (2011) *Understanding and Measuring Women's Economic Empowerment: Definition, Framework and Indicators*, Washington, DC: International Centre for Research on Women.

Innovative Development Strategies (Pvt.) Ltd (2014) *Performance Evaluation Impact Assessment: Pakistan Entrepreneurs Project* [online], Islamabad, Pakistan, May 2014 <www.meda.org/impact-assessment-report/file> [accessed 1 February 2015].

Jones, L. (2012) *Discussion Paper for an M4P WEE Framework: How can the Making Markets Work for the Poor Framework work for poor women and for poor men?* Durham, UK: Springfield Centre.

Kabeer, N., Mahmud, S., and Tasneem, S. (2011) *Does Paid Work Provide a Pathway to Women's Empowerment? Empirical Findings from Bangladesh*, IDS Working Paper 375, Brighton, UK: Institute of Development Studies.

Markel, E., and Jones, L. (2014) *Women's Economic Empowerment: Pushing the Frontiers of Inclusive Market Development* [pdf] <https://www.microlinks. org/sites/default/files/resource/ files/WEE_in_Market_Systems_Framework_ final.pdf> [accessed 27 January 2015].

SEEP Network (2014) 'USAid calls for practitioner learning from push/pull and inclusive market development' [blog] <www.seepnetwork.org/blog/ LEO-call-project-examples-inclusive-market-development-2> [accessed 27 January 2015].

About the authors

Christine Faveri (cfaveri@meda.org), Director, Women's Economic Opportunities at Mennonite Economic Development Associates, Canada.

Kerry Jane Wilson (wilsonkerryjane@gmail.com), Director, Zardozi – Markets for Afghan Women at Zardozi, Afghanistan.

Perveen Shaikh (ecdi_pak@yahoo.com), President, Entrepreneurship and Community Development Institute, Pakistan.

CHAPTER 11

Digital agriculture and pathways out of poverty: The need for appropriate design, targeting, and scaling

Carolyn Florey, Jon Hellin, and Jean Balié

Abstract

Digital technologies range from 'low-tech' tools such as mobile phones and computers to more 'high-tech' solutions such as blockchain, Internet of Things (IoT), and artificial intelligence. Digital technologies can help smallholder farmers increase their yields and incomes if they are effectively targeted to facilitate agriculture as a 'pathway out of poverty'. For digital agriculture to deliver on its promise, it is critical not only to design digital agriculture interventions that consider the target populations' needs, constraints, and appropriateness, but also to ensure that digital technologies do not exacerbate social and economic inequalities. Cognizance of these risks is essential if practitioners are to ensure that digital agriculture fulfils its potential and makes significant contributions to the Sustainable Development Goals (SDG). We use the example of a digital agriculture decision support tool, Rice Crop Manager (RCM), to illustrate the challenges of designing, targeting, and scaling digital tools to support rural development.

Keywords: digital agriculture, Rice Crop Manager, gender, equity, poverty

Introduction

Previously, agricultural researchers and practitioners' primary objective was feeding the world's growing population, utilizing scientific research to increase yields and food production. The Green Revolution, for example, is considered a success when assessed in terms of an increase in food production and, hence, a greater supply of food to support growing human populations. This approach was relatively straight-forward: develop new agricultural technologies such as higher-yielding crop varieties and transfer them to farmers through government extension services. However, the context has dramatically changed, as global trends of population growth, climate change, urbanization, labour scarcity, yield stagnation, food insecurity, conflict, and resource degradation have shifted the agricultural and food landscape.

http://dx.doi.org/10.3362/9781788530576.011

For the past few decades, the focus on agriculture and pro-poor rural development has garnered remarkable interest within international policy, research, and development agendas. Since the 1990s, development economists and policy professionals have focused on 'making markets work for the poor' (Markelova et al., 2009). Scholars and policy practitioners have emphasized the economic, social, and cultural role of the agricultural sector and the need to revitalize it to combat poverty effectively. In the last two decades, numerous efforts have been directed at removing policy-induced distortions in financial and agricultural product markets, including exchange rate misalignment, prohibitive tariffs, ineffective subsidies, and inadequate price interventions. Policy reforms have stimulated the supply side of the rural economy, through better functioning markets, to generate and capture value addition and on-farm investments to increase agricultural productivity (e.g. through new varieties, improved cropping systems, and better post-harvest processing) (Gómez et al., 2011).

The need to make agriculture more profitable, productive, efficient, sustainable, and attractive to new groups, while making food more nutritious, provides a key opportunity for innovation in the field of digital agriculture. Digitization of the economy, or 'cyber-physical' merging of human and machine, is often presented as the fourth industrial revolution (Schwab, 2017). Digital technologies such as blockchain, big data, robotics, and the Internet of Things (IoT) are changing the way people access information, interact with others, provide services, sell and purchase products, and, ultimately, how they make decisions. The digitization of agricultural value chains is an opportunity to generate wealth, save time, and improve livelihoods throughout the world. The utilization of low and high technology solutions for agriculture has enormous potential to transform the agriculture sector. Currently, at least 96 per cent of the world's population is within range of a mobile signal (International Telecommunication Union, 2018).

Digital technologies have the potential to revolutionize agriculture and transform the sector and rural livelihoods. The integration of digital technology in agriculture can potentially lead to the modernization of the sector through better connected, informed farmers who have access to new information and markets while reducing hardships and ultimately improving their livelihoods (Kos and Kloppenburg, 2019; Basso and Antle, 2020). Agricultural researchers and implementers are actively developing new tools and solutions in agriculture that leverage digital technologies. Service provision of drones for seed sowing, blockchain for traceability and certification, site-specific nutrient recommendations sent via text message, 3D printing of spare parts for farm machinery, and artificial intelligence algorithms that identify pests and diseases are a handful of examples that could lead this transformation.

Other examples of digital technologies and innovation practices in agriculture include:

- Internet of Things-based decision support tool for irrigation scheduling and carbon footprints labelling;

- site-specific nutrient precision management that enhances resource-use efficiency;
- geospatial tools to estimate rice production and rapidly assess damage from floods and droughts to tie in the data to insurance schemes;
- drone-based improvements in agronomic practices.

In sub-Saharan Africa alone, almost 400 digital agriculture tools were identified in 2018 (Technical Centre for Agriculture and Rural Cooperation (CTA), 2019). These tools incorporate digital technologies ranging from 'low-tech' tools such as mobile phones and computers to more 'high-tech' solutions such as blockchain, IoT, and artificial intelligence. The application of these technologies along the agricultural value chain has been equally diverse and varied: from market information on mobile phones, to drones that monitor pests and disease, to sensors that provide actionable irrigation and water management recommendations. Digital technologies can help smallholder farmers increase their incomes and yields if utilized effectively and efficiently (Kos and Kloppenburg, 2019). Meanwhile, economists and policy analysts are developing relevant policies to foster digital technology adoption at scale in an interoperable, scalable, and affordable manner.

The evidence for the transformative potential of digital agriculture continues to grow. Countries across South Asia, Southeast Asia, and Africa launch new digital agriculture platforms each year across the agricultural value chain. In India, for example, states such as Andhra Pradesh, Odisha, and Telangana are at the forefront of the digital transformation (Boettiger and Sanghvi, 2019; Bouton, 2019). Sri Lanka, Vietnam, and the Philippines seek to partner with international and domestic technology companies to reap the potential benefits of digital agriculture. India and Sri Lanka, for example, have official programmes to double farmers' incomes through the adoption of technology-advanced agricultural innovations and more particularly digital technologies (Department of Agriculture, Cooperation and Farmers' Welfare, 2020).

In the case of sub-Saharan Africa (SSA), the Malabo Montpellier Panel (2019) reported that:

> *How African countries position themselves to harness and deploy digital technologies will determine the future competitiveness and sustainability of African agriculture and its contribution to African economies ... In fact, the so-called Fourth Industrial Revolution can be an opportunity for African countries to leapfrog and lead the way in the application of digital technologies along the agriculture value chain. While some technologies may be out of reach for most value chain actors for now, this is an opportune moment to devise appropriate strategies to equip the next generation of farmers with the right set of digital skills to be able to harness those digital solutions and services still on the horizon* (Malabo Montpellier Panel, 2019: iv, 1).

However, the realities and constraints that exist in agricultural production in the global South temper the optimism that often accompanies unbridled advocacy of the potential promise of digital agriculture. Increasing agricultural productivity, for instance, has certain limitations. In geographies where markets for increased inputs do not exist because the private sector initiative and participation have not been sufficiently stimulated (Ricker-Gilbert et al., 2011; Ghins et al., 2017), pushing for higher-yielding technologies (such as modern crop varieties) to increase productivity merely ensures that input prices can be more readily controlled by the low number of agro-dealers. As a result, the market power exercised by too few operators will lead to depressed farm-gate prices because of continuing high input prices.

Furthermore, many of the binding constraints faced by smallholder farmers centre on basic capacity issues that may be exacerbated, not alleviated, by digital technologies: they are not organized collectively, they have limited experience of market negotiation, and little appreciation of their capacity to influence the terms and conditions upon which they engage with the market, and they have little or no information on market conditions, prices, and quality of goods (Shiferaw et al., 2011). There is also the key issue of farmers' aspirations; there are many farmers for whom increasing productivity and greater access to markets are not a priority, instead, they focus on off-farm or non-farm activities with a view to temporarily or permanently exiting from farming (Mausch et al., 2018).

Ultimately, improved preliminary assessments and targeting will maximize the likelihood that the spread of digital agriculture will contribute to improved access to markets and higher incomes for smallholder farmers. Farmers are a heterogeneous group and for the poorest of the poor, digital agriculture will be an insufficient pathway out of poverty. Digital agriculture, like other technologies, should best be targeted at those farmers who aspire and are able to improve their livelihoods via farming, those farmers best placed to 'step up' according to the typology proposed by Dorward et al., (2009). There also remains the challenge that has plagued agricultural development for decades, namely the scaling of technologies (Faure et al., 2018; Woltering et al., 2019). In the following section and using the example of a digital tool, Rice Crop Manager, we illustrate how digital agriculture can provide realistic and actionable solutions when it is combined with context-specific, targeted interventions, in partnerships with a plethora of different stakeholders.

Rice Crop Manager

A digital decision support tool known as Rice Crop Manager (RCM) enables farmers to calculate field-specific rates of fertilizer N, P, and K for rice. The International Rice Research Institute (IRRI) and its partners developed the science behind RCM, site-specific nutrient management, in the 1990s to identify the best nutrient management practices for specific rice fields. RCM has been adapted for geographies such as the Philippines, India, Indonesia, Myanmar, and Bangladesh. To date, RCM has scaled in the Philippines and in various Indian states such as Eastern Uttar Pradesh, Odisha, and Bihar. In these geographies, the tool, which is available as a web-based tool, has proven to help farmers achieve higher yields, positive net benefit, and less risk of financial loss when they followed the RCM recommendation compared with farmers' fertilizer practice, and a blanket fertilizer recommendation (Sharma et al., 2019).

In the Philippines, IRRI works with the Department of Agriculture – Bureau for Agricultural Research (DA-BAR) and Agricultural Training Institute (DA-ATI), the Philippine Rice Research Institute (PhilRice), and multiple DA agencies, regional field offices, and local government units. The vision statement for RCM Philippines is 'RCM Philippines as the Department of Agriculture ICT platform to make Filipino rice farmers competitive through science-based crop management recommendations for increased yields and incomes'. RCM, which began in 2013 and will conclude with the final transition to the DA at the end of 2021, has gone through all stages of programmatic readiness and institutionalization, from developing the core science of site-specific nutrient management (SSNM), to building robust partnerships and proven results within the government, to final integration into the Philippines Rice Industry Roadmap.

RCM is primarily a web-based decision support tool whose target audience is agricultural extension workers (AEWs). In March 2020, IRRI released an Android app version of RCM for the Philippines as well. In most dissemination and scale models, AEWs are trained to operate the RCM application. In addition, they and DA counterparts are trained in the underlying SSNM science that underlies RCM to be able to explain and interpret the recommendations when interacting with farmers. Farmers are then interviewed using the RCM application (either web-based or Android app) and their responses are used to compute and determine the RCM recommendation. The interviews are conducted in either online or offline mode, depending on the connectivity of the AEW. However, connectivity is still required to generate the recommendation. Using a cloud-based server, the RCM algorithm then determines the RCM recommendation, which is printed out in a central location and provided to the farmers to be used throughout the season (Figure 1). The recommendation provides advisories on the source, timing, and amount of fertilizer selected by the farmers, crop cycle, weed management, organic fertilizer, and nursery preparation. Reminders on nutrient management and package and practices are also sent through SMS and voice calls, depending on what is appropriate for the target geography and population.

Data show that RCM has the potential to increase both yields and incomes for farmers. Sharma et al., (2019) compared field-specific nutrient management calculated by RCM with farmers' fertilizer practice and a blanket fertilizer recommendation in Odisha State in India. The authors found that grain yield was consistently higher with RCM fertilization recommendations and there were financial net benefits (Sharma et al., 2019). In the Philippines, Banayo et al., (2018) and Buresh et al., (2019) showed that SSNM provided by RCM improved productivity and profitability in rain-fed lowlands of the

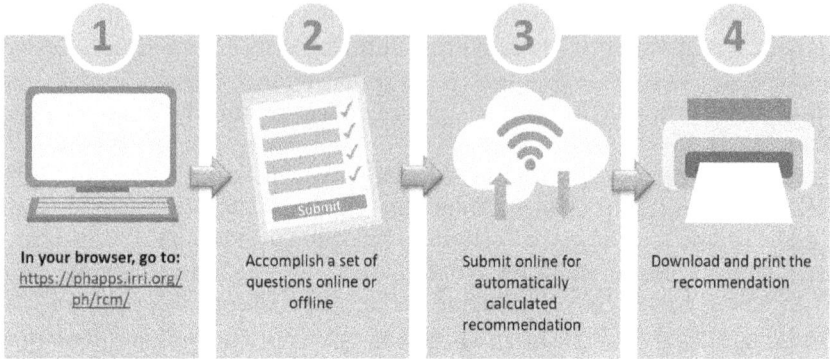

Figure 1 Rice Crop Manager process.

Philippines. Utilization of the RCM recommendations in the Philippines has led to an average yield increase of almost 400 kg/ha/crop and a net benefit of US$107/ha/crop. In the Philippines, over 2 million recommendations have been generated, approximately 117,000 farmers and 189,000 fields have been registered and almost 84,000 fields (44 per cent of registered fields) were measured using global positioning (GPS) equivalent to 57,000 hectares.

Scaling RCM is a challenge in all of the geographies where it is being disseminated and promoted. The categories of challenges include enabling environment, human resources and capacity, partnership, technology platform, and monitoring, evaluation, and learning (MEL). The full institutionalization and scaling of RCM have required buy-in and coordination among government institutions, and critically, connectivity. In the Philippines, for example, internet users represent only 60 per cent of the population, while 64 per cent are unique mobile subscribers. The lack of widespread connectivity has affected the design, dissemination, and scale of the project. It has meant that recommendations, while generated through a website, are then printed on paper and given to farmers. This increases the danger that: 1) the recommendation gets lost or is not delivered; and/or 2) farmers do not receive the reminders in real time, something that could be accomplished through SMS, Interactive Voice Response (IVR), or voice calls.

In some cases, farmers are unable to follow RCM recommendations because they are not able to afford the cost of the recommended inputs. In the Philippines, the cost of inputs is one of the primary reasons why farmers are unable to adopt fully the RCM recommendation. To mitigate this challenge, IRRI has piloted a finance module that would calibrate the recommendation according to what the farmer could afford. The RCM team is also considering partnerships with banks, loan agencies, and crowdsourcing companies to complement and provide the needed financial resources to be able to afford these inputs.

Human resource capacity is another challenge for the widespread dissemination of RCM. AEWs are the target users of the RCM application in most of the geographies where it is being implemented. For countries with strong agricultural institutions and small ratios of AEW to farmers, this dissemination model can be effective. However, in countries where institutions are weak, or AEWs are responsible for more than 1,000 farmers, it is difficult to incorporate the 15 minutes per farmer required for an RCM interview into already overstretched workloads. Further, it is important that AEWs understand the underlying SSNM science of RCM to be able to convince and explain to farmers why they should follow recommendations. In the new geographies where RCM is being piloted, more work is being done to consider RCM as a farmer-facing platform to avoid the bottlenecks and dependencies built into a system that relies on AEWs as the primary dissemination agents. One recently tested idea is the use of high school students to act as RCM information providers to their farmer-parents (Manalo et al., 2019).

The inclusion of realistic, measurable, and robust MEL systems is important for a holistic understanding of the reach and impact of digital agriculture platforms such as RCM. When RCM was launched in the Philippines, the primary indicator of success was initially the number of recommendations generated. Numbers per se reveal little about adoption and behaviour change. MEL systems evolved to include an in-depth review of why farmers were not adopting the RCM recommendation as well as the rate of adoption among farmers. Results suggested that only 27 per cent of targeted farmers adopted some part of the RCM recommendation. A focus on adoption and behaviour change has changed incentives for regional field offices and AEWs.

The RCM technology platform has its own unique challenges for scaling nationwide. As a web-based platform that requires internet connectivity to generate recommendations, it is difficult for AEWs to provide recommendations in real time. These obstacles can be mitigated, for example, by bringing all farmers together in a common meeting place that has internet connectivity and then providing recommendations on site. There are, however, major cost implications of these types of meetings.

Finally, RCM is based on SSNM, and continued research is required to ensure that the content provided is science-based and validated. IRRI scientists and partners from national government research institutes conduct a series of nutrient omission plot trials (NOPT) and farmer field trials and incorporate the findings from these trials into the RCM algorithm. This research updating and leadership takes time to identify research gaps and develop actionable, easy-to-use farming advice. In order for RCM to be effective, the underlying science has to be frequently updated. While there have been a number of challenges for scaling and sustaining Rice Crop Manager, strong partnerships with the government and being able to show results through increased yields and incomes have been key to RCM's success to date. Consideration of scaling, sustainability, and user targeting have continuously been tested, iterated, and updated as part of RCM implementation. The challenge remains as to whether RCM can be sustained without donor support and/or government subsidies, and it is clear that there is a need to move beyond numbers per se and to improve the targeting of RCM while also investigating the extent to which farmer uptake is mitigating or exacerbating social and gender inequities.

Digital technology is not a panacea

Digital technology, such as RCM, has the potential to transform agriculture in emerging markets, but like all technologies, it is not a panacea. The challenges of scaling faced by RCM are ones that almost all initiatives to promote agricultural technologies have to contend with (Glover et al., 2016; Woltering et al., 2019) including digital agriculture (Kos and Kloppenburg, 2019). Another Achilles heel of agricultural technologies is that they can lead to a further marginalization of the most vulnerable populations. Information has always been a critical component of agricultural production as farmers exchange best practice, suggestions, and counsel. If the primary channel for information dissemination shifts to digital technology, farmers without access will face increased information asymmetries. Exacerbating the digital divide generally and the social/gender divide more specifically, are two of the top risks of promoting digital agriculture, both of which have direct impacts on social and gender equity and parity.

Digital divide: social and gender equity

Behind the enthusiasm for this current wave of innovation and sophisticated technological advances, the experience with RCM illustrated the danger of marginalizing farmers who do not have the financial resources to access digital technologies, thereby exacerbating the digital divide. There is a risk that some farmers will not get information about these new technologies at an early stage. Further, these farmers would neither have the physical and/or financial capacity to access new technologies nor would they receive sufficient capacity building and training to effectively use these technologies to transform not only their production system but also their lives and that of their families. As a result, the benefits of digital agriculture may not accrue to the remote and marginalized communities and poorer farmers within them. Several factors underlie the digital divide, including, but not limited to, a lack of connectivity infrastructure, affordability, electricity, education, knowledge, skills, gender, age, and location.

Access to extension information has positive impacts on knowledge, productivity, and technology adoption. Although 80 per cent of people living in developing countries have access to mobile connectivity, only 30 per cent of them have ever accessed the internet (Pathways for Prosperity Commission, 2019). In this case, the technology is accessible, but any intervention that utilizes the mobile web would still result in a digital divide because a majority is not using the digital technology to its full capacity in a meaningful way. Technologies are neither inherently gender neutral nor gender ambivalent (Faulkner, 2001; Wajcman, 2009; Azar and Sandén, 2011). Likewise, model farmers used to disseminate improved farming practices, Climate-Smart Agriculture practices, for example, become power brokers controlling access to opportunities, thus reinforcing inequalities by favouring male and excluding female farmers (Taylor and Bhasme, 2018).

Taking the example of RCM, this technology relies on extension services to provide farmers with recommendations. However, it is well documented that women are less likely to have access to agricultural extension information than men (Taylor and Bhasme, 2018). Part of the problem is that women are more than 21 per cent less likely to own a mobile phone than men in low- and middle-income countries. Regionally, this number increases to 23 per cent in sub-Saharan Africa, 24 per cent in the Middle East, and up to 37 per cent in South Asia (GSMA mWomen, 2011). Furthermore, extension messages are seldom tailored for women. A study of 97 countries found that a mere 5 per cent of extension resources were directed at women (FAO, 2011). Furthermore, the lack of female extension agents can be both an overt and a subtle barrier to access information/knowledge because of gender and family norms in communicating with males outside the family (FAO, 2011). Extension information delivered to the male in the household will not automatically trickle down to his female counterpart. Considerations of low literacy and education levels and entrenched gender norms can result in gendered extension resources that can be tailored to a female audience.

Digital agriculture has the potential to facilitate change and increase access to information and services for women. Used appropriately, women can leverage technology for the benefit of the entire household while increasing their decision-making power (Quisumbing et al., 1996; Gates, 2014), building skills, and increasing both agricultural and human capacity investments. A clearer understanding of usage by farmers in target geographies is critical to design more appropriate interventions. Such analyses could result in more appropriate, targeted, and inclusive interventions that could be digital-first, hybrid digital and analogue, or only analogue with the potential for integrating digital at a more appropriate point. Digital agricultural research for development (AR4D) initiatives such as RCM, however, need to address explicitly the issue of gender equity. The handful of publications to date on RCM demonstrate a failure to do so (see Banayo et al., 2018; Buresh et al., 2019; Sharma et al., 2019; Manalo et al., 2019).

The gender digital divide highlights the larger issue of social equity, with respect to how outcomes are distributed across society and how consequences will play out for future generations. Technologies affect different social groups in different ways, even in the same geographical/agro-ecological context. This leads to consideration of potential trade-offs between efficiency and fairness, which are policy relevant and that policy makers should be aware of. Inequalities extend beyond gender in society-specific ways. For example, in India, farmers belonging to marginalized castes have less access to public extension services that may facilitate increased annual crop income (Krishna et al., 2019). Failing to address issues of social equity can result in a number of unintended negative externalities, including demotion of social groups, tensions across communities, institutional instability, and market distortions or inefficiencies. Through these channels, inequities could ultimately threaten the contribution of agriculture to the achievement of economic and social development goals. The development community, mobile network operators, regulatory agencies, and national governments must recognize these constraints and ensure that a lens combining gender and social equity is used in designing, implementing, and assessing digital programmes.

Scaling

The biggest challenge when it comes to RCM is scaling. This is a challenge for all those engaged in AR4D and is not confined to RCM or digital tools. The growing interest in digital agriculture (and the example of RCM above) suggests that the scaling issue be properly addressed in AR4D initiatives. Too often, international development interventions are designed *for* target populations and not *in consultation with* them. The traditional linear approach for new technology development and dissemination involves three main stages: 1) upstream research institutions that engage in discovery and proof of concepts; 2) transfer of the validated research outputs to downstream 'development agents' who are generally responsible for piloting; and 3) transfer to extension services that are usually responsible for scaling out/up. This linear approach has long been criticized as it does not capture the multifaceted and complex impact pathways observed in reality. Therefore, the focus along the AR4D continuum has shifted and puts the emphasis on interdisciplinary approaches and interconnectedness recognizing the need for learning, feedback loops, partnerships, and joint action in multi-stakeholder settings within the context of agricultural innovation systems (Schut et al., 2015).

Scaling is more likely as a result of systems-thinking generated by agricultural innovation systems. Digital technologies such as RCM can contribute more to development impact by conceptualizing the scaling process as a multifaceted one that catalyses three interconnected and complementary pathways – technology development; capacity development; and policy influence pathway – overseen by inter-disciplinary research teams and trans-disciplinary networks (Douthwaite et al., 2017). These networks facilitate the fostering of organizational, governance, and policy environments that encourage scaling. This is a challenge not just for researchers but for all stakeholders as they clarify and agree on their different roles and responsibilities. In the case of RCM, now that the technology has been developed and proven, much of the focus in the Philippines and states in India is now on scaling. Ideally, a scaling strategy would have been built into the technology and development strategies from the beginning.

In summary, in the case of RCM and other digital agricultural technologies, reporting increased yields and incomes is only part of the story. More attention has to be given to the issue of scaling in the context of sustainable business models; whether digital agriculture (and agriculture in general) offers the targeted populations a pathway out of poverty; and the extent to which reported yield and income increases may be masking growing social inequalities among the targeted populations.

A way forward for digital agriculture

In the medical profession, one of the first lessons doctors learn is to 'do no harm', and the same should be true for any development sector when the lives and livelihoods of people are at stake. For digital agriculture, the demand for evidence of what works and what does not work is getting increased attention (Kos and Kloppenburg, 2019; Klerkx et al., 2019). The evidence base for digital agriculture will guide further understanding of the enabling conditions for specific populations and geographies, advancing understanding of the maturity of digital agriculture interventions, and providing impact and improved outcome data. Given the current evidence base, it is unclear whether digital technology will be accessible to most small farmers and automatically lead to increases in yields, income, and overall prosperity. Furthermore, the design of agricultural interventions does not inherently focus on social equity, which must be a deliberate focus in the future (Eriksen and Brown, 2011; Collins, 2018; Hellin and Fisher, 2019).

The rapidly evolving digital technology space will require agile, flexible structures to integrate and test the application of new technologies in a way that does no harm. Guidelines are available; the Principles for Digital Development ('Digital Principles') were created in 2012 by a group of donors and implementing development organizations. They are intended as guidelines to integrate best practices into technology-enabled programmes as they provide parameters for ensuring that digital solutions are designed with the target beneficiaries, with scale and sustainability in mind, and with consideration of the enabling environment where they will be implemented, among others (Principles for Digital Development, n.d.). Consideration of the Digital Principles can improve the design and deployment of digital agriculture and help to ensure that targeted farmers are best positioned to benefit from a digitized agricultural value chain.

The FAO and ITU have produced a toolkit specific to E-Agriculture Strategy and Policy which examines a context across leadership and governance; strategy and investment; services and applications; infrastructure; standards and interoperability; content, knowledge management, and sharing; legislation, policy, and compliance; and workforce and capacity development (FAO and ITU, 2016). Other generic resources for digital development are also readily available and can be tailored for the agriculture sector. For example, USAID's recent *Digital Investment Tool: An Approach to Incorporating Digital Development Best Practices in Your Activity* links all assessments to the Digital Principles and assesses the maturity of digital systems in order to make them more adaptive and efficient (USAID, 2019).

A consideration of the social, spatial, and economic inclusivity of digital agriculture interventions will ensure that the interventions 'do no harm' and reach the most marginalized and vulnerable populations. There is also increased discussion in the digital development community about formalizing a human rights-based approach to the internet and digital technology (Baú and Calandro, 2019). An inclusive approach to digital agriculture recognizes the interconnectedness of social, economic, and cultural impacts of digital technology. As advocated by international organizations such as FAO and ITU (2016) and the Pathways for Prosperity Commission (2019), the development of comprehensive digital strategies, and digital agriculture strategies more specifically, will provide the strategic guidance and frameworks for policies that will facilitate digital agriculture integration. Effective strategies will consider issues such as connectivity, meaningful use, equity, access, and affordability, among many others, and do so in a holistic way that links policies such as infrastructure investment with rural farmer connectivity, for example.

Conclusions

The utilization of low and high technology digital tools has enormous potential to transform the agriculture sector. Countries across South Asia, Southeast Asia, and Africa already promote new digital agriculture platforms across the agricultural value chain. For digital agriculture to deliver on its promise of increasing farmers' yields and incomes, it is critical to design interventions that consider the target populations' needs and constraints, and to assess whether a digital technology solution is appropriate. Technologies affect different social groups in different ways, even in the same geographical/agro-ecological context. This leads to consideration of potential trade-offs between efficacy, efficiency, and fairness.

Exacerbating the digital divide generally and the digital gender divide, more specifically, are two of the top risks of integrating digital tools in agricultural value chain development. In addition, using technology for knowledge dissemination can further entrench the information asymmetries in the agricultural production chain that already exist. It is incumbent upon implementing, research, and funding organizations as well as governments that the enthusiasm and funding for digital agriculture considers the potential further marginalization of the most vulnerable populations they allegedly seek to benefit in the end. Furthermore, as is the case with any technology, attention needs to be directed at scaling.

RCM illustrates that integrating the globally recognized Principles for Digital Development are critical in programme design, development, and deployment. Scientific and technological advances in digital technology are already transforming agriculture around the world, helping to address challenges such as labour shortages and improve farming efficiency and sustainability. Digital agriculture can also advance progress on the agricultural sector's contribution to realizing the Sustainable Development Goals (SDGs), but there are trade-offs, specifically with respect to agricultural productivity, poverty reduction, and social equity. When it comes to digital agriculture's contribution to the SDGs, there are two key issues to assess:

- The extent to which digital technologies can help farmers move up the development ladder when an enabling environment for adoption is properly and consciously generated and maintained.
- Even when the right technologies are identified and the enabling environment is in place, such new technologies are potentially socially, spatially, and economically disruptive and as a result can lead to the exclusion of some categories of farmers that are not equipped to successfully engage and reap the expected benefits. This raises the fundamental issues of social and gender equity and whether digital agriculture can and will mitigate or exacerbate these inequities.

For digital agriculture to deliver on its promise, it is critical to design digital agriculture interventions that consider the target populations' needs and constraints, as well as the possibilities within the existing enabling environment to determine what – if any – digital technology solution is appropriate.

References

Azar, C. and Sandén, B.A. (2011) 'The elusive quest for technology-neutral policies', *Environmental Innovation and Societal Transitions* 1(1): 135–9 <https://doi.org/10.1016/ j.eist.2011.03.003>.

Banayo, N.P.M.C., Haefele, S.M., Desamero, N.V. and Kato, Y. (2018) 'On-farm assessment of site-specific nutrient management for rainfed lowland rice in the Philippines', *Field Crops Research* 220: 88–96 <http://dx.doi.org/10.1016/j.fcr.2017.09.011>.

Basso, B. and Antle, J. (2020) 'Digital agriculture to design sustainable agricultural systems', *Nature Sustainability* 3(4): 254–6 <http://dx.doi.org/10.1038/s41893-020-0510-0>.

Baú, V. and Calandro, E. (2019) 'Digital media and information rights', *The International Encyclopedia of Media Literacy*, pp. 1–13, Wiley Online Library <http://dx.doi.org/10.1002/ 9781118978238.ieml0234>.

Boettiger, S. and Sanghvi, S. (2019) 'How digital innovation is transforming agriculture: lessons from India' [online], McKinsey & Company. Available from: https://www.mckinsey.com/ industries/agriculture/our-insights/how-digital-innovation-is-transforming-agriculture-lessons-from-india [accessed 9 June 2020].

Bouton, M. (2019) 'The digital route to transforming farm sector', *The Hindu Business Line* [online]. Available from: https://www.thehindubusinessline.com/opinion/the-digital-route-to-transforming-farm-sector/article26006290.ece [accessed 9 June 2020].

Buresh, R.J., Castillo, R.L., Dela Torre, J.C., Laureles, E.V., Samson, M.I., Sinohin, P.J. and Guerra, M. (2019) 'Site-specific nutrient management for rice in the Philippines: calculation of field-specific fertilizer requirements by Rice Crop Manager', *Field Crops Research* 239(May): 56–70 <http://dx. doi.org/10.1016/j.fcr.2019.05.013>.

Collins, A. (2018) 'Saying all the right things? Gendered discourse in climate-smart agriculture', *Journal of Peasant Studies* 45(1): 175–91 <http:// dx.doi.org/10.1080/03066150. 2017.1377187>.

Department of Agriculture, Cooperation and Farmers' Welfare (2020) 'Doubling of farmers' income' [online], Government of India. Available from: http:// www.agricoop.nic.in/doubling-farmers [accessed 3 March 2020].

Dorward, A., Anderson, S., Bernal, Y.N., Sánchez, E., Rushton, J., Pattison, J. and Paz, R. (2009) 'Hanging in, stepping up and stepping out: livelihood aspirations and strategies of the poor', *Development in Practice* 19(2): 240–7 <http://dx.doi.org/10.1080/09614520802689535>.

Douthwaite, B., Mur, R., Audouin, S., Wopereis, M., Hellin, J., Saley Moussa, A., Karbo, N., Kasten, W. and Bouyer, J. (2017) *Agricultural Research for Development to Intervene Effectively in Complex Systems and the Implications for Research Organizations* [pdf], KIT Working Paper 2017-12 <http://agritrop. cirad.fr/584543/1/Douthwaite_al_AR4D_Research_organizations-2017_ v6.pdf> [accessed 9 June 2020].

Eriksen, S. and Brown, K. (2011) 'Sustainable adaptation to climate change', *Climate and Development* 3(1): 3–6 <http://dx.doi.org/10.3763/ cdev.2010.0064>.

FAO and ITU (2016) *The E-agriculture Strategy Guide – Piloted in Asia-Pacific Countries*, Food and Agriculture Organization of the United Nations and International Telecommunication Union, Bangkok.

Faulkner, W. (2001) 'The technology question in feminism: a view from feminist technology studies', *Women's Studies International Forum* 24(1): 79–95 <http://dx.doi.org/10.1016/ S0277-5395(00)00166-7>.

Faure, G., Barret, D., Blundo-Canto, G., Dabat, M., Devaux-Spatarakis, A., Le Guerroué, J.L., Marquié, C., Mathé, S., Temple, L., Toillier, A., Triomphe, B. and Hainzelin, E. (2018) 'How different agricultural research models contribute to impacts: evidence from 13 case studies in developing countries', *Agricultural Systems* 165: 128–36 <http://dx.doi.org/10.1016/ j.agsy.2018.06.002>.

Food and Agriculture Organization of the United Nations (FAO) (2011) *The State of Food and Agriculture, 2010–11. Women in Agriculture: Closing the Gap for Development*, FAO, Rome.

Gates, M.F. (2014) 'Putting women and girls at the center of development', *Science* 345(6202): 1273–5 <http://dx.doi.org/10.1126/science.1258882>.

Ghins, L., Mas Aparisi, A. and Balié, J. (2017) 'Myths and realities about input subsidies in sub-Saharan Africa', *Development Policy Review* 35: O214–33 <http://dx.doi.org/10.1111/ dpr.12258>.

Glover, D., Sumberg, J. and Andersson, J. A. (2016) 'The adoption problem; or why we still understand so little about technological change in African agriculture', *Outlook on Agriculture* 45(1): 3–6 <http://dx.doi.org/10.5367/ oa.2016.0235>.

Gómez, M.I., Barrett, C.B., Buck, L.E., De Groote, H., Ferris, S., Gao, H.O., McCullough, E., Miller, D.D., Outhred, H., Pell, A.N., Reardon, T., Retnanestri, M., Ruben, R., Struebi, P., Swinnen, J., Touesnard, M.A., Weinberger, K., Keatinge, J.D.H., Milstein, M.B. and Yang, R.Y. (2011)

'Research principles for developing country food value chains', *Science* 332(6034): 1154–5 <http://dx.doi.org/10.1126/science.1202543>.

GSMA mWomen (2011) *GSMA mWomen Programme: Policy Recommendations to Address the Mobile Phone Gender Gap*, GSMA, London, UK.

Hellin, J. and Fisher, E. (2019) 'The Achilles heel of climate-smart agriculture', *Nature Climate Change* 9(7): 493–4 <http://dx.doi.org/10.1038/s41558-019-0515-8>.

International Telecommunication Union (2018) *Measuring the Information Society Report*, ITU, Geneva, Switzerland.

Klerkx, L., Jakku, E. and Labarthe, P. (2019) 'A review of social science on digital agriculture, smart farming and agriculture 4.0: New contributions and a future research agenda', *NJAS – Wageningen Journal of Life Sciences* 90–91: 100315 <http://dx.doi.org/10.1016/ j.njas.2019.100315>.

Kos, D. and Kloppenburg, S. (2019) 'Digital technologies, hyper-transparency and smallholder farmer inclusion in global value chains', *Current Opinion in Environmental Sustainability* 41: 56–63 <http://dx.doi.org/10.1016/j.cosust.2019.10.011>.

Krishna, V.V., Aravalath, L.M. and Vikraman, S. (2019) 'Does caste determine farmer access to quality information?', *Plos One* 14(1): e0210721 <http://dx.doi.org/10.1371/journal. pone.0210721>.

Malabo Montpellier Panel (2019) *Byte by Byte: Policy Innovation for Transforming Africa's Food System with Digital Technologies*, Malabo Montpellier Panel, Dakar, Senegal.

Manalo, J.A., Pasiona, S.P., Bautista, A.M.F., Villaflor, J.D., Corpuz, D.C.P. and Biag-Manalo, H.H.M. (2019) 'Exploring youth engagement in agricultural development: the case of farmers' children in the Philippines as rice crop manager infomediaries', *Journal of Agricultural Education and Extension* 25(4): 361–77 <http://dx.doi.org/10.1080/1389224X.2019.1629969>.

Markelova, H., Meinzen-Dick, R., Hellin, J. and Dohrn, S. (2009) 'Collective action for smallholder market access', *Food Policy* 34(1): 1–7 <http://dx.doi.org/10.1016/j.foodpol.2008.10.001>.

Mausch, K., Harris, D., Heather, E., Jones, E., Yim, J. and Hauser, M. (2018) 'Households' aspirations for rural development through agriculture', *Outlook on Agriculture* 47(2): 108–15 <http://dx.doi.org/10.1177/0030727018766940>.

Pathways for Prosperity Commission (2019) *The Digital Roadmap: How Developing Countries Can Get Ahead*, Final Report of the Pathways for Prosperity Commission, Oxford.

Principles for Digital Development (no date) 'Principles for Digital Development' [website]. Available from: https://digitalprinciples.org/ [accessed 9 June 2020].

Quisumbing, A.R., Brown, L.R., Feldstein, H.S., Haddad, L. and Peña, C. (1996) 'Women: the key to food security', *Food and Nutrition Bulletin* 17(1): 1–2 <http://dx.doi.org/10.1177/15648 2659601700116>.

Ricker-Gilbert, J., Jayne, T.S. and Chirwa, E. (2011) 'Subsidies and crowding out: a double-hurdle model of fertilizer demand in Malawi', *American Journal of Agricultural Economics* <http://dx.doi.org/10.1093/ajae/aaq122>.

Schut, M., Klerkx, L., Sartas, M., Lamers, D., Campbell, M.M., Ogbonna, I., Kaushik, P., Atta-Krah, K. and Leeuwis, C. (2015) 'Innovation platforms:

experiences with their institutional embedding in agricultural research for development', *Experimental Agriculture* 52(4): 537–61 <http://dx.doi. org/10.1017/S001447971500023X>.

Schwab, K. (2017) *The Fourth Industrial Revolution: What It Means and How to Respond*, Penguin Books, New York.

Sharma, S., Rout, K.K., Khanda, C.M., Tripathi, R., Shahid, M., Nayak, A., Satpathy, S., Banik, N.C., Iftikar, W., Parida, N., Kumar, V., Mishra, A., Castillo, R.L., Velasco, T. and Buresh, R.J. (2019) 'Field-specific nutrient management using Rice Crop Manager decision support tool in Odisha, India', *Field Crops Research* 241: 107578 <http://dx.doi.org/10.1016/ j.fcr.2019.107578>.

Shiferaw, B., Hellin, J. and Muricho, G. (2011) 'Improving market access and agricultural productivity growth in Africa: what role for producer organiza- tions and collective action institutions?', *Food Security* 3(4): 475–89 <http:// dx.doi.org/10.1007/s12571-011-0153-0>.

Taylor, M. and Bhasme, S. (2018) 'Model farmers, extension networks and the politics of agricultural knowledge transfer', *Journal of Rural Studies* 64: 1–10 <http://dx.doi.org/10.1016/ j.jrurstud.2018.09.015>.

Technical Centre for Agriculture and Rural Cooperation (CTA) (2019) *Digitalisation of African Agriculture Report, 2018-2019*, CTA, Wageningen, The Netherlands.

USAID (2019) *Digital Investment Tool: An Approach to Incorporating Digital Development Best Practices in Your Activity* [pdf], USAID, Washington, DC <https://digitalprinciples.org/ wp-content/uploads/Digital_Investment_ Review_Tool_Final_20191021-1.pdf>.

Wajcman, J. (2009) 'Feminist theories of technology', *Cambridge Journal of Economics* 34(1): 143–52 <http://dx.doi.org/10.1093/cje/ben057>.

Woltering, L., Fehlenberg, K., Gerard, B., Ubels, J. and Cooley, L. (2019) 'Scaling – from "reaching many" to sustainable systems change at scale: a critical shift in mindset', *Agricultural Systems* 176: 102652 <http://dx.doi. org/10.1016/j.agsy.2019.102652>.

About the authors

Carolyn Florey (c.florey@irri.org), Digital Tools Cluster Leader, Sustainable Impact Platform, International Rice Research Institute (IRRI), Los Baños, Philippines.

Jon Hellin, PhD (j.hellin@irri.org), Platform Leader, Sustainable Impact, International Rice Research Institute (IRRI), Los Baños, Philippines.

Jean Balié, (j.balie@irri.org), Platform Leader, Agri-Food Policy, International Rice Research Institute (IRRI), Los Baños, Philippines.

CHAPTER 12

Value chain development for rural poverty reduction: A reality check and a warning

Dietmar Stoian, Jason Donovan, John Fisk, and Michelle F. Muldoon

Abstract

Over the past decade, the value chain development approach has increasingly been adopted by governments, donors, and NGOs to reduce rural poverty. The design of related interventions often assumes that poor households: 1) have sufficient resources to effectively participate in value chain development; 2) do not face substantial trade-offs when using these resources; and 3) are able to assume higher risks when reinvesting capital and labour. However, insights from our own experiences and the literature show that these assumptions often do not reflect the realities and the needs of the poor. We argue that value chain development with poor and vulnerable populations, particularly in rural areas, requires additional conceptual frameworks, analyses, and interventions. In particular, we encourage donor agencies and development practitioners to adopt an asset-based approach to the design, implementation, and assessment of target value chains and to identify the non-market interventions needed for enabling particularly disenfranchised groups to meet the minimum asset thresholds for their successful participation in value chain initiatives.

Keywords: value chain development, very poor, poverty reduction, asset-based approach, vulnerable populations

In the late 1990s, a sense of urgency over the need to reinvigorate development processes led to the formulation of the Millennium Development Goals which incorporated the view that increased income is a prerequisite to livelihood security and a decent standard of living. To date, however, notable progress in poverty reduction – measured in terms of income and passing the $1 a day absolute poverty threshold – has mainly been made in Southeast and East Asia, especially China, while significant poverty pockets continue to persist in the rural areas of sub-Saharan Africa, South Asia, and Central and South America (UN, 2011). In search of viable alternatives to reducing poverty, value chain development emerged in the early 2000s as: 1) a market-based approach

http://dx.doi.org/10.3362/9781788530576.012

to meet poverty-related Millennium Development Goals; and 2) a response to new opportunities in international markets signalling stronger demand for agricultural and forest products and services produced with environmental and social responsibility.

Value chain development has generally been defined as an 'effort to strengthen mutually beneficial linkages among firms so that they work together to take advantage of market opportunities, that is, to create and build trust among value chain participants' (Webber and Labaste, 2010). Key concepts related to value chain development are: win–win relationships, upgrading, innovation, and added value. 'Pro-poor' value chain development has been defined as a 'positive or desirable change in a value chain to extend or improve productive operations and generate social benefits: poverty reduction, income and employment generation, economic growth, environmental performance, gender equity and other development goals' (UNIDO, 2011). It is principally from the latter perspective that many development agencies, donors, and governments have adopted value chain development as a key element of their rural poverty reduction strategies (see DFID and SDC, 2008; Humphrey and Navas-Alemán, 2010). In addition to targeting poor and vulnerable populations in the rural sector as primary beneficiaries, some value chain initiatives seek to link to the macroeconomic environment by broadening their approach towards resource-constrained enterprises in the upstream segments of a value chain, and the promotion of changes in the political-legal, institutional, and regulatory frameworks (see Kula et al., 2006).

Despite the prominent role of the value chain development approach in current development agendas, surprisingly little is known about its impacts on rural poverty. The urgency of making tangible progress towards the poverty-related Millennium Development Goals and the uncertainty about the actual and potential contributions from value chain development call for taking stock in terms of what we already know about its design, implementation, and impact, and what we have yet to learn to better direct growing investments in such initiatives and ensure substantial effects on poverty. In this chapter we call for an asset-based approach to design, implementation, and assessment of value chain development and the need for non-market interventions to help particularly disenfranchised groups to meet the minimum asset thresholds for their successful participation in value chain development.

What we know

1. Actors promoting value chain development vary widely, as do their motives. NGOs often pursue explicit poverty reduction goals, while the private sector may see them as a by-product.

The strengthening of mutually beneficial business relationships between two or more chain actors, including producers, distributors, processors, wholesalers, and/or retailers, requires improved interactions between them, often facilitated by the provision of technical, business, and financial services from outside of the chain. Related interventions aim at strengthening capacities and enhancing mechanisms for sharing information, benefits, and risks. The stronger the win–win nature of such relations, the more likely they are to endure over time. While pro-poor value chain initiatives have an explicit focus on poverty reduction, other value chain initiatives may not. This, however, does not mean that they could not have an important, though unintended, poverty impact. Further, in many cases, a diverse set of stakeholders from within and outside of the value chain invest in the chain, at times with little or no coordination between them. Private companies, for example, may invest in their relationships with poor producers in an effort to improve their environmental and social credentials, while an NGO may provide technical and financial assistance to the producers and other chain actors. From the company's perspective, value chain development is one among several types of business strategy pursued to ensure a positive image, market positioning, and the sourcing of scarce raw materials (Box 12.1).

From the NGO's perspective, their work with upstream chain actors is in explicit pursuit of poverty reduction goals.

2. Value chain development involving the poor needs to account for their diversified livelihood strategies and related risks and trade-offs.

A review of value chain methodologies and case studies (see, for example, Kula et al., 2006; Tanburn and Sen, 2011) shows that the poverty reduction potential of value chain development is often based on the assumption that poor households: 1) have sufficient resources to effectively participate in value chain development; 2) do not face substantial trade-offs when using these

---

Box 12.1. Private sector initiatives that link to the poor

An alternative approach is the base-of-the-pyramid (BoP), where large companies aim to involve the poor in markets as providers of raw materials and/or as customers of affordable products. Such approaches often aim at producing more with less and ensuring long-term business viability. Concerns have been raised that BoP approaches underappreciate heterogeneity among the poor, as well as the intricacies of participatory partnerships between transnational companies and poor communities (Arora and Romijn, 2009). Other approaches go beyond economic goals by incorporating environmental and social goals. Corporate social responsibility (CSR) strategies call for exceeding legal mandates by involving ethical standards, stakeholder claims, and international norms in the business model. Pioneers of CSR have made notable investments in determining and improving their carbon, poverty, and other environmental or social footprints in pursuit of company or industry-wide goals. Lately, though, CSR has been criticized by Porter and Kramer (2011) for not being a solution, as social issues remain at the periphery, not at the core. Instead, they advocate creating shared value (CSV) as a strategy to generate value for both companies and society by reconceiving products and markets, redefining productivity in the value chain, and enabling local cluster development.

resources; and 3) are able to assume higher risks when reinvesting capital and labour. In reality, however, many poor households pursue diversified livelihood strategies by combining subsistence and market-oriented agriculture with off-farm labour and other non-agricultural income-generating activities. In contrast, participation in value chain development often requires them to pursue a specialization strategy, with higher investments of capital, labour, and other resources in a given chain. Involving the rural poor in value chain development therefore calls for a sound approach to address the complex trade-offs between income generation, food security, gender equity, sustainable natural resource management, and overall livelihood resilience.

According to empirical evidence, threats for the rural poor are much greater and opportunities more limited where the competitiveness of the domestic business sector lags far behind international standards (Altenburg, 2007). Under these conditions a 'multi-chain approach' to value chain development as suggested by Stoian and Donovan (2007) for agricultural and forest sectors helps to minimize risks and to maximize poverty reduction potential by strengthening not only the most promising, often export-oriented value chain, but also a variety of domestic or regional chains to which smallholders have access. Charette (2011) argues on a similar line when advocating a 'portfolio approach' to value chain development programmes that stretches across sectors, in particular where the agricultural sector is highly subject to price and weather shocks, and where the manufacturing and/or services sectors show strong potential for growth and development. Despite these recent conceptual advances in value chain development, it is still common practice to focus on a single value chain without due attention to the impact of value chain participation of the rural poor on overall livelihood resilience and related trade-offs. In any case, value chain development is only part of the solution to rural poverty reduction. A complementary focus on rural infrastructure and services, food security, and local markets for traditional products, such as basic grains, is necessary as part of a comprehensive strategy for rural development.

3. Pro-poor value chain development has both advocates and sceptics. Both sides lack sound evidence to substantiate their claims.

It does not come as a surprise that this approach has both advocates and sceptics. The former argue that the most promising option for lifting rural people out of poverty, other than rural–urban migration, is linking poor farming households to lucrative markets through skills development and new institutional arrangements along the chain. Sceptics, on the other hand, regard value chain development as unsuitable for working with the very poor, given its perceived emphasis on risk-taking and entrepreneurship, and the additional challenges faced by the very poor when responding to economic incentives (Fowler and Brand, 2011). The history of stimulating export-oriented production of non-traditional agricultural products illustrates some of the challenges faced when seeking to integrate the poor into more demanding markets (although not all value chain development programmes target export markets). From the sceptics' perspective, such an approach may be seen as an example of failed pro-poor value chain development, while advocates would hold that precisely the absence of good value chain development practice has limited the impact of non-traditional agricultural export programmes on poverty (Box 12.2).

When looking for evidence of the impact of poverty-focused programmes it becomes evident that 'despite the pressure for measuring and reporting on results, most development agencies have in effect failed to measure and report on significant results in eradicating poverty' (Tanburn and Sen, 2011). As a result, neither advocates nor sceptics can base their claims regarding the efficacy of value chain development on sound impact assessment. In fact, most methodologies used for assessing the impact of value chain development on poverty are fairly simplistic and yield partial information on its strengths and limitations as a pathway out of poverty. Assessments typically focus on the generation of employment and income, rather than broader changes in terms of critical livelihood and business assets (see Humphrey and Navas-Alemán, 2010). Resulting reports thus provide an incomplete and potentially biased picture of value chain development impact on the livelihoods of the poor and the viability of smallholder enterprises of which they may be a part. For example, a given initiative may have increased the income derived from

---

Box 12.2. Struggles of smallholders to participate in non-traditional agricultural exports

Beginning in the 1970s and through the 1990s, governments and donor agencies promoted non-traditional agricultural exports (NTAE) in Latin America and Africa through trade liberalization, cooperative development, export promotion, fiscal incentives, subsidized credit, technical assistance, and infrastructure development. These initiatives were often geared towards medium and large-scale agribusinesses, while smallholders participated with varying levels of intensity without being the primary beneficiaries of NTAE interventions. In some cases, the private sector has taken the lead in organizing the production of non-traditional export goods. Food processors and super-markets in Europe and the United States have redirected part of their sourcing of raw materials to traders, processors, and producers in developing countries. There is ample evidence that the conditions for smallholder participation in NTAE were often inadequate to allow for poverty reduction, and many of them dropped out of programmes because of low productivity, high input costs, falling export prices, and limited access to farming inputs and credit. In other cases, smallholders were pushed out as a result of their limited ability to meet the quality or volume requirements of traders and processors. Over the years, consensus has emerged that NTAE development programmes generally lacked economic sustainability, and did not adequately address poverty or the environmental and social costs of export-oriented production by large agribusinesses. Value chain development today, with its focus on both supply and demand factors for the design of sustainable market linkages, responds to the lessons learned from earlier NTAE experiences. However, there is urgent need for those that fund and implement value chain initiatives to address the poverty implications of their interventions in a more integrated way.

commercializing crop production, while at the same time it has compromised household food security and induced gender inequalities in terms of labour division and decision making; or a smallholder enterprise may have increased permanent staff, though increased payroll costs undercut the prices paid to producer members.

4. Current assessments of value chain development tend to provide an incomplete picture of their impact.

The limited utility of one-dimensional assessments follows a general trend of ineffective design and implementation of monitoring and evaluation for development interventions, including those in agriculture (Haddad et al., 2010). Discussions in the grey literature on private sector development have advocated traditional logframe-based project assessment for understanding value chain development poverty implications, with emphasis on enterprise rather than household-level impacts (see Tanburn and Sen, 2011). While logframes and similar tools for 'rigorous' planning, monitoring, and evaluation may serve the reporting needs of project managers and donors, they are inappropriate for understanding complex development processes (Jones, 2011), as they assume that the implementing organization has the capacity to achieve the targeted outcomes and impacts on its own. The failure to adequately account for external factors, such as changes in the political-legal or market context, or the effects of value chain interventions by others, provides an incomplete and potentially distorted picture of value chain development impact. The reported impact is made more questionable if household-level impacts are deduced from enterprise-level outcomes rather than by measuring them.

What we think we know

This section addresses our own insights or those of others that are yet to become part of the mainstream discussion on value chain development.

1. Conceptual models underlying pro-poor value chain development tend to lack a holistic perspective.

Many value chain initiatives involving the poor are based on fairly simple conceptual models focusing on a few variables (output, employment, income, production practices, infrastructure), while minimizing or omitting other critical, albeit complex, factors (e.g. social and human capital building, vulnerability). Such initiatives often aim to achieve greater productivity and better prices for poor households, and the resulting increase in income is seen as a proxy for poverty reduction, if not overall development. On the upside, the simplified design of a value chain initiative reduces both monitoring and evaluation, and implementation costs and makes the results easy to communicate across the chain and to other stakeholders. On the downside, such an approach does not recognize the full set of assets needed by poor households to effectively participate in value chain development, nor does it address how these assets can be built over time to permanently escape from poverty and ensure livelihood resilience, or deal with the trade-offs the rural poor face when making decisions about their allocation of time and resources between a specific value chain and other livelihood activities.

2. Poor households and smallholder enterprises require minimum assets to success-fully participate in value chain development.

Despite the warning that poor households vary in their asset levels, income flows, social networks, and abilities to cope with shocks (Fowler and Brand, 2011), many value chain initiatives treat poor rural households as a uniform stakeholder group with the same response capacity. In reality, however, both external factors such as access to basic infrastructure and services, common pool resources, and social stability, and internal factors, such as asset endowments, interests, and power, ultimately determine the extent to which poor households are 'ready' to participate in specific value chains. Similarly, the 'value chain readiness' of SMEs requires adequate policies to improve overall investment conditions, attract foreign investment, and provide better business services to increase their competitiveness (Altenburg, 2007). Minimum asset thresholds for successful participation in value chain development thus apply at both household and enterprise levels, as illustrated by an example of a coffee cooperative in Nicaragua (Box 12.3). Below these thresholds, specific, non-market-based interventions are needed to create the necessary

---

Box 12.3. Evidence of asset thresholds for successful participation in certified coffee markets

The Nicaragua-based coffee cooperative, Soppexcca, links roughly 500 smallholder producers to international buyers of certified fair-trade and organic coffee. Following the coffee crisis – a period between 1999 and 2004 when prices fell below the cost of production for many producers in Central America – donors and NGOs invested US$2.1 m in building the capacity of Soppexcca and its members to expand their output and better meet the quality demands of international buyers. Donovan and Poole (2011) assessed the changes in tangible and non-tangible assets for both Soppexcca and a representative sample of its members between 2006 and 2009. For the cooperative, interventions enabled major expansion of infrastructure and processing machinery, increased coverage of its technical assistance, and higher ability to engage with new fair-trade coffee buyers in the United States. Related investments provided an option for generating income through expanded service provision to members, and thus were considered critical for the co-op's long-term survival. Most co-op members benefited in terms of increased income flows and greater resilience through their membership in the cooperative. Nearly a quarter of the households were able to take advantage of credit provided by Soppexcca and others to expand their landholdings, diversify their agricultural production, and/or rejuvenate their coffee plantations. However, important weaknesses and gaps in assets remained unaddressed by the interventions and by Soppexcca itself. For example, financial assets remained seriously underdeveloped during the assessment period, while long-term debt increased significantly. Extension services expanded during the period but had difficulties in responding to members' needs. One-third of the sampled households faced major barriers to intensify coffee production, access crucial inputs and services, and increase or diversify their production of basic grains. These households tended to be strongly constrained in their endowment with or access to assets, as reflected in very small landholdings, insecure land tenure, and high dependence on off-farm income for their livelihoods. They were also more likely to have older household heads or to be headed by a female. The Soppexcca case shows that greater attention needs to be paid to the asset endowments of smallholders and the related dynamics, if value chain development is to reduce rural poverty in an integrated and significant way.

preconditions for poor households and resource-constrained enterprises to become value chain ready.

3. Value chain development stakeholders would benefit from an asset-based approach, clear impact models, and sound metrics for understanding poverty impacts and identifying options for improved pro-poor value chain development.

There is a growing consensus that conventional poverty definitions need to be broadened to account for critical livelihood assets and vulnerability (see, for example, McKay, 2009). These definitions allow for the endowments of and changes in human, social, natural, physical, and financial capital, and their effects on livelihood resilience. When applied in value chain development, such an asset-based approach is critical to determine whether value chain readiness is reached by meeting minimum asset thresholds. It also permits us to prove the existence of positive feedback loops; that is, processes in which the building of one asset (e.g. financial capital) leads to the building of others (e.g. human or physical capital). These would be understood as indicators of broad-based and lasting impact on rural livelihoods in pursuit of well-being and resilience.

Despite advances in thinking about the nature and causes of poverty, most sceptics and advocates of value chain development rely on a limited set of indicators and data to substantiate their poverty claims. The former tend to describe the limited poverty impact of value chain development by focusing on either the limited *relative* share of benefits captured by the poor in a given chain, or the exclusion of the poorest sections of the rural population. Advocates, on the other hand, argue that the contribution of value chain development to poverty reduction needs to be measured as an *absolute* increase in income through interventions in a value chain, and that employment effects among the poor are relevant irrespective of the overall distribution of benefits. In both cases, clear impact models with plausible cause–effect relationships, or refined metrics that allow for both positive and negative effects of value chain development are largely absent.

There is an urgent need and an opportunity for public and private investors in value chain development to promote the adoption of an asset-based approach to the design and implementation of value chain initiatives, based on

---

Box 12.4. International collaboration to design an asset-based approach to value chain development assessment

Between 2008 and 2011, an international group of development practitioners and researchers, representing Bioversity International, CATIE, CRS, ICRAF, Intercooperation, LWR, MEDA, Swisscontact, TechnoServe, and Winrock's Wallace Center, among others, collaborated on the design and testing of the *5CapitalsToolkit* – an asset-based approach to assess the poverty impacts of value chain development (see Donovan and Stoian, 2010). In collaboration with local NGOs and consultants, and with financial support from the Ford Foundation, the toolkit was designed and validated through 23 case studies in Latin and North America, Africa, and Asia. The aim was to design a tool that would: 1) assess the impact of a whole set of value chain development interventions, rather than that of a particular intervention; 2) consider changes in assets among both households and the enterprises that maintained links with them; and 3) differentiate between the impacts of the combined value chain development interventions vis-à-vis those induced by external factors. Experiences gained in tool testing demonstrated the potential of an asset-based approach to value chain development assessment, along with related challenges. Case study collaborators agreed that: 1) such an approach is very useful to gain in-depth insight into value chain development-related poverty impacts; 2) the focus on both household and enterprise assets sheds additional light on poverty impacts; 3) the context analysis as the first step of the methodology is critical to isolate value chain development-related impact from context-induced change; and 4) the results of impact assessment have highest value when used for redesigning value chain development interventions. At the same time they found that this approach: 1) implies investments of human and financial resources that are reasonable but not low-cost; 2) requires a flexible handling of the enterprise assessment due to the varied nature of 'linked enterprises'; and 3) depends on systems thinking to make the most out of it. The final version of the toolkit (in English and Spanish) and an edited case study volume will be made available on the CATIE and ICRAF websites in 2012 (www.catie.ac.cr and www.icraf.org)

---

well-defined impact models, and to develop sound metrics that help demonstrate under which conditions value chain development generates high poverty impact. Recent work by an international coalition of development practitioners and researchers highlights the opportunities and the challenges for the application of an asset-based approach to value chain development (Box 12.4).

4. Value chain development requires adequate linking of technical, business, and financial services.

In addition to successful collaboration between public and private sectors and civil society, pro-poor value chain development requires a combination of technical, business, and financial services. Some of these services are available from within the chain, particularly those that help improve quality or efficiency. Such 'embedded services', typically provided by downstream actors to their upstream business partners, have the advantage of focusing on clearly identified needs and upgrading opportunities in the chain. On the other hand, certain services may not be readily available from within the chain, especially those that help improve environmental and social performance or that address long-term issues related to capacity building and skills development among the poor. These services may need to be sourced from external service providers, such as government agencies, NGOs, development projects, and consulting firms. The diverse nature of the services needed poses a challenge to their effective and efficient delivery. Technical services related to production and, to a lesser extent, processing technologies tend to be readily available for traditional products, either from downstream actors or from external service providers. Financial services may be provided in the form of advance payments or credits within the chain, or through government-funded programmes and microfinance projects from outside the chain. Usually, however, they are not available to highly resource-constrained smallholders. Business services often turn out to be the Achilles heel in value chain development as specialized business service providers for the rural sector are largely absent. A further challenge for value chain development-related services is their provision in an isolated fashion. Service providers are typically specialized in one of these three types of service and rarely make an effort to partner with those who provide complementary services. Effective and efficient services for value chain development require a sound demand analysis and a concerted approach to the delivery of technical, business, and financial services that are well-linked and complement each other in a logical fashion. Following the subsidiarity principle, only those services would be provided from outside the chain that cannot be sourced from within the chain.

What we still need to know and do differently

The number of rural people living in desperate conditions under various degrees of vulnerability remains high. Undoubtedly, we have advanced our understanding of poverty issues and there is a growing consensus on the importance of pro-poor interventions in value chains. Yet there are a number of crucial issues on which our knowledge is still insufficient. In the absence of an asset-based approach to designing, implementing, and monitoring value chain initiatives, related impact models and theories of change are incomplete. Under these conditions, it is virtually impossible to identify the best options for helping poor people to *exit* from poverty, let alone to *stay* out of poverty. In addition to these knowledge gaps, there are a number of 'action gaps' related to areas that require forms of engagement in value chains in addition to, or other than, those applied to date.

Need for improved knowledge

1. *How to determine value chain readiness?* If the goal of the intervention is to reduce vulnerability and lift people out of poverty, how can we determine whether poor households and their business organizations are ready to participate in value chain development? Which minimum . asset thresholds do they need to meet and, if not available, what are the best options to help them become value chain ready?

2. *Can asset building at the level of smallholder enterprises spur asset building at the household level?* Since business organization of smallholders is often considered a prerequisite for their successful participation in value chains, we need to understand under what conditions asset building at the level of the smallholder enterprises positively influences household assets and reduces vulnerability, and how value chain development can help to create more synergy in this respect.

3. *How to ensure that assessing value chain development impact is both effective and efficient?* Current impact assessment of value chain programmes tends to be low-cost and fairly one-dimensional, whereas an asset-based approach to assessment yields more robust results while requiring higher investments. There is a clear need for experimenting with differentiated approaches to impact assessment, for example the routine measuring of outputs, the assessing of outcomes to the extent possible, and full-fledged impact assessment through in-depth case studies. The Donor Committee for Enterprise Development (DCED), for example, recommends three 'universal' impact indicators (scale, income, and jobs) for ongoing results measurement; at the same time it acknowledges that this cannot replace rigorous impact assessments, nor evaluations, as these ask broader questions (Tanburn and Sen, 2011).

4. *How best to use an asset-based approach for planning, implementing, and assessing value chain development?* In particular, we need to better understand what indicators within each asset type – typically including human, social, natural, physical, and financial capital – tell us the most about reducing poverty and vulnerability. Which proxies can be used to make assessment manageable and cost effective? How do we adapt or tailor value chain development to different contexts and varying asset levels in given populations? How can we best deal with non-linear asset pathways (asset building followed by asset erosion or vice versa)?

5. *Which roles correspond to private, public, and civil society sectors in promoting value chain development?* What can the private sector do alone? Under what conditions will the private sector invest in the long term, or go the extra mile for pro-poor value chain development? What can realistically be expected from private sector initiatives, such as base of the pyramid, corporate social responsibility, or creating shared value? Where and how do public–private partnerships work best and where are their limits? What is the specific role of NGOs in helping build assets beyond the contributions from public and private sectors?

Need for improved action

1. *Account for the evolution of income and asset objectives.* Value chain development programmes need to account for the dynamics and variations of asset endowments and livelihood objectives among poor and vulnerable populations. Different measures are needed in each stage when following

a pathway out of poverty from: '(i) stabilizing household consumption/ stemming asset loss, to (ii) smoothing household consumption/ protecting assets, to (iii) smoothing household income/acquiring assets, to (iv) expanding household income/leverage assets, and to (v) stabilized income-generation and asset accumulation' (Fowler and Brand, 2011).

2. *Differentiate between those who are value chain ready and those who are not.* Market-based interventions work for those who meet minimum asset thresholds and, hence, are value chain ready. Those who are not require specific, non-market-based interventions to create the necessary preconditions for their participation in value chain development. These include, but are not limited to, customized technical assistance and training to build human and social capital, rehabilitation of natural capital where eroded, investments in basic infrastructure and services, and resolution of land tenure conflicts where existing. These interventions fall outside the realm of value chain development but are critical for its success, if the poorest sections of the rural population are to benefit from it.

3. *Follow logical sequence of asset building.* There are plentiful examples of programmes where donors have given processing equipment to farmer organizations, but the initiatives have failed because of lacking business skills. In many cases, human and social capital needs to be built before considering investments in physical capital. In other cases, eroded natural capital needs to be rebuilt before meaningful business development is possible.

4. *Ensure synergies among public and private sectors and civil society, promoting value chain development.* Based on the subsidiarity principle, public sector and civil society should only engage in those interventions that cannot be performed by the private sector. This requires determining which services can be provided from within the chain ('embedded services') and which need to be sourced from external service providers (in many cases government agencies or NGOs). For example, rather than donating equipment, donors might link farmers to credit agencies to buy the equipment. If necessary, agencies could subsidize the cost of credit.

5. *Improve the quality of and the linking between technical, business, and financial services.* In the absence of integrated service providers, we need to make major efforts to link technical, business, and financial services in ways that allow for meaningful asset building at household and smallholder enterprise levels. At the same time, we need to ensure that these services are geared to the requirements identified by the chain actors rather than outside agents from public sector or civil society.

6. *Create awareness among donors and development practitioners about the advantages of adopting an asset-based approach to the design, implementation, and assessment of value chain development.* There is a need to provide evidence that the increased costs and complexity of an asset-based

approach are outweighed by tangible benefits in terms of higher impact on poverty reduction, livelihood resilience, and viability of smallholder enterprises.

7. *Promote comprehensive strategies to rural development.* There is both a need for and an opportunity to combine value chain development with other approaches to rural development, such as sustainable rural livelihoods, territorial development, and investments in rural infrastructure and services.

8. *Innovate in partnerships for joint learning and continuous improvement.* The diverse nature of stakeholders in value chain development provides a great opportunity for joint learning. Each of them brings specific perspectives, skills, and experiences to the table, but we need to define appropriate forums and mechanisms for sharing and capitalizing on these. The outcome of such learning alliances and communities of practice will be highest if nurtured by genuine interest in learning and authentic commitment to continuous improvement.

Conclusions

Our current knowledge of the poverty impacts of value chain development is limited. Regardless of whether related initiatives are driven by private, public, or civil society sectors, the use of sound metrics to determine their impact at both the enterprise and the household level, and to isolate value chain development from contextinduced change should be the rule rather than the exception. If value chain development is to be effective in addressing rural poverty, it must embrace the complex needs and realities of the rural poor. This includes the recognition that market-oriented activities are important but not exclusive elements of rural livelihood strategies. Particular attention needs to be paid to the specific challenges and needs of the very poor given their higher risk and vulnerability. Otherwise there is a substantial risk that pro-poor value chain development does not live up to expectations and causes undue trade-offs in the livelihood strategies of the rural poor.

An asset-based approach to the design, implementation, and assessment of value chain development is a powerful vehicle to address these challenges and risks. Not only does it provide an appropriate measure of the multiple dimensions of poverty and vulnerability, but it also helps to determine which households and smallholder enterprises are ready for value chain development, and which require specific preparatory interventions to become value chain ready. An asset-based approach to value chain development comes at a price, though. Related planning, data collection, and analysis are relatively time-consuming, complex, and costly. At the same time, such an approach helps forgo higher expenses to mitigate unintended effects of interventions in value chains. It provides public sector and civil society organizations with the necessary information to justify the investment of taxpayers' money, and holds the potential to improve the environmental and social credentials of private sector companies pursuing base of the pyramid, corporate social responsibility, creating shared value, or similar strategies.

Value chain development is not a panacea to rural development. When seeking impact beyond poverty reduction on resilience of livelihoods and ecosystems, it needs to be paired with complementary approaches. Comprehensive strategies for rural development would include improvements in local infrastructure and services, political-legal frameworks, food security, local markets for agricultural and forest products, and income generation through services and off-farm employment. Appropriate design, implementation, and monitoring and evaluation of such strategies, again, will best be achieved by pursuing an asset-based approach.

Much remains to be learned about the best possible design and implementation of value chain programmes and pertinent combinations with other approaches. Undoubtedly, however, an asset-based approach to pro-poor value chain development is a critical piece of such strategies. Governments, donors, development agencies, NGOs, and private sector agents committed to poverty reduction will need to invest in pilot projects, tool development, and capacity building; engage in multi-stakeholder platforms for joint learning; and commit to continuous improvement. Without the adoption of an asset-based approach to value chain development, poor households and smallholder enterprises in the upstream segments of the chain will continue to be exposed to high uncertainty and risk and, in particular, to potentially harmful trade-offs between value chain optimization and resilience at the household and business level.

References

Altenburg, T. (2007) *Donor Approaches to Supporting Pro-poor Value Chains* [website], report prepared for the Donor Committee for Enterprise Development – Working Group on Linkages and Value Chains, German Development Institute (DIE), Bonn, Germany <www.value-chains.org/dyn/bds/docs/568/DonorApproachestoPro-PoorValueChains.pdf> [last accessed 24 January 2012].

Arora, S. and Romijn, H. (2009) *Innovation for the Base of the Pyramid: Critical Perspectives from Development Studies on Heterogeneity and Participation* [website], United Nations University/Maastricht Economic and Social Research and Training Centre on Innovation and Technology, Maastricht, the Netherlands <www.merit.unu.edu/publications/wppdf/2009/wp2009-036.pdf> [last accessed 24 January 2012].

Charette, D. (2011) *A Portfolio Approach to Value Chain Development Programs*, MicroREPORT #169, USAID, Washington, DC.

DFID (Department for International Development) and SDC (Swiss Development Corporation) (2008) *A Synthesis of the Making Markets Work for the Poor (M4P) Approach*, SDC, Berne, Switzerland.

Donovan, J. and Poole, N. (2011) 'Asset building in response to value chain development: Evidence from specialty smallholder coffee producers in Nicaragua', *ICRAF Working Paper* 138,World Agroforestry Centre, Nairobi, Kenya.

Donovan, J. and Stoian, D. (with contributions from Antezana, I., Belt, J., Clark, S., Harper, M., Poole, N., Ruddick, S. and Waagbo, J.) (2010) *Assessing the Impact of Value Chain Approaches on Rural Poverty*, Methodological Guidelines for Development Practitioners and Private Sector Representatives, CATIE, Turrialba, Costa Rica.

Fowler, B. and Brand, M. (2011) *Pathways Out of Poverty: Applying Key Principles of the Value Chain Approach to Reach the Very Poor*, Discussion Paper/ Microreport #173, USAID, Washington, DC.

Haddad, L., Lindstrom, J. and Pinto, Y. (2010) 'The sorry state of M&E in agriculture: Can people-centred approaches help?' *IDS Bulletin* 41: 6-25.

Humphrey, J. and Navas-Alemán, L. (2010) 'Value chains, donor interventions and poverty reduction: A review of donor practice', *IDS Research Report* 63, IDS, Brighton, UK.

Jones, H. (2011) 'Taking responsibility for complexity: When is a policy problem complex, why does it matter, and how can it be tackled?' *ODI Briefing Paper* 68, ODI, London.

Kula, O., Downing, J. and Field, M. (2006) 'Value chain programmes to integrate competitiveness, economic growth and poverty reduction', *Small Enterprise Development* 17: 23-35.

McKay, A. (2009) 'Assets and chronic poverty: Background paper', *Chronic Poverty Research Centre Working Paper* 100, University of Sussex, Brighton, UK <www.chronicpoverty.org/uploads/publication_files/WP100%20 McKay_1.pdf> [last accessed 24 January 2012].

Porter, M.E. and Kramer, M.R. (2011) 'Creating shared value: How to reinvent capitalism – and unleash a wave of innovation and growth', *Harvard Business Review* (Jan-Feb 2011): 2–17.

Stoian, D. and Donovan, J. (2007) 'Value chain development from a livelihoods perspective: A multi-chain approach for coffee and cacao producing households in Central America', in E. Tielkes (ed.), *Utilisation of Diversity in Land Use Systems: Sustainable and Organic Approaches to Meet Human Needs. Tropentag 2007 – International Research on Food Security, Natural Resource Management and Rural Development*, Kassel-Witzenhausen, Germany, 9–11 October 2007.

Tanburn, J. and Sen, N. (2011) *Why Have a Standard for Measuring Results? Progress and Plans of the Donor Committee for Enterprise Development*, DCED, London.

UN (United Nations) (2011) *The Millennium Development Goals Report 2011*, UN, New York.

UNIDO (United Nations Industrial Development Organization) (2011) *Pro-poor Value Chain Development: 25 Guiding Questions for Designing and Implementing Agroindustry Projects*, UNIDO, Vienna, Austria.

Webber, C.M. and Labaste, P. (2010) *Building Competitiveness in Africa's Agriculture: A Guide to Value Chain Concepts and Applications*, World Bank, Washington, DC.

About the authors

Dietmar Stoian, PhD (d.stoian@cgiar.org), Lead Scientist, Value Chains, Private Sector Engagement and Investments, World Agroforestry (ICRAF), Bonn, Germany.

Jason Donovan, PhD (j.donovan@cgiar.org), Senior Economist, Research Theme Leader for Markets and Value Chains, International Maize and Wheat Improvement Center (CIMMYT), Texcoco, Mexico.

John Fisk, Winwork International, Arlington, USA.

Michelle F. Muldoon (michelle@veritasdevelopment.biz), Veritas Marketing & Business Consulting, Arlington, VA, USA.

PART III

Assessment and outcomes of VCD

CHAPTER 13

Microfinance plus for ecosystem services: A territorial perspective on Proyecto CAMBio in Nicaragua

Johan Bastiaensen, Frédéric Huybrechs, Davide Forcella, and Gert van Hecken

Abstract

Drawing from discussions on the panacea problem in microfinance and natural resource management, we scrutinize a 'green microfinance plus' programme – Proyecto CAMBio – in a specific setting in Nicaragua, focusing in particular on its interaction with local development pathways. The programme was designed to promote biodiversity-friendly land uses through the combination of credit provision, technical assistance and conditional economic incentives. In our case study, we highlight the focus on individual producers, the implicit targeting of more established medium-sized producers, and the uncritical promotion of a particular technical model of production. The project might thereby have failed to identify and revert some negative processes of environmental degradation and did not consciously engage with the dynamics and political arenas of sustainable development. We call for a more holistic territorial perspective that is conducive to more strategic thinking about the interactive socio-technical dynamics and ensuing opportunities and constraints for different producer types and technical-commercial models. Such strategic reflection is both inevitable and political, as it impacts on the opening and closing of avenues for more or less socially inclusive and environmentally sound development pathways.

Keywords: green microfinance, coffee, environmental services, microfinance plus, microcredit, Nicaragua, sustainable development, development pathways

Introduction

As the social impact of microfinance continues to be the subject of heated debate and contestation, the sweeping claim that it is a panacea for poverty has clearly become unsustainable. In the light of the ongoing discussion on poverty impact, does it make sense to burden the microfinance agenda with yet another, at least as large, challenge, namely that of promoting

http://dx.doi.org/10.3362/9781788530576.013

environmentally friendly development? Is this perhaps yet another example of 'microfinance narcissism' (Bastiaensen et al., 2013), whereby microfinance is seen as the linchpin of global change? Successions of contradictory impact studies (Bauchet et al., 2011; Banerjee et al., 2015) have been unable to demonstrate the effects of microfinance. Indeed, the realization that its impact (or lack thereof) inevitably depends on complex, dynamic interactions – making a system's evolution intrinsically non-linear and unpredictable – renders futile any attempt to unequivocally attribute outcomes to microfinance alone.

One response to this insight has been the plea for a 'microfinance plus' approach (Sievers and Vandenberg, 2007; Bastiaensen and Marchetti, 2011), whereby financial and non-financial services are combined. This could offer better perspectives for promoting beneficial change to interconnected social, economic, cultural and ecological systems. In the present chapter, we consider a 'green microfinance plus' initiative: the Central American Proyecto CAMBio (Central American Markets for Biodiversity) in Nicaragua, as implemented by the Fondo de Desarrollo Local (FDL). The innovative project skilfully combined conditionally subsidized agricultural microcredit with technical assistance and payments for environmental services (PES) for the purpose of inducing environmentally sound land-use changes. This case study highlights the inevitability and the political character of complex interactions between green microfinance interventions and local development pathways. We call for a more holistic territorial perspective that is conducive to strategic thinking about the interactive socio-technical dynamics and ensuing opportunities and constraints for different producer types. Further, by linking our findings to broader debates about the need to go beyond panaceas in microfinance and natural resource management, we reflect more broadly on the potentials and pitfalls of green microfinance plus programmes.

Microfinance, complexity and sustainable development

Before turning to our case, let us briefly reflect on the panacea problem and microfinance plus. Again, the controversy surrounding the supposed poverty impact of microfinance provides an interesting starting point, particularly Susan Johnson's observation that what is lacking from the debate is an adequate theory of the mechanisms and processes that generate poverty, as it commonly adopts a residual approach to poverty (Johnson, 2012). This stands in the way of more adequate understanding of the roles of the different actors involved. Johnson rightly asserts that poverty is not residual at all, but a reality resulting from collective relational processes that distribute aspirations, burdens and opportunities for social groups in society.

With the rise of 'green microfinance' – microfinance taking environmental considerations into account (Muñoz Araya and Christen, 2004; Hall et al., 2008; Schuite and Pater, 2008; Allet, 2012; Huybrechs et al., 2015) – it also becomes necessary to reflect on the analysis of human–nature interactions. In that realm, too, Johnson's argument about poverty remains valid. An adequate approach to the world's environmental challenges requires an analysis of productive economic systems as embedded in and interacting with both the life-support system of nature and the socio-cultural system of human society (Ropke, 2005). The (im)balance of the emerging dynamics and the associated challenges need to be seen as the outcome of complex relational processes mediated by social institutions, at multiple scales.

In rural regions, one can usually discern the emergence of one or a few dominant development pathways, connected to agricultural or other economic activities, which create opportunities and impose constraints for distinct groups (de Haan and Zoomers, 2005; Bastiaensen et al., 2015). This is the emergent outcome of power-laden territorial collective action by interacting groups of actors in multiple organizations and social networks, inspired by certain sets of (sufficiently shared) ideas and motivations, and governed by particular 'rules in use' or 'practical norms' (Bastiaensen et al., 2015).

These complex socio-ecological dynamics cannot be captured in straight-forward predictive models, especially not in the context of profound systemic change, which usually requires a more thorough reshuffle of social networks, ideas, motivations, and 'rules in use'. Yet, it is common practice among scientists and practitioners alike to approach these complexities with simplified, reductionist models in laying the foundation for policy design and action. It is this tendency that Ostrom and Cox (2010) have dubbed the 'panacea problem'. Simplified, manageable and often unidisciplinary models of reality create an appealing semblance of control. This often results in decontextualized, one-size-fits-all policy recommendations, however, and ineffective and unjust policies (Leach et al., 2010; Ramalingam, 2013). Ostrom and Cox (2010) therefore suggest to embrace more holistic heuristic frameworks that try to make sense of contextualized complex interactions.

The economic conceptualization of society as a set of rational individuals, responding to price signals and interacting with each other through markets, is a well-known and influential example of a reductionist model. The initial microfinance model is also derived from a reductionist model of the world, where financial capital is the key constraint facing poor 'entrepreneurs' (Johnson, 2012; Aitken, 2013; Mader, 2014; Schwittay, 2014). The provision of microcredit to excluded sectors is seen as an obvious and comprehensive solution. At the same time, in natural resource management there is a tendency to relate the depletion or provision of environmental services (ES) to the (in)effective pricing of environmental costs and benefits. The introduction of adequate payments for ES (PES) is assumed to restore the balance in provisioning ES (Ferraro and Simpson, 2002). And in yet another model, where a lack of producer knowledge about ecosystem-friendly production technologies is considered the key problem, technical assistance is held to provide the solution.

The three aforementioned models might be amalgamated into a single framework: a combination of microcredit with PES and TA, as in the green microfinance intervention analysed in this contribution. However, a mere aggregation of three supposed solutions to partial problems does not necessarily guarantee an adequate holistic understanding of and response to the problems facing the evolving socio-ecological systems as a whole. A 'complex' worldview rather requires these proposed solutions to be understood in their mutual interactions as well as their interaction with the prevailing system more generally.

These insights form the basis for our case study, where we discern prevailing opportunities and constraints for different social groups; look at how the implementation of the green microfinance project interacted with this setting; and reflect on the emerging outcomes in terms of environmental performance. To take a significant step beyond panaceas, we suggest a more proactive and conscious engagement with these complex interactions, and a recognition of the inevitably political role herein.

Development pathways and socio-ecological systems

The Macizo de Peñas Blancas (hereafter Peñas Blancas) is located in the northern central highlands of Nicaragua. Declared a nature reserve 25 years ago, it is part of the Mesoamerican Biological Corridor and one of six conservation nuclei in the Bosawás Biosphere Reserve. Its exceptional status set it apart as a priority area for the implementation of Proyecto CAMBio in Nicaragua. The climatological and topographical features of this 'cloud forest' make it suitable for coffee cultivation, an economic activity that strongly characterizes the local development pathway.

Peñas Blancas is part of the 'old agricultural frontier' (Maldidier and Marchetti, 1996). Farmers first arrived there in search of unclaimed land in the 1940s, having been pushed east by the expansion of the major coffee estates in consequence of government policy to boost coffee production (Rocha, 2001). Upon their arrival, the displaced farmers would typically clear forest to grow staple crops and raise fowl and pigs for subsistence. Whenever savings or credit permitted, they would generally plant coffee shrubs.

The construction of a road in the 1970s improved opportunities for the commercialization of coffee and opened up the region to newcomers, pushing the agricultural frontier even further. This process was interrupted during the 1980s, when the country was gripped by an armed conflict between the Sandinista regime and the counter-revolutionary Contras. The coffee industry, which had been nationalized in the 1980s, was liberalized again in the 1990s, as state credit was withdrawn and cooperatives and state-led production units were dismantled. This created opportunities for larger entrepreneurs to purchase land. Increasingly, growers chose to cultivate newer coffee varietals, which are more densely sown and are more resistant to sunlight. They also offer higher yields, though this requires more intensive use of agrochemicals.

Over the past 15 years, the coffee region has been hit by two severe crises. In 2000, international coffee prices plummeted, affecting farmers' incomes and their access to credit (credit provision was cut by 70–90 per cent the next year) (Rocha, 2001). More recently, the 'coffee rust' fungus decimated mainly weaker plantations and less resistant and older varietals. After the 2011–12 harvest, the disease left 20 per cent of the national coffee fields in need of renovation (Avelino and Rivas, 2013). The epidemic strongly affected the least privileged coffee farmers, in part because of their different approach to coffee production: they tend to use fewer agrochemicals, to cultivate in more shaded areas, and generally try to benefit from the long productive life of coffee. Moreover, smaller farmers tend not to have access to longer term commercial credit from banks. Instead, they must rely on forward sales to middlemen or coffee exporters (Mendoza et al., 2013), or on mostly short-term microfinance loans. Longer term credit is key to renovating plantations, however, as it takes three years before newly sown coffee plants become productive.

The 2000 coffee crisis drew attention to the plight of small coffee farmers, resulting in various projects and initiatives, including 'fair trade' coffee certification. However, as certification demands high fees and alternative commercialization channels, the scheme is not readily accessible to small family farmers, with the exception of farmers who managed to organize themselves in cooperatives, often as part of a project or external support programme. Other labels, such as Rainforest Alliance, UTZ and 4C, currently tend to benefit mostly large-scale estates (Gómez et al., 2011).

These historical evolutions – mediated by a differential access to credit, markets, projects, certification, and social and political support – have resulted in the following local typology of producers (based on Maldidier and Marchetti (1996) and Arribard (2013)):

- 'Poor peasants with land' rely exclusively on family labour, sometimes complementing agricultural revenues with remunerated work on other farms. They produce subsistence staple crops, keep fowl and pigs, and install small plots of coffee. Their holdings are generally smaller than 3 hectares.
- 'Small-scale coffee farmers' hold areas between 3 and 30 ha and employ temporary workers during harvest. They have easier, yet limited, access to credit. In lower-lying areas, some of these farmers also engage in small-scale cattle raising. Like the 'poor peasants with land', they sell their coffee mostly to intermediaries or to the main export companies in the region.
- 'Medium-scale coffee farmers' own between 30 and 100 ha and complement family labour with the employment of both temporary and permanent workers. These farmers tend to devote most of their land to coffee production, though some, particularly those operating at lower altitudes, engage in medium-scale cattle rearing and milk production.
- The 'coffee estates' are the largest actors in the region, with holdings measuring up to 350 ha. Their approach is based on an entrepreneurial model of production and they often operate as part of a larger, more integrated enterprise that is also involved in the processing and trade stages of the value chain.

The majority of farmers in the region belong to the first two groups, with more than half their farms measuring under 7 ha (Gómez et al., 2011). The largest 10 per cent of producers own over half the available arable land.

While the proposed typology is inevitably a simplification, it does allow us to reflect on the territorial development pathway in a more synthesized and yet sufficiently diversified way. Considering the environmental concerns that Proyecto CAMBio tried to address, it is important to note that smaller farmers tend to cultivate coffee with denser and more diversified shade cover, and to use fewer agrochemicals (Cuadra Mayorga and Alvarado Narváez, 2011). They also generally diversify their economic activities as a mitigation strategy for their vulnerability to coffee crises. Even though small-scale coffee farming in this region is economically viable, such crises are a recurring threat. They can force smaller producers to reduce their coffee areas – eliminating the shade and replacing coffee with staple crops or renting out land for vegetable contract farming – or even to sell their holding altogether. Conversely, such crises create opportunities for the larger farmers to acquire additional land at bargain prices, leading to an even greater concentration of land holdings. This may, in turn, result in landless farmers moving to the new agricultural frontier in search of new farmland, a process previously observed in other regions in Nicaragua (Polvorosa, 2015). Hence, the privileged position of the larger estates, the economic vulnerability of the smaller farmers, and the general trend towards production methods involving more agrochemicals and less shade – as a merely technical response to the aforementioned crises – may be seen as important dynamics within the currently dominant development pathway.

From an ecological perspective, this reflection on development pathways would seem to point towards the need for strategies to strengthen the viability and stability of smaller producers in the face of increasing land concentration and in reaction to a yield-oriented entrepreneurial approach to coffee production. In this context, opportunities may present themselves in connecting such producers to rewarding markets. This would require, among other things, a degree of organization among farmers and the questioning of current market relations, as well as careful reflection on how to enhance their diversified farming activities. Such a strategy would not only seek to promote more environmentally friendly coffee production, but it would also strive to support farmers who, under the current development pathway, feel like 'a species at risk of extinction', as one farmer poignantly put it. In other words, it would need to take account not just of biodiversity, but also social diversity, as well as any interactions between these two dimensions.

Microcredit for ecosystem services/biodiversity: Proyecto CAMBio

Proyecto CAMBio was implemented in Guatemala, Honduras, El Salvador, Costa Rica and Nicaragua between 2008 and 2013. It was financed by the Central American Bank for Economic Integration (CABEI), the United Nations

Development Programme (UNDP) and the Global Environment Facility (GEF). The aim of Proyecto CAMBio was to support biodiversity-friendly activities by 'removing barriers' for financial institutions and micro, small and medium-scale enterprises to engage with these practices (Proyecto CAMBio, 2013). With the guiding idea that pro-environmental change can be achieved through economic incentives (GEF, 2005; UNDP, 2006; Ervine, 2010), the project provided credits, conditional biopremiums and technical assistance (TA) for promoted practices.

The project allied with 24 intermediary financial institutions (including banks, credit cooperatives and microfinance institutions) in the five target countries. In practice, there were variegated implementation modes (Forcella, 2012; Lucheschi, 2014; Proyecto CAMBio, 2014; Forcella and Lucheschi, 2015). Here, we focus on Proyecto CAMBio as implemented by the Nicaraguan microfinance institution Fondo de Desarrollo Local (FDL) in association with its partner organization Nitlapan. The implementation mode of FDL–Nitlapan has been described as 'exemplary' and worthy of emulation (Vargas et al., 2011; Mendoza et al., 2012; Proyecto CAMBio, 2014). We do not imply that the specific outcomes of this case apply to the rest of Proyecto CAMBio, and we do not purport to make an analysis of the whole project. Rather, we rely on our conceptual framework of complex local dynamics and development pathways to present an in-depth analysis of the case at hand (Flyvbjerg, 2006). Our critical analysis aims to further improve the valuable green microfinance plus strategy of FDL-Nitlapan.

In its implementation of Proyecto CAMBio, FDL combined credit, TA and the so-called biopremium. For the provision of credit, FDL had access to a credit line from the CABEI at a 4.5 per cent annual interest rate. This enabled it to provide CAMBio loans at a slightly cheaper interest rate of 20 per cent annually, as compared to FDL's average rural interest rate at the time around 27 per cent. The loans were provided to finance investments in agroforestry and silvopastoral practices. They were capped at US$10,000 and averaged $2,070 per credit, which is low in comparison to many other implementations of Proyecto CAMBio.

Upon ex post verification of the agreed ecological goals (or transformations) – chosen from a list of possibilities provided by CABEI – the producer would receive a cash premium equal to 14 per cent of the loan. These conditional biopremiums were seemingly inspired by the notion of PES, with GEF acting as a biodiversity 'buyer'. Further reference to the notion of PES in the project is implied in its name, 'Central American Markets for Biodiversity' (neatly abbreviated as CAMBio, which is Spanish for 'change'). It is worth noting that Nitlapan had previous experience with the implementation of a supposedly successful PES pilot project in Nicaragua, namely the Regional Integrated Silvopastoral Ecosystem Management Project (RISEMP) (Van Hecken and Bastiaensen, 2010; Huybrechs et al., 2015). In addition, among the participating intermediary financial institutions, FDL was the one that gave the most biopremiums (Proyecto CAMBio, 2013).

When a producer successfully obtained the premium for the agreed trans-formations, FDL would also receive an amount equal to 6 per cent of the loan; hence both the producer and FDL had an incentive to comply. Finally, the project also provided funds for TA, helping producers make the envisaged ecofriendly investments. The funds amounted to 10 per cent of the disbursed loans and this money was used to pay Nitlapan for the provision of the TA.

Analysis of Proyecto CAMBio in the Macizo de Peñas Blancas area

Given the limited funds and the struggle to maintain client relations during a severe repayment crisis in Nicaragua at the time (Bastiaensen et al., 2013), FDL focused CAMBio on selected loyal, long-term clients. Hence, in addition to its ecological objectives, the project was used to reward clients with a good credit record. Furthermore, most probably due to perceived risks and concern with financial indicators, there was an additional bias towards somewhat larger, medium-sized farmers. This can be seen in Table 13.1, which shows the distri-bution of the types of farmer in our survey sample (consisting of 88 Proyecto CAMBio beneficiaries and a control group of 42 other FDL clients), according to the evolution of stated farm characteristics between 2008 and 2013. The bias is also reflected in the average size of the farms: 31.3 ha for the Proyecto CAMBio group compared to 22.2 ha for the other group (for details on the survey and its quantitative analysis, see Forcella and Huybrechs, 2015).

The bias towards medium-sized farmers may also have been induced by the CAMBio incentive system. In particular, the 10 per cent for TA and mon-itoring was deemed insufficient for clients with smaller loans, while the 6 per cent premium for FDL was also more easily earned on fewer loans of larger amounts. Few considered the focus on medium-sized farmers to be problem-atic, as this was believed to guarantee a greater environmental impact. As we will see, however, targeting certain types of farmer also impacts on how the project engages with local development pathways.

In Proyecto CAMBio, farmers received credit for investing in either silvo-pastoral cattle farming (21 per cent of the contracts) or (mainly coffee-related) agroforestry (79 per cent). Considering the relative importance of coffee-re-lated credit, and the fact that our fieldwork was carried out in areas closest to

Table 13.1 Distribution of types of farmer in the survey sample (n = 130)

	Proyecto CAMBio beneficiaries (%)		Other FDL clients (%)	
	2008	*2013*	*2008*	*2013*
Poor peasant with land	18	8	39	14
Small-scale coffee farmer	42	47	39	60
Small-scale cattle farmer	14	11	15	14
Medium-scale coffee farmer	19	27	5	10
Medium-scale cattle farmer	7	7	2	2

the core of the nature reserve and best suited to coffee cultivation, our analysis focuses primarily on coffee farmers.

In order to analyse the interactions between Proyecto CAMBio and the envisaged environmentally friendly practices, we applied the Ecosystem Services Index (ESI) in our survey. This index attributes quantitative values per hectare in terms of biodiversity and carbon capture to different land uses (see Murgueitio et al., 2003). ESI is just one of several possible indicators and it does not allow measurement of all elements of ES or biodiversity. However, for the analysis at hand it hints at possible evolutions on the surveyed farms, and its adoption is inspired by the above-mentioned GEF-funded RISEMP project. We will look at this proxy's evolution for the farms as a whole (but dividing the ESI by the number of hectares for reasons of comparability), not just for the areas targeted by the project within the participating farms. This allows us to take better account of the types of farmer reached and the land-use evolutions promoted in interaction with the local development pathway.

Conditions for eligibility to the biopremium were set on a farm-by-farm basis, as farmer and technician agreed on one or more targets, based on a list of options provided by CABEI. These included the installation of live fences, the conservation of forest around water springs, filters for treating water contaminated by coffee husking, and the planting of shade trees in coffee fields or pastures. Many participants indicated that they had already applied most of these practices prior to the intervention (80 per cent). All indicated that they would continue to do so afterwards. Strikingly, eight in 10 responded that they would have made the investments regardless of the project incentives. Insofar as the planting of shade trees is concerned (a condition specified in 90 per cent of the coffee-related contracts), the conditionality did not compel producers to go far beyond common practice. Medium-sized producers were not systematically required to attain the denser levels of shade commonly applied by the more diversified poor and small farmers. They were also offered the option of adopting the dominant yield-enhancing model.

Analysis of the biopremium payments indicates that some farmers obtained the premium even though their ESI/ha had diminished. Furthermore, the distribution of the predominant tree-related biopremium (which ranged from $0.34 to $12 per tree planted) was found to be erratic. The higher biopremiums were received by farmers owning larger holdings and with better access to credit, while the biopremium paid per tree correlates negatively with the evolution of the farms' environmental index. Thus, the link between the biopremium paid and the ES provided is weak and biased towards relatively larger producers. On this basis, the system can be questioned in terms of both the innovativeness of the promoted practices and their effectiveness. These findings are in line with other studies of Proyecto CAMBio in Nicaragua (Forcella, 2012) and Guatemala (Lucheschi, 2014).

More generally, the survey data indicates an overall tendency towards land concentration as well as an improved ESI on most farms in the region. Logically, these dynamics cannot be attributed wholly to Proyecto CAMBio, as they depend mainly on other farm characteristics and their interactions with existing development pathways. An important driver of evolutions in ESI is change in the farmer's main economic activity. Our quantitative analysis indicates a positive effect from switching to coffee cultivation and a negative one from changing to cattle raising. As hinted at in Table 13.1, the 'control' group had a higher proportion of farmers who, over the five years, evolved from being 'poor peasants with land' to becoming small-scale coffee farmers. This implies a switch to more environmentally friendly land-use practices in the non-CAMBio clients, related to a transition from staple crops to coffee as a main economic activity, as shown in Figure 13.1. This leads to the paradoxical conclusion that the normal, unconditioned credit without subsidies might have had a greater ecological impact than did the subsidized Proyecto CAMBio credit, through its greater engagement with farmers making the switch from staple crops to coffee, although we do not pretend credit is the only factor explaining this change in livelihood trajectory. Hence, the choice for the more established medium-sized coffee farms – which was inspired by a combination of financial, marketing and ecological concerns – might not have been the most ecologically rewarding option after all.

This conclusion is further corroborated if we look at the promoted technical approach to coffee farming. Smaller coffee farmers tend towards a more traditional way of producing coffee, with less use of agrochemicals and more diversified shading. Our interviews with this group indicated that they valued the TA promoted by CAMBio (and beyond) in response to the devastating coffee rust crisis, in particular the choice for the presumably more resistant catimor varietal, but that they often found the technical recommendations for fertilizer and pesticide use to be unattainable. One can hypothesize that

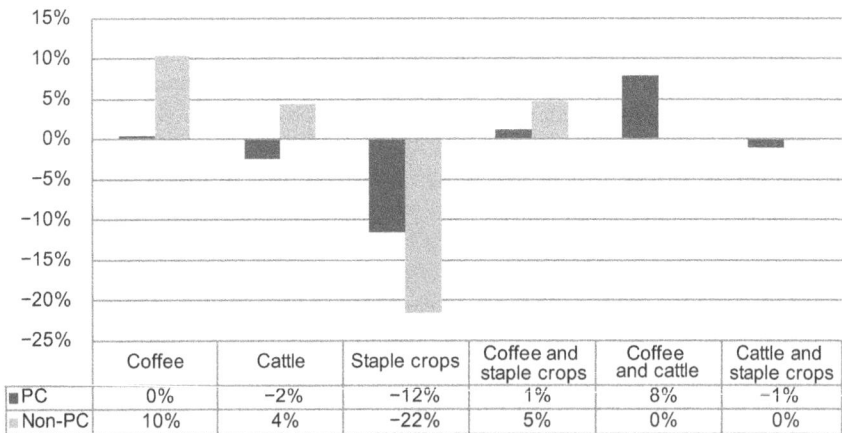

	Coffee	Cattle	Staple crops	Coffee and staple crops	Coffee and cattle	Cattle and staple crops
■ PC	0%	-2%	-12%	1%	8%	-1%
▨ Non-PC	10%	4%	-22%	5%	0%	0%

Figure 13.1 Evolution in main economic activity of CAMBio and non-CAMBio clients between 2008 and 2013.

smaller farmers' preferences were not met by the promoted technical model. Still, there might be opportunities for an alternative pathway, supporting collective action among small-scale producers to renew their more traditional approach to coffee farming and helping them to obtain certification or access to specialty coffee markets, as in other regions of Nicaragua (though certification in itself is not unproblematic: see Mendoza and Bastiaensen, 2003; Westphal, 2008; Valkila, 2009). Collective engagement might also generate new opportunities for other crops, like cocoa, which could be incorporated into diversification and climate-change adaptation strategies.

Given our overall analysis, more decisive priority to actual and potential small-scale coffee farmers in our study region and in the current coffee crisis is strongly advisable, ecologically as well as socially. It would contribute to reducing the conversion of devastated coffee fields into staple or vegetable-growing land; avoid distress sales of land and possible outmigration to other agricultural frontiers; and represent a counterweight to the expansion of the input-intensive entrepreneurial approach to coffee production. Small-scale coffee production might in particular also offer better prospects in terms of interconnectivity in the necessary (yet overlooked) landscape approach to the biodiversity corridors in Central America. The individual approach stands in the way of critically assessing the logic of the intervention in terms of more or less desirable territorial pathways and related social dynamics among different types of producer, erroneously concentrating efforts on larger farmers for the sake of generating a greater impact.

From this angle, one might also worry about the indirect effect of the implementation of the CAMBio project, particularly at a political and cognitive–motivational level. The current implementation of CAMBio – including the relatively high-profile public distribution of the biopremium to relatively more established and 'modern' coffee farmers – might indeed contribute to legitimizing the current pathway of coffee development, which is possibly environmentally and socially sub-optimal. Indeed, it rewards entrepreneurial production, and input-intensive and yield-optimizing (sun-exposed) coffee technologies as being ecologically friendly, while implicitly and probably unintentionally denying support for the arguably ecologically more interesting practices of smaller farms.

This at once brings us to a crucial issue: that concepts such as 'environmental friendliness', 'biodiversity', and 'environmental concern' – which may seem unproblematic and which, indeed, we have used unquestioningly throughout this chapter – are inevitably ambivalent and intrinsically politically contentious, as they do not mean the same to all people; nor do they affect all in the same manner or to the same extent. Our argument for a territorial approach inspired by a socio-ecological perspective thus inevitably requires engagement with the political struggles around the definition of environmental problems and solutions, their relation to other objectives, and the distribution of the ensuing costs and benefits (Fabinyi et al., 2014). A further analysis of Proyecto CAMBio would, for example, need to engage with the a priori focus on biodiversity. We wonder to what extent projects can meaningfully engage with local problems of environmental governance without prior reflection on how those problems are perceived locally and on which practices are most likely to yield worthwhile social and ecological outcomes given the broader local dynamics.

It would also be worth exploring further the dynamics and political arenas between and within different institutions in the process of defining and implementing programmes and their evaluation. The consideration of Proyecto CAMBio as a 'success' by its executors might also relate to other objectives and valuations beyond the environmental objective, such as the fact that the project provided 'green' credits in a financially sustainable way, bringing together different donors, financial institutions and their clients. Further, there may not be much room for manoeuvre to go against the tide of the financialization of poverty and nature, which is enforced through epistemic communities, funding opportunities and the prevalent political–economic structure (Sullivan, 2013; Mader, 2014; Schwittay, 2014; Van Hecken et al., 2015).

Conclusion

This chapter analysed Proyecto CAMBio – an innovative rural 'green microfinance plus' project that strives to go beyond mere credit provision by adding components of TA and PES – in the specific context of its implementation by FDL–Nitlapan in the Macizo de Peñas Blancas area in Nicaragua. Our analysis indicates that such an integrated microfinance plus approach can be a step in the right direction towards inducing relevant ecological (and social) transformations. However, the mere addition of a biopremium (PES) and TA to individual investment credit provides no guarantee for optimal targeting and attainment of the ecological goals set, even if important positive results are achieved by individual client-beneficiaries. In our case study, the implicit priority given to more established medium-sized coffee producers led the project to ignore relatively more rewarding opportunities offered by engaging more strongly with smaller producers, where normal, non-subsidized credit provision paradoxically generated relatively greater ecological impact and contributed towards the social objectives by consolidating poor peasant producers under threat of losing their land due to the coffee crisis. The rather uncritical adoption of an input-intensive, yield-enhancing technical model as the most adequate socio-technological solution to the current coffee crisis might also be questionable.

Therefore, a more holistic territorial perspective needs to be adopted whereby greater attention is paid to strategic reflection on the interactive socio-technical dynamics and emerging pathways in terms of predominant producer types and the associated 'good' technical-commercial models. Such reflection is both inevitable and inevitably political. Any choice made will generate different responses insofar as the perspectives, values and opportunities of determinate groups are concerned. It will thus open and close different avenues for their respective development, as it provides or denies access to credit, subsidies, technological and business assistance, while at the same time promoting certain types of research and development. Additionally, it promotes or hinders particular ideas (e.g. about the 'good' and the 'ecologically sound' technical model of coffee production) and engages with alliances among local and external actors. A more substantial transformation of the current – often socially and ecologically detrimental – development pathways requires the promotion of more drastic structural changes in the ideas and processes of development than has been in evidence thus far in Proyecto CAMBio. Going beyond the individual approach and adopting a more explicit and holistic territorial perspective might be a further step in the right direction.

References

Aitken, R. (2013) 'The financialization of micro-credit', *Development and Change* 44: 473–99 <http://dx.doi.org/10.1111/Dech.12027>.

Allet, M. (2012) 'Why do microfinance institutions go green?' CEB Working Paper No. 12/015, Brussels: Université Libre de Bruxelles – Solvay Brussels School of Economics and Management Centre Emile Bernheim.

Arribard, L. (2013) *Analyse diagnostic du système agraire à l'ouest du massif de Peñas Blancas*, Master thesis, Paris: Agroparistech.

Avelino, J. and Rivas, G. (2013) 'La roya anaranjada del cafeto' <http://hal.archives-ouvertes.fr/ hal-01071036> [accessed 20 July 2015].

Banerjee, A., Karlan, D. and Zinman, J. (2015) 'Six randomized evaluations of microcredit: introduction and further steps', *American Economic Journal: Applied Economics* 7: 1–21 <http:// dx.doi.org/10.1257/app.20140287>.

Bastiaensen, J., Marchetti, P., Mendoza, R. and Perez, F. (2013) 'After the Nicaraguan non-payment crisis: alternatives to microfinance narcissism', *Development and Change* 44: 861–85 <http://dx.doi.org/10.1111/Dech.12046>.

Bastiaensen, J. and Marchetti, P. (2011) 'Rural microfinance and agricultural value chains: strategies and perspectives of the Fondo de desarrollo local in Nicaragua', in B. Armendáriz and M. Labie (eds), *Handbook of Microfinance*, Singapore: World Scientific.

Bastiaensen, J., Merlet, P., Craps, M., De Herdt, T., Flores, S., Huybrechs, F., Mendoza, R., Steel, G. and Van Hecken, G. (2015) 'Making sense of territorial pathways to rural development: a proposal for a normative and analytical framework', IOB Discussion Paper 2015.04, Antwerp: University of Antwerp Institute of Development Policy and Management.

Bauchet, J., Marshall, C., Starita, L., Thomas, J. and Yalouris, A. (2011) 'Latest findings from randomized evaluations of microfinance', *Access to Finance Forum*, Washington, DC: CGAP.

Cuadra Mayorga, L.C. and Alvarado Narváez, U.P. (2011) *Evaluación de tres servicios ambientales de café agroforestal en fincas con diferentes tipos de manejo ubicadas en el Macizo de Peñas Blancas, Jinotega-Matagalpa*, Master thesis, Managua: Universidad Nacional Agraria.

de Haan, L. and Zoomers, A. (2005) 'Exploring the frontier of livelihoods research', *Development and Change* 36: 27–47 <http://dx.doi.org/10.1111/j.0012-155X.2005.00401.x>.

Ervine, K. (2010) 'Participation denied: the global environment facility, its universal blueprint, and the Mexico-Mesoamerican Biological Corridor in Chiapas', *Third World Quarterly* 31: 773–90 <http://dx.doi.org/10.1080/01436597.2010.502694>.

Fabinyi, M., Evans, L. and Foale, S.J. (2014) 'Social-ecological systems, social diversity, and power: insights from anthropology and political ecology', *Ecology and Society* 19 <http:// dx.doi.org/10.5751/Es-07029-190428>.

Ferraro, P.J. and Simpson, R.D. (2002) 'The cost-effectiveness of conservation payments', *Land Economics* 78: 339–53 <http://dx.doi.org/10.3368/le.78.4.465>.

Flyvbjerg, B. (2006) 'Five misunderstandings about case-study research', *Qualitative Inquiry* 12: 219–45 <http://dx.doi.org/10.1177/1077800405284363>.

Forcella, D. (2012). *Payments for environmental services and microfinance – Proyecto Cambio in Nicaragua*, European Microfinance Programme Master thesis, Brussels: Université Libre de Bruxelles.

Forcella, D. and Huybrechs, F. (2015) 'Green microfinance for ecosystem services – an empirical quantitative study of a project's results, the variables influencing its outcomes and the effectiveness of the related conditional payments' <http://dx.doi.org/10.2139/ssrn.2635228> [accessed 26 August 2015].

Forcella, D. and Lucheschi, G. (2015) 'Microfinance and ecosystems conservation – how green microfinance interacts with socio-ecological systems – lessons from Proyecto Cambio in Nicaragua and Guatemala' <http://dx.doi.org/10.2139/ssrn.2635421> [accessed 26 August 2015].

Global Environment Facility (GEF) (2005) 'Central American Markets for Biodiversity (CAMBio): Mainstreaming biodiversity conservation and sustainable use within micro-, small, and medium-sized enterprise development and financing', Project Executive Summary, Washington, DC: GEF.

Gómez, L., Ravnborg, H.M. and Castillo, E. (2011) 'Gobernanza en el uso y acceso a los recursos naturales en la dinámica territorial del Macizo de Peñas Blancas – Nicaragua', Documento de Trabajo No. 82, Santiago de Chile, Chile: Programa Dinámicas Territoriales Rurales RIMISP, Centro Latinoamericano para el Desarrollo Rural.

Hall, J.C., Collins, L., Israel, E. and Wenner, M.D. (2008) 'The missing bottom line: microfinance and the environment', <http://www.microfinancegateway.org/library/missing-bottom-line-microfinance-and-environment> [accessed 20 July 2015].

Huybrechs, F., Bastiaensen, J., Forcella, D. and Van Hecken, G. (2015) 'Enfrentando la vía ganadera extensiva: potenciales y limitaciones de los pagos por servicios ambientales y de las microfinanzas verdes', in J. Bastiaensen, P. Merlet and S. Flores (eds), *Rutas de desarrollo en territorios humanos: las dinámicas de la Vía Láctea en Nicaragua*, Managua: UCA Publicaciones.

Johnson, S. (2012) 'From microfinance to inclusive financial markets: the challenge of social regulation', *Oxford Development Studies* 41: S35–S52 <http://dx.doi.org/10.1080/ 13600818.2012.734799>.

Leach, M., Scoones, I. and Stirling, A. (2010) *Dynamic Sustainabilities: Technology, Environment, Social Justice*, London: Earthscan.

Lucheschi, G. (2014) *Payment for Environmental Services and Microfinance: Proyecto Cambio in Guatemala*, Master thesis, Brussels: Université Libre de Bruxelles.

Mader, P. (2014) 'Financialisation through microfinance: civil society and market-building in India', *Asian Studies Review* 38: 601–19 <http://dx.doi.org/10.1080/10357823.2014.963507>.

Maldidier, C. and Marchetti, P. (1996) *El campesino-finquero y el potencial económico del campesinado nicaragüense: Tipología y regionalización agrosocioeconómica de los sistemas de producción y los sectores sociales en el agro nicaragüense*, Managua: Nitlapán.

Mendoza, R. and Bastiaensen, J. (2003) 'Fair trade and the coffee crisis in the Nicaraguan Segovias', *Small Enterprise Development* 14: 36–46 <http://dx.doi.org/10.3362/0957-1329.2003.020>.

Mendoza, R., Dávila, O., Fonseca, F. and Cheaz, J. (2012) 'Modelo de Adaptación al Cambio Climático a través de la Reconversión Productiva y transformación territorial. Proyecto CAMBio en Nicaragua', in RIMISP (ed.), *Alianzas para el empoderamiento económico*. Santiago.

Mendoza, R., Fernández, E. and Kuhnekath, K. (2013) 'Institución patrón-dependiente o indeterminación social? Genealogía crítica del sistema de habilitación en el café' *Encuentro* 92: 87–102.

Muñoz Araya, M.C. and Christen, R.P. (2004) 'Microfinance as a tool to protect biodiversity hot-spots', Annual Global Roundtable Meeting on Finance and Sustainability, Rio de Janeiro <http://www.microfinancegateway.org/library/microfinance-tool-protect-biodiversity-hot-spots> [accessed 20 July 2015].

Murgueitio, E., Ibrahim, M., Ramirez, E., Zapata, A., Mejía, C. and Casasola, F. (2003) 'Usos de la tierra en fincas ganaderas: Guía para el pago de servicios ambientales en el Proyecto Enfoques Silvopastorales Integrados para el Manejo de Ecosistemas', Calí: CIPAV, CATIE, Nitlapán.

Ostrom, E. and Cox, M. (2010) 'Moving beyond panaceas: a multi-tiered diagnostic approach for social-ecological analysis', *Environmental Conservation* 37: 451–63 <http://dx.doi.org/10.1017/ s0376892910000834>.

Polvorosa, J.C. (2015) 'Ruta de desarrollo ganadero lechero: el caso de Matiguás', in J. Bastiaensen, P. Merlet and S. Flores (eds), *Rutas de desarrollo en territorios humanos: las dinámicas de la Vía Láctea en Nicaragua*. Managua: UCA Publicaciones.

Proyecto CAMBio (2013) 'Lecciones aprendidas del proyecto CAMBio', Tegucigalpa: BCIE, PNUD, FMAM <http://www.proyectocambio.org/categoria_1394581282> [accessed 20 July 2015].

Proyecto CAMBio (2014) 'Experiencias exitosas producto de la incidencia de la asistencia técnica otorgada por el Proyecto CAMBio', Tegucigalpa: BCIE, PNUD, FMAM [PDF] <www. proyectocambio.org/admin/documents/224> [accessed 20 July 2015].

Ramalingam, B. (2013) *Aid on the Edge of Chaos: Rethinking International Cooperation in a Complex World*, Oxford: Oxford University Press.

Rocha, J.L. (2001) 'The chronicle of coffee: history, responsibility and questions', *Envío* 241 <http://www.envio.org.ni/articulo/1523> [accessed 20 July 2015].

Ropke, I. (2005) 'Trends in the development of ecological economics from the late 1980s to the early 2000s', *Ecological Economics* 55: 262–90 <http://dx.doi.org/10.1016/j.ecolecon.2004.10.010>.

Schuite, G.-J. and Pater, A. (2008) 'The triple bottom line for microfinance', <http://www. microfinancegateway.org/library/triple-bottom-line-microfinance> [accessed 20 July 2015].

Schwittay, A. (2014) 'Making poverty into a financial problem: from global poverty lines to kiva.org', *Journal of International Development* 26: 508–19 <http://dx.doi.org/10.1002/Jid.2966>.

Sievers, M. and Vandenberg, P. (2007) 'Synergies through linkages: who benefits from linking micro-finance and business development services?' *World Development* 35: 1341–58 <http:// dx.doi.org/10.1016/j.worlddev.2007.04.002>.

Sullivan, S. (2013) 'Banking nature? The spectacular financialisation of environmental conservation', *Antipode* 45: 198–217 <http://dx.doi.org/10.1111/j.1467-8330.2012.00989.x>.

United Nations Development Programme (UNDP) (2006) 'Central American Markets for Biodiversity (CAMBio): Mainstreaming biodiversity conservation and sustainable use within micro-, small, and medium-sized enterprise development and financing', UNDP project document, New York: UNDP.

Valkila, J. (2009) 'Fair Trade organic coffee production in Nicaragua – sustainable development or a poverty trap?' *Ecological Economics* 68: 3018–25 <http://dx.doi.org/10.1016/j.ecolecon.2009.07.002>.

Van Hecken, G., & Bastiaensen, J. (2010) 'Payments for Ecosystem Services in Nicaragua: Do Market-based Approaches Work?' *Development and Change* 41: 421-44 <http://dx.doi.org/ 10.1111/j.1467-7660.2010.01644.x>

Van Hecken, G., Bastiaensen, J. and Huybrechs, F. (2015) 'What's in a name? Epistemic perspectives and payments for ecosystem services policies in Nicaragua', *Geoforum* 63: 55–66 <http:// dx.doi.org/10.1016/j.geoforum.2015.05.020>.

Vargas, E., Ramírez, L. and Vallejo, M. (2011) 'CAMBio: tranversalización de la conservación y el uso sostenbile de la biodiversidad en el desarrollo y financiamiento de las micro, pequeñas y medianas empresas', Evaluación de medio término, New York: UNDP.

Westphal, S.M. (2008) 'Coffee agroforestry in the aftermath of modernization: diversified production and livelihood strategies in post-reform Nicaragua', in C.M. Bacon, E.V. Mendez, S.R. Gliessman, D. Goodman and J.A. Fox (eds), *Confronting the Coffee Crisis: Fair Trade, Sustainable Livelihoods and Ecosystems in Mexico and Central America*, Cambridge: MIT Press.

About the authors

Johan Bastiaensen, Professor, University of Antwerp Institute of Development Policy and Management (IOB), and Associate Researcher at Instituto Nitlapan, Universidad Centroamericana, Managua, Nicaragua.

Frédéric Huybrechs, PhD candidate, University of Antwerp Institute of Development Policy and Management (IOB), funded by Flemish Interuniversity Council (VLIR-UOS).

Davide Forcella, Post-doctoral Researcher, Université Libre de Bruxelles (ULB) and Associate Researcher, Centre for European Research in Microfinance (CERMi).

Gert Van Hecken, Post-doctoral Researcher, University of Antwerp Institute of Development Policy and Management, and Flemish Fund for Scientific Research (FWO), and Associate Researcher, Instituto Nitlapan, Universidad Centroamericana, Nicaragua.

CHAPTER 14

Impact of an agricultural value chain project on smallholder farmers, households, and children in Liberia

Diana Duff Rutherford, Holly M. Burke, Kelly K. Cheung, and Samuel H. Field

Abstract

We explore the impact of a rural agricultural value chain project in Liberia on smallholder farmers, their households and children in order to better understand the link between household economic welfare and child wellbeing. Drawing on longitudinal field-based quasi-experimental survey data, we estimate the causal effect of the project on the use of modern farming techniques and production, household assets and food security, and child education, health and nutrition. Mixed-methods include multiple rounds of focus groups with farmers, key informant interviews with community leaders, and project monitoring farmer diaries. Treatment farmers showed increased use of modern farming techniques and improved production, households experienced greater access to food, and while no significant changes were found for children, for the outcomes of interest, treatment children outcomes trended in the positive direction. The evaluation suggests that participation in agricultural value chain interventions contributes to positive farm outcomes and social assets, but economic-focused activities alone are insuffcient to improve children's lives. Since improving the lives of children from birth is critical to breaking the intergenerational cycle of poverty, economic strengthening programs like value chain interventions, must monitor their effects on children: to do no harm and to identify and take advantage of opportunities to improve the lives of children.

Key words: economic development, program evaluation, panel data, value chain, household economic welfare, child wellbeing

Introduction

More than two billion people live on less than US$2 a day (World Bank, 2015b). For most rural poor, agriculture is the main occupation and source of income (World Bank, 2015a). Market-based solutions such as agricultural value chain interventions have become increasingly popular to reach this population and facilitate their entrance into larger markets, providing

http://dx.doi.org/10.3362/9781788530576.014

a means to improve their economic welfare (Staritz, 2012). At the same time, the development field increasingly recognizes that building a strong foundation in childhood is more likely to interrupt the transmission of poverty from one generation to the next (Alderman, 2012; PEPFAR, 2012). Recent research shows that household economic status and child well-being are highly correlated (Campbell, Handa, Moroni, Odongo, & Palermo, 2010). It behooves economic development policy makers and practitioners to better understand the connection between house-hold economic welfare and child well-being, as well as the interventions that affect positive change for households and those living within them.

This chapter examines the impact of one such intervention—the agricultural value chain project Agriculture for Children's Empowerment (ACE)—in rural Liberia. ACE was designed to build relationships among actors in agricultural value chain networks and increase crop volume, thereby increasing sales for farmers and food security for households. Increasing income from farms was expected to increase spending on children's education, and improve nutrition and access to health care.

This chapter is organized as follows. The rest of this section provides background information on the evidence-based impact of agricultural value chain projects, the link between household economic welfare and child well-being, the agricultural context in Liberia, and the ACE project. Section 2 describes the study methods and Section 3 provides mixedmethods results for smallholder farms, households, and children, including the potential for contamination. Section 4 is a discussion of results, Section 5 describes study limitations, and Section 6 provides a conclusion.

Agricultural value chain interventions with vulnerable populations

Few agricultural value chain programs with vulnerable populations have been rigorously evaluated for impact, and none of the evaluations have examined the effects on children. The challenges of evaluating these complex programs are well documented (Creevey, Dunn, & Farmer, 2011). Yet this type of intervention has become increasingly common in the past 10 years. This is likely because of its systemic approach for sustainable development, including positive results at the farm or enterprise level, with large outreach and positive spillover effects (Dunn, 2014). Therefore, it is critical for the development field to understand the impact of these interventions on multiple levels.

Krieger (2014a, 2014b, 2014c) has reported results from three impact evaluations, as part of the World Food Programme's Purchase for Progress (P4P) 20-country, five-year pilot initiative. P4P tested ways to link smallholder farmers to formal commodity markets, using a model that depended on the local context and enabling environment. In Ethiopia and Tanzania, P4P worked with farmer organizations, agricultural cooperatives, and savings and credit cooperatives. In Ethiopia, results included a significant increase in maize (staple) yield at the farmer level. In Tanzania, households that received the interventions were more likely to sell maize through savings and credit cooperatives and received a higher average price for maize. In El Salvador, P4P's model included working with farmer organizations to improve assistance packages, build extension services' capacity to deliver packages, and facilitate access to finance the purchase of packages. Krieger found statistically significant improvements in all of the maize production indicators measured, including likelihood to plant maize, average area under production, use of certified maize seed, yield, and quantity and quantity sold. Despite farm-level improvements in some cases, none of the three studies found statistically significant differences with regard to key household outcomes: income, assets, livestock, and food consumption.

Humphrey and Navas-Alema´n (2010) have examined reports on 30 value chain interventions, not all in agriculture, finding that the majority did not conduct impact evaluations to determine if the programs had any effect on poverty. Of those programs that engaged in agriculture linkage activities, only one (Bringing Knowledge to Vegetable Farmers in Rangpur, Bangladesh) included a quantitative impact evaluation, but no report has been found beyond an early assessment (Gibson, 2005).

A recent review of findings on the impact of agricultural value chains on vulnerable populations concludes that although there is some evidence to indicate that smallholders may experience an increase in enterprise profit, this may not translate into an increase in household income (Dunn, 2014). One possible reason for this is that household income is a more distal outcome (Dunn, 2014). Other known contributors include the lack of sensitivity in measurement tools (such that small changes in income are not statistically significant) and that with money being fungible, it is diffcult to accurately collect data across all potential household sources of income and expenditure.

A quasi-experimental impact assessment of three value chain interventions—horticulture, maize, and dairy—in Kenya found a positive impact on poverty reduction but no statistically significant impact on household income (Oehmke, Jayne, Aralas, & Mathenge, 2010). Creevey et al., (2011) found that two additional value chain program assessments with counterfactuals showed positive outcomes at the farm level with increased productivity or revenue from the sale of produce.

Child well-being and economic welfare

Research shows a strong correlation between household economic welfare and child well-being. Campbell et al., (2010) examined an array of socioeconomic outcomes including nutrition and education. After controlling for other possible intervening factors, they found that "household wealth is the single most important correlate of better outcomes." Low household economic status was a stronger predictor of negative outcomes than was orphan status, which is particularly relevant given the number of HIV/AIDS-related orphans. Akwara et al., (2010) found that both household economic status and parental education levels were the most consistent predictors of negative outcomes for children. They too found that household economic condition was a stronger predictor of negative outcomes for children than was orphan-hood.

The U.S. President's Emergency Plan for AIDS Relief's (PEPFAR's) Guidance for Orphans and Vulnerable Children Programming states that a positive foundation for children would increase the likelihood of interrupting "the transmission of poverty from one generation to the next" (Alderman, 2012; PEPFAR, 2012). The U.S. Government Action Plan on Children in Adversity (United States Government, 2012) is the first ever U.S. government system-wide strategy for international assistance for children. Driven by evidence illustrating that failing to address children's needs results in negative social and economic outcomes, the plan's primary goals are to build strong beginnings for children, protect them from violence and exploitation, and keep them in or return them to family care so they grow up in the best environment possible. The plan seeks to strengthen child welfare and protection systems, integrate the plan throughout U.S. government agencies, and promote evidence-based policies and programs. This chapter supports the latter and calls for more research to improve our understanding of what interventions work best for both households and the children living within them and how systemic programs like value chain interventions can be tailored to have greater impact for children, their families, and their communities.

Study region

The challenges left in the wake of the 15-year civil war in Liberia have profound implications for all aspects of recovery and reconstruction, and have created obstacles to the development of the country. Issues such as limited economic opportunities for youth and the presence of unemployed excombatants at ACE project inception in 2008 need to be addressed in order to promote an effective and sustainable reintegration and reconstruction process (United Nations, 2006). In 2013, Liberia was ranked 174 out of 185 countries on the Human Development Index scale, with 83.8% of the population below the US$1.25 per day poverty line and 63.8% below the national poverty line (UNDP, 2013).

Agriculture is the mainstay of the rural economy, and at the time of ACE project inception, agricultural activities employed close to 70% of Liberia's population (Liberia Institute of Statistics & Geo-Information Services LISGIS, 2009). This has changed little since project inception, as illustrated by the Comprehensive Food Security and Nutrition Survey (CFSNS), which states that 67% of the population relies on agriculture as their primary livelihood. Most people living in rural Liberia depend on a combination of "food and cash crop production, petty trading or street vending, hunting/gathering, casual labor, palm oil, charcoal production or rubber tapping" (World Food Programme, 2013). Households generally adopt livelihood strategies based on the natural resources available to them, and it is not uncommon to find several generations of farmers or rubber tappers. However, this cycle now appears to be shifting, with young people reluctant to become farmers, despite the opportunities in the sector and rising food prices (Education Development Center et al., 2012). Though possessing abundant arable land and opportunities in the agricultural sector, Liberia continues to import about half of its staple foods (World Food Programme, 2013).

Initial post-conflict donor programs focused on asset replacement to create a foundation for the transition to a more market-based agriculture system, which is essential to reduce Liberia's continuing dependence on food imports. Yet this transition has been hampered by years of relief handouts and direct subsidies of essential agricultural inputs. These have contributed to a culture of donor dependence and high expectations for food and farming inputs to be given at no cost. Recognizing this, ACE activities were designed to contribute to a new focus on self-reliance and a break with donor dependency—in particular, increased rural access to commercial inputs and services and to multiple market channels.

ACE project

ACE was one of four projects funded by the U.S. Agency for International Development's (USAID's) Displaced Children and Orphans Fund (DCOF) under the Supporting Transformation by Reducing Insecurity and Vulnerability with Economic Strengthening (STRIVE) program. STRIVE, implemented from 2007 to 2015, was designed to use market-led economic strengthening initiatives to benefit vulnerable children. STRIVE sought to examine the links between economic strengthening programs, household economic welfare, and child well-being. The key questions were whether and how economic strengthening programs affected households and children.

In Liberia, the ACE project, implemented by ACDI/VOCA with STRIVE funding, was founded on the premise that increased household economic security, resulting from increased farm production and linkages with buyers, would stimulate more consistent investments in child well-being via longer term social investments in education, health, and nutrition.

ACE adopted a dynamic, value-chain facilitation approach (Campbell, 2014), which was expected to lay the foundation for sustainable commercial activities by identifying agricultural upgrading opportunities and building relationships among value chain actors. Networks of economic actors rely on such relationships. However, the agriculture network was nearly non-existent in Liberia in 2008, in part because of a lack of trust between farmers and buyers and between farmers and input suppliers (ACDI/VOCA, 2014). ACE was designed to develop the network by stimulating the entrepreneurial skills and mindsets of farmers, and by building essential relationships in profitable value chains. ACE worked with Monrovia-based input suppliers and buyers to provide inputs, and to develop linkages and forward-buying contracts to farmer groups. However, the location of ACE farmers in rural communities was challenging for buyers and input providers. Some suppliers and buyers made in-roads, but the volume was not suffcient for them to remain operational in the rural areas. ACE instead shifted its approach and worked with existing local suppliers in towns with market centers, where farmers sell produce, and with buyers at those markets.

Interventions with smallholder farmers (typically with no more than two acres for crops) included Farming as a Business curriculum, introducing farming for profit, teaching farmers modern growing methods, and food and seed preservation, which together were expected to increase crop quality and yield. ACE helped farmers form groups or clusters of approximately 40 farmers with a self-elected cluster head. Cluster heads were lead farmers who acted as change agents, sharing information and establishing demonstration plots. Clusters were encouraged to aggregate crops for sale under the assumption that forward-buying contracts and better prices would be forthcoming, as well as for the bulk purchase of inputs. ACE field offcers held monthly meetings with each cluster. ACE introduced input suppliers and buyers to ACE farmers and trained farmers on input quality and use. The training applied to most crops, though ACE focused on common local vegetables (pepper and bitter ball) known to rural farmers in Bong and Nimba Counties after an early attempt to introduce high-value vegetables (tomatoes, lettuce) in demand in the capitol had failed. Many of the vegetable farmers in the sample also grew rice (staple crop) and later in the project obtained high-yield rice seed made available through a rice seed bank facilitated by ACE and a local partner.

The ACE causal model hypothesized that this combination of supply- and demand-side efforts would increase farm income, either through increased harvest size and crop sales, or through household consumption of more crops, thereby saving on food expenditure. The potential for savings is noteworthy given that food expenditure accounted for 66% of household expenditure in 2007 (Government of Liberia, 2007) and 60% in 2010 (Owadi, Kendle, & Koiwu, 2010).

The model further assumed that increased household economic security would stimulate more consistent investments in child well-being via longer term social investments in education, health, and nutrition. The evaluation therefore measured changes in children's school enrollment and attendance, incidence of common illnesses and their treatment, and food access and dietary diversity. The project began in September 2008. Following recommendations in an October 2009 assessment report expressing concern that ACE was not reaching suffcient numbers of farmer households, ACE revised its approach from a systemic, community-based model to direct strategic technical assistance to smallholder farmers, as described above. Field operations ended in December 2013.

Methods

The evaluation used a mixed-method, quasi-experimental design with a matched comparison group. Research methods and timing are presented in Table 14.1. In April 2011, the research team attempted to panel all of the households that had signed up to join the ACE project or that had been with the program for less than 1 year (293 households), in addition to similar comparison households in nearby towns with access to the same services: roads, health care, schools, and markets. Following implementation of this baseline survey, the sampling frame for all subsequent qualitative methods was the survey database of paneled households and their members.

Survey sampling and recruitment

According to lists provided by ACE at the time of the baseline survey in April 2011,[1] there were 293 farming households participating for less than 1 year in ACE or expected to soon be involved in the ACE project. Given the small number of participants, a census was conducted. Of the 293 households, 291 agreed to be interviewed at baseline, but a review of the data found duplicate households and false names (hoping to gain something from the interviewers), resulting in 274 paneled households.

To identify farming households that could serve as comparators, at the time of the baseline survey we identified non-project villages that lay within 10 km (typically less than 5 km) of project villages located along the same roadsdifferences in farm capacity due to rainfall, sun exposure, soil quality, and access to markets. An advance team from the firm engaged to implement the survey was dispatched to collect information about each candidate village, including information on available services, the number of vegetable farmers and common crops, and ongoing nongovernmental (NGO) or government activities. This process of identifying potential communities was the same process ACE used when selecting potential intervention sites: villages were eliminated if they had only a small number of vegetable farmers or high levels of NGO activity.

The advance team collected lists of vegetable farmers in each of the eligible villages. The study aimed to develop a pool of potential comparison households with similar attributes as the project households. The overall pool of comparison households that was selected was 1.5 times larger the group of treatment households.

The study used an untreated control group design with dependent pretest and posttest samples. Regression models were used to produce adjusted comparisons across treatment (ACE) and comparison (non-ACE) households for select outcome variables. For each outcome examined, our estimate of the causal effect of being assigned to the ACE intervention was based exclusively on the difference-in-difference estimator (i.e., the mean difference between treatment and comparison households in the outcome over the post-treatment period).

The difference-in-difference estimator adjusted for baseline non-equivalence across treatment and comparison households (i.e., selection bias) in all unobserved, time-stable confounders that had associations with the outcome that did not vary across treatment and post-treatment periods. Though not as

Table 14.1 Research methods and timing

Timing	Method	Sample size	Domains of inquiry & purpose
April 2010	Focus groups with ACE participants, randomly selected within farmer cluster. Key informant interviews with community leaders	24 focus groups in 8 ACE communities (217 participants) 8 key informant interviews with community leaders and school staff	Understand nutrition, social networks, and farming activities in project communities and households
April 2011	Baseline survey (panel): census of treatment households. Untreated farmer household comparison group	274 treatment households; 416 comparison households	Farming methods, production, inputs, sales outlets, income, poverty, shocks; household access to food, assets, house materials; child education (enrollment & attendance), child health (preventive care, incidence & treatment of common illnesses), and nutrition (dietary diversity & food security measures). Household member demographics; participation in programs
April 2011	Focus groups with ACE farmers, randomly selected within farmer cluster	6 FGs with 53 treatment farmers in 6 communities	Ascertain the linkages between treatment farmers and others in the value chain
October 2012	Focus groups with paneled treatment and comparison farmers; random within clusters. Stratified sample: (1) 14 towns with a minimum of 15 paneled study participants, (2) matched treatment and comparison pairs, and (3) FG participants randomly selected from study list	8 FGs with 109 treatment farmers 7 FGs with 97 comparison farmers	Assess the extent of treatment spillover; describe farmer networks and linkages; and determine how farmers understand linkages
2011– 13	Farmer financial diaries with random sample of ACE farmers	115 vegetable treatment farmers, with replacement by ACE over time	Farmer recorded production and sales (quantities and values) for common crops. Diaries were part of the ACE project monitoring system. ACE provided the data to the research team

(continued)

Table 14.1 Continued

Timing	Method	Sample size	Domains of inquiry & purpose
April 2013	Endline survey (panel)	252 treatment households; 378 comparison households	Same as baseline
April 2013	Key informant interviews with community leaders based on location of paneled households, 2–3 per town	67 interviews	Understand other factors that might affect impact measures including program activity in study areas, participant level in those programs, substance of the programs, and major changes in access to services: health, education, water and sanitation, and roads
June 2013	Community debriefs for *outreach* purposes; 2–3 members of each treatment and comparison community	Two county-level debrief sessions with 35 study participants in each	Study results discussed and evaluation design disclosed to comparison group, making efforts to link them with treatment farmers

rigorous as a randomized control trial, this analytical approach was feasible within the project's implementation strategy and provided credible evidence of the ACE project's impact.

The difference-in-difference estimates reported in this chapter are regression-based. In addition to the fixed effects needed to identify difference-in-difference estimates, the model included a few additional fixed effects:

(a) a set of dummy regressors that captured variation in the outcome across the seven geographic clusters, defined as a cluster of geographically proximate villages;

(b) a regressor representing the change (i.e., difference between baseline and endline) in the natural log of family size (i.e., number of household members). Models involving child-level outcomes also included regressors that indicated the child's sex and the natural log of a child's age in years;

(c) terms representing two-way interactions between each of these regressors and measurement occasion (baseline vs. endline).

Additional details regarding the model specification depended on the measurement scale of the outcome (e.g., count, binary indicator, continuous), and whether the outcome was measured at the household or household-by-child level. With respect to the measurement scale of the outcome, we estimated generalized linear models with appropriate link functions (e.g., logistic for binary data) and response distributions (e.g., Poisson for count data). The choice of link function and response distribution for each outcome variable is indicated in the tables containing the impact estimates. With respect to the different levels of analyses, the longitudinal sampling design was assumed to induce residual dependence between observations nested within the same household.

For outcome measures at both the household and household-by-child levels, we adopted a marginal approach to modeling this dependence and assumed a simple block-diagonal structure for variance/covariance residual matrices. For observations purely at the household level, the blocks represented individual households and the correlations represented the stability in the responses from a single household over the two measurement occasions. In the case of outcome variables at the child level, the blocks represented household-by-time observations and the correlations represented the correlation in the outcome among children sampled from the same household at the same measurement occasions. Observations from the same household but separated by time, on the other hand, were assumed to be independent.

This simplification of the residual dependence structure was necessary for two reasons. First, attempts to relax this restriction did not consistently converge across all outcomes—particularly when the outcome was categorical. Secondly, the data did not include child-level identifiers that would allow us to identify observations linked to the same child over the two measurement occasions. Nonetheless, we believe that our modeling approach accounted for the most important source of non-independence in the child-by-household level outcomes—the nesting of children within households. Finally, the estimation procedure depended on whether the outcome was categorical or continuous. We used generalized estimation equations (GEEs) for the categorical outcomes and maximum likelihood estimation (MLE) for continuous outcomes.

The survey instrument covered household member demographics, housing materials, household assets, poverty (measured with the Liberia Poverty Assessment Tool), and access to food (measured on a modified household food insecurity access scale) to measure household well-being as context and potential intermediaries between farm yield and income and child outcomes. The survey also captured agriculture shocks (i.e., drought, flood, crop disease/pests, crop price, family illness) and participation in any program (i.e., ACE and others). In addition, the survey collected data on farm size, farming methods, farm production by crop type, inputs (i.e., tools, fertilizer, seeds, and labor), sales outlets, and sales. For children, the survey collected data on school enrollment and attendance for all school-age children, because they are the most likely areas to be affected by economic well-being. Also likely to be affected are access to and use of medicines and medical treatment. With regard to child health, data were collected on vaccinations, common supplements, and medicine for common illnesses (e.g., oral rehydration salts). Incidence and treatment of common illnesses such as diarrhea, fever, and cough were measured. With regard to child nutrition, data were collected for up to three children in each household: a child between 0 and 5 months, the youngest child between 6 and 23 months, and the youngest child between 2 and 18 years. Data included dietary diversity based on the Food and Nutrition Technical Assistance (FANTA) Individual Dietary Diversity Score and adapted by the Food and Agricultural Organization of the United Nations (FAO) (FAO, 2008), and access to food measured by the number of missed meals.

Financial diaries

In addition to the survey, the study team used data from farmer financial diaries collected by ACE as part of their project monitoring during 2011–13. The study team conducted the sampling of ACE farmers, 115 of whom were asked to complete the diary. Some farmers dropped out (mostly due to relocation) and had to be replaced by ACE, and ACE also lost some data, resulting in some missing quarterly data. ACE collected the data quarterly by capturing on a computer what farmers recorded in their chapter diaries. Farmers were challenged by poor literacy and numeracy skills, which ACE attempted to mitigate by providing some training to farmers' middle-school-aged children and by encouraging farmer cluster heads to review diaries with individual farmers at monthly meetings. The diaries captured data about input costs, harvest amounts, and sales to create a farm balance sheet for select crops supported by ACE (bitter ball and pepper).

ACE then provided the data to the study team, who used it in two ways. First, a basic analysis was done to determine if we agreed with the ACE project's conclusion that ACE farmers, based on the diary, experienced increases in production, sales, and farm income. The second was to match farmers in the diary database with farmers in the survey database to determine if the reported data were similar.

Qualitative methods

As described above, prior to the baseline survey, an initial round (April 2010) of focus group discussions (FGDs) were conducted with ACE farmers and community members in eight communities. FGDs were conducted as follows: six with ACE farmers about linkages between farmers and input providers and buyers, six about farmers' perception of the effects of the project, and 12 with community members about their social networks (six with men, six with women). In addition, eight key informant interviews were conducted with community leaders and school staff. When combined with project monitoring data, this information helped us to eliminate early adopters of ACE from the survey sample frame to accommodate the late-starting baseline. The findings also contributed to the questionnaire design, as they provided a detailed portrait of farmers' socio-economic context.

FGDs conducted at the same time as the baseline survey (April–May 2011) provided information about the linkages between treatment farmers and others in the value chain, including input providers and buyers. FGDs were conducted by members of the survey team, hired and managed by a local research firm. They were conducted in towns that had a large enough cluster of farmers to create a focus group. Participants were invited randomly from a list of treatment farmers provided by ACE by location. The list included early adopters of ACE, as well as those included in the survey sample frame. The ACE lead farmer was approached first, and he invited those requested by the survey team. FGDs with approximately nine participants each were conducted in English and local dialects as needed based on the needs and preferences of participants. In Bong and Nimba Counties, English is commonly spoken, and there are two tribes, whose members speak different dialects. No recordings were made. A summary report of each FGD was written by the FGD facilitators. The research team conducted a thematic analysis.

The baseline quantitative findings gave rise to 2012 qualitative field work, as ACE expressed concern about potential spillover of the treatment into comparison groups due to their close proximity. In addition, there was some concern about the timing of the baseline compared with treatment timing, as some of the research participants had participated in ACE activities in mid-to-late 2010 and others had not begun until 2011. FGDs with both treatment and comparison communities were therefore designed to examine these issues, as well as farmer networks and farmers' perceptions of linkages with others in the value chain and their relative importance.

The 2012 FGDs were conducted with farmers (approximately 13 per FGD) in both treatment and comparison communities by two Liberian facilitators trained by the research team, with two members of the team as recorders, in English and dialects as needed. As with the previous FGDs, participants were based on random selection within paneled treatment and comparison groups. Invitations were made in person by the ACE lead farmer or someone of his choosing in treatment groups, and by the village head or proxy in comparison groups. Recordings were made, but the quality was poor given that most groups were held outside and participants tended to sit in long rows. Each FGD was written up the day it was conducted with discussion among the team. Thematic analysis was done later by the research team with input from the Liberian facilitators.

In order to understand the potential effects of other programs on this evaluation's impact measures, key informant interviews were conducted in each village concurrent with the endline survey in April 2013. These included interviews with village chiefs, school principals, development chairmen, and other community leaders to discuss changes in their villages during the preceding 2 years. Topics included road improvements, any changes that would affect access to health care and education, and how non-ACE programs may have affected study participants. Interviews were conducted by a local survey firm, which provided written summaries of the interviews. The research team analyzed these in stages: thematic analysis, coding, review of data by treatment/ comparison location, re-coding based on those results, and a weighted analysis (described below) of agriculture programs to determine the level of exposure to agriculture assistance in treatment versus comparison communities.

Information about each program mentioned in interviews was gathered based on the research team's existing awareness of the programs, Internet searches, and communication with the programs or field advisors. With this information, each program was weighted based on its level of agriculture programing: 1 if the agriculture content was high (i.e., agriculture was a key component of the program), 0.5 if it was modest, and 0 if there was no agriculture component. No other components of the programs—such as education, health, water and sanitation, and food—were weighted.

Two community debriefs were conducted (one in each study county) by ACE project staff, one of the lead researchers, and two members from the local survey firm. One to three members of each community attended, so that they could share the information with others in their communities. Each debrief consisted of approximately 35 study participants. Debriefs served multiple purposes: (1) to describe findings to research participants, (2) to get their input on how results were or should be interpreted, (3) to disclose the evaluation design to the comparison group, and (4) to create linkages between members of treatment and comparison groups for the purpose of knowledge sharing.

Results

We present both quantitative and qualitative findings at each level of analysis: farm, household, and child. Qualitative findings are interwoven to correspond with each quantitative indicator. A total of 78 households from the baseline sample were unable to be interviewed at endline, representing an attrition rate of 9%. The most common reason for attrition was relocation.

Smallholder farmers

ACE sought to improve farmers' use and management of inputs such as seeds, fertilizers, and pesticides and improve links to input providers. The project also sought to help farmers use modern farming methods to increase yield and quality, to improve crop and seed preservation, to see farming as a business, to aggregate crops for sale, and to expand their access to buyers.

Though most households reported owning a plot at baseline (89%, data not shown), all did so at endline. The average self-reported agricultural land was about two acres, with farmers reporting planting between one and 50 acres. ACE staff commented that many farmers did not know the size of their plots and the data reflected that most farmers (82–91% across the two time periods) reported less than five acres in production.

Ownership of agricultural tools was common among households. Over time, ownership of key tools increased across all groups. One unexpected result concerned watering cans. Though many more treatment households than comparison households had a watering can at baseline, the proportion that had a watering can decreased among treatment households and increased among comparison households over time. ACE facilitated five farmer groups that, with cash and support from ACE to link with a micro-finance institution, organized to buy gasoline-powered water pumps. Other farmers could rent the pump to water their crops. The decreased availability of watering cans among treatment households may have been due in part to the increased availability of water pumps for irrigation.

Treatment farmers used about one more modern farming technique than comparison farmers. The survey asked households about their use of 10 modern farming techniques from which we created an index that ranged from 0 (used none of the techniques) to 10 (used all of the techniques). The index included: (1) composting fertilizer, (2) planting according to calendar, (3) harvesting according to calendar, (4) planning plot layout, (5) planting in rows or lines, (6) irrigation or watering, (7) drying crops for preservation, (8) keeping records of farming costs and production, (9) measuring when mixing fertilizer or other chemicals, and (10) timely weeding.

Treatment and comparison farmers both experienced an increase in the number of modern techniques used, but the increase among treatment households was significantly greater ($p < .10$) than that among the comparison households (Tables 14.2a and 14.2b). This finding was supported by the results of the 2012 FGDs. For example, out of 15 FGDs, planting in line was mentioned by seven treatment and three comparison groups, planting according to a calendar was raised as important in six treatment groups and only two comparison groups, and record keeping was discussed in six treatment groups and none of the comparison groups. By contrast, in one comparison group, nearly everyone agreed they *"use more labor"* to increase yield, and they would use fertilizer but *"we have no money to buy it so what can we do with that? So we need labor."*

As noted, another key input for farming is labor, which consists of family labor, cooperative labor groups locally called "koos," and other hired labor, sometimes children. Though not statistically significant, the proportion of households that hired labor stayed relatively stable over time for treatment households, but declined slightly for comparison households.

Rice was the most commonly grown crop, with bitter ball, hot pepper, and cassava the next most common crops. Rice was rarely sold by farmers in Liberia as it is the staple food, whereas the other three common crops were frequently sold. Sales of common crops increased more for treatment groups than comparison groups based on survey data. The medians for treatment and comparison groups differed by US$40 at baseline and by US$108 at endline. Due to data-quality challenges at baseline in the section of the survey on farm production, and on high standard deviation for crop sales in particular (results available upon request), we examined the trends for treatment farmer yield and sales using the survey data and ACE's farmer diary data. Though we were able to match households in the survey and diary samples, the data were not

Table 14.2a Farming methods—adjusted† percentages and means

	Intervention				Comparison			
	Baseline		Endline		Baseline		Endline	
Household owns watering can (n/%)	262	40%	252	33%	381	13%	378	19%
Farming techniques index (proportion of techniques out of 10)	255	0.25	225	0.44	367	0.23	315	0.37
Household used hired labor (n/%)	273	66%	223	67%	412	64%	313	57%

†Controlling for geographic cluster and family size.

Table 14.2b Farming methods—treatment effects and model specification

	Adjusted† impact estimate Estimate (95% CI)	Model specification		
		Link function (treatment effect)	Distribution of response	Block-diagonal dependence structure
Household owns watering can (n/%)	0.477 (0.271–0.838)**	Logistic (odds ratio)	Binary	Compound symmetric
Farming techniques index (proportion of techniques out of 10)	1.169 (0.98–1.394)*	Logistic (odds ratio)	Binomial	Compound symmetric
Household used hired labor (n/%)	1.365 (0.796–2.341)	Logistic (odds ratio)	Binary	Compound symmetric

†Controlling for geographic cluster and family size.
**p < .05.
*p < .10.

correlated, meaning that farmers reported different numbers in the survey than they did in the more frequently captured information in the diaries. We concluded that the diary data were more dependable, though available only for treatment farmers since the diaries were an ACE monitoring tool. Farmer diary data showed increasing vegetable yield (average 314 kg/ farmer at first diary entry to 458 kg at last diary entry) and farm income from sale of common vegetables between last diary entry and a pre-treatment last crop season diary entry (Wilcoxon Rank Sum $p < 0.001$). Without comparison data, the quantitative data were inconclusive with regard to impact on farm yield and sales. From the 2012 FGDs, however, half the treatment groups reported increases in farm yield and income, and no comparison groups reported change.

The outlets for selling crops resulted in increases in sales to relatives and NGOs and decreased sales to market ladies— known locally as Gobachop, who are also members of the Liberian Market Association (LMA)—and friends and neighbors. The expectation was that treatment farmers would have both more and "better" linkages (e.g., buyers from Monrovia, where prices for produce are higher). FGD findings from 2012 found that treatment farmers had stronger linkages with buyers in the capital (the major outlet) than did comparison farmers. For participants in four of six treatment FGDs (compared with two of seven comparison FGDs), Gobachop and the LMA—both Monrovia-based outlets—formed the key outlet; for one group, the key outlet was a local buying agent, which was also the most important outlet for three of seven comparison groups.

Moreover, based on the 2012 FGDs, treatment farmers had more outlets for their crops. They also cited the benefit of what they call "bucket sales"—aggregating produce among farmers, as described by a treatment group: *"We put all the goods together, bring to the chairman, the goods are plenty... Makes business, brings money. We bring goods, record your name with the number of bags. Chairman calls LMA, and you get money for the number of bags you brought."* By aggregating produce, they reportedly arranged more lucrative sales agreements with buyers. No comparison groups reported produce aggregation and sales or cooperation beyond the typical labor groups.

Farmers referred to the dangers of being cheated by buyers throughout the project: two of six FGDs in 2010, one of six FGDs in 2011, and six of 15 FGDs in 2012. As described by one 2012 participant: *"Marketers [buyers] are trying to cheat us. If you know the expenditures from your farm, they know we are someone who knows something now."* Farmers also described unbalanced power relationships with buyers in each round of FGDs: four of six in 2010, one of six in 2011, and six of 15 in 2012. From one comparison FGD in 2012, farmers agreed that *"buyers make the price. You are forced to give in; you have to agree to it."* Other examples of the disadvantage to farmers were descriptions of how farmers must sell to whoever is present to buy, regardless of price, or the produce will spoil. There are no options to maintain fresh produce in the study areas.

A new, additional description of the relationship with buyers was observed in 2012 FGDs, whereby farmers described the need to have a good, long-term relationship with a buyer. This was stronger for treatment groups (six of eight FGDs) than comparison groups (three of seven FGDs). As some treatment group farmers described the relationship: *"We market before we produce. Now we know the time when a particular good is scarce and will make money."* Comparison group farmers referred more frequently to the buyer knowing their condition, being able to reach the buyer if local, and being extended credit. For example, in one comparison group, a farmer said, *" [It's] best to sell to local buyers because [you] can reach them anytime, [they] live in the area, and give credit. Sometimes Monrovia buyer will not buy or give us credit."*

In summary, in FGDs, treatment farmers reported using modern farming techniques, which led to increased yield and consistency/quality of crops. They reported more and better links to buyers and more farm income from vegetable crop sales. Relationships with buyers improved over time for the treatment group, but remained challenging.

Households

The following provides a descriptive summary of the demographic and socioeconomic characteristics of surveyed households. In order to assess the representativeness of the sample, we compared our results against nationally representative demographic and health data. Data were gathered for 5,254 individuals at baseline and 5,307 at endline with the population equally divided among men and women.

Almost half (50% at baseline and 47% at endline) of all household members were under 15 years of age. The 2011 Liberia Malaria Indicator Survey (LMIS) found a similar rate, with 49.8% of the rural population below 15 years of age (National Malaria Control Program (NMCP) [Liberia] et al., 2012). The average dependency ratios for our sample (104.6 and 101.6 at baseline and endline, respectively) were smaller than the rural average of 115.1 found in the LMIS (NMCP et al., 2012), but higher than the national average of 86. In Liberia and other countries where the majority of households depend on agriculture to make a living, the dependency ratio is typically above 100.

Table 14.3 shows the characteristics of households and household heads at baseline. The average household size in our baseline sample was 6.3 persons.[2] Seventy-six percent were male-headed households, a common characteristic of Liberian households (National Malaria Control Program (NMCP) [Liberia] et al., 2012). These results were slightly larger than the average household size of 5.7 persons and average maleheadship of 73.4% for rural households found in the 2009 LMIS (National Malaria Control Program (NMCP) [Liberia] et al., 2009). The majority (78%) of household heads were 25–54 years old with a mean age of 43. About 83% of household heads were married or in a common law union at baseline.

Though about half (56%) of male heads of household had completed primary school, most female heads of household (61.4% for treatment and 58.1% for comparison) had had no schooling. This strong disparity in educational attainment between men and women was also reflected in the preliminary results of the 2013 Liberia Demographic and Health Survey, which showed that approximately one of three women have no education, a little more than one of three women (35.7%) have a secondary or better education, and more than half of men (57.9%) have a secondary or better education (Liberia Institute of Statistics and Geo-Information Services LISGIS et al., 2014).

In terms of poverty, most households (85.4% at baseline) were below the international poverty line (US$1.25 per day or 57.57 Liberian dollars in 2008 prices), and 80.6% were below the national poverty line. The value of the national poverty line is 68.66 Liberian dollars per adult equivalent [3] per day. The Liberia USAID Poverty Assessment Tool (PAT) was applied to measure the share of households who were very poor. The PAT is a short, country-specific survey that gathers household data on indicators that have been identified as the best predictors of whether a given set of households is very poor.

From the survey data, we examined changes over time between treatment and comparison groups with regard to household ownership of productive and non-productive assets. Results are shown in Tables 14.4a and 14.4b. Household assets served as a proxy for economic well-being beyond the farm, and are a more sensitive measure than household poverty. Household food insecurity, measured using a modified Household Food Insecurity Access Scale

Table 14.3 Household and household head characteristics at baseline

	Treatment n = 274	Comparison n = 416	Total n = 690
Household characteristics			
Mean household size (sd)	6.3 (3.0)	6.3 (2.7)	6.3 (2.8)
Male-headed households (%)	83.6	76.7	79.4
Below international poverty line (%)	82.1	87.0	85.0
Below national poverty line (%)	76.3	81.2	79.2
House walls are mud & sticks (%)	57.9	60.9	59.7
House roof is corrugated iron (%)	87.2	91	89.5
Earth flooring material (%)	60.1	62.9	61.8
Toilet facility is bush or none (%)	65.6	60.9	62.8
Household head characteristics Mean age (sd)	42 (13.2)	43 (12.8)	43 (13.5)
Household head has no schooling (%)	28.6	36.6	32.8
Household head completed primary school (%)	56.3	48.4	51.6
Agriculture as main occupation (%)	97.8	97.1	97.4

Values are given as percentages or mean (SD) unless otherwise specified. Nonresponses vary across items.

Table 14.4a Assets and food insecurity—adjusted[†] means

	Treatment		Comparison	
	Baseline N = 273	*Endline N = 252*	*Baseline N = 409*	*Endline N = 378*
Productive assets index	1.4	1.7	1.4	1.6
Non-productive assets index	2.1	2.4	2.2	2.5
Food insecurity index	0.56	0.45	0.51*	0.50

†Controlling for geographic cluster and family size.
*Based on 412 households; different *N* is due to missing values.

Table 14.4b Assets and food insecurity—treatment effects and model specification

	Adjusted[†] impact estimate Estimate (95% CI)	Model specification		
		Link function	*Distribution of response*	*Block-diagonal dependence structure*
Productive assets index	1.094 (0.941–1.272)	Natural log (count ratio)	Poisson	Compound symmetric
Non-productive assets index	1.012 (0.845–1.213)	Natural log (count ratio)	Poisson	Compound symmetric
Food insecurity index	−0.104 (−0.193 to −0.016)**	Identity (mean difference)	Gaussian	Unstructured

**p < .05; *p < .10.
†Controlling for geographic cluster and family size.

(HFIAS; Coates, Swindale, & Bilinsky, 2007), served as an intermediary outcome between improved farm yield/income and child nutrition.

Ownership of productive assets (e.g., mobile phones, radios, motorcycles) and non-productive assets (e.g., mattresses, beds, coal irons, coal pots, cassette players) increased over time for both treatment and comparison households with no significant differences observed between the groups.

Food security is a complex issue and challenging to quantify. The World Health Organization (WHO) describes three pillars of food security (World Health Organization, 2015): food availability, access to food, and food use, to which the FAO adds stability of food availability, access, and use over time (FAO, 2008). Quantitatively, we looked most closely at household food access and availability, herein described as self-reported food insecurity using the heretofore mentioned modified HFIAS. We created an index by asking how often in the last 4 weeks households experienced the following:

1. Worry that you or your household would not have enough food?
2. Was there ever no food to eat of any kind in your household because of lack of resources to get food?
3. Did you or any household member go to sleep at night hungry because there was not enough food?
4. Did you or any household member go a whole day and night without eating anything because there was not enough food?

The index ranges from 0 to 2, with larger numbers indicating greater food insecurity. Food insecurity decreased over time for treatment households, but remained relatively stable among comparison households—a difference that was statistically significant (Tables 14.4a and 14.4b). This was supported by the qualitative findings, ACE staff reports, and monitoring of rice harvests over time. The importance of rice as a staple crop, as perceived by household decision makers, was clearly shown by the qualitative research. Participants may have stated that they had not eaten, even after consuming full meals that lacked rice. Conversely, caregivers may have reported having eaten a full meal, while consuming rice only. Though rice fills the belly, it is insuffcient for good nutrition and therefore overall health.

In all FGDs from 2010 through 2012, farmers clearly stated that the purpose of farms was to sustain their families. Food was grown to *"eat some, and sell some,"* a phrase repeatedly made by farmers. Among two of the seven comparison FGDs in 2012, most of the participants said they did not have enough to sell. Another comparison group agreed that "[we] *keep most of the rice; sell sometimes because of hard times"* (e.g., to take care of an emergency). These were considered the most vulnerable households, because selling a little produce is a means to obtain cash to purchase things for which barter is not feasible, like medicine, health care, and school fees.

Though 2012 comparison groups were likely to discuss rice, treatment groups were less likely to do so. Treatment groups discussed savings (four treatment versus one comparison group) and income (six treatment versus three comparison groups) far more and in positive ways than did comparison groups. These FGDs indicated that though comparison group households were stagnant with regard to farm outcomes and largely with regard to their standard of living and child wellbeing, treatment households were better off than they used to be. The treatment groups referred to buying land on which to build a house in town, improving their existing house structures, and sending children to school regularly because they could afford fees and children's shoes. Overall, we concluded from the 2012 FGDs that treatment farmers were more able to provide for their families in terms of food, housing, and sustainability, as exemplified by this statement from a treatment group participant: *"Through my garden [proceeds], I send children to school and bought zinc to build a house. At first I didn't have a plan, now I have a plan."*

Children

There were 2,879 children aged 18 or younger living in the households sampled at the time of the baseline survey and 2,899 at the time of the endline survey. We did not find any statistically significant differences between children from treatment and comparison households over time on any of the quantitatively measured outcomes. Many of the outcomes, however, were trending in the expected direction (i.e., the treatment group having better outcomes over time) (Tables 14.5a and 14.5b). For example, chronic food insecurity, which is seasonal and predictable, remained a challenge, especially with regard to economic and physical access to food. The proportion of children who missed one or more meals in the last 7 days decreased over time for all groups. The trend was stronger for children in treatment households than for those in comparison households. Conversely, the children in both groups were found to be eating a less diverse diet over time. In June 2013 debriefs, treatment and comparison farmers indicated that their ability to trap and hunt bush meat had become increasingly diffcult. The dietary diversity breakdown showed a decrease in meat protein, as well as a decrease in fruits and vegetables; the latter was largely explained by a later harvest at endline of vitamin-A rich fruits.

Health outcomes for children 0–18 years living in treatment and comparison households. In terms of health outcomes for children up to 18 years old, none of the changes were statistically different between the treatment and comparison groups over time. However, some interesting trends were observed (Tables 14.6a and 14.6b). In both treatment and comparison groups, the proportion of days children lost to fever or cough in the 2 weeks prior to the survey decreased over time, as did the proportion of children with fever who received treatment outside the home. The proportion of days children lost to diarrhea in the past 2 weeks also decreased in both groups.

The three educational outcomes examined were enrollment, attendance, and expenditures—all three of which improved for all children. Though none of the changes in individual outcomes were statistically significant between children of treatment and comparison households, all of the outcomes trended

Table 14.5a Child nutrition—adjusted[†] percentages and means

	Treatment				Comparison		
	Baseline		Endline		Baseline		Endline
Percent who missed one or more meals in the last 7 days (n/%)	230	31.9	234	13.3	367	32.1	349	16.4
Individual dietary diversity score (IDDS) (n/adjusted mean)	235	3.83	236	3.47	365	3.78	351	3.40

[†]Controlling for geographic cluster and family size.

Table 14.5b Child nutrition—treatment effects and model specification

	Adjusted[†] impact estimate Estimate (95% CI)	Link function	Model specification		
			Distribution of response	Block-diagonal dependence structure	
Percent who missed one or more meals in the last 7 days (n/%)	0.787 (0.403–1.54)	Logistic (odds ratio)	Binary	Compound symmetric	
Individual dietary diversity score (IDDS) (n/adjusted mean)	0.026 (−0.231 to 0.283)	Identity (mean difference)	Gaussian	Unstructured	

**$p < .05$; *$p < .10$.
[†]Controlling for geographic cluster and family size.

Table 14.6a Child health—adjusted† percentages

	Treatment		Comparison	
	Baseline	Endline	Baseline	Endline
Percent of days of activity lost to fever or cough in past 2 weeks for those sick (n/%)	347 22.3	299 20.8	526 22.8	498 20.0
Percent treated outside the home for fever (n/%)	347 91.9	299 86.3	526 85.9	499 85.3
Percent of days of activity lost to diarrhea in past 2 weeks for those sick (n/%)	206 20.4	180 17.5	294 20.5	277 18.7
Percent given ORS for diarrhea (n/%)	206 60.0	180 63.2	294 58.3	276 53.0
Percent treated outside home for diarrhea (n/%)	206 87.2	180 83.7	294 77.8	276 77.8

†Controlling for geographic cluster and family size.

Table 14.6b Child nutrition—treatment effects and model specification

	Adjusted† impact estimate Estimate (95% CI)	Model specification		
		Link function	Distribution of response	Block-diagonal dependence structure
Percent of days of activity lost to fever or cough in past 2 weeks for those sick (n/%)	1.080 (0.838–1.393)	Logistic (odds ratio)	Binary	Compound symmetric
Percent treated outside the home for fever (n/%)	0.585 (0.238–1.436)	Logistic (odds ratio)	Binary	Compound symmetric
Percent of days of activity lost to diarrhea in past 2 weeks for those sick (n/%)	0.925 (0.663–1.29)	Logistic (odds ratio)	Binary	Compound symmetric
Percent given ORS for diarrhea (n/%)	1.420 (0.698–2.889)	Logistic (odds ratio)	Binary	Compound symmetric
Percent treated outside home for diarrhea (n/%)	0.759 (0.283–2.035)	Logistic (odds ratio)	Binary	Compound symmetric

$**p < .05$; $*p < .10$.
†Controlling for geographic cluster and family size.

in a positive direction for the children of treatment farmers (Tables 14.7a and 14.7b).

Farmers and other members of their communities listed children as the number one priority for expenditures in FGDs conducted in 2010. As described by one participant of a treatment FGD in 2010, *"The rationale is that your goods are sold, you have more money and this money will be used to send your children to school and take care of other expenses."* The same was seen in 2011 when participants in three of five FGDs mentioned children's school fees first and two other groups mentioned "family and children" and households and children. So it was not surprising when in 2012, 13 of 15 FGDs participants mentioned school fees or furthering education as the primary benefit of the harvest.

Potential for contamination

A common issue in impact evaluation is the potential to under- or overestimate impact. Potential sources of misestimation include spillover between treatment and comparison groups and contamination, often resulting from other programs attempting to affect the same or similar outcomes as the assessed program. We used the 2012 FGDs with treatment and comparison groups to address spillover and the 2013 key information interviews with community leaders to address contamination from other programs.

In FGDs in 2012, participants discussed the people with whom farmers communicate about their farming practices. Farmers' answers ranged from buyers and input suppliers to friends, family, and neighbors. More treatment farmers (in five of eight groups) than comparison farmers (in one of seven groups) mentioned that they share farm-specific information with buyers, input suppliers, or agents representing them. Information shared tended to be limited to pricing and making arrangements to buy inputs on credit, not farming techniques.

The other potential source of spillover was sharing information with friends, family, and neighbors. Participants in five of eight treatment FGDs specifically mentioned sharing information about their farming practices with others, either within or outside of their community. This ranged from teaching family members in other communities to giving advice to friends whose crops were not as plentiful. Participants in two of seven comparison FGDs said that they share information about farming practices specifically.

Farmers were asked to provide locations of those with whom they share information about farming. Each group developed a list of towns, which were reviewed against the locations of treatment and comparison study participants. Five comparison groups were on the list of places where information is shared by treatment farmers. A review of the FGD reports found that one such comparison group mentioned that ideas are shared with them, but they have no tools to carry out what they hear. Another comparison group had a farmer who attended an FAO training where he learned new farming practices, but noted that no one has addressed the community as a group (and thus the practices

Table 14.7a Educational outcomes—adjusted† percentages and means

| | Treatment | | Comparison | |
	Baseline	Endline	Baseline	Endline
Percent currently enrolled in school (n/%)	899 40.3	939 47.1	1476 43.7	1475 45.8
Percent of days attended school last month (n/%)	595 53.5	655 59.1	1017 55.5	1017 57.5
Total Liberian dollars spent on education in last year (natural log)	578 48.86	661 79.59	995 53.13	1026 70.64

†Controlling for geographic cluster, family size, child age and sex.

Table 14.7b Educational outcomes—treatment effects and model specification

	Adjusted† impact estimate Estimate (95% CI)	Link function	Model specification Distribution of response	Block-diagonal dependence structure
Percent currently enrolled in school (n/%)	1.212 (0.805–1.825)	Logistic (odds ratio)	Binary	Compound symmetric
Percent of days attended school last month (n/%)	1.159 (0.78–1.723)	Logistic (odds ratio)	Binary	Compound symmetric
Total Liberian dollars spent on education in last year (natural log)	1.225 (0.679–2.211)	Identity (mean difference)	Gaussian	Unstructured

$**p < .05$; $*p < .10$.
†Controlling for geographic cluster and family size.

have not been taken up). A third comparison group talked about wanting to get inputs, but if they were given to them, they said there would be no knowledge of how to use them, as described by a comparison farmer who said, *"If NGOs give you something, you don't know how to use it, so you're just getting information."*

In a community with both treatment and comparison farmers, members of the comparison group mentioned some "modern" farming techniques such as weeding, spacing plants, and identifying insects. However, they also reported practicing traditional techniques, including burning to clear their land, and not making seeds or drying vegetables. The data indicated that though there was information sharing, most of the information was not acted upon. Farmers preferred seeing a new technique successfully used by someone else before they risked adopting it themselves.

We examined contamination resulting from other programs with data from key information interviews with community leaders undertaken at the time of the endline survey. Leaders were asked about their awareness of programs in their communities in the past 2 years. Sometimes programs were named and other times described. We researched all programs to determine the level of agricultural activities and assigned weights to them as described in the methods section. The results showed that comparison communities had more exposure (9.5 score) to agricultural activities than treatment communities (8 score) during the assessment period.

With regard to other programs that may have affected the evaluation's findings, five comparison communities and no treatment communities reported exposure to health programs. Similarly, food programs were reportedly available in three comparison communities and no treatment communities. Therefore, health and nutrition outcomes for children in the treatment groups may have been underestimated. Treatment and comparison communities were similar in their exposure to education programs (two and three communities, respectively) and with regard to a Food for Peace program addressing food security, nutrition, and child health (eight and seven communities, respectively). Finally, with regard to water and sanitation programs, more treatment communities (five) than comparison communities (two) were exposed, which could mean that certain child-level health outcomes could have been overestimated.

Discussion

Lessons arising from this research relate to (1) the ability to change children's lives with economic strengthening programs, (2) the project implementation approach, and (3) evaluation design choices. As predicted by the ACE project causal model, the ACE project approach met the needs of farmers through training, mentoring, and linking them with input suppliers and buyers, thereby resulting in improved farming methods, farm yield, and income as illustrated by the combination of results from surveys and FGDs (with comparison groups) and farmer diaries (monitoring data).

The evaluation illustrates how the link between economic welfare and child well-being is not as straightforward as described in the ACE causal model. This is evident in the observed uptake of modern farming techniques by treatment farmers and their effects on farm production, which led to increases in households' access to food but no significant changes for children, despite a quantitative trend toward improvements in children's education and health.

It is possible that children's nutrition would have been improved if the project had monitored child nutrition throughout the project, and addressed child nutrition as an issue as opportunities arose (e.g., in community meetings). Had ACE systematically monitored the desired child outcomes, it would have known that children continued to eat mostly rice-laden meals with palm oil. Had ACE's approach been community-based, ACE might also have been aware of the challenges farmers faced in obtaining meat. Interestingly, ACE initially proposed to test whether economic strengthening alone was suffcient to improve child well-being by engaging half of participant communities in a public information campaign to sensitize them to children's issues, and the other half of communities in agricultural interventions only. Following project start-up, ACE proposed several modifications, including taking the vegetable value chain approach with intensive engagement through local schools. (Their initial approach had used school gardens as demonstration plots to promote agricultural technical assistance and training, and a hands-on approach to nutritional education for children and community members.)

The school-based approach proved to be resource intense, as is the case with community (or systems) approaches. What is commonly referred to as participant uptake was perceived to be slow. Field visits by the funder in 2009 resulted in recommendations to de-emphasize the school-based activities to increase the resources expended on the economic drivers of change—farming as a business and the vegetable value chain. An additional recommendation in 2010 included accelerating rice activities to improve food security, and simultaneously reducing household expenditures on rice. Following these recommendations, ACE approached smallholder farmers directly. Given that child outcomes were not seen to significantly improve, a systems approach may be more successful at changing children's lives if given a longer time frame than was initially provided to ACE. In addition, the systems approach might also have increased ACE's outreach over time, as interest in ACE's work and perceived effects might have led to positive spillover among other communities and community members. It is unknown if ACE's initial approach would have eventually reached as many farmer households as the modified project reached, so the resource intensity observed in 2008–09 might have eventually abated, resulting in no more expense than what was incurred.

In terms of the project approach, based on the guidance given to ACE to inform the intervention activities in 2010 and thereafter, and on the findings from across all of the information sources, ACE's consumer-oriented (see Goletti, 2005) or market linkage approach (Humphrey & Navas-Alemán, 2010), was appropriate and necessary in this context. In post-conflict Liberia, the value chain network was too weak, lacking a variety of input providers, buyers, and other business service providers, and lacking trust between actors (ACDI/ VOCA, 2014). A lack of trust among value chain actors may be a key constraint in market system development (Campbell, 2013). ACE illustrates the importance of developing network linkages, which are known to increase effciency and social capital (Creevey et al., 2011). "The literature to date indicates that small, low-risk investments to increase quality and yields are the most effective path for generating behaviors that promote value chain competitiveness among the poor" (Campbell, 2013, p. 12).

Some additional lessons around project monitoring for economic strengthening programs are also worth examining. One lesson learned is the essential need for all economic programs to monitor improvements in key program-defined outcomes among children and to make sure the interventions do no harm. In the case of ACE, child labor comes to mind. Though not closely examined in this evaluation, economic strengthening programs have had mixed results on child labor, and some have been linked to increased child labor (CPC Livelihoods & Economic Strengthening Task Force, 2011). This is especially important in agricultural contexts as described by Bandara, Dehejia, and Lavie-Rouse (2014), who found that agricultural shocks had a negative effect on child labor, especially for boys, in Tanzania. As with the lesson about child nutrition, it behooves practitioners to be aware of both the potential benefits and the potential risks to children and to monitor them. In terms of access to food and nutrition, additional public messaging around the nutritional needs of children and the links among education, health, and child nutrition might change food choices. This recommendation is similar to that found in another recent economic strengthening program that improved household economic welfare and reduced household food insecurity, but did not improve child nutrition (Brunie, Fumagalli, Martin, Field, & Rutherford, 2014). This also lends weight to the need to understand decision making within the household, especially since evidence suggests that agriculture value chains have the potential to positively affect nutrition (Hawkes & Ruel, 2011). More research is needed to understand what complementary interventions are needed to improve child nutrition.

Lessons learned on evaluation design are addressed below under study limitations.

Study Limitations

The mixed-methods evaluation yielded an immense body of results and cross-validated findings from which to draw conclusions. At the same time, it is important to keep in mind the limitations of interpreting data given the evaluation design, sample size, and other constraints resulting from both project and research implementation.

Though contamination between treatment and comparison groups appeared to be minimal, the high prevalence of other agriculture programs, especially among comparison groups, suggests that our evaluation may have underestimated the impact of ACE activities on key farm and household outcomes. Food assistance/nutrition programs and health programs were also more accessible to comparison households than to treatment households, which may have resulted in an underestimation of impact on child well-being indicators such as adequate food (missed meals), dietary diversity, and experience and treatment of diarrhea, fever, and cough. Since there were more sanitation and water programs reportedly available to treatment households than to comparison households during the 2 years between baseline and endline, the potential for the overestimation of impact exists for child health outcomes, since access to improved toilets and safe water affects the prevalence of illnesses, especially diarrhea.

Though impact could have been underestimated for farm and household outcomes, it could also have been undetectable because of the small sample size. The smaller the size of the study, the larger the impact has to be in order to be observed using statistical methods. The use of mixed-methods and considerable triangulation among multiple data sources was our effort to mitigate this limitation. Indeed, the strength of the evaluation was the mixed-methods approach to collecting data at multiple levels—farm, household, and child— which yielded a more complete picture of the complex relationship between economic strengthening and child outcomes than could have been obtained otherwise, and revealed innovative ways to improve future program impact and sustainability for reducing children's vulnerability.

Given the paucity of impact evaluations of agricultural value chain programs with vulnerable populations, it is nearly impossible to compare our results with those from the few evaluations that exist, as the contexts and subsectors vary. What we can say for certain is that research and impact evaluations are needed to understand the value of agricultural value chain interventions. New studies would do well to include longer time frames. It is worth noting that the P4P impact evaluations ranged from 2 years between baseline and endline in Ethiopia to 3 years in El Salvador and 4 years in Tanzania. Though P4P did not examine child-level outcomes, it found no statistically significant improvements on non-farm household outcomes (Krieger, 2014a, 2014b, 2014c).

As with other impact evaluations of value chains, traditional impact evaluation methods are insuffcient, and a search for an appropriate counterfactual will remain challenging for market-based interventions (Dunn, 2014). We recommend a mixed-methods approach and the use of repeated measures for farm enterprise, household, and child outcomes. Diaries are feasible if they are done with assistance, especially in low-literacy contexts. Systematic project monitoring and evaluation are also recommended.

Conclusion

This evaluation's findings support the growing recognition that increasing agricultural productivity is insuffcient to improve household economic welfare and child health and nutrition. The value chain systemic approach has the potential to increase farm productivity, household economic welfare, and other social assets like human and social capital, and did so in the case of ACE in Liberia. It remains to be seen if, in the absence of child-focused complementary interventions, children will also see positive impacts. Understanding pathways for child well-being are critical to breaking the intergenerational cycle of poverty. It is also critical that projects monitor their effects on children so as to do no harm, and also to take advantage of opportunities to improve child outcomes. Though it is possible that the impact on children may require a longer evaluation time than 2 years, it is also possible that we do not adequately understand how intra-household dynamics affect decisions that in turn affect outcomes for children. Unpacking the household to understand the dynamics around financial decision making, food preparation, parenting styles, violence between adults or toward children, and how and with whom children spend their time is essential to our ability to design effective programs with this generation and the next in mind.

Notes

1. The baseline survey was conducted after ACE's intervention strategy was adjusted in late 2009 through 2010. Smallholder farmers in the treatment group at the time of baseline either had received no treatment beyond a meeting to explain the program and decision to participate or had begun forming farmer groups in their towns with initial meetings with ACE field workers. No agricultural information would have had any effect on their farms in that season.
2. A household is defined as a group of people who pool their resources, eat from the "same pot", and have lived together for at least six of the last 12 months.
3. Adult equivalence scale was recommended by FAO (scale proposed in National Research Council (1989)) for use in Africa whereby each household member counts as some fraction of an adult male. The household size is the sum of the fractions. See Backiny-Yetna, Wodon, Mungai, and Tsimpo (2012) for an explanation of its use in deriving Liberia's poverty estimates based on the 2007 CWIQ survey.

Acknowledgement

Funding for this project was provided by the U.S. Agency for International Development (USAID) under the terms of associate agreement DFD-AA-00-07-00251-00, the Supporting Transformation by Reducing Insecurity and Vulnerability with Economic Strengthening (STRIVE) project. The contents are the responsibility of the authors and do not necessarily reflect the views of FHI 360, USAID or the United States Government. The authors thank Jennine Carmichael, Jessica Bachay, Alissa Bernholc, Helen Bristow, Thomas Grey, Steve Sortijas and Whitney Moret, and the University of Liberia Pacific Institute for Research and Evaluation for their research support, and Marvelous

Queejay-Weah, Laveto Akoi-Forkpa and the ACE Liberia team for their collaboration. Reprinted with the permission of Elsevier.

First published as: Rutherford, D.D., Burke, H.M., Cheung, K.K., and Field, S. H. (2016) 'Impact of an Agricultural Value Chain Project on Smallholder Farmers, Households, and Children in Liberia' *World Development* 83, pp 70-83, <https://doi.org/10.1016/j.worlddev.2016.03.004>

References

ACDI/VOCA (2014). *Agriculture for children's empowerment (ACE): Value chain network analysis*. Washington, DC: ACDI/ VOCA.

Akwara, P. A., Noubary, B., Lim Ah, K. P., Johnson, K., Yates, R., Winfrey, W., ... Luo, C. (2010). Who is the vulnerable child? Using survey data to identify children at risk in the era of HIV and AIDS. *AIDS Care, 22*(9), 1066–1085.

Alderman, H. (2012). The response of child nutrition to changes in income: Linking biology with economics. *CESifo Economic Studies, 58* (2), 256–273. http://dx.doi.org/10.1093/cesifo/ifs012.

Backiny-Yetna, P., Wodon, Q., Mungai, R., & Tsimpo, C. (2012). Poverty in Liberia: Level, profile, and determinants. In Q. Wodon (Ed.), *Poverty and the policy Response to the economic crisis in Liberia* (pp. 9–34). Washington, DC: World Bank.

Bandara, A., Dehejia, R., & Lavie-Rouse, S. (2014). The impact of income and non-income shocks on child labor: Evidence from a panel survey of Tanzania. *World Development, 67*, 218–237. http://dx.doi.org/10.1016/j.worlddev.2014.10.019.

Brunie, A., Fumagalli, L., Martin, T., Field, S., & Rutherford, D. (2014). Can village savings and loan groups be a potential tool in the malnutrition fight? Mixed method findings from Mozambique. *Children and Youth Services Review, 47*(2), 113–120. http://dx.doi.org/ 10.1016/j.childyouth.2014.07.010.

Campbell, P., Handa, S., Moroni, M., Odongo, S., & Palermo, T. M. (2010). Assessing the "Orphan Effect" in determining development outcomes for children in 11 eastern and southern African countries. *Vulnerable Children and Youth Studies, 5*(1), 12–32.

Campbell, R. (2013). *Feed the future learning agenda literature review: Expanded markets, value chains, and increased investment*. Rockville, MD: Westat.

Campbell, R. (2014). *A framework for inclusive market system development*. ACDI/ VOCA.

Coates, J., Swindale, A., & Bilinsky, P. (2007). *Household food insecurity access scale (HFIAS) for measurement of food access: Indicator guide VERSION 3*. <http://www.fantaproject.org/sites/default/files/resources/HFIAS_ENG_v3_Aug07.pdf>.

CPC Livelihoods and Economic Strengthening Task Force (2011). *The impacts of economic strengthening programs on children: A review of the evidence*. CPC Livelihoods and Economic Strengthening Task Force.

Creevey, L., Dunn, E., & Farmer, E. (2011). *Outreach, outcomes and sustainability in value chain projects microREPORT #171*. ACDI/ VOCA.

Dunn, E. (2014). *FIELD Report No. 18: Smallholders and inclusive growth in agricultural value chains*. Washington, DC: FHI 360.

Education Development Center (EDC), Mercy Corps, YMCA Liberia (2012). *Advancing youth project: Labor market assessment – Liberia*. <http://www. youtheconomicopportunities.org/sites/default/files/up-loads/resource/ Advancing%20Youth%20Project%20-%20Labor%20Market%20 Assessment%20Report.pdf>.

FAO (2008). *Guidelines for measuring household and individual dietary diversity*. Rome, Italy: Food and Agriculture Organization.

Gibson, A. (2005). *Bringing knowledge to vegetable farmers: Improving embedded information in the distribution system*. The Springfield Centre for Business in Development.

Goletti, F. (2005). *Agricultural commercialization, value chains, and poverty reduction: Making Markets work better for the poor*, Discussion paper No. 7. Hanoi: Asian Development Bank.

Government of Liberia (2007). *Greater monrovia comprehensive food security and nutrition survey (CFSNS)*. Monrovia, Liberia.

Hawkes, C., & Ruel, M. T. (2011). *Value chains for nutrition*, Paper presented at the leveraging agriculture for improving nutrition and health, New Delhi, India. <http://www.ifpri.org/sites/default/files/ publications/2020anhconf-paper04.pdf>.

Humphrey, J., & Navas-Alema´n, L. (2010). *Value chains, donor interventions and poverty reduction: A review of donor practice*. Brighton, UK: Institute of Development Studies (IDS).

Krieger, D. (2014a). *The impact of P4P on FOs and smallholder farmers in El Salvador*. World Food Programme, P4P Global Learning Series.

Krieger, D. (2014b). *The impact of P4P on FOs and smallholder farmers in Ethiopia*. World Food Programme, P4P Global Learning Series.

Krieger, D. (2014c). *The impact of P4P on SACCOs and smallholder farmers in Tanzania*. World Food Programme, P4P Global Learning Series.

Liberia Institute of Statistics and Geo-Information Services LISGIS (2009). *2008 National population and housing census: Preliminary results*. Government of Liberia.

Liberia Institute of Statistics and Geo-Information Services LISGIS, Ministry of Health and Social Welfare [Liberia], National AIDS Control Program [Liberia] & International, I. (2014). *Liberia demographic and health survey 2013*. Monrovia, Liberia: Liberia Institute of Statistics and GeoInformation, Services (LISGIS) and ICF International.

National Malaria Control Program (NMCP) [Liberia], Ministry of Health and Social Welfare (MOHSW), Liberia Institute of Statistics and GeoInformation Services (LISGIS) & ICF International (2012). *Liberia malaria indicator survey 2011*. Monrovia, Liberia.

National Malaria Control Program (NMCP) [Liberia], Ministry of Health and Social Welfare (MOHSW), Liberia Institute of Statistics and Geo-Information Services (LISGIS) & ICF Macro (2009). *Liberia malaria indicator survey 2009*. Monrovia, Liberia.

National Research Council (1989). *Recommended dietary allowances* (10th ed.). National Academy Press.

Oehmke, J. F., Jayne, T. S., Aralas, S. B., & Mathenge, M. K. (2010). *Impacts of USAID/Kenya supported agricultural productivity interventions on household income and poverty reduction*. Nairobi, Kenya: Tegemeo Institute of Agricultural Policy & Development.

Owadi, B., Kendle, A., & Koiwu, T. (2010). *Impacts of USAID/Kenya supported agricultural productivity interventions on household income and poverty reduction*. Comprehensive Food Security and Nutrition Survey.

PEPFAR (2012). *Guidance for orphans and vulnerable children programming*. Washington, DC: PEPFAR: The U.S. President's Emergency Plan for AIDS Relief.

Staritz, C. (2012). *Value chains for development? Potentials and limitations of global value chain approaches in donor interventions*, Working paper. Austrian Foundation for Development Research (Ö¨ FSE).

UNDP (2013). *Human development report 2013 the rise of the south: Human progress in a diverse world*. New York, NY.

United Nations (2006). *Common country assessment Liberia: Consolidating peace and national recovery for sustainable development*. Monrovia, Liberia.

United States Government (2012). *United States government action plan on children in adversity: A framework for international assistance: 2012– 2017*.

World Bank (2015a). *Agriculture & rural development*. Retrieved April 29, 2015, from <http://data.worldbank.org/topic/agriculture-and-rural-development>.

World Bank (2015b). *Poverty overview*. Retrieved April 29, 2015, from <http://www.worldbank.org/en/topic/poverty/overview>.

World Food Programme (2013). *Liberia comprehensive food security and nutrition survey (CFSNS)*.

World Health Organization (2015). *Food security. Trade, foreign policy, diplomacy and health*. Retrieved April 29, 2005, from <http://www. who.int/trade/glossary/story028/en/>.

About the authors

Diana Duff Rutherford, independent consultant.

Holly M. Burke, Scientist, FHI 360, North Carolina, USA.

Kelly K. Cheung, Mars, Incorporated.

Samuel H. Field, FHI 360, North Carolina, USA.

CHAPTER 15

Practical lessons on scaling up smallholder-inclusive and sustainable cassava value chains in Africa

Richard Lamboll, Valerie Nelson, Helena Posthumus, Adrienne Martin, Kolawole Adebayo, Francis Alacho, Nanam Dziedzoave, Grace Mahende, Vito Sandifolo, Lateef Sanni, Louise Abayomi, Andrew Graffham, Rory Hillocks, and Andrew Westby

Abstract

Developing more inclusive and sustainable agricultural value chains at scale is a development priority. The 'Cassava: Adding Value for Africa' project has supported the development of value chains for high quality cassava flour (HQCF) in Ghana, Tanzania, Uganda, Nigeria, and Malawi to improve the incomes and livelihoods of smallholder households, including women. The project focused on three key interventions: 1) ensuring a consistent supply of raw materials; developing viable intermediaries as secondary processors or bulking agents; and 3) driving market demand. Scaling-up experiences are presented, guided by an analysis of drivers (ideas/ models, vision and leadership, incentives and accountability), the enabling context (institutions, infrastructure, technology, financial, policy and regulations, partnerships and leverage, social context, environment), and the monitoring, evaluation, and learning process. Lessons for scaling up of similar value chain interventions are presented. These highlight the tension between rapid development of value chains and achieving equity and sustainability goals; the need for holistic approaches to capacity strengthening of diverse value chain actors; the role of strengthening equitable business relationships and networks as a vital element of scaling processes; and how informed engagement with government policy and regulatory issues is key, but often challenging given conflicting pressures on policymakers. The scaling process should be market-led, but the level and type of public sector and civil society investment needs careful consideration by donors, governments, and others, in particular less visible investments in fostering relationships and trust. Addressing uncertainties around smallholder-inclusive value chain development requires adaptive management and facilitation of the scaling process.

Keywords: cassava, value chain, smallholder, scaling, Africa

http://dx.doi.org/10.3362/9781788530576.015

Developing more smallholder-inclusive and sustainable agricultural value chains at scale is a development priority. This chapter presents new practical lessons from a development programme in five African countries (Ghana, Nigeria, Uganda, Tanzania, and Malawi), which seeks to build smallholder-inclusive cassava value chains.

Cassava in sub-Saharan Africa

Cassava is an important staple crop in sub-Saharan Africa (SSA). Most cassava is produced on smallholder farms with family labour using hand tools and without use of external inputs. Across SSA, cassava is mainly used for human consumption. Cassava is Africa's second most important food staple in terms of calories consumed per capita and is a major source of calories for roughly two out of every five Africans (IFAD/ FAO, 2005; Rosenthal and Ort, 2012).

Traditionally cassava was seen as a food security crop, but production has expanded rapidly in SSA in response to increasing demand (rapidly expanding and urbanizing population), particularly in Ghana and Nigeria (Nweke, 2004), and supply factors (higher yielding varieties, post-harvest technologies, and switching to cassava in areas of high land pressure) (IFAD/FAO, 2005; Fermont et al., 2008). The area planted to cassava increased almost threefold in Ghana and Nigeria from 1961 to 1999. IFAD/FAO (2005) argue that one of the key factors influencing the expansion of the cassava area was the availability of improved processing equipment. Processing reduces bulkiness of fresh cassava roots by removing water, resulting in improved storability and lower transport costs to urban market centres.

While many have considered cassava an inferior food crop (IFAD/FAO, 2005), this situation varies with location (e.g. cassava is more widely consumed in West Africa than East and Southern Africa) and is rapidly changing. Domestic food production and/or food imports will have to increase to meet the growing and changing food demand due to population growth, urbanization, and – although poverty levels remain high – growing middle classes (UN, 2013; AfDB, 2011; Chandy et al., 2013). Global food concerns in the light of climate and other changes are renewing the urgent challenge facing African nations to increase domestic and regional food production. Alongside this trend, in addition to traditional food uses (Westby, 2002), cassava is also being considered as a raw material for a wide range of food and non-food industrial uses.

Smallholder-inclusive staple food value chains in sub-Saharan Africa

Smallholder farms in SSA number around 33 million, represent 80 per cent of farms in the region, and contribute up to 90 per cent of food production in some SSA countries (Wiggins and Keats, 2013). Developing smallholder agriculture can be effective in reducing poverty and hunger in low-income countries, particularly in the short to medium term, but sustainable access to markets is needed (Wiggins and Keats, 2013), as well as the ability to engage and benefit from market access (Barrett, 2008; Seville et al., 2010).

The majority of smallholder households in SSA are net deficit in food production terms and only a minority sell food staples in an average year (Hazell and Poulton, 2007). Most poor farmers are not linked to markets (Wiggins and Keats, 2013) or deal with markets (buying inputs and selling produce) in small amounts (Wiggins and Keats, 2014). In the case of staple food grain producers in eastern and southern Africa, a relatively small share of households sell food grains and many of those selling are still net purchasers over the year. Farmers must have access to productive technologies and adequate private and public goods in order to produce a marketable surplus. Those with access to appropriate assets and infrastructure, together with suitable incentives, typically engage in markets, while those lacking one or more of those three elements generally do not (Barrett, 2008). Disincentives for SSA root crop producers result from extremely disconnected value chains, infrastructural constraints, and policymakers paying little attention to these commodities (Angelucci et al., 2013). In contrast to high value export crops (an option for only a minority of smallholders), for staple crops there seem to be few private initiatives that address the lack of smallholder access to domestic and regional markets (Wiggins and Keats, 2013).

There is an ongoing debate concerning the nature and extent of public interventions and the role of the private sector in agricultural development. A neo-classical economic view emphasizes the role of market forces as the main mechanism for efficient resource allocation and considers public sector intervention as having price-distorting effects. This view was strongly advocated by the World Bank and the international Monetary Fund (IMF) (the Washington Consensus) in Africa through structural adjustment programmes and radical reforms in agriculture that were centred on privatizing production and delivery of services and restricting governments to legislative and regulatory roles and delivering core public sector goods and services. However, for countries in which markets are yet to emerge or are underdeveloped and frequently fail, applying the Washington Consensus policies produced mixed social and economic results (Chang, 2009). The realities of the developing world include market failures, capability constraints, and risk management issues (Smith, 2009).

Following agricultural market liberalization in SSA, private traders have taken up opportunities to purchase output from producers, although this varies geographically, while private sector provision of pre-harvest services has been more limited. Incentives for investment in service provision for food crops have been much weaker than for export cash crops. Private investment in crop storage has been low, contributing to increased price volatility post-liberalization (Poulton et al., 2010; Poulton and Macartney, 2012).

The reasons for these outcomes are contested. Some argue that states have not fully withdrawn from many markets and this discourages private investment. Others emphasize the impact of low public investment in basic infrastructure on private investment in agricultural marketing. Some commentators point to the lack of important institutions required to support efficient private markets. Finally, coordination issues have been identified as a key area to address 'low level equilibrium traps' constraining agricultural production and marketing activities (Poulton and Macartney, 2012).

The conceptual and empirical evidence on smallholder market participation, with a focus on staple food grains in eastern and southern Africa, suggests that interventions aimed at facilitating smallholder organization, reducing the costs of intermarket commerce, and improving poorer households' access to improved technologies and productive assets are central to stimulating smallholder market participation and escape from semi-subsistence poverty traps (Barrett, 2008). Appropriate institutions and endowments are needed as well as 'getting the prices right' in order to induce market-based development (Barrett, 2008).

Public support may be necessary to encourage private investment and innovation in agriculture. Market failures (i.e. a situation where market forces fail to allocate resources efficiently or result in a net social welfare loss) justify a public intervention. For example, enterprises may not have the information or experience necessary to invest without undue risk. Such risks are often especially high to innovators. Public agencies might share some of the high transaction costs and associated risks constraining private sector activity. However, key influences on private investment in agricultural supply chains are the existence of an enabling rural investment climate and rural public goods (Wiggins and Keats, 2014). While a sharing of transaction costs and risks could partly compensate for high costs due to the lack of an enabling environment, it is unlikely to stimulate greater private investment where unpredictable state policies are discouraging investment (Poulton and Macartney, 2012). As well as market failure, there may be government or state failure (Poulton and Macartney, 2012) which may also justify public support to private enterprise (Wiggins and Keats, 2014).

'Cassava: Adding Value for Africa': description of the interventions

Smallholders producing cassava in SSA have restricted market access for their produce, not least because roots are perishable, bulky, and expensive to transport. High quality cassava flour (HQCF) has multiple market outlets for food and industrial uses and is a new opportunity for smallholder farmers and processors. Less capital equipment investment is needed than, for example, starch; it builds on existing processing knowledge. Processing of cassava roots to HQCF involves peeling, washing, grating, pressing, disintegration, sifting, drying, milling, screening, packaging, and storage.

Cassava is traditionally grown by large numbers of smallholders; each farmer usually cultivates less than 2 ha. Meanwhile, emerging markets for HQCF make orders and expect deliveries of consistent quality product in large quantities from systems that are not currently set up to accommodate a large number of suppliers. The key challenge to linking cassava farmers to the large markets for HQCF, therefore, is aggregation and facilitation of delivery of HQCF to factories through a value chain originating from many smallholders combined with meeting quality standards.

There are a number of ways to overcome this challenge and the preferred option will vary from one country or region to another. Where value chains are relatively well established (like Nigeria and Ghana), the introduction of artificial dryers capable of processing 1–3 metric tonnes of HQCF/day (single shift) could help to locate intermediary processing closer to the sources of fresh cassava roots and/or provide intermediate aggregation and transportation services, in addition to maintaining an acceptable quality of products delivered to the end use market. Where the value chain is relatively new and the technology gap is more difficult to overcome in the short run, the services of aggregation of high quality cassava grits (grated, pressed, and sun-dried, but not milled) will have to be provided by an entity such as a farmers' association or an entrepreneur, who could also provide a milling service. This is because grits can be more easily collected from a large number of farmer-processors for bulking and the quality parameters for grits are more easily maintained than for flour. A further option is for communitylevel processors to target smaller, more localized markets such as rural or small town bakers.

The 'Cassava: Adding Value for Africa' project (C:AVA; http://cava.nri.org/) has developed value chains for HQCF in Ghana, Tanzania, Uganda, Nigeria, and Malawi (phase 1, 2008–14). Funded by the Bill & Melinda Gates Foundation (the Foundation), the project aims to improve the livelihoods and incomes of smallholder households as direct beneficiaries, including women and disadvantaged groups. It promotes the use of HQCF as a versatile raw material for which diverse markets exist. Three key value chain strategies form the basis of C:AVA, namely: 1) ensuring a consistent supply of raw materials; 2) developing viable intermediaries who can act as secondary processors or bulking agents in value chains; and 3) driving market demand and building market share (in, for example, bakery industry, components of traditional foods, or plywood/chapterboard applications).

C:AVA has made multi-point interventions in the value chain, which differ by location and time. Project country offices based in universities and other research centres have played the key role of facilitation of the value chain. Partnerships have been essential to progress.

Interventions with smallholder farmers have focused on improving root supply. This has included working with community groups to build capacity in cassava root production (agronomy training, introducing new high-yield cassava varieties) and business and organization management training and mentoring.

Interventions with processors to improve quantity and quality of HQCF produced has involved: support at community level and various sized enterprises on HQCF processing; introducing new processing technologies or improving existing ones; and business and organization management training and mentoring.

A third set of interventions has been at the market level including identifying potential new markets for HQCF and providing business and technical support to make a case for using HQCF.

Capacity strengthening of diverse service providers has been an important part of this process. This was a key consideration with respect to sustainability of the value chains being developed.

C:AVA has facilitated the development of HQCF uses and value chains supplying a range of markets including: wheat replacement for flour millers, biscuit manufacturers, and local bakeries; in plywood and paperboard manufacturing, replacing wheat flour and maize starch, respectively; and novel traditional products e.g. instant *fufu*; and domestic use of cassava flour. There are two main types of drying processes in HQCF value chains: artificial drying using flash dryers or bin dryers and sun drying. While there is an overall broad project approach, within each country there have been varied strategies and experiences reflecting different contexts.

This chapter presents reflections of C:AVA's scaling-up experience to date and implications for similar value chain development interventions; that is, value chains based on a staple food crop – particularly cassava – supplying domestic or regional markets in SSA.

Method

Our working definition of scaling up draws on the definitions of Hartmann and Linn (2008) and IIRR (2000). Hartmann and Linn (2008) define scaling up as 'expanding, replicating, adapting and sustaining successful policies, programs or projects in geographic space and over time to reach a greater number of rural poor'. IIRR (2000) presents the following definition: 'Scaling up brings more quality benefits to more people over a wider geographical area, more quickly, more equitably, and more lastingly.' In this chapter we will include the following dimensions: the expansion and adaptation of cassava value chains over time and space; the number of target beneficiaries reached; and the quality, equity, and sustainability of benefits.

To draw practical lessons from across the project in different countries, a study was undertaken which aimed to: 1) clarify what has/is being scaled up; 2) analyse pathways to scale and impact and the approaches used; 3) identify key drivers and enabling/constraining factors; and 4) identify lessons for scaling up and scaling out of similar smallholder-inclusive value chains.

To examine the C:AVA scaling-up process we used a conceptual framework (Figure 15.1) that was adapted from a generic value chain scaling-up framework developed by Hartmann et al., (2013) and Linn (2012). To scale up cassava value chains to benefit a larger number of smallholder farming families requires an alignment between various drivers and enabling or constraining factors within the overall value chain system and context within which it is based. While implementing an intervention, a learning process involving some form of monitoring and evaluation (M&E) is needed to inform the scaling-up pathway so it can be adapted in light of the lessons learnt.

Drivers push the scaling-up process forward, and Linn (2012) identifies the following elements: ideas and models that have worked at a small scale or have been promoted successfully elsewhere; vision and leadership which has recognized that the scaling up of an idea is necessary, desirable, and feasible; external catalysts such as political and economic crises or pressure from outside actors (donors, NGOs, and so forth) which may drive the scaling-up process forward; and incentives and accountability for results which are needed to drive actors and institutions.

The key steps in the study method were as follows:

- A review of C:AVA documentation to gather information on the project in each country, including changes in strategy and the evolution of the value chains being developed. Project documentation included: the original project proposal; value chain, gender, and situation analysis scoping studies in each country; annual and quarterly country progress reports; project annual reports; annual meeting presentations; and

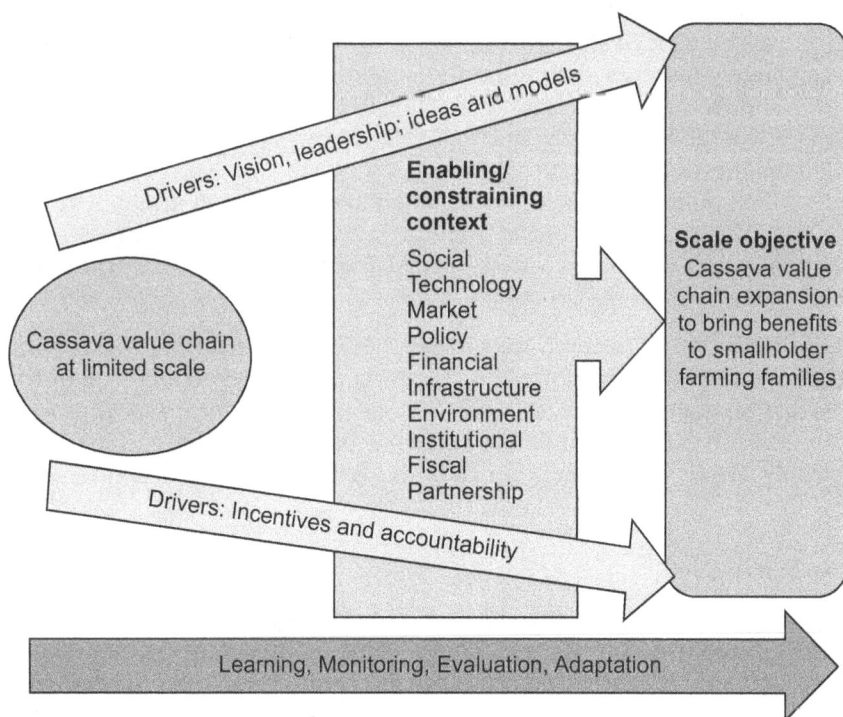

Figure 15.1 Scaling up cassava value chains: pathways, drivers, and enabling and constraining factors.
Source: Adapted from Hartmann et al., (2013) and Linn (2012)

monitoring and learning reports. This information was used to map out C:AVA scaling process/pathways to scale for each country.

- Interviews with C:AVA personnel to identify drivers, enablers, and constraining influences in each country and for the project as a whole. The study facilitation team interviewed: the overall project managers (two, based in Nigeria and UK), country managers (five, based in Ghana, Nigeria, Uganda, Tanzania, and Malawi), subject specialists who also had a country focus (four, based in UK and Nigeria), and one m&e specialist (based in UK). A checklist based on the conceptual framework (Figure 15.1) was used to ascertain for each country: the overall project evolution (scaling strategies, value chains being supported, actual C:AVA activities, target groups); key drivers and key enhancing/constraining factors; and the M&E and learning processes. The information collected was recorded in summary tables for each country.
- Participatory analysis by country managers and coordinators of the relative importance and influence of the drivers and enabling or constraining influences identified. Country teams were asked to: 1) verify the summary tables making corrections and adding any key omissions; 2) prioritize, as high, medium, or low, the listed drivers and factors (enablers or constraints) in terms of their influence on scaling-up process for HQCF value chains to bring benefits to smallholders and other target groups for their respective countries to date; and identify which of these drivers and factors (enabling or constraining) are still key influences for future scaling of HQCF value chains to bring benefits to smallholders and other target groups.
- The results were shared for validation in a C:AVA team meeting, including the programme officer from the Foundation.
- A project working paper was prepared, which contributed to the development of a C:AVA phase II.

In the following sections we present the findings of the study according to the conceptual framework above, drawing on experiences from across the five project countries, starting with the scale objective for the C:AVA project, then the drivers, followed by the enabling/constraining context. Finally, we identify lessons and draw out conclusions emerging from the analysis.

Scale objective

The original project objective in relation to scaling was based on bringing income benefits to 90,000 smallholder families. This objective was refined in country strategy workshops following a number of initial project studies (value chains, scoping studies, gender situational analysis, and baseline surveys). These studies identified the diversity within the broad category of 'smallholder', which informed project planning in a general sense, but did not result in specifically targeted interventions for different types of smallholder.

Figure 15.2 outlines the broad situation regarding different types of cassava farmers and how they may engage in new cassava value chains. Larger, better resourced, male members of rural communities are typically in a better position to respond to, and manage the risks offered by, new commercial opportunities. Significant support will be needed for women and less well-resourced members of rural communities, many of whom are food insecure, to benefit from new cassava value chain development. Enterprises may also need help to source from these target groups. In Nigeria, for example, only 45 per cent of the female-headed households working with C:AVA had more than one hectare of farmland, compared to 87 per cent of male-headed households (Figure 15.3).

Drivers

Vision and leadership/Ideas and models

C:AVA is a key driver of smallholder-inclusive HQCF value chains development in all five countries. In Nigeria and Ghana there are also a number of other important cassava value chain policy and programme interventions. The overall vision of

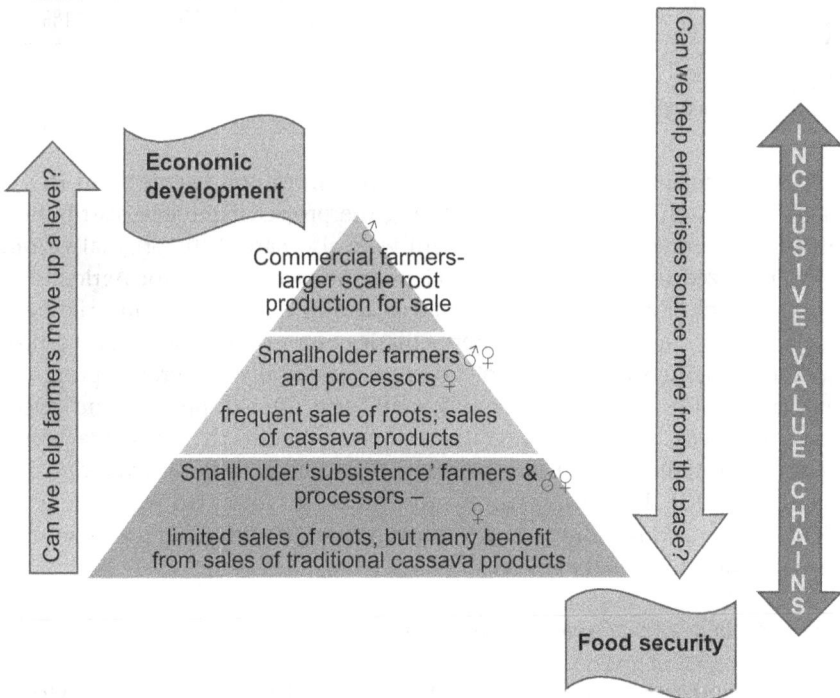

Figure 15.2 How can different smallholder farmers or processors be included in cassava value chains?
Source: Adapted from Seville et al., (2010) and Woodhill (2012) cited in Hartman et al., (2013)

Female (42) ■ Male (149)

	No Land	≤1	>1–3	>3–5	>5–10	>10
Female (42)	5%	50%	26%	12%	7%	0%
Male (149)	0%	17%	38%	21%	13%	11%

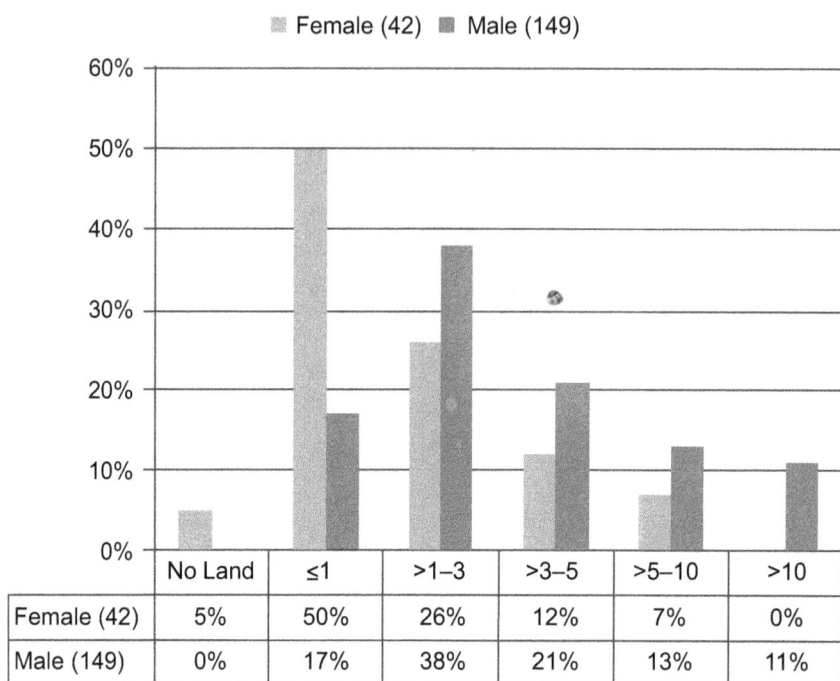

Figure 15.3 Farm size (ha) by gender of heads of households working with C:AVA in Nigeria.
Source: Data from C:AVA Impact Study in Nigeria

C:AVA – of smallholder households benefiting from improvements in HQCF value chains – has been sustained during the project. Equitable distribution of benefits and women's empowerment were also part of the original vision, as emphasized in the Foundation's Gender Impact Strategy for Agricultural Development (2008). The overall strategy was to build on and upscale pilot initiatives through support to intermediaries as a means of aggregating produce and linking smallholders to end users. Specifically, the project proposed that smallholder farmers sell cassava roots, grits (grated, pressed, and dried, but not milled), and wet cake (grated and pressed), directly or via village processors, to intermediaries for onward sale to end users in cassava value chains based on HQCF. The focus was on substitution for imported wheat flour by HQCF in the baking industry and improvement of traditionally processed cassava products for urban markets.

Flexibility in project management and ongoing support along the value
chains has allowed diverse value chain models to emerge
Country-level trajectories have varied from the initial C:AVA strategic vision through an iterative process, initiated in the country strategy workshops. A variety of 'value chain models' have emerged in the various countries in response to different contextual constraints and opportunities (Table 15.1).

Table 15.1 Emerging HQCF value chain models

Emerging HQCF value chains	Ghana	Nigeria	Malawi	Tanzania	Uganda
Farmer-processor groups to small local end users			√	√	√
Farmer-processor groups to large urban end users				√	
Farmer-processor associations to local small end users			√		√
Farmer-processor associations to large urban end users					√
Small enterprises (sun drying) to local small end users	√		√	√	
Small enterprises (sun drying) to large urban end users	√			√	
Small enterprises (bin drying) to small local end users	√				
Small enterprises (bin drying) to large urban end users	√				
Medium/large enterprises (flash drying) to large urban end users	√[1]	√	√		

Note: [1]Currently understood to be producing industrial grade cassava flour

This involved investments, often invisible to those outside the process, in problem solving iteration, learning by doing, and mentoring. The project focused on a range of different types and scale of intermediaries, using sun drying and artificial drying in different countries. Mid-term, in 2010, there was a switch in emphasis and resource allocation to improving the artificial drying capacity and fuel efficiency of intermediaries in Nigeria in order to increase the scale of HQCF production and numbers of smallholders supplying roots. There were also renewed efforts to identify diverse end markets.

Champions of smallholder-inclusive value chains are emerging
There are examples of private sector players who are helping to drive the value chains to achieve scaling up. A large company in Malawi has stated that they want to support smallholders and the director of a Tanzanian small- or medium-scale enterprise (SME) is a potential role model for small-scale (female) entrepreneurs to enter the value chain. It is likely that in several countries, scaling up will involve a wider identification of such potential entrepreneurs.

Different models for linking farmer (processor) organizations to buyers in cassava value chains are emerging, with differing challenges and opportunities in terms of scaling up (see Table 15.2). These relate to dimensions such as the criteria for participation, formal and informal contractual arrangements, responsibilities of different parties, provision of resources, access to market information, continuity and building trust, and the nature of and exposure to risk.

Table 15.2 Organizational models of smallholder production and examples in C:AVA countries

Model	Driver of organization	Rationale	C:AVA country cassava examples
Producer-driven (association)	Producers, when formed into groups such as associations or cooperatives	Access new markets Obtain higher market price Stabilize and secure market position	Producer associations and cooperatives in Uganda (and in Malawi)
Buyer-driven	Processors Retailers Traders, wholesalers, and other traditional market actors	Assure supply Increase supply volumes Supply more discerning customers – meeting market niches and interests	SME out-growers, Ghana
Facilitator-driven	NGOs and other support agencies National and local governments	'Make markets work for the poor' Regional and local development	Community processing groups in Tanzania, Ghana, Malawi (and Nigeria prior to 2010)
Integrated supply chain	Lead firms Supermarkets Multinationals	New and higher value market Low prices for good quality Market monopolies	Some interest is emerging

Source: Based on Miller (2011)

Incentives and accountability

Commercial incentives vary greatly among the different countries, value chain models, and over time

Incentives and commercial motivation for private sector investment in value chains (and hence scaling up) are affected by prices, access to credit, quality, and volumes. Commercial and other incentives along the value chain can change dramatically over time. Profitability of HQCF production and the attractiveness of HQCF in relation to alternatives/substitutes vary seasonally and from year to year, depending on the fluctuating prices for cassava roots, wheat, and fuel costs for artificial drying. The project invested to improve incentives and profitability, in order to improve cassava productivity of farmers; to increase efficiency and reduction of intermediary processors' costs; and to develop awareness of product attributes among end users. There has been little investment so far by the private sector in improving profitability along the chain. Interest has been reported by some companies in buying from smallholder farmers/processors for reasons beyond short-term commercial interests, such as corporate social responsibility and encouraging brand loyalty.

Competitiveness of HQCF compared to alternative raw materials is a key driver for end users
HQCF was competitively priced in relation to imported wheat and maize starch prices in Malawi and Uganda. Malawi also had foreign exchange short-ages, which further contributed to interest among large enterprises to invest in HQCF value chains. In other countries, HQCF was less competitive compared with alternative raw materials (mainly wheat flour), but interest in HQCF and other cassava-based products has increased in all countries nevertheless. A growing middle class provides opportunities for sales of quality products uti-lizing HQCF, such as composite flour and instant *fufu*.

Motivating farmers in the short term without fostering dependency, while working towards longer-term value chain benefits is a challenge
Farmers and community-level processors are motivated by prospects for income generation and livelihood security. Better-off farmers are in a position to respond on the basis of their existing assets. The limited capacity at start up and limited working capital of asset-poor farmers, combined with small margins on sales, can be a major disincentive to their participation, but the provision of support to build capacity and fast track implementation risks creating dependency.

Enabling and constraining context

Institutional context: the entire value chain

Developing sustainable smallholder-inclusive value chains is a long-term process involving the entire chain
Ongoing support to the chain actors, as well as the linkages between them, has been necessary to build value chains in each country. This required invest-ments by C:AVA in value chain relationships, addressing problems and iden-tifying opportunities in the value chain. Such investments may not be highly visible to donors or other actors seeking to facilitate value chain creation or strengthening, but they are crucial for success.

Value chain actors sharing a similar business ethos are likely to find it easier to do business together and linking these actors offers greater likelihood of sustainable chains
Mutual understanding of expectations, business norms and practices, capac-ity, and needs among the suppliers and buyers along the value chain is crucial. There are examples of enterprises whose managers have experience of working with smallholder suppliers, together with knowledge of what smallholders need in terms of advice and inputs. In these circumstances there is less need for external support and greater likelihood of a sustainable value chain. C:AVA has facilitated links between actors in value chains – providing a space for improved understanding and negotiation to take place.

Increased demand for cassava needs to be carefully balanced with increased supplies of cassava roots
Improved varieties and crop husbandry can rapidly lead to increased yields. It is necessary to avoid a cassava glut, but it is equally important not to completely cut investments in cassava production to avoid shortages that may cause the value chain to collapse. This matching of supply and demand is a critical balancing act which may be addressed by, for example, involving cassava producers of various scales of operation, and regular feedback of market intelligence on price movements and production costs. Another aspect of the imbalance between supply and demand is seasonality of production (see Environmental context). Increased demand for cassava for alternative uses reduces the supply for the HQCF value chain and, unless production increases, results in higher prices. The competition for cassava roots for alternative cassava value chains exists in all countries, but is particularly challenging in Ghana and Nigeria, and has also been the case in periods of food shortages at regional level influencing Uganda and parts of Malawi.

Institutional context: farmers/processors

Skills in business management, group dynamics, leadership, and accountability at farmer-processor organizations are key to successful participation in value chains
The lack of these skills in farmer-processor groups was a constraining factor in each country. Stronger farmer-processor organizations possessing such skills have benefited most from the new HQCF value chains. Project support encouraging networks of farmer-processor groups and intermediaries for information sharing were seen as positive.

Constraining factors at farmer level can be overcome with technical support and organizational capacity building
At farmer level, a number of factors were said to be constraining scaling up of HQCF value chains, including smallholder farmers' lack of access to improved planting materials or seed systems, inability to respond to the spread of cassava diseases, and side-selling of cassava to other markets. More structural issues such as access to land and gender inequalities were not raised in the interviews yet may have had a significant impact on farmers' ability to participate and benefit from HQCF value chain development.

Prior investments in institutional development provide a launch pad for integrating smallholder farmers into value chains
Where there has been success in working with farmer cooperatives/associations that can manage cassava processing and marketing operations, as in Uganda, there had been significant *prior* investment by donors and NGOs in institutional development. C:AVA has successfully built upon this previous investment in organizational farmer development in Uganda. In southern Tanzania and Malawi, there had also been some previous investment in

organizational development through the formation of community processing groups.

Institutional context: intermediaries

Smaller enterprises have shown more interest in entering the HQCF value chain than larger organizations
There are different types and scales of intermediaries associated with different value chains (Table 15.1) and operating with different technologies. There has been interest shown by larger enterprises, but generally – outside of Nigeria – they have not invested in artificial drying as anticipated. Smaller entrepreneurs are joining value chains in Tanzania and Malawi, using sun-drying technology for which entry costs are much lower.

Procurement of cassava roots exclusively from smallholder farmers can involve significant risks for medium- and large-scale processors
Intermediary processors face challenges (high costs of logistics, coordination of purchases, side-selling in contract farming, etc.) when they procure cassava roots from smallholder farmers only. Spreading procurement of cassava roots from different types of cassava growers (e.g. of different scales) reduces the risk for medium- to large-scale processors who require a consistent and reliable root supply (see Table 15.3). One of the future strategies identified was the potential for engaging smallholder farmers in contract farming, in order to improve their access to inputs and technical advice, and their ability to provide a reliable supply, including by joining forces with large-scale farmers.

Practical knowledge and skills combined with business skills are needed for successful participation in value chains
Potential intermediaries need exposure to information on the opportunities presented by HQCF processing and trading and the opportunity to learn the business through exchange visits, access to advice and/or mentoring, hands-on practice, etc. In Tanzania, an accessible learning site at a parastatal responsible for small-scale industry development enabled a local entrepreneur to try out HQCF processing in a practical way and led to significant investment.

Institutional context: end users

Awareness-raising among potential end users of HQCF creates interest, but their decision making depends on their capacity (technical knowledge, equipment and skills)
C:AVA was successful in raising awareness with end users such as local bakers, agri-food companies, and paperboard manufacturers, through workshops, media, personal visits, etc. However, the end user's decision on whether to use HQCF appears to be highly dependent on the capacity of their organization. For example, a paperboard manufacturer in Uganda who had hands-on

Table 15.3 Types of intermediary, sources of supply, and risks to intermediaries

Intermediary	Source of supply	Nature of risk
Medium – large enterprises (flash drying)	Buy on open market Source from own farms Contract/outgrower schemes Farmer groups (roots)	Source markets may be at a distance Undersupply of roots results in operation below capacity, which reduces income to repay investment loans; may jeopardize ability to meet contracts Weather conditions affect root production Side-selling in contract arrangements
Small enterprises bin/sun drying	Buy on open market Source from own farms Farmer processing groups (roots and/or grits)	Undersupply of roots results in operation below capacity and reduced income to repay investment loans Weather conditions affect production (and processing)
Farmers associations	Members of association use own roots, purchase from other members or from farmers in locality	Equipment often received as grant, therefore less commercial pressure to operate to capacity Weather conditions affect production and processing

technical knowledge was provided with a sample of HQCF and made a rapid decision to start using it, with little or no further project support. In contrast, a paperboard manufacturer in Malawi implemented joint trials with C:AVA personnel over a period of time in order to make an assessment of the suitability of HQCF.

There are few examples of provision of services by end users to other actors in the HQCF value chain, although in other sectors, end users have engaged in providing inputs, credit, and advice to their suppliers (e.g. breweries supporting sorghum producers in Uganda; Wiggins and Keats, 2014). An example for HQCF is an agro-processing company in Dar es Salaam that is providing credit to a community processing group in Mtwara that supplies it with grits.

Institutional context: service providers

There are different ways for strengthening farmer and processor capacity, involving private, NGO, and public sectors. Private sector-led approaches can provide strong motivation and resources, enterprise management skills, and a guaranteed market. NGOs often have well-motivated staff, strong accountability structures, an ethos of farmer empowerment and gender inclusivity, and are used to targeting more vulnerable groups. The public sector has the advantage of continuity of presence and technical skills and policy linkages.

Service providers require capacity building in value chain development, business management, and farmer organizational strengthening
Service providers have played an important role in all countries, but the experience has been mixed, depending upon their capacities. In Tanzania

and Nigeria, for example, the service providers felt a sense of ownership and continued to provide services despite the ending of their contracts. But understanding and expertise in value chain development and business management is often limited among local NGOs (e.g. Ghana, Uganda) and government agricultural extension organizations; strengthening the capacity of the service providers in business management requires time and resources.

Relationships between service providers need to be strengthened to enhance knowledge sharing, learning, and ownership
In some countries (e.g. Tanzania, Nigeria, Ghana), the relationships between service providers have been strengthened; they see themselves as a team taking ownership of cassava development activities. This network of service providers provides opportunities to replicate and scale-out the C:AVA intervention. In other countries (e.g. Malawi), service providers tend to work in isolation, which hampers sharing of information and knowledge.

Infrastructural context

Infrastructural challenges (roads, electricity, and water supplies) are important constraints to cassava value chains
Access to suitable roads was a key constraint across all countries. Access to reliable/affordable electricity was ranked as a highly important constraint in Nigeria and Uganda. Water supply is a significant constraint for processing in Nigeria and Tanzania and to a certain extent in Uganda. Many of the infrastructural constraints are unlikely to change without significant public investment, but it is an important issue for consideration in siting new processing facilities, as well as establishing where there can be a reliable supply of cassava.

Mobile phone technology facilitates trade of cassava products in rural areas
Mobile phone coverage was said to be a highly important enabling factor in Tanzania and Uganda to facilitate trade (by sending or receiving orders and payments).

Technological context

Efficient technology is key to making cassava processing profitable, but requires technological innovation and capacity building of local equipment fabricators
C:AVA made available improved equipment for sun drying, and has demonstrated that efficiencies can be obtained for smallholders. In Nigeria, major improvements have been made in energy efficiency and conversion to renewable energy resources in flash-drying technology.

C:AVA investments in improved processing technology and strengthening the capacity of fabricators in different countries have been positive and provide significant opportunities for South–South learning. Too often it has been assumed in the past that it is sufficient to hand out processing equipment without regard for dependency issues, sustainability, or the technical advice and maintenance inputs required. The capacity of local equipment fabricators to maintain and manufacture processing equipment was a challenge in all C:AVA countries. Strengthening capacity among suppliers of equipment is necessary to produce quality processing equipment and also to provide support for installation and maintenance.

Sun-drying technology is suitable for smallholders and starting SMEs but poses logistical challenges for scaling up HQCF production
Producing high volumes of HQCF based on sun drying is challenging, particularly in West Africa, but also to some extent in Tanzania and Malawi; limiting factors vary but may include climate, lack of drying space, limited capacity for collective action, and poor infrastructure. Production of high volumes of HQCF of consistent quality through sun drying requires strong quality management systems and coordination of processing activities. Farmer-processors often lack such logistical skills. However, it is a relatively low-cost (and low-risk) technology suitable for smallholders and starting SMES who enter the HQCF value chain and target buyers that can accommodate small quantities.

Financial context

Working and investment capital for intermediaries and processors is a constraining factor and requires more engagement from industrial end users
The experiment with a loan portfolio guarantee fund in Ghana was not very successful as the banks did not provide loans to the intermediaries at lower interest rates, despite receiving a C:AVA guarantee. There are few examples of credit being made available to farmers and processors from actors higher up the value chain.

Policy and regulatory context

The policy and regulatory environment in the five C:AVA countries has not been strongly conducive to cassava value chain development
In Malawi, the government's fertilizer subsidy programme for maize, for food security reasons, has encouraged farmers to shift from cassava to maize, resulting in reduced production. In Nigeria a specific policy on HQCF inclusion in wheat flour was reversed and subsequently reintroduced following changes in government. This instability created an unpredictable environment for investment in cassava development. C:AVA staff played a big role in advocacy, contributing to presidential initiatives on cassava involving heads of state of Nigeria and Malawi.

C:AVA Uganda was instrumental in suggesting the standards and specifications for seven cassava products, including HQCF, which were legally approved and gazetted by the East Africa community. This provides longer-term opportunities for scaling up, although in the shorter term, despite project support for farmer-processor associations to meet requirements, the Uganda National Bureau of Standards did not issue certifications. This created a (temporary) block on HQCF supplies to biscuit manufacturers.

Partnerships and leverage

Experiences with partnerships with other organizations have been mixed, but are important to support value chains successfully
NGOs with similar missions and target groups are potential agents to achieve scaling. C:AVA's relationship with NGOs (those already working with the project and others) contributed to the scaling process. Although the public sector often lacks the means to contribute to scaling up, government policies can influence value chain development. Partnerships with NGOs and the public sector have been beneficial in all countries, but a lack of partnerships with financial institutions was noted.

Leverage can be a key aspect of a scaling process and C:AVA is just starting to show some success
The World Bank defines the basic concept of leverage as: 'the ability of a public financial commitment to mobilise some larger multiple of private capital for investment in a specific project or undertaking' (Griffiths, 2012). However, others consider the mobilization of resources from any sector as leverage.

In Malawi, a large domestic private company invested in a flash drier facility following a range of project interventions to encourage investment (provision of planting material, a soft loan, a study tour to Nigeria to see flash driers, business plan development, links to the paperboard market, and other associated information). In southern Tanzania, a small-scale female entrepreneur built a small processing centre in a village and planted a large area of cassava. C:AVA provided hands-on experience through a parastatal processing centre, supplied a grater and press and made linkages to markets in Dar es Salaam. In Tanzania, District Agricultural Development Plan funds have been used to support community processing groups. In Malawi, lessons from C:AVA helped source support from government and NGO partners to reach more beneficiaries.

Social and cultural context

Cultural patterns in food consumption can pose either a challenge or an opportunity to new cassava value chains
In Ghana and Nigeria, most consumers prefer traditional cassava products (e.g. garri, *fufu*) and local processors are less interested in the less profitable HQCF. In Uganda, on the other hand, consumers are interested in cassava-based products and traditional value chains are less well developed, creating an opportunity for HQCF inclusion in food products. Companies can capitalize on this interest by promoting local and patriotic products that include cassava as an ingredient. This is more than a corporate social responsibility issue – it

can be a good example of a business case facilitating a positive development impact.

Cassava value addition can empower women, but gender-related obstacles to women's participation need to be addressed promptly and adequately
Cassava value addition was identified as a promising intervention, which aligned with the priorities of the Foundation to support women's empowerment. C:AVA has brought benefits to women, particularly through the added value created in sun-dried HQCF value chains. In order to scale up and reach more women, sustainable mechanisms will be necessary to improve women's access to equipment, finance, and to support their participation in sun-drying value chains.

Environmental context

Environmental issues are largely constraining
Limited access to water, climate and climate change issues, and the environmental impact of waste water from processing (the latter noted in Ghana, Nigeria, and Malawi) were all noted as constraining factors to cassava processing.

Seasonality is an important consideration in the supply of cassava roots and sun drying processing
Most cassava roots are harvested during the wet season in West Africa when the moist ground makes harvesting easier and in the dry season in East/southern Africa. This, together with the demand to make other cassava-based products, results in considerable variation in availability and price of roots over the year.

Monitoring, evaluation, and learning

cross-country learning, although limited, was considered valuable by participants. Cross-country lesson learning with Nigeria has been beneficial for C:AVA Malawi and Malawian investors. Fabricators of processing equipment from Uganda, Tanzania, and Malawi attended a training event in Malawi run by a Nigerian fabricator. Learning occurred among country managers at annual meetings. More crosscountry learning between different actors would have been beneficial.

Lessons learned by C:AVA

1. There is a potential tension between the *rapid* development of cassava value chains and the realization of benefits to smallholders, addressing gender disparities and sustainability.
   - Scaling-up objectives should clearly articulate the target groups and nature of the benefits and be at the core of intervention strategy.

- Scaling up requires the commercial 'pull' of end user markets (as stressed by Campbell, 2010), but crucially they must be aligned with interventions that give a 'push' to smallholders, as argued by others such as Barrett (2008) and Seville et al., (2010).
- Longer-term horizons and an adaptive problem solving approach are needed (consistent with Wiggins and Keats, 2013) in building capacity along the entire value chain and aligning the key elements of these complex systems.

2. Smallholders are not a homogeneous group and face different risks, challenges, and opportunities.
   - Understanding of and engagement with the rural communities with whom interventions are working is critical. Country-level typologies of small-holders based on their resources and market access (see Figure 15.2) help in the development of interventions and the assessment of impact. Although not a novel point (see for example seville et al., 2010; Donavan et al., 2015), it does need to be emphasized if the position of stated target groups is to be improved.

3. *Scaling-up strategies need to be informed by local and national stakeholders and context, but draw on cross-country learning.* There is no one simple model for scaling up value chains, but a diversity of 'value chain models' relating to local and national contexts. Circumstances matter (Wiggins and Keats, 2014; Donavan et al., 2015; Smith, 2009). These imply different scaling strategies, including leverage, partnerships, capacity building, etc. Flexibility to adapt the strategy and resources in the light of changes in policy (donor and government) and market conditions, among others, is key in the scaling process.
   - Ensure scaling-up strategies are developed through a participatory stakeholder planning process. The views of smallholder men and women, as well as other actors, are needed to identify their interest, their views on business, economic, and social viability, and their capacity strengthening needs.
   - Stakeholder inclusive mechanisms for adapting the strategy in the light of changing circumstances need to be established.

4. *Individual and organizational capacity of target beneficiaries needs to be strengthened as they engage in more commercial pre- and post-harvest farming activities.* Strong farmer organizations allow individual smallholder farmers and processors to benefit from value chains through collective action. Farmer organizational capacity building takes time and resources; among the issues are governance, trust, internal communication, transparency, and leadership.
   - Cost-effective approaches for strengthening individual capacity at scale and the potential of different farmer organizations are needed.
   - Resources need to be invested in service providers that have demonstrated practical ability to strengthen farmers' organizational capacity for engagement in value chains. To be more effective, service

providers need access to learning networks and best practice on management and governance of farmers' organizations, financial transparency, and resolving challenges of collective action (e.g. Ton, 2010; Francesconi and Wouterse, 2011). Public, private, and NGO sector actors with their associated strengths are needed to secure resources and provide sustainable services.

- An innovative response is needed to address potential gender-related obstacles to women's participation (e.g. training of female village-based mechanics, peer-to-peer learning, and role models).

5. *A range of institutional arrangements between farmers and actors higher up the value chains emerged* to address the challenge of smallholder capacity to deliver large quantities of roots to large-scale processors. Contract farming and outgrower schemes are subjects of intense debate (Prowse, 2012). They can present advantages and disadvantages to smallholder farmers, depending on the business model, degree of formality, objectives, source of technical assistance, credit, inputs, other partners involved, and minimum land or other resource requirement per participant.

- Interventions should be informed by recent experiences with different institutional arrangements. This would ensure awareness of the options available and the associated implications in terms of: roles and responsibilities, capacity requirements, likely distribution of benefits, and wider impact in the shorter and longer term.
- It is important to analyse the conditions in which schemes can work for target groups. Whatever arrangements are in place, they have to work for both farmers and intermediaries. It will be important to monitor closely the potential risks and benefits to smallholder groups.

6. *In decision-making about scaling up value chains it is important to understand the anticipated benefits in terms of both the extent of coverage and degree of individual benefit.* Some value chain models are more smallholder and women friendly than others. For example, large-scale mechanized HQCF processing can create a high demand for cassava roots, potentially bringing benefits to many smallholders. However, the benefits may be of limited additional value per individual, especially where resources are constrained. Other value chains, targeted to specific groups, e.g. women processors, may make a large difference, changing the trajectory of a household and raising them out of poverty, but for fewer people.

7. *Monitoring, evaluation, and learning systems are required to meet a range of different expectations.* Quantitative modelling is useful for analysis of economic variables and is important for measuring aspects of scale, e.g. inputs, outputs, numbers of beneficiaries, and level of income benefit. Other key aspects in a scaling process require other forms of qualitative and process-orientated monitoring in order to meet the learning objective.

- *Supporting the scaling up of value chains needs effective learning, communication, and adaptation.* C:AVA has shown the importance of learning from the experience of value chain development and having the flexibility to adapt as circumstances change. This is in agreement with others, such as Wiggins and Keats (2014), who stress the value of loose-coupled management that allows learning. A systematic learning and communication strategy needs to be implemented at different levels for: 1) different participants to access information and engage in shared learning; 2) sharing with potential investors in smallholder-inclusive value chains to encourage take-up of relevant lessons from C:AVA; and 3) engaging with decision-makers influencing the enabling context.

- More use of ICT and innovative communication approaches would facilitate shared internal learning and enhance communication with external stakeholders.

8. The scalability and sustainability of value chain interventions should be considered against the available financial resources.

- Financial resources are needed at various points along the value chain (for capital investment, working capital, transport, marketing, etc.). In going to scale, wider access to equipment and finance for its purchase are needed, as well as arrangements for repair and maintenance. Options for finance should be explored for different scales of operation in emerging value chains, e.g. loans, credit from linked value chain actors, joint ownership, and development funds used to purchase equipment, among others.

9. *It is important to recognize the role of relationships and networks for scaling processes.* Developing smallholder-inclusive value chains requires support and investment in developing value chain relationships and aligning key actors and elements. Building relationships and networks along and around the value chain creates trust and develops understanding of interests and clarifies expectations.

- There should be appropriate levels of investment (financial and skills) in the relationship development aspects of value chain development. The greater the social difference between value chain actors, the greater the investment needed in relationship building.
- The value chain 'models' that are being scaled up need to make explicit to donors and the wider development community, the degree of relationship building needed to establish effective business arrangements among value chain actors, including the time taken and risks involved.

10. *Partnerships and leverage have been increasingly recognized as a means of taking HQCF value chains to scale.* Partners in different (public, private, and third) sectors bring different interests and resources. In C:AVA there has been emphasis on building informal partnerships with actors along the value chain and, to an extent, partnerships with public sector organizations and NGOs for extending to new geographical areas.

- Systematically consider, at country and project levels, the enabling opportunities *that can be created and constraints that can be addressed through partnerships and leverage.*

- *Further analysis* is needed of government policy and regulatory issues affecting scaling of cassava value chains in order to guide engagement with policymakers. Working as far up the hierarchy of issues as possible would help to draw attention to more systemic problems and address national conditions (Vorley et al., 2012; Wiggins and Keats, 2014).

Conclusions

Scaling up smallholder-inclusive, resilient agricultural value chains is a priority for many development actors aiming to meet a variety of social, economic, and environmental objectives (e.g. improving rural incomes, local economic development, poverty reduction). Cassava, in particular, is a climate-resilient crop. It is also widely grown by smallholders and there is expanding demand for more and different types of agri-food products in Africa. All of this means that there is significant potential to develop cassava-based value chains in which smallholders participate and benefit.

Value chain development – as opposed to interventions which focus on a particular aspect or aspects of the chain only – may be considered as inherently part of a scaling process. Developing inclusive value chains – such as for HQCF – involves significant uncertainty and risk, not least because it entails decision-making by and functioning linkages between a wide range of actors. Hence, significant investments are needed to support actors along such emerging value chains, which can be very vulnerable to shocks and stresses. Scaling such inclusive value chains involves a process of both aligning and influencing a range of drivers within changing contexts. There is also a need to learn from failures as well as successes in an iterative process. The level and type of investment required for success needs careful consideration by donors, governments, and others working in the field, in particular the less visible investments in fostering relationships and building trust along the value chain.

Although scaling up should be market-led, public sector and civil society interventions are needed to reach more disadvantaged social groups if the effects are to be transformative rather than marginal (e.g. a slightly improved income for betteroff producers). These may be direct investments such as co-financing, building capacity, infrastructure (e.g. roads, energy) or indirect policy levers influencing the agri-food investment environment and value chain governance.

Our experience shows that the tension between the rapid development of cassava value chains and achieving equity and sustainability goals can be challenging. To increase the participation of smallholders, particularly those less well-off, in cassava value chains going to scale, requires a holistic approach to investment in capacity building. This capacity strengthening is needed most probably along the value chain, at individual and organizational levels, although types of support required will vary. Strengthening equitable business relationships and networks is vital for scaling processes that can be sustained over time. Informed engagement with government policy and regulatory issues is also important, but we recognize the challenges involved given the often conflicting pressures on policymakers.

Addressing the uncertainties around smallholder-inclusive value chain development needs *adaptive management and facilitation of the scaling process.* This involves longer timescales in planning and capacity strengthening, challenging of assumptions, strong co-learning and feedback processes to inform decision-making, fostering relationships, and building trust.

Acknowledgements

This work was supported by the Bill & Melinda Gates Foundation 'Cassava: Adding Value for Africa (C:AVA)' project and the European Union Food Security Thematic Programme 'Improving the livelihoods of smallholder cassava farmers through better access to growth markets (cassavagmarkets)' project grants to the University of Greenwich's Natural Resources Institute. The views expressed are not necessarily those of the Foundation or the European Commission.

References

African Development Bank (AfDB) (2011) *The Middle of the Pyramid: Dynamics of the Middle Class in Africa* [pdf], Market Brief, 20 April 2011, Abidjan: AfDB <www.afdb.org/fileadmin/ uploads/afdb/Documents/Publications/The%20 Middle%20of%20the%20Pyramid_The%20Middle%20of%20the%20 Pyramid.pdf> [accessed 4 May 2014].

Angelucci, F., Balié, J., Gourichon, H., Mas Aparisi, A. and Witwer, M. (2013) *Monitoring and Analysing Food and Agricultural Policies in Africa: Synthesis Report 2013* [pdf], MAFAP Synthesis Report Series, Rome: FAO <www.fao. org/docrep/019/i3513e/i3513e.pdf> [accessed 9 May 2015].

Barrett, C.B. (2008) 'Smallholder market participation: concepts and evidence from eastern and southern Africa', *Food Policy* 33(4): 299–317 <http://dx. doi.org/10.1016/j. foodpol.2007.10.005>.

Campbell, R. (2010) *Implementation Best Practices for Value Chain Development Projects*, MicroREPORT #167, September 2010, Washington, DC: USAID.

Chandy, L., Ledlie, N. and Penciakova, V. (2013) *The Final Countdown: Prospects for Ending Extreme Poverty by 2030* [pdf], Policy Paper 2013-04, Washington, DC: The Brookings Institution <www. brookings.edu/~/media/research/ files/reports/2013/04/ending%20extreme%20poverty%20   chandy/the_ final_countdown.pdf> [accessed 4 May 2014].

Chang, H.-J. (2009) 'Rethinking public policy in agriculture: lessons from history, distant and recent', *Journal of Peasant Studies* 36: 3,477–515 <http:// dx.doi.org/10.1080/03066150903142741>.

Donovan, J., Franzel, S., Cunha, M., Gyau, A. and Mithöfer, D. (2015) 'Guides for value chain development: a comparative review', *Journal of Agribusiness in Developing and Emerging Economies* 5(1): 2–23 <http://dx.doi.org/10.1108/JADEE-07-2013-0025>.

Fermont, A.M., van Asten P.J.A. and Giller, K.E. (2008) 'Increasing land pressure in East Africa: the changing role of cassava and consequences for sustainability of farming systems', *Agriculture, Ecosystems and Environment* 128: 239–50 <http://dx.doi.org/10.1016/j.agee.2008.06.009>.

Francesconi, G.N. and Wouterse, F. (2011) *The Renewed Case for Farmers' Cooperatives: Diagnostics and Implications from Ghana* [pdf], IFPRI Discussion Paper 01129, Washington, DC: International Food Policy Research Institute <www.ifpri.org/sites/default/files/publications/ifpridp01129.pdf> [accessed 4 May 2014].

Griffiths, J. (2012) *'Leveraging' Private Sector Finance: How Does it Work and What are the Risks?* [pdf], London: Bretton Woods Project <www.brettonwoodsproject.org/wp-content/ uploads/2013/10/leveraging.pdf> [accessed 2 June 2015].

Hartmann, A. and Linn, J. (2008) *Scaling Up: A Framework and Lessons for Development Effectiveness from Literature and Practice* [pdf], Wolfensohn Center for Development Working Paper 5, Washington, DC: Brookings Institution <www.brookings.edu/~/media/research/files/ papers/2008/10/scaling%20up%20aid%20linn/10_scaling_up_aid_linn.pdf> [accessed 4 May 2014].

Hartmann, A., Kharas, H., Kohl, R., Linn, J., Massler, B. and Sourang, C. (2013) *Scaling up Programs for the Rural Poor: IFAD's Experience, Lessons and Prospects (Phase 2)* [pdf], Global Economy & Development Working Paper 54, Washington, DC: Brookings Institution <www.brookings. edu/~/media/research/files/papers/2013/1/ifad%20rural%20poor%20kharas%20linn/ifad%20 rural%20poor%20kharas%20linn.pdf> [accessed 4 May 2014].

Hazell, P. and Poulton, C. (2007) 'Experiences with commercial agriculture', case study on food staples, All-Africa Review of Competitive Commercial Agriculture in sub-Saharan Africa Study, Rome: FAO; Washington, DC: World Bank.

International Fund for Agricultural Development, Food and Agriculture Organization of the United Nations (IFAD/FAO) (2005) 'A Review of Cassava in Africa with Country Case Studies on Nigeria, Ghana, the United Republic of Tanzania, Uganda and Benin', in: *Proceedings of the Validation Forum on the Global Cassava Development Strategy*, volume 2, Rome: IFAD/FAO <ftp:// ftp.fao.org/docrep/fao/009/a0154e/A0154E00.pdf> [accessed 9 May 2015].

International Institute of Rural Reconstruction (IIRR) (2000) *Going to Scale: Can We Bring More Benefits to More People More Quickly?* Conference highlights 10–14 April, Philippines: IIRR.

Linn, J.F. (2012) 'Overview: pathways, drivers and spaces', in J.F. Linn (ed.), *Scaling up in Agriculture, Rural development and Nutrition* [pdf], IFPRI 2020 vision, Washington, DC: IFPRI <http://ebrary.ifpri.org/utils/getfile/collection/p15738coll2/id/126977/filename/127188.pdf> [accessed 9 may 2015].

Miller, C. (2011) *Agricultural Value Chain Finance Strategy and Design* [pdf], Technical Note, Rome: Food and Agriculture organization of the United Nations <www.ruralfinance.org/ fileadmin/templates/rflc/documents/AgVCF_Tech_note_pdf.pdf> [accessed 9 may 2015].

Nweke, F. (2004) *New Challenges in the Cassava Transformation in Nigeria and Ghana*, EPTD Discussion Paper 118, Washington, DC: International Food Policy Research Institute.

Poulton, C. and Macartney, J. (2012) 'Can public–private partnerships leverage private investment in agricultural value chains in Africa? A preliminary review', *World Development* 40(1): 96–109 <http://dx.doi.org/10.1016/j.worlddev.2011.05.017>.

Poulton, C., Dorward, A. and Kydd, J. (2010) 'The future of small farms: new directions for services, institutions, and intermediation', *World Development* 38(10): 1413–28 <http://dx.doi. org/10.1016/j.worlddev.2009.06.009>.

Prowse, M. (2012) *Contract Farming in Developing Countries: A Review*, A savoir 12, paris: Agence Française de Développement (AFD).

Rosenthal, D.M. and Ort, D.R. (2012) 'Examining cassava's potential to enhance food security under climate change', *Tropical Plant Biology* 5(1): 30–8 <http://dx.doi.org/10.1007/ s12042-011-9086-1>.

Seville, D., Buxton, A. and Vorley, B. (2010) *Under What Conditions are Value Chains Effective Tools for Pro-Poor Development?* Sustainable Food Lab, report prepared for the Ford Foundation, Hartland, VT, London: IIED.

Smith, A.M. (2009) 'Fair trade, diversification and structural change: towards a broader theoretical framework of analysis', *Oxford Development Studies* 37(4): 457–78 <http://dx.doi. org/10.1080/13600810903305208>.

Ton, G. (2010) *Resolving the Challenges of Collective Marketing. Incentive Structures that Reduce the Tensions between Members and their Group* [pdf], Policy Brief no. 4, Wageningen: LEI Wageningen ur <www.esfim.org/wp-content/uploads/esFim-research-Brief-n04-collective-marketing.pdf> [accessed 9 may 2015].

United Nations, Department of Economic and Social Affairs, Population Division (2013) *World Population Prospects: The 2012 Revision*, CD-ROM edition, New York: UNDESA.

Vorley, B., Cotula, L. and Chan, M.-K. (2012) *Tipping the Balance: Policies to Shape Agricultural Investments and Markets in Favour of Small-scale Farmers* [online], London: IIED/Oxford: Oxfam <http://policy-practice.oxfam.org.uk/publications/tipping-the-balance-policies-to-shape-agricultural-investments-and-markets-in-f-254551> [accessed 9 may 2015].

Westby, A. (2002) 'cassava utilization, storage and small-scale processing', in R.J. Hillocks and A. Belloti (eds), *Cassava Biology, Production and Utilization*, Wallingford, UK: CABI.

Wiggins, S. and Keats, S. (2013) *Leaping and Learning: Linking Smallholders to Markets in Africa*, London: Agriculture for Impact, Imperial College and Overseas Development Institute.

Wiggins, S. and Keats, S. (2014) *Smallholder Engagement with the Private Sector* [pdf], Economic and Private Sector Professional Evidence and Applied Knowledge Services, london: ODI <www. value-chains.org/dyn/bds/docs/868/TopicGuideonSmallholderEngagementwithprivatesecto.pdf> [accessed 9 may 2015].

About the author

Richard Lamboll (r.i.lamboll@gre.ac.uk), Principal Researcher.
Valerie Nelson, Reader in Rural Development.
Adrienne Martin, Director of Programme Development.
Louise Abayomi, Senior Research Fellow, Postharvest.

Andrew Graffham, Principal Scientist.

Rory Hillocks, Principal Scientist.

Andrew Westby, Director at the Natural Resources Institute, University of Greenwich, Chatham, UK.

Helena Posthumus, Senior advisor at KIT Royal Tropical Institute, Amsterdam, the Netherlands.

Kolawole Adebayo, Professor of Rural Development Communication.

Lateef Sanni, Professor of Food Science and Technology, Federal University of Agriculture, Abeokuta, Nigeria.

Francis Alacho, Country Manager, C:AVA, African Innovations Institute, Kampala, Uganda.

Nanam Dziedzoave, Director, Council for Scientific and Industrial Research-Food Research Institute, Accra, Ghana.

Grace Mahende, Country Manager, C:AVA, Tanzanian Food and Nutrition Centre, Dar es Salaam, Tanzania.

Vito Sandifolo, Country Manager, C:AVA, Chancellor College, the University of Malawi, Zomba, Malawi.

CHAPTER 16

Gender mainstreaming in value chain development: Experience with Gender Action Learning System in Uganda

Linda Mayoux

Abstract

There is an emerging consensus that promoting gender justice in value chain development is not only a rights issue for women, but makes 'business sense' for households, enterprises, and ultimately the national economy. This chapter discusses experiences using a community-led methodology, Gender Action Learning System (GALS), with producers and traders of coffee, maize, fruits (avocados, pineapples, and passion fruit), and beans in Kasese District, Western Uganda. This community-led value chain development methodology has brought about profound changes for significant numbers of people in a relatively short period of time, on sensitive and potentially conflictual issues such as gender-based violence and land ownership as well as decision-making, division of labour, and women's access to health and education. These changes have taken place with the full support of many men who have become enthusiastic promoters of gender equality as part of their own vision of happiness and social justice. Addressing gender inequalities at all levels of the chain forms a 'win–win strategy' which has increased incomes and contributed to upgrading whole value chains and developing the local economy.

Keywords: Gender Action Learning System, Uganda, value chain development, gender inequality

The Convention on the elimination of All Forms of Discrimination Against Women (CEDAW) was adopted by the UN General Assembly in 1979 and by 2010 had been ratified by 186 out of 193 countries. CEDAW states that, like men, women have the right to freedom from violence and freedom of movement; equal rights in decisionmaking and to own property; the right to freedom of thought and association; to work, rest and leisure; and to an adequate standard of health and education. Most national governments have gender policies, strategies, and legislation based on some variant of CEDAW. Most development agencies have an official commitment to gender equality and gender mainstreaming across their other interventions as part of their

http://dx.doi.org/10.3362/9781788530576.016

mandate. Many have position papers on gender and the key importance of women's empowerment in economic growth and/or poverty reduction.

There is an extensive body of research by World Bank, IFPRI, and others, which shows that gender inequalities are a key constraint on economic growth and food security, and a key cause of poverty, not only for women themselves, but also for their families and communities (Farnworth and Ragasa, 2008; Mayoux and Mackie, 2009). Women's importance in supplying national and international markets with both traditional and high-value products such as textiles, coffee, and cocoa has increased significantly over the past few decades. However, gender inequalities and discrimination at all levels mean that women are marginalized or excluded from the more profitable agricultural and manufacturing chains and/or the profitable parts of these chains. Women-owned businesses face many more constraints than those of men, and receive fewer financial and non-financial services (see Farnworth and Ragasa, 2008; Mayoux and Mackie, 2009; and the many studies of women's enterprise commissioned for ILO's WEDGE programme, which can be found on www.ilo.org). Gender inequalities in control of productive assets, such as land, mean that even where women do the majority of the work in cultivation they are generally invisible as 'helpers' of 'male farmers'. Women rarely control household income, particularly from crops marketed by men, even where production is dependent on women's unpaid role in cultivation and care work.

Despite the importance of women in most value chains and official commitments to gender mainstreaming, 'gender' continues to be widely seen as a sideline 'women's issue' in most value chain development – an additional 'problem' on top of all the other competing objectives and priorities in economic development interventions (environment, HIV/AIDS, etc.). Gender analysis remains weak in most 'mainstream' livelihood, market, and value chain analyses, and largely ignored in manuals and capacity building (Farnworth and Ragasa, 2008; Solidaridad, 2009). As a result, women are not only often excluded from value chain development (VCD) interventions, but gender inequalities may actually increase, exacerbating the unacceptably high gender disparities on all human development and rights indicators.

This is the case even in interventions which claim to be 'ethical', such as cooperative development, fairtrade, and organic farming (see, for example, Farnworth and Ragasa, 2008; Solidaridad, 2009). Women are assumed to automatically benefit from interventions targeting 'household heads' – assumed in turn to be any man present. Requirements for traceability in supply chains generally involve documenting assets in men's names, which further consolidates their rights, and may even undermine food security for the household. The change to organic cultivation often increases women's labour more than that of men without increasing women's control of income or assets. Women's incomes may even decrease as they, already overworked, spend less time on their own economic activities because they are unable to reduce the time spent on food crops (Bolwig and Odeke, 2007). In households involved in fairtrade, men often take over areas of decision-making in production and household expenditure that formerly were a woman's domain (Solidaridad, 2009). Women traders may be displaced as markets are developed in large urban centres and for export – as for example in markets for fruits such as mangoes and green leafy vegetables in Uganda (Farnworth and Ragasa, 2008). Government regulations in Côte d'Ivoire on cooperativization in the cocoa industry have made participation by women's groups very difficult, further marginalizing women coffee producers (Solidaridad, 2009).

There have been some notable recent innovations:

- The development of women's entrepreneurship in industries dominated by women, which has been promoted through interventions such as ILO's Growth-oriented Women Entrepreneurs' project and MEDA's work with women entrepreneurs in Pakistan supported by USAID.
- The establishment of women's cooperatives in economic activities dominated by women. Some chains where women have benefited and improved their position on a large scale are Café Femenino and Las Hermanas coffee cooperatives in Latin America (Melendez, 2008), shea nut production in Mali, and cashew nut production in Mozambique (KIT et al., 2006).
- Household mentoring approaches that work with men and women to understand the benefits of addressing gender inequalities in work and decision-making in order to increase household incomes, such as ACDI/ VOCA's 'Farming is a Family Business' and IFAD's District Livelihoods Support Programme (Farnworth, 2012).
- Toolkits and resources for mainstreaming gender in value chain analysis and market development produced by USAID, ILO, Agri-ProFocus, and the M4P Hub.

Updated reports and resources on these initiatives can be found on the Gender in Value Chain Agri-ProFocus Learning Network (see Website resources at the end of the chapter).

This chapter discusses experience using the Gender Action Learning System (GALS), which can be used on its own or integrated with any of the above to increase inclusion, empowerment, and sustainability.

Gender Action Learning System: overview of the process

GALS is a flexible but structured community-led empowerment methodology which works with both women and men to help them gain more control over their lives. It is different from many other participatory and gender methodologies in that it starts with women and men as individuals rather than households or communities. It develops skills in life and livelihood planning as the basis for cooperation within households, community collective action, and gender advocacy. After an initial 'catalysing intervention' of 1–2 years it becomes organizationally and financially sustainable through peer dissemination and integration into other interventions and decision-making processes.

GALS originated in a generic methodology: Participatory Action Learning System (PALS), developed from 2002 by the author for livelihood development and participatory impact assessment. From 2004, PALS tools were used for gender analysis and gender planning in India, Pakistan, Sudan, and Kenya. The resources and manuals for this earlier work can be found on the WEMAN Resources website. Funding for PALS as a livelihoods and participatory impact assessment methodology came from Hivos, Trickle-Up US, and Kabarole Research Centre (KRC) in Western Uganda in 2002, and DFID's Enterprise Development Information Assessment Information Service (EDIAIS) (Mayoux, 2006). Adaptation for gender planning was mostly funded by Southern NGOs: ANANDI in India, Learning for Empowerment Against Poverty (LEAP) in Sudan, and Aga Khan Foundation for work with Pakistan Microfinance Network. PALS tools were also used in gender training with ILO's GOWE project (Mayoux and Mackie, 2009).

The systematization of this experience as GALS to promote women's rights in CEDAW started in December 2007, funded under Oxfam Novib's Women's Employment Mainstreaming and Networking (WEMAN) programme. GALS was then adapted specifically for mainstreaming gender justice in value chain development from August 2009 as part of a joint IFAD and Oxfam Novib (ON) pilot project in Uganda, focusing on coffee, maize, fruits, and beans.

This paper focuses on the experience of two organizations whose farmer members (called entrepreneurs) and staff have been at the forefront of development of the PALS livelihoods methodology since 2004/05 and lead partners in WEMAN since 2007, although most of the widespread changes discussed here date from the VCD project in August 2009.

Bukonzo Joint Cooperative Microfinance (BJ) is a successful member-managed cooperative with a well-established savings and credit programme, and profitable coffee marketing. As part of the IFAD/ON value chain project it focused on coffee and maize chains. In July 2012 BJ had 3,237 members: 2,399 women and 838 men, all of whom were using GALS in some form. BJ has organizational regulations on gender balance in senior as well as other positions on the staff and the member board. It also gives preferential conditions to women members in share dividends and savings and credit. Gender awareness is a key consideration in staff recruitment and is under constant review by the member board, but there is no written gender policy or gender-focused staff.

Green Home Women's Development Association (GH) is a local community-based organization (CBO) with neither an effective microfinance nor marketing organization. In the IFAD/ON project, GH focused on fruits and beans value chains. In 2009 GH had around 1,000 members of whom the majority were women. Gender issues were prominent in organizational documents and at one point there was a written gender policy in English. But most senior staff were men and member involvement in the board was minimal. By the time of writing in 2012 GH was in the process of trying to reinvent itself in the face of (as yet unproven) allegations of mismanagement and malpractice by some senior management and staff. A core of 100 members were in the process of setting up a new organization, New Home Network (NHN), and expanding membership using the GALS methodology.

The methodology, as it was developed and implemented in the organizations discussed here, is summarized in Box 16.1, and described in detail elsewhere (Mayoux et al., 2011). However, the precise way in which each stage is conducted and the timing of moving from one stage to the next depends on the characteristics of the particular value chain concerned, particularly the length of the chain, types of power relations involved, the amount of knowledge at different levels, and the purpose of the particular intervention.

The first stage of the process is scoping the chains along with the use of adapted value chain mapping tools to identify key stake-holders and key priority starting points based on a gender analysis of existing information. In BJ and GH, value chains were selected through existing meetings with entrepreneur members because of significance in terms of income (coffee, maize, and some fruits), numbers of farmers (coffee and beans), and/or potential for profitable upscaling (maize). BJ and the process consultants already had considerable experience with these chains through other work and their clear mandate was to promote their members within these chains. The preliminary mapping was therefore done very quickly through informal meetings with a few key people before moving on to the more participatory and in-depth action learning in Stage 2.

Stage 2 is a longer process with different stakeholder groups who are then brought together to identify win–win strategies in Stage 3. The initial focus is on the most vulnerable stakeholders, particularly women. The aim from the very first session is for individuals to identify immediate strategies which can bring about tangible positive improvements in their lives and livelihoods, to start progress towards their vision. The individual-level tools are also designed to identify immediate steps to address inefficiencies and unnecessary unhappiness caused by gender inequality – for men as well as women. In BJ and GH those trained in initial workshops learned and applied the GALS methodology over a period of about six months for the chain/s in which they were most involved. They then used the same tools to develop strategies in other value chains where they saw potential for profitable livelihood diversification in production and/or trade. Stage 2 involved the range of local chain stakeholders from the beginning because members already knew these people as members of the same families and communities. In the case of coffee, Bukonzo Joint had already made contact with traders up the chain as they were setting up the marketing cooperative. Relationships were characterized by lack of trust and poor communication, and exclusion of women from more profitable activities and trading relationships. This meant that it was easier to bring stakeholders together and discuss common interests in removing misunderstandings and inefficiencies than might initially be the case in other more conflictual chains.

Box 16.1. Overview of the GALS value chain process

Gender justice vision

A world where women and men are able to realize their full potential as economic, social, and political actors, free from all gender discrimination, for empowerment of themselves, their families, their communities, and global humankind.

Approach to pro-poor value chain development

Value chain upgrading to improve incomes for those most vulnerable within the value chain through improvements in quality and/or productivity and/or relations with others in the chain.

Livelihood diversification for those most vulnerable in the chain to improve negotiating power and, if necessary, to enable them to leave the chain.

Focus on underlying gender inequalities in access to power and resources at all levels which constitute discrimination and violation of women's human rights as well as leading to inefficiencies in household livelihoods at all levels of the value chain.

GALS stages and tools

Stage 1: Preliminary scoping and mapping to select the value chains, and then for each chain to map the main chain activities, stakeholders, value distribution, governance, and gender inequalities in all these based on existing knowledge and secondary source material.

Stage 2: Participatory action research with vulnerable stakeholder groups and, where feasible, more powerful stakeholders, to identify poverty and gender issues at each level, identify immediate change strategies and strengthen collaboration and peer sharing.
Tool 1: Gender balance tree (individual/collective)
Tool 2: Market map (individual/collective)
Tool 3: Income challenge action tree (individual/collective)
Tool 4: Gender challenge action tree (individual/collective)
Tool 5: Individual livelihood and gender road journeys with monitoring calendar
Tool 6: Stakeholder collective road journeys

Stage 3: Identification, planning, and negotiation of multi-stakeholder win–win strategies through value chain multi-stakeholder events, resulting in a multi-stakeholder strategic plan towards a vision of common interests.
Tool 7: Multi-stakeholder win–win tree or diamond
Tool 8: Multi-stakeholder win–win road journey

Stage 4: Sustainable action learning process through peer upscaling and integration in other interventions. This includes monitoring change through integration of individual and group level learning into management information systems as the basis for policy advocacy and establishment of participatory planning in annual general meetings, value chain fairs, and local government.

The core of the upscaling process in Stages 2 and 3 is voluntary peer training within families and existing support networks – those receiving training have a personal interest in helping. This includes integration into group meetings and any supply chain training by traders. In both BJ and GH, outreach targets through peer training were consistently exceeded. Many members had trained other members in their households and communities so, although outreach to organization members has been tracked, total outreach is much greater, but not known. The main role for organization staff is support for emerging collective actions on gender issues such as land ownership and gender-based violence, and assigning value to the process through aggregation and dissemination of monitoring information for advocacy. This involves making links as soon as possible with local leaders, local government, and other powerful chain actors in order to promote communication and speed up the development of win–win strategies between stakeholders.

GALS is self-monitoring from individual level up to organization level as an ongoing learning and reflection process. (A description of the GALS information system can be found in Mayoux, 2012a, b and forthcoming.) Capacity-building and planning workshops are structured to produce reliable quantitative as well as qualitative information for all participants on context, strategies, and changes. Baseline information is collected on the individual diagrams for later aggregation and analysis. Further information on issues where respondents are likely to know and verify information is collected retrospectively. The information is then tracked over time in ways most useful for the empowerment process at individual and group levels. Information from a number of sources is combined in this paper:

- Quantitative and qualitative impact information in Bukonzo Joint on women's land ownership, division of labour, and coffee quality, collected since 2009 and now regularly collected for over 3,500 members and reported back at board meetings as part of their routine planning process.
- Quantified diagram outputs and qualitative information on gender relations and strategies from a series of 10 stakeholder capacity-building and planning workshops in 2009–2010.
- A participatory survey in BJ in February 2010 as part of the peer capacity-building collected information on literacy levels and changes in land-holding for 204 men and 296 women.
- Participatory pictorial surveys of changes in income, livelihood diversification, and peer training conducted for 476 participants in the four multi-stakeholder meetings in September 2010.
- Interviews conducted by BJ in 2011 for 2,717 households as part of the organic and fairtrade certification processes.
- Qualitative information on the above from the author's own field notes and reports to Oxfam Novib and IFAD (Reemer and Oxfam Novib, 2011).
- Qualitative information from an eight-day qualitative external study of BJ for Oxfam Novib and GIZ in October 2011 (Farnworth and Akamandisa, 2011). (As is often the case with short studies of this type, the authors missed some important aspects of implementation in Bukonzo Joint. It also conflates the potential of the GALS methodology per se with the

ways in which practical implementation was constrained by lack of capital and external funding for the complementary microfinance and coffee marketing. As discussed in more detail elsewhere (Mayoux, forthcoming) these errors make some of the conclusions and recommendations unreliable.)

- Qualitative and quantitative research using GALS tools with GH as well as BJ members in July 2012.

Undoubtedly, much of the information is incomplete and many unanswered questions remain. In what follows, the author analyses the available information in the light of her contextual understanding and in-depth qualitative questioning alongside her long-term support role. The A4 diaries and quantified workshop outputs provide the basis for more rigorous qualitative and quantitative research to be conducted by the organization or external agencies if and when funds are available for such a study.

Changing gender inequalities makes business sense

Participatory analysis with men as well as women using GALS tools at the initial stakeholder workshops in 2009 identified a clear gender division of tasks, roles, and power. Use of the gender balance tree to analyse work input and expenditures highlighted the conclusion that women did the majority of cultivation work in all crops. In crops such as beans women did all the work apart from preparing land. In coffee-producing households women did about 70 per cent of the main cultivation work and processing tasks such as hulling, alongside cultivation of food crops and unpaid household work.

In about 70 per cent of households, men had migrated to town in search of work. Men were typically only involved in very occasional heavy tasks, coming back to harvest and market the coffee beans when they wanted cash. They 'took' any coffee beans from the trees, drying them on the ground or stored in a sack around the house, sold the them to local buyers (near bars), and used the money for their own purposes (often alcohol or women in town). Seventy per cent of 495 men, followed up through individual research at the time of capacity-building, openly admitted to taking all the money from coffee production, and even stealing their wives' money, wasting much of this on drink and other women. Polygamy (59 per cent of men interviewed in 2009) increased the level of dependency on increasingly fragmented plots of land, and also reduced men's income and labour input into any one household. There was a high level of marital instability, domestic violence (40 per cent of 887 men interviewed), male alcoholism (58 per cent), and drug addiction. In some households, men's expenditure on alcohol in one month was equal to the costs of the school fees for a term.

Women had no power over decision-making because of their economic and social dependence on men and their vulnerable situations. Typically women drew themselves kneeling down in front of their husbands to hand over all their money. Women had the main responsibility for their children and making sure that there was food for the family, including the husband when he was there. This limited their time and mobility to earn an income. When children (or other members of the extended family) were sick, women often had to take care and pay for hospital bills or medicines. Women took the main interest in education for their children and could not rely on their husbands to pay the school fees. Relations between co-wives were often very competitive because husbands typically favoured one wife over the other. One wife might work more hours but the husband would tell the other wife to pick the coffee and sell it to buy a nice dress and go to the hairdresser. This instability meant women were also keen to use any means they could to retain control of crops or cash for healthcare and education as well as food.

The market maps showed how the women's role varied between the different crops. In fruits and beans, women were involved in marketing, especially from their homes, along the road, and in village markets. In some households, the men took the fruit and/or beans to market or sold them to male middlemen, and shopkeepers (mostly male) came from neighbouring trading centres to buy fruits from the village. Shops for beans and groundnuts were often owned by women. In coffee, all traders were men except very small-scale women barter-traders, because women had insufficient capital. Their ability to move up the trading chain was seriously constrained by their lack of control over income from the coffee, and lack of savings and access to credit because they did not own land. They also had limited time to spend away from the household to seek out the best prices.

Participatory analysis using the increasing incomes challenge action tree concluded that gender inequalities were not only a problem for women, but a key cause of low productivity, low quality, and low prices at the farm level. In the case of coffee, unripe beans or beans which were not fully processed, or still wet, were frequently sold by both husband and wife even though they fetched a lower price, in order to prevent the other from taking it. Men took any coffee they could when they wanted money – including unripe and unprocessed coffee – before women were able to sell it. Men sold non-harvested coffee in advance, and even the coffee flowers before beans were formed, in order to get cash. Much of the cash was spent in bars conveniently located next to the trader shops. In some cases they did not even tell their wives and the trader simply came and took the coffee. Women, who did most of the work, had little power over decision-making or investment in production or efficient processing such as hulling. Much of the coffee was dried in the dust on the ground leading to mixing with impurities which further reduced the quality. Women said that because their benefits from the work or any investments were limited, their motivation to produce/pick/process good quality coffee was small.

Gender inequalities can be changed

The main aim of the GALS process is gender justice and women's human rights as stated in CEDAW, rather than improved quality or productivity of crops per se. As in other methodologies, such as the household approaches of

IFAD and ACDI/VOCA, enabling women and men to analyse clearly the negative business consequences of gender inequalities for themselves was a key factor in enlisting broad stakeholder support for a gender justice process. The combination of gender analysis with value chain development promotes the involvement of men as well as women, and this can lead to very significant changes in dimensions of gender inequality which are often considered too 'culturally embedded' or personally sensitive or conflictual to address.

Significant reductions in gender-based violence and increases in women's participation in many areas of decision-making are reported in member diaries, workshop presentations, and testimonies as well as external studies (Farnworth and Akamandisa, 2011). Both women and men now typically draw themselves sitting on an equal level at a table making decisions instead of the earlier images of women kneeling in front of men and handing them all the money. There have been significant reductions in male alcoholism with men now having their own savings or contributing to those of women. Interactive theatre role plays, where couples explore the most significant changes to their relationship as a result of GALS, highlight a change from conflict and mistrust to love and affection.

There have been significant changes in division of labour. These changes have only been monitored for Bukonzo Joint, but anecdotal evidence suggests they have also occurred for members of Green Home. Of 887 men interviewed by BJ in 2009, 55 per cent thought men should not help their wives because of culture. By June 2012, out of 3,568 members and non-members using GALS (in the same 8 out of 13 parishes), 40 per cent (1,435) reported working together across the full range of productive and reproductive tasks, 29 per cent (1,041) reported sharing at least three tasks which had not happened before, and 30 per cent (1,092) were unchanged. These percentages are similar to those in 2011 for 2,717 households interviewed as part of the certification process, indicating a possible levelling off of impact once the receptive households have changed. It may also be that women overstate some changes, and men understate changes in work allocation (Farnworth and Akamandisa, 2011).

What is distinctive about GALS is its ability to bring about very tangible changes in more sensitive and/or conflictual areas such as land ownership. As noted above, the fact that women did not own land was identified early in the GALS VCD process as a cause of family disunity and hence poor quality coffee. In short-term low investment crops, such as beans, maize, and some fruits, land ownership was less of an issue because women could hire in land and thereby have more control over the proceeds. But in all households, because men owned or controlled the land and had paid a dowry of 12 goats to the woman's father, they considered themselves entitled to control any money in the household and decide how much work they want to put into what activities. Increasing women's ownership and control of land was therefore identified as a high priority, particularly by women.

However, land ownership is a complex issue with differences between clan land (about 80 per cent land) which is governed, but not owned, by male family elders, and land registered to individuals through customary or formal legal arrangements or purchase (see detailed discussion in Farnworth and Akamandisa, 2011). There are also differences in a woman's entitlement to her husband's property depending on religion and type of marriage, with the highest status and entitlement for the minority of women having a church or civil marriage, where in theory women have an equal right to all their husband's property from the day of marriage. In other cases, women have customary access to land for cultivation through their relations with men, who subdivide their plots between wives. On divorce, in theory, women can go back to cultivate land belonging to their parents, though some remain on their husband's property, particularly if many children are involved. There is increasingly intense pressure on land, with rapid population growth creating a trend to formally register plots from clan land as government leases (encouraged by the government). But there is continuing resistance from many clan elders to the fragmentation of clan land as it is supposed to be a safety net for future spouses and generations. They insist that their children should buy their own land rather than taking family land. Local leaders and traders made frequent reference to cultural norms and also to fears that if women could get land from their husbands in their own right, this would lead them into serial marriages with men just to get more land.

This already complex set of rights is further complicated by the fact that each of the land arrangements is interpreted in different ways by local land officials, and actual implementation is very varied and subject to various forms of corruption. Although regulations state that there must be at least two women on local land boards, many of the male land officials were of the (incorrect) opinion that it was illegal for women's names to go on any land agreements, despite the fact they were supposed to have had gender training. Local land boards have no records of women owning land before the start of GALS in 2009, and land officers said that before the lobbying by BJ they had not thought of this. Women owned land in only two households out of 419 interviewed by BJ at the beginning of the GALS process in 2009. A number of women had purchased land with loans from GH or BJ, but the land had been registered in the man's name.

As a result of the GALS process, combined with other interlinked strategies by BJ, there have been significant increases in women's land ownership in the area. Firstly, use of the GALS challenge action trees, for individual and collective analysis of the potential benefits of joint ownership of land by men as well as women, started the change in attitudes and behaviour at the household level for a significant number of lead households. Secondly, sustained lobbying of the local authorities and clan elders by staff and members of Bukonzo Joint through the thematic meetings convinced members of the local land board that change was desirable – and even led to dismissal of members of the board judged to be ineffective. Thirdly, in 2011 as part of the fairtrade certification process, BJ decided to encourage the inclusion of women's names on certification documents – not a legally binding document but as a form of awareness-raising to boost the more formal registration process. The passing of the long-awaited Domestic Relations Act in late 2011 may have also boosted the process with some people, though at the time of writing there was very little publicity for the Act in this area, the land official still had no copies, and there had still not been any training for land officials in what the Act means.

By July 2012 out of a total of 3,057 members monitored by BJ, 102 had fully signed joint or individual women's land agreements; and 1,362 had applications in process which had been signed at the local level or by family elders. This covered all members and some non-members reached by GALS in 8 out of 12 parishes covered by BJ. At the time of writing the other four were due to report. So a total of 1,464 or 48 per cent of households had some form of document on women's or joint ownership of land. Joint ownership was further encouraged as part of a certification process in which out of 2,717 households visited, 2,068 had signed joint certification documents and 66 women had individual ownership – a total of 76 per cent. The process was also dynamic with members seeking new solutions where they encountered resistance. For example, in Kanyatsi parish, members discovered that many of them had problems obtaining a land lease. If they applied individually it was difficult to deal with the local government and they had to pay UGS180,000 (US$70) for any area of land, because of costs related to documents, forms, processing time, etc. They decided to apply for the land lease as a group (10 people) and negotiated with the local government. In the end they paid only UGS67,000 ($26) each. In Green Home there were also significant changes, and impact trees used in June 2012 indicated that in one group, six out of 24 members had signed land agreements following GALS, one had already signed at an earlier sensitization meeting, and the others were on family land.

Surprisingly these changes have received increasing support from men. The GALS diagrams and testimonies of men provide evidence of why they have changed and men assert that they are much happier now. Many men are also at the forefront of working with other men to change, having set up men's groups to address issues of alcoholism. Male elders and members of the local land boards are now promoting joint registration on land agreements.

Win–win strategies

A key part of the GALS value chain strategy is to work with more powerful stakeholders and traders up the chain. Gender justice in VCD requires strategies beyond the household level to deal with discrimination within markets, value chains, and support institutions. This discrimination was most evident in the coffee value chain where both women producers and traders were discriminated against in the market, and larger coffee traders from Kasese town or Kampala would not deal with women. Even if women had good quality coffee, they depended on the male village traders for the marketing to Kasese traders, who gave them lower prices for the reasons outlined above. Because the land belonged to their husbands, women were not eligible to join cooperatives (apart from BJ) or receive bank credit and were not targeted in technical training. They had also been excluded from certification processes in the area.

Rather than seeking to displace traders (male or female), the GALS process aims to harness their skills, energies, and resources to develop the markets and chains. From this process it is expected that the traders will themselves gain, and thus be motivated to continue. But through increased demand and competition, coupled with removal of discrimination, benefits will go disproportionately to those most vulnerable in the chain – in this case women producers. As noted above, in all four value chains, local traders, trade associations, and traders from Kasese town were involved in the GALS process very early on.

Men and women traders have voluntarily given up their time to attend the GALS trainings. It quickly became clear from the initial capacity-building workshops with traders that gender inequalities were fundamental to inefficiencies affecting the quality of supply not only in their supplier households, but also in their own households and businesses. In the case of coffee traders, access to capital to buy coffee and time to negotiate with buyers up the chain are necessary to get the best prices and are the main determinants of income. Small traders buy coffee with credit from traders higher up the chain. Much of the reason why they sold bad quality coffee and could not earn so much was because they did not have sufficient savings to invest and buy quality coffee in bulk. In order to bulk up the coffee they mixed in impurities, which further added to the bad reputation and low market price of coffee from this area on global markets. The other issue was poor measuring scales, which meant small traders were often cheated. But they also agreed that decreasing their own expenditure on alcohol (in some cases 10 bottles a day costing UGS2,000 each ($0.78)) would go a long way to boosting the necessary savings to get them out of the cycle of debt to middlemen higher up the chain, and to invest in more reliable weighing equipment and better storage. Between initial workshops in September 2009 and follow-up workshops in December that year, significant changes had occurred in the households of all 14 traders attending the workshop. Some examples are given in Box 16.2, but these are not unique. All the traders agreed that they would like more gender training, and also business training for their wives so that they could do business together and save to improve their income.

Working with multiple stakeholders has not only benefited participants in the process, but has also led to improvements in the local economy. Before the GALS value chain process, the quality of coffee and other products in the Bukonzo area was extremely low and could only command low prices on the market, and productivity was also low. As a result of combined work to reduce the gender-based inefficiencies in decision-making, work allocation, and expenditures at the household level through GALS and the related promotion of technical improvements and Fairtrade linkages, Bukonzo Joint coffee is now ranked third in Uganda for unwashed coffee (druga). Kampala traders

---

Box 16.2. Some examples of changes in gender relations in coffee trader households

Trader A has three wives, four gardens, and two commercial premises. Before the GALS workshop he bought and did everything without consulting any of his wives. After the workshop he called a meeting with his wives and other clan members, and they made a family agreement that from that time on they would all be sharing. He signed an agreement for one plot of land for each of two wives, and started to purchase a plot for the third wife. He said he used to treat his wives like children, like people who can't think. Now it is much better for him. He feels he has much more freedom. Before he had responsibility for everything and his wives would complain. Now they have their own responsibilities and trust. If there is no money, they understand. He also thinks it is a mistake not to put a wife's name on the land agreements because if he dies then not only his wife, but also his children will suffer because his brothers will take the land.

Trader B did not allow his wife to pick or handle coffee before the September workshop, only cassava, beans, and other food crops. He controlled all the money and spent part of it himself in town. After the workshop he discussed with his wife how to work together. They both take the coffee to the store and his wife now knows exactly how much they have. Ninety per cent of the income is now with her, he no longer spends so much in town, and they have been able to buy a goat (but in his name).

---

are now coming direct to farmers, and prices for farmers have significantly increased relative to world coffee prices. In 2012 BJ was looking to diversify its marketing strategy to include maize and possibly other value chains alongside its successful strategy for exporting Fairtrade and certified organic coffee, having succeeded in combining funding from a range of sources to purchase and install all the coffee-processing equipment planned in the organizational road journey at the beginning of the GALS project. Members of NHN were joining with Bukonzo Joint's Fairtrade marketing in coffee and maize. Using the same diagram and drawing tools provides a universal language for communication between stakeholders and increases stakeholder participation, as well as cutting through verbose and lengthy definitions and concepts at higher levels. The participatory methodology also develops the analytical, participatory, listening, and communication skills of institutions and policy-makers, to increase the effectiveness of their pro-poor interventions, as well as the personal reflections of staff and planning. The GALS process has led to a mushrooming of information sharing and informal forms of collaboration, and a strengthening of member associations, some of which have been established as a result of the GALS process itself. This is particularly noticeable in the reorganization of GH members as New Home Network, which brings together both producers and traders in beans and fruits. Not only have they developed their own individual plans, but organizational plans too.

Some remaining challenges and wider implications

The experience with GALS reinforces the conclusions of other methodologies that changing gender inequalities and discrimination makes 'business sense' for households, enterprises, and ultimately the local and national economy. Some profound and easily monitored changes in gender inequality can take place relatively quickly, even in households where men have been violent, alcoholic, and adulterous. The explicit and very graphic nature of much of the pictorial information around issues of gender-based violence, alcohol, and prostitution makes it very difficult for people at any level to dismiss gender strategies as externally imposed or 'culturally inappropriate'. Men who are able to address negative dimensions of their 'masculine' role, such as violence and alcoholism, are happier and feel more valued by their families and community. Male as well as female community leaders can become important promoters of change. Working first with those who are most vulnerable constitutes a powerful start for improving communications between chain actors and chain efficiency, and demonstrates the business case for gender mainstreaming and women's empowerment. Addressing the gender inequalities that cause inefficiencies in livelihoods at many levels of the chain can make a significant contribution to upgrading the whole value chain and developing the local economy.

A distinct advantage in GALS is that once learned, use of the tools in individual diaries and group meetings to analyse, plan, and track progress is cumulative and ongoing. In Stage 4, the methodology becomes organizationally and financially self-sustaining and selfupscaling at different levels – adapted as needed to different purposes and integrated as far as possible into other activities. The same processes and skills can also be integrated to mainstream gender and increase effectiveness in other interventions. In Bukonzo Joint all the costs of GALS capacity building are now covered by the increased profits from microfinance and/or coffee. In NHN there is very little external funding. The considerable skill and initiative which very poor people who cannot read and write demonstrate during this process, and the constructive strategies they propose, are often an eye-opener to other chain stakeholders. Organizational replication is also occurring between CBOs in the local area, generally without external funding, as a result of people's interest in the success cases.

This is not to say that there are no challenges to be addressed. Firstly, there may be some levelling off of impact in any one community once the members most receptive or in need of change have been reached. A particular challenge is to address the needs of the large numbers of women whose husbands are in polygamous relationships, not only discouraging men from multiple relationships but helping existing polygamous families to reconcile differences and work together so that all wives benefit. Some work has been done on this, but it needs to be more widely upscaled through some readjustment of tools. This may also require some counselling adaptations and newer techniques, such as interactive theatre and participatory video, that may also be useful to regain people's interest (see WEMAN 'Making Gender FUN'). There is a need to further extend and deepen the GALS analysis over the full range of CEDAW rights. Now members and staff are confident with the basic tools, they can use the more advanced diagrams for much more detailed analysis and tracking, and advocacy research (see Mayoux, 2012a, b and forthcoming).

There are signs that commercial success has also led to increasing participation of men, leading in turn to changes in governance. There is a need to revisit BJ's original PALS poverty analysis now that many previously poor members have become better off, to ensure that poorer people in the community are not being left out and to develop strategies for inclusion. There is anecdotal evidence that where men are elected to leadership positions in primary cooperatives, women are leaving. In addition, men are favouring men in allocation of loans, and are failing to observe the differential policy on shares whereby women currently get 60 per cent and men get 40 per cent. It is increasingly considered unfair that men should be penalized in this way, but the equalization could be made conditional on men producing a legal joint land agreement – that is, equality at home is required before equality in the organization. Similar requirements could also apply to any man standing for elected office within the organization. The earlier idea of a women's coffee cooperative as a specific niche brand could also be reconsidered as a way forward to assist single women – particularly the roasted coffee BJ is able to produce with its new processing equipment.

Some of these challenges are a consequence of constraints under which BJ and NHN are operating rather than GALS per se. Some of these challenges are now addressed in the revised versions of the methodology being used elsewhere (updated Manuals will be available by December 2012 on the WEMAN Resources website). Evidence from replications so far elsewhere in Uganda, Rwanda and Nigeria indicates that significant changes can occur in some people's lives from the first sessions. Peer training is also occurring at a significant rate. It is estimated that in new organizations where there is some sort of group activity through microfinance or cooperatives, adapting and implementing the methodology as it now stands would take about two years. This does, however, inevitably depend on the levels of organizational commitment to both gender justice and a community-led process, and their willingness to follow up on governance and advocacy issues, such as land, which emerge from the GALS process.

Acknowledgment

She is very grateful to the members of the Bukonzo Joint GALS team, particularly Teddy, Annette, Polonia, Asasio, and David who spent time to check all the quantitative information in this chapter. She would also like to thank fellow GALS consultants, Paineto Baluku and Janet Biira, and WEMAN Programme Officer Thies Reemer for filling in information from earlier reports and their comments on the first draft of this paper. Responsibility for the analysis, and any errors, lie entirely with the author.

References

Bolwig, S. and Odeke, M. (2007) *Household Food Security Effects of Certified Organic Export Production in Tropical Africa*, Epopa, Netherlands. Available at: www.grolink.se/epopa/Publications/EPOPA%20Report%20on%20 Food%20Security%20impact%20of%20organic%20production.pdf [accessed 23 October 2012].

Farnworth, C.R. (2012) *Household Approaches Synthesis Paper*, Rome: IFAD.

Farnworth, C.R. and Akamandisa, V. (2011) *Report on Gender Action Learning System (GALS) Approach to Value Chain Development in Bukonzo Joint in Uganda*, for Oxfam Novib and GIZ.

Farnworth, C. and Ragasa, C. (2008) *Gender and Agricultural Markets Gender in Agriculture Sourcebook*, Washington, DC: World Bank, FAO and IFAD: 173–256.

KIT, Faida MaLi, IRRI and Peppelenbos, L. (eds) (2006) *Chain Empowerment: Supporting African Farmers to Develop Markets*, Amsterdam: Royal Tropical Institute; Arusha: Faida Market Link; Nairobi: International Institute of Reconstruction.

Mayoux, L. (2006) 'Road to the foot of the mountain: but reaching for the sun: PALS adventures and challenges', in K. Brock and J. Pettit (eds), *Springs of Participation: Creating and Evolving Methods for Participatory Development*, Practical Action Publishing, Rugby.

Mayoux, L. (2012a) *Designing a GALS Action and Advocacy Learning System*, The Hague: Oxfam Novib.

Mayoux, L. (2012b) 'Rocky road to diamond dreams: GALS Stage 1 community design process and participatory review' [website] <www.wemanresources.info>.

Mayoux, L. (forthcoming) *Equal and Together: GALS Overview Manual*, Rome: IFAD.

Mayoux, L. and Mackie, G. (2009) *Making the Strongest Links: A Practical Guide to Gender Analysis in Value Chain Development*, Geneva: ILO.

Mayoux, L., Baluku, P., Biira, J. and Reemer, T. (2011) *Growing the Diamond Forest: Community-led Action Learning for Gender Justice in Wealth Creation*, Gender Action Learning System Manual 3, The Hague: Oxfam Novib.

Melendez, F.V. (2008) *Cafe Feminino: Experiencias de mujeres emprendedoras*, San Juan, Peru: Centro de Investigacion Capacitacion Asesoria y Promocion (CICAP).

Reemer, T. and Oxfam Novib (2011) *Gender Justice in Pro-poor Value Chain Development*, Final report, IFAD small grant R1161 (June 2009–June 2011).

Solidaridad (2009) *The Role of Certification and Producer Support in Promoting Gender Equality in Cocoa Production*, Solidaridad and Oxfam Novib.

WEMAN (no date) 'Making Gender FUN' [website] <www.wemanresources.info/5_MakingGenderFun/5_0_MakingGenderFun.html> [accessed 18 October 2012].

Websites

Gender in Value Chain Agri-ProFocus Learning Network: http://genderinvaluechains.ning.com ILO: www.ilo.org

M4P Hub: http://m4phub.org

MEDA's work in Pakistan: www.meda.org.pk/meda-donors/usaid-pakistan GAMEchangeNetwork resources: https://gamechangenetwork.org/

About the author

Linda Mayoux (gamechangenetwork@gmail.com), independent consultant.

www.ingramcontent.com/pod-product-compliance
Lightning Source LLC
Chambersburg PA
CBHW070902030426
42336CB00014BA/2290